EROS AND TRANSFORMATION

SEXUALITY AND MARRIAGE
An Eastern Orthodox Perspective

William Basil Zion

UNIVERSITY
PRESS OF
AMERICA

Lanham • New York • London

Copyright © 1992 by
University Press of America®, Inc.
4720 Boston Way
Lanham, Maryland 20706

3 Henrietta Street
London WC2E 8LU England

Library of Congress Cataloging-in-Publication Data

Zion, William Basil, 1931–
Eros and transformation : sexuality and marriage : an Eastern
Orthodox perspective / William Basil Zion.
p.   cm.
Includes bibliographical references and index.
1. Marriage—Religious aspects—Orthodox Eastern Church.
2. Sex—Religious aspects—Orthodox Eastern Church.
3. Love—Religious aspects—Orthodox Eastern Church.
4. Orthodox Eastern Church—Doctrines.
5. Orthodox Eastern Church—Membership.
6. Christian ethics—Orthodox Eastern authors.   I. Title.
BX378.M2Z56   1992   92–7242—dc20   92–7242 CIP

ISBN 0–8191–8647–3 (cloth : alk. paper)
ISBN 0–8191–8648–1 (pbk. : alk. paper)

 The paper used in this publication meets the minimum requirements of
American National Standard for Information Sciences—Permanence
of Paper for Printed Library Materials, ANSI Z39.48–1984.

Acknowledgements

Father Thomas Hopko of St. Vladimir's Seminary read a version of this manuscript and offered invaluable assistance which enabled me to make important changes. This does not, of course, mean that he agreed with all that I said, but his encouragement has been ever present. My friend, Prof. Charles Lock, and my colleague, Prof. Millard Schumaker, also read the work in manuscript and were of considerable assistance. Perhaps I owe most to another friend, Andrew Taylor, whose intelligent reflections and salutory influence made it necessary for me to rewrite the entire manuscript. I believe that the result is a vision of love as God's appearance in our midst rather than the moralistic treatise that I had first attempted. It is to my wife Rhoda that I owe her belief in what I was doing and its inherent value. She worked long and hard on the initial manuscript. So, also, I owe much to Dorothy Schweder who retyped chapters when my amateurish efforts at the computer resulted in their loss. Finally, my son Peter has taught me what I have learned about computer skills and often salvaged what I had thought irreparably lost. And, of course, there is so much joy from my daughter Katherine, whose smile and charm speak of love's delight.

It is to my bishop SERAPHIM of Ottawa that I owe the most, for his encouragement of my work, his patience, and his vision of Orthodox theology which is both faithful to the tradition and yet tries to address the problems of modernity.

EROS AND
TRANSFORMATION

Table of Contents

Preface

This work, which has been six years in the making, is essentially an interpretation of marriage and sexuality from an Eastern Orthodox perspective. It is in no sense a statement of *the* Eastern Orthodox position on either sexuality or marriage, if only because of the lack of a definitive synthesis of a theology of sexuality within Orthodoxy. I have sought to examine the particular theology of marriage which has emerged within Eastern Christianity and to examine some modern problems in moral theology from that particular standpoint.

In teaching courses on Christian ethics and specializing in the area of sexual ethics, I became aware that everything written on this topic in the Christian West ignores the alternative approach taken by the Eastern Orthodox tradition. Having myself been formed in the discipline of moral theology and ethics as taught in Anglican and Roman Catholic institutions, I slowly became aware of the parochial parameters of Western theological thought and the heavily Augustinian or Thomistic assumptions which pervaded much moral theology.

It was with my conversion to Eastern Orthodoxy and my decision to live in the world which it provided that I came to undertake the task of exploring a sexual ethic built on Orthodox rather than Western, heterodox presuppositions. Whereas the discovery of an alternative to the debates between deontic and teleological ways of doing moral theology brought me to a new realization of how one might find alternatives, I discovered that many of the complex issues regarding concrete moral decisions could not be taken without exploring the theological foundations on which they might be resolved. In other words, it was not enough to accept or dismiss the teleological grounds on which the papal strictures against contraception might be based. I had to look for alternative grounds on which a decision about contraception might be carried out. This, of course, carried me to fundamentals. In reading Orthodox discussions of the issues at hand, as, for example, Philip Sherrard's on Paul VI's encyclical *Humanae Vitae*, there is inevitably a return to the Fathers of the Church and specifically in this instance to a theology of sexuality based on Gregory of Nyssa's theology rather than that of Augustine.

There is no way in which an Orthodox writer can ignore the Fathers, but equally it is impossible to ignore the Holy Scriptures. The task of reading the latter by way of the former is no longer acceptable in the academic world in the simplistic fashion in which it was once done. The recognition of the specific genres of the varying works, their locality and time, all depend upon historical scholarship in a way which was not available to the Fathers. This is not to deny the continuity between the Scriptures and the writings of the Fathers. I accept as a fact the continuity between the various writers of the New Testament gospels and epistles and the thought worlds of early patristic literature. The flow between the Johannine literature and the thought of St. Irenaeus of Lyon is apparent to all who may read them.

I have sought to explore not only the foundations of an Eastern Orthodox sexual ethic but the goal of that ethic, which is the placing of human sexuality within the great sacramental mystery of Christ in marriage. Since Orthodox people have never done theology outside the setting of the liturgy, it has been equally important to unveil the liturgical theology of marriage. This way of doing theology differs radically from that found in Western Christianity. This theology affirms that marriage is good, even an avenue into the Kingdom of God, and that the unitive and procreative purposes of marriage are both instituted by God.

The return to the Fathers, part of the legacy of Father

Georges Florovsky, can never be a fundamentalist one, since the Fathers are available to us only through our experience of life and Orthodox faith, not by some miraculous trip by which we can put ourselves back into the second or third centuries after Christ. Those advocating a patristic theology never include all the Fathers but their own select few. The judgment on which Fathers are normative depends upon the decision of the Orthodox Church. Thus, one must avoid not only a biblical fundamentalism but a patristic fundamentalism. Equally one must avoid an ecclesial fundamentalism which would isolate the authority of the Church from the currents of thought and culture in which the Church lives. As the Greek Fathers were not immune to the Platonism of their time, so we are not immune to the intellectual currents in which we live.

I have insisted, as a Western Orthodox Christian, on using the scholarship of Western bibilical scholarship, patristics, and occasionally the expertise of contemporary clinical sexology. I hope to show that my own Orthodox faith is compatible with these approaches. Just as one cannot study sexuality without a knowledge of psychoanalysis, so one cannot do moral theology without a knowledge of the methodological conflicts found in moral theology today. The awareness that proportionalism is used by Orthodox theologians in their considerations of divorce and remarriage tells me that it just may be possible to use similar approaches with regard to other controversial areas where traditionally deontic absolutes have dominated the field of discourse. However, the lack of legal absolutism within the Orthodox world and the willingness to allow for compromise carry us beyond the impasse erected by traditional Roman Catholicism in their integration of deontic absolutes and naturalistic teleology.

This book originally began as an attempt to achieve a modern manual for Orthodox confessors, who have had nothing of this sort for many years. Such manuals existed in previous centuries: lists of sins with their gravity and penances. It became evident to me when I was a parish priest in Toronto for three years that the sexual sins and agonies that were brought to me in confession were not easily dealt with by the simple code of whether the particular sin was forbidden or not. Inevitably I was driven back to the fundamentals, to ask whether coitus before marriage was morally acceptable, to formulate responses to requests for godly counsel about masturbation, homosexual relations, or contraception. The issues have all turned out to be more complex than I had imagined, and the result is far from being the manual that I had hoped for. Indeed, the results are exploratory and intended for both the clergy and for the intelligent and informed lay persons of whom there are many within the Orthodox Church today. I put them forth for consideration, nothing more.

Some may ask why I have not made greater use of two very important works about sexuality and Orthodox Christianity. The first is Peter Brown's study *Body and Society.* I know of no other work of such profundity and learning, but it remains an essay in social history as reflected in the context of the theologies of particular Church Fathers. That, of course, means that it is invaluable, coming, as it does, from a very great historian. But my work is that of a moral theologian who is interested in historical theology, and most particularly in Orthodox theology. Thus, I have not addressed the theology of Augustine, who, though a holy bishop of Hippo, wrote books that were never received in the East as Orthodox. They were in many instances the sources of gravely heterodox teachings within the context of Roman Catholicism and later Calvinism. The other work, perhaps more germaine, is that of Eve Levin, *Sex and Society in the World of the Orthodox Slavs, 900-1700.* Again, the magisterial quality of the work is such that none can read it without having his or her own understanding radically altered. My own impression after reading it was one of unmitigated gloom since Levin clearly shows how the sanctification of sexuality in marriage had been reduced to a set of strictures imposed by families upon their children, often before puberty, so as to control their lives. Indeed, Levin intimates that the second marriage was often the only possible expression of a personal and loving relationship between two people. At least the Orthodox Christian world allowed this whereas the Latin West permitted nothing of the kind. The absence of any regard for the personal situation before the force of rigid canons; the lack of any awareness of romantic or personal love when it came to sexuality; and the entirely negative stance toward sexual expression other than as copulation for the purpose of procreation - all point to the loss of the vision of the Kingdom of God in and through marriage. That vision became something hoped for in the other world. If obedience to the Holy Canons means that we return to such legalism, I want no part of it. Anyone who thinks that there can bo an easy and compatible integration of theology and canonical practice should read Levin's book carefully.

Finally, I would say that my persistence in carrying out this task has bordered on presumption. That a convert (and a fairly recent convert) should venture to interpret the Eastern Christian mind on marriage and sexuality is nothing short of precarious. Yet no one else has done this, and only one with the curiosity to ask the appropriate questions can begin this exploration. To explore them triumphalistically and uncritically will help no one in the end. Orthodox are living in the modern world, and if they are not to secumb to a ritualism imposed on an underlying paganism, they must ask the kind of questions that I have raised. Modern questions will not go away, and the fact that the Fathers knew nothing of the steroid pill does not mean that we can avoid our questions about its morality. Theology must not be thought to have ceased at the end of the patristic period. As Orthodox Christians our commitments to the faith of the councils does not mean that we repeat their answers unthinkingly. What I have done I offer to a dialogue within the Church in confidence that the Holy Spirit will guide the Church. I pray that the same Spirit will show me the errors into which I have fallen so that I may duly repent of them.

The contemporary reader will note that I have not addressed the contemporary issues of gender. Such problems as to whether women can be or will be ordained as Orthodox priests raise these questions rather acutely. These issues are very deep, and as Bishop Gregory (John Zizioulos) of Thyrateia has insisted, we must have theological discussions of these issues, not anathemas. Modern Orthodox thought will have to explore what we now know about gender as a cultural construct built on biological and genetic bases. Since these questions are too complex to be addressed in a chapter, I have sought on the whole to ignore them or to raise them in subsequent publications.

Foreword

Fr. Basil Zion has given us a study of marriage and sexuality within the tradition of the Orthodox Church, seeking to open up within the Church a discussion of the many questions that have been raised. Questions of contraception, pre-marital sexual relations, masturbation, divorce and remarriage, and homosexual relations are being debated throughout society today. Orthodox Christians cannot respond to these concerns without a knowledge of what the Church teaches, and shy she teaches it. Fr. Basil has sought both scriptural and pastristic sources, but he has addressed them by using the tools of contemporary scholarship. His dialogue is, therefore, not only with Orthodox Christians, but with other Christians and persons of good will in the therapeutic communities.

Not everyone will agree with all that Fr. Basil writes. He is in manay ways a first in exploring the foundations of an Orthodox theology of sexuality. His contribution will assist the dialogue that is taking place, both in the Church and in society. It will assist those who are tempted to fall away into secularism to understand why the Church has taken the positions that she has.

Fr. Basil is a priest of the Orthodox Church in America, serving within the Archdiocese of Canada. He is also a professor in the Department of Religious Studies at Queen's University in Kingston, Ontario. He is trained in moral theology as well as in contemporary psychoanalytic thought.

I would commend Fr. Basil's work to those who read it, not as a definitive answer to every problem, but as a point from which to begin this important discussion. It is through the debate that we will by God's help see more clearly. He brings to his work not only his academic training and experience, but ten years of pastoral experience in Toronto and Kingston.

+ SERAPHIM
Bishop of Ottawa and Canada

Introduction

The purpose of this book is to explore the distinctive characteristics of the Eastern Orthodox approach to sexual ethics. It is an essay in moral theology, but the distinctive note of the Orthodox way of doing theology is based on scripture and tradition rather than on natural law analyzed rationally according to a hierarchy of ends. The consequence of this methodology lies in the importance and space given here both to exploring what the tradition has said about sexuality and how that tradition is based on the Old and the New Testaments of the Bible.

Four chapters of the book are devoted to marriage. Two chapters are given to problems surrounding marriage: contraception and divorce. The prominence given to marriage lies in the fundamental Orthodox conviction that God's purpose for human sexuality lies in marriage or the monastic life. Other problems in the area of sexual ethics, namely, masturbation and homosexuality are approached as difficulties particularly, though not exclusively, experienced by single people. Accordingly, our approach must incorporate much of the wisdom entrenched in the monastic tradition in order to address these questions adequately.

My discussion of marriage begins with the New Testament. The focus is placed on the teachings of Jesus and those of St. Paul, culminating in the fifth chapter of the epistle to the Ephesians, verses 20-33. This passage is not only the

1

most positive and exalted discussion of marriage in the New Testament, but it is used as the liturgical epistle in the Orthodox ritual for marriage. Eph 5:20-33 is explored critically with regard to what it says about the sacramental character of marriage, the relations of the sexes, and the ethical character of those relations (subordination of both sexes to one another, fear and reverence on the part of the woman, and love of the man for the woman). The thesis of this book is that the sexual union of the couple, performed in the context of love, signifies a participation in the love of Christ for His Church. Few outside the Eastern Orthodox tradition have viewed marriage as realistically as a sacramental participation in God through the union of the couple.

I explore the mystery of marriage in the writings of the Fathers of the Church in the second chapter. The center of discussion lies in the defense of marriage against the Encratists. The natural theology of Clement of Alexandria is examined to reveal the principle which made justification of sexual love in marriage rest upon procreation. The basic Orthodox case against Encratism was made to depend upon the purpose of marriage as procreative. The affirmation of the Church's stance against Encratism was to become a criterion of true Orthodoxy, as we see from the treatises on virginity by Gregory of Nyssa and John Chrysostom. Nevertheless, the superiority of virginity was upheld and marriage often disvalued as second best. The thesis of this book is that both with Gregory and John this has been much exaggerated. Gregory had a very positive doctrine of marriage, as Mark D. Hart has convincingly argued, and contrary to Peter Brown, John Chrysostom reversed his highly polemical attack on marriage and sexuality in his later writings. In Chrysostom's early work marriage is little more than a state permitted to avoid fornication in the weak. However, the mature Chrysostom exalts marriage as a sign of the real presence of Christ and His Kingdom in our midst, speaking of the union of the man and the woman as itself creating a "little church."

The liturgical tradition of the Orthodox Church shows how the various rites for marriage, coming out of a Jewish background as well as the Hellenistic setting of the fourth century, manifest a constant witness to the goodness of marriage. The history of marriage as a familial ceremony coming more and more under ecclesiastical supervision finally culminates in the Eastern Orthodox doctrine that marriage is a sacrament bestowed by the Church on the couple (in contrast to the Western view where the man and the woman are the ministers of the sacrament). I explore the various theories regarding the minister of the sacrament of marriage, whether this is the couple or the priest, and the question as to what rites actually bestow the sacrament. The movement of the betrothal and the crowning into essentially one event, both presided over by a priest, has the effect of eliminating the contractual understanding of marriage latent in the separate betrothal. Orthodoxy has no basis on which to legitimize unions outside the ecclesiastical setting, so that pre-ceremonial unions discussed in Western churches, are entirely foreign to her tradition. I conclude that there are no marriages for Orthodox believers apart from the blessing of the Church.

The modern theologies of marriage provided by two Greeks, Stephanos Charalambidis and Christos Yannaras, and two Russians, Pavel Evdokimov and Evgueny Lampert, are examined in chapter four. In addition, the work of Philip Sherrard, an English Orthodox theologian, is explored. The characteristic note of Greek theology lies in the emphasis given to the Incarnation of Christ which unites the man and the woman in the flesh. The link between this theology, which is personalist as well as sacramental, and the interpretation of love as reflecting the love of Christ crucified is significant. Yannaras clearly rejects both a naturalist and a legalist understanding of marriage. The Russian tradition, on the other hand, is deeply influenced by the philosophy of Soloviev which is clearly a form of love-mysticism. The movement beyond any utilitarian basis in procreation or family life all comes from Soloviev and from the unique experiences of all three theologians as lovers. Each had a very special relationship with a woman to whom he was married - unlike Soloviev who remained single but emotionally involved in romantic relationships as well as semi-gnostic experiences of the Eternal Feminine. In any event, Evdokimov, Lampert, and Sherrard correct Soloviev by giving an importance to marriage and sexual union that was foreign to Soloviev. Lampert is particularly important since he worked out an Orthodox theology of sexuality which legitimized and recognized the transforming power of physical love within the context of married love.

Whereas many put aside the sophiological interests of Soloviev and Bulgakov as remote and unintelligible to modern people, I have found them a precursor to modern feminism. One sees this very clearly in the book of Joan Engelsman, *The Feminine Dimension of the Divine* where *sophia* opens the door to the feminine aspects of the Deity. Questions of gender have become paramount in contemporary theological discussions, and I have resisted entering into the debate in this book. However, it is the openness to the questions posed by modernity, even if in the somewhat dated German Idealism espoused by Bulgakov, and Florenski, that we can see how Eastern Orthodoxy need not remain captive to the thought forms of Greek Antiquity in order to remain faithful to her vision.

The Eastern Orthodox approach to divorce and remarriage has always remain opaque and paradoxical to Western theologians. I scrutinize both Roman Catholic and Protestant objections to the Orthodox position along with the biblical and patristic evidence. Orthodox Christianity has affirmed both the indissolubility of marriage and the possibility under certain conditions of a second marriage even if the first spouse is still alive. The evidence remains ambiguous, both in the Bible and the Fathers, but second marriages began to be accepted from the time of Origen to that of St. Basil the Great in the Eastern Church. This practice was made canonically acceptable by the Quinisext Council in Constantinople where it became normative for Orthodoxy. The legitimation of the practice is justified by modern Orthodox theologians on the basis of (1) the affirmation that once a marriage is dead it cannot be said to have any validity, (2), a second marriage is often a lesser of evils, and (3) the practice of economy by Orthodox bishops. Several Roman Catholic moral theologians, including Bernard Häring and Richard McCormick, have argued in similar fashion. Orthodox practice, therefore, is not unfaithful to the gospel but is based on an awareness that we still live in the age of this world, though raised into the Kingdom of God in the Eucharist and in the crowning of marriage. Orthodox moral theology manifests a flexibility in regard to divorce and remarriage which is not so evident in other areas of sexual ethics, though perhaps it might be so if the underlying principles are made evident. This is what I have tried to do.

In a chapter on contraception various opinions from Orthodox theologians favoring the practice are contrasted with those opposed. The opinions of the Fathers regarding contraception are examined, though they often confuse contraception with abortion or licentiousness. The argument in favor of contraception within the context of marriage is set forth and affirmed as morally correct since the fundamental objection to contraception lies in a form of physiological teleology and ecclesiastical authoritarianism foreign to Orthodox tradition.

The moral problems of masturbation are investigated in the light of both patristic and canonical references. The theological objections to masturbation within the Christian tradition have been based either on alleged references in Holy Scripture forbidding the practice, on the normative character of procreation for the use of the sexual organs, or on the evil inherent in concupiscence outside the context of marriage. On the basis of clinical evidence, it appears that masturbation is often reparative and a response to anxiety or depression. We must, accordingly, relate masturbation to a person's vocation. For the monk masturbation is a breakdown of the prayer of the heart and is inspired by demonic influences. For the man or woman who intends to marry, masturbation may be anticipatory or remedial in character. On the other hand, masturbation may reflect the symptoms of marital breakdown. The designation of masturbatory acts as "grave sin" depends upon a teleological understanding of sexuality which is foreign, we are convinced, to the thrust of Orthodox moral theology. In an Orthodox moral theology masturbation must be seen as a complex phenomenon, often sinful, but not necessarily destroying the graceful union with God. The remedy for masturbation lies in affective relationship, both with God and the loved one. It is more symptomatic of an underlying disorder than itself the disorder.

The objective evil of homosexual acts is based on both biblical and patristic texts. When examined, these texts reveal both a cultural identification of homosexuality with the forms of pederasty practiced in the Hellenistic world and the forms of decadence and excess which prevailed in late antiquity. The modern discovery of psychological homosexuality is entirely foreign to the discussions of a previous age. I consider various theories of the etiology and meanings of homosexuality. In particular, the views of Dr. Elizabeth Moberly, an Orthodox psychotherapist and theologian, are examined. Moberly finds in homosexual feelings and orientation a search for healing based on a need for love from the same-sex parent. The remedial character of homosexuality does not allow a lax or permissive attitude toward homosexual acts since Moberly rules them out as incestuous in character. Finally, the position of the Orthodox Church is upheld insofar as homosexual acts cannot be expressive of the loving union which the sacrament of matrimony seals and celebrates. Nevertheless, both compassion and awareness of the involuntary nature of most homosexual activity would mitigate the harshness of traditional Christian attitudes toward homosexuals. The involuntary nature of most homosexual sin is another reason for mitigating the traditionally negative judgments made on homosexual persons who act on their orientation.

The final chapter "Eros and Transformation" is a synthesis of the entire work, affirming the goodness of sexuality as uniting through the energies of God what is separated and alienated. An understanding of *eros* as moving persons toward one another to friendship and self-giving love is set forth using the thought of Olivier Clément, Pavel Florensky, and Christos Yannaras as grounds for this perspective. From self-centeredness one moves toward the other and toward the other sex. A theology based upon the energies that draw persons to one another is grounded in the fundamentals of Orthodox theology, from St. Maximus the Confessor to St.

Gregory Palamos. Love, fueled by *eros* moves under the influence of the grace of the Holy Spirit so that the self turns outward from desire to possess to the mutuality of friendship, and from mutuality to *agape*.

A natural law grounding for love is found in the work of Giroian and Yannaras. Over against the scholastic understanding of natural law based on reason discerning the ends of human action, Yannaras established freedom as the heart of human nature. It is the meeting of persons in freedom, communicating in the language of love, which is the realization of the potentialities of human nature.

The character of sexuality as a language is taken from the work of Olivier Clément to affirm that the moral norm is authenticity and truthfulness rather than activity fulfilling the purposes of procreation. The work of two non-Orthodox moral theologians (André Guindon and Robert Solomon) is brought forward to fill out the interpretation of sexuality as a language. Both Soloviev and Clément, as Orthodox thinkers, also posit sexual relating as a form of speaking.

It is the fundamental thesis of this book that sexuality becomes a way of entering the Kingdom of God when it is exalted into forms of love which are sanctifying. The importance of the Incarnation and the sacramentality of marriage mean that a repressive repudiation of sexuality as "the evil impulse" must be excluded. The ambivalence of Orthodoxy on this issue has been evident since the beginnings of Christianity, but the full development of a theology of marriage means that speaking the sexual language to the beloved other is of equal value to the life of virginal monasticism. The due understanding of the sanctifying power of marriage is a recognition that those who have persevered from the time of their crowning can hope for an entry into the Kingdom of God like unto the holy martyrs themselves.

Chapter One:

Marriage and the New Testament

The teaching of the Orthodox Church on marriage is part of the Holy Tradition of the Church. This teaching is based on the scriptures of the Old and New Testament as interpreted by those Holy Fathers recognized by the Church as authoritative. This interpretation is not and never can be carried out in a way which would displace the scriptures by the Fathers or the Fathers by the scripture. Just as a non-historical fundamentalism may ignore and displace the authority of the Church by placing the Bible above and outside the tradition of the community, so Orthodox may sometimes appear to displace the study of the scriptures by substituting patristic authorities. The patristic writings are interpretations, and interpretations depend upon that which is to be interpreted. So, the Bible exists within a historical context which is distinct both culturally and temporally from the patristic witness and reading of the biblical text.

In my study of sexuality and marriage in the Orthodox tradition, I have envisioned my task as an examination of both the scriptural and the patristic development. One cannot be reduced to the other without serious confusion. This procedure necessitates the use of a critical, historical method. Neither the Bible nor the Fathers can be adequately understood without being placed in their temporal and cultural setting. This involves, also, a willingness to use modern critical method. Such a method may well be suspect insofar as it has emerged in non-Orthodox circles and may be thought to involve a skepticism foreign to the believing context of the Orthodox Church. But skepticism may be and must be distinguished from a questioning method and its consequences. A critical attitude does not necessarily flow from unbelief. Those who, for example, would argue that as Orthodox we must believe that Dionysius the Areopagite lived in the first century are not only indulging in a pious obscurantism but make it impossible to grasp the meaning of his work in the milieu in which it came to be in the early sixth century. The same critical scholarship must be applied if we are to grasp the particular theology of the Letter to the Hebrews. This is clearly not a Pauline work since its theology and context are radically different from those revealed in the authentic Pauline letters. Following the imperative of this methodology, we can no longer naively assume that a patristic interpretation provides us with all we need to know about a scriptural text. The text must be judged on its own within its own historical context. Patristic views are important to grasp how the church understood the text and how particular judgments were made regarding its meaning in the controversies and discussions that occurred at a later point in the history of the Church. A correct methodology would recognize that the commentary of St. John Chrysostom on Eph 5:30 has a theological validity and importance even if the words "of his flesh and of his bones" are a variant in the text and not part of the original text of the author, St. Paul. A patristic fundamentalism which would require us to accept these words as original to Paul is uncalled for and is based on incorrect methodology, namely, a reading back of a variant phrase into the earlier text in which it did not appear.

There is no doubt that both positive and negative judgments exist within the New Testament regarding sexuality and marriage. There are severe judgments against those in the early Christian community who are governed by their corrupt bodily desires, as in 2 Pt 2:10, 18. In Rv 14:4, we read of "these who have not defiled themselves with women, for they are virgins; it is these who follow the Lamb whereever he goes." Jesus himself speaks of the evils that flow from the hearts of men. In Mk 7:21 he says: "What comes out of a man is what defiles a man. For from within, out of the heart of man, come evil thoughts, fornication, theft, murder, adultery, coveting, wickedness, deceit, licentiousness, envy, slander, pride foolishness. All these evil things come from within, and they defile a man."

The teaching of Jesus on marriage is found in all the Synoptic Gospels but with interesting variations in the Gospel of Matthew. When asked by the Pharisees whether it is against the law for a man to divorce his wife (a question of debate among the factions of Judaism at that time. Jesus responds by asking what the law of Moses commands (Mk 10:3). The Pharisees stated that Moses allowed a writ of dismissal and consequently a divorce.

But Jesus said to them, "For your hardness of heart he wrote you this commandment. But from the beginning of creation, 'God made them male and female.' For this reason a man shall leave his father and mother and be joined to his wife, and the two shall become one flesh.' So they are no longer two but one flesh. What therefore God has joined together, let not man put asunder." A comparison with the versions of Matthew (Mt 5:32 and Mt 19:1-9) makes it clear that Mark is reflecting Roman law rather than Jewish law in speaking of a woman divorcing her husband, which was not permitted in Judaism. Clearly, at least this part of the narrative has been expanded from the original Jewish context as it was expressed in Matthew's gospel. On the other hand, the parallels in Matthew contain the phrase "except on the ground of unchastity "*parektos logou porneias* (Mt 5:32) and "except for unchastity" (Mt 19:9). Most scholars think that the exception has been added by the author of Matthew's gospel. The phrase "except for fornication" clearly reflects in a literal way the technical term used in Dt 24:1 (*ereweth dabhar*). Schillebeeckx writes: "It is also clear that the entire context of Mt 19:9 was dominated by the heated controversy that was raging in Jesus' time between the school of Rabbi Hillel and that of Rabbi Shammai."[1] Rabbi Shammai regarded adultery or other indecent acts as the only grounds for divorce, while Rabbi Hillel provided wide and various grounds for divorce.

It is evident that the questions posed to Jesus were put forth to "test" him in what was a lively controversy in rabbinical circles. In essence, Jesus states that there are no grounds for divorce and remarriage, so that any who divorces his wife and marries another is guilty of adultery. The grounds for this judgment are found in the law of creation rather than the law of Moses which permitted divorce "For your hardness of heart Moses allowed you to divorce your wives, but from the beginning it was not so" (Mt 19:8).

Jesus is appealing beyond the law of Moses to the order of creation. The implication is that this Mosaic law was given because of the hardness of heart of mankind. Eric Fuchs writes: "Notice that Jesus does not criticize Moses, but rather only restores the intention of the text from Deuteronomy, thereby clarifying the social status of the law: it is a response to the unfortunate fact of human wickedness and its function is to deflect the catastrophic consequences that can come from the presence of evil in man and in society."[2] Indeed, the attack made by Jesus is not against the law itself but against the establishment of a law which was contingent upon the perception of evil as expressing God's will for mankind for all time. Francis Beare thinks that since Gn 2:24 is from the J narrative, it points back to the story of woman being made from the rib of man.[3] Gn 2:23 gives us the reason behind the injunction that a man leave his father and mother and become one flesh with his wife. In other words, since they were originally one in creation, in marriage they return to this unity. One may, however, question the relevance of this observation to the teaching of Jesus who combines the two passages of Gn 1:27 and Gn 2:24 in Mt 19:5-6. The reality of a union which creates "one body" is based on God's differentiation of mankind into male and female and the call to leave the parents for this new bond. The basic affirmation is the statement of Jesus: "They are no longer two, therefore, but one body. So then, what God has united, man must not divide" (Mt 19:6). Creation is here linked to the gracious act of God since the same God who unites is the creator of all. As already noted, the exceptions present in Matthew's versions of Jesus' teaching on divorce and remarriage (Mt 5:32

and Mt 19:9) are generally read as additions to the text, not the actual words of Jesus. The claim made by Roman Catholic scholars that these words allow separation but not remarriage will be examined later in reference to divorce and remarriage. What is evident in the teachings of Jesus is that marriage is indissoluble in its promise and reality. Fuchs thinks that we must not legislate at this point since clearly Jesus' appeal was not to a new law. The law had provided a way out of marriage as a way of avoiding the reality of the marital relationship. In referring to Genesis Jesus is referring to the reality of marriage as against the legalization of marriage. It is lust which contradicts marriage by reducing the woman to an object, an object of desire. Thus the teaching of Jesus is revealed when he states: "You have heard that it was said, 'You shall not commit adultery.' But I say to you that everyone who looks at a woman lustfully has already committed adultery with her in his heart" (Mt 5:27-28). This difficult saying makes sense within the discussion of divorce and remarriage. As Fuchs puts it, "This is the very heart of the matter in the sexual and conjugal relationship: the struggle is not between 'permitted' and 'forbidden,' but between lust, fear, and refusal--as opposed to acceptance of the other and discovery of the presence of a creative and forgiving love."[4]

The section of Matthew's gospel which follows these sayings of Jesus about divorce and remarriage tells of the reaction of the disciples to what He had said. They ask: "If such is the case of a man with his wife, it is not expedient to marry." (Mt 19:10). Jesus replies: "Not all men can receive this precept, but only those to whom it is given. For there are eunuchs who have been so from birth, and there are eunuchs who have been made eunuchs by men, and there are eunuchs who have made themselves eunuchs for the sake of the kingdom of heaven. He who is able to receive this, let him receive it." (Mt 19:10-12). Many New Testament scholars find these statements about eunuchs displaced and difficult to comprehend. Fuchs thinks that the disciples saw Jesus' teaching as a new legalism which would make of marriage a state of total bondage. However, that was not the intention of His teaching. It would appear that the intention is revealed by the statement that His teaching can only be accepted by those to whom it is granted. In other words, the reality of marriage is a gift of grace. The sayings about eunuchs point to conditions which are unnatural, two of which were cursed by Judaism. At the level of the natural we find ourselves like eunuchs limited and unable to attain sexual fulfillment in a happy marriage, but at the level of grace even the eunuchs may find a place in the kingdom of God. Beare writes: "But it is probable that in a document as early as the Gospel of Matthew the words are rightly interpreted (as in the whole tradition) as the acceptance of voluntary celibacy for the sake of greater freedom in the service of the gospel. Paul is the example that at once comes to mind (I Cor 9:5)."[5]

The tendency on the part of Catholic scholars to interpret the sayings of Jesus about marriage as implying adherence to a natural law over against the law of Moses fails to grasp the link between creation and grace revealed in Jesus' teaching here. Similarly, some Protestants set up a tension between law and grace which depends more on the problematic of Reformation and Counter-Reformation than upon the *sitz im leben* of Jesus' discussions with the Pharisees. Catholics may do this by setting up a new law, more inflexible and more demanding than any beforehand. Protestants, for their part, live within the dialectic of law and grace that would make all law a condescension to the hardness of men's hearts and grace only a forgiveness of the sin of that hardness of heart. What we find, rather, in the teachings of Jesus is the radical power of grace that flows from the kingdom of God. The reality of "one flesh" (quite impossible for human beings) and something so humanly absurd as celibacy for the sake of the kingdom are both possible within the context of the gift of God's Holy Spirit. Herein we find the two poles of Orthodox theology and practice: Marriage is a sign of the kingdom and celibacy is also a sign of the kingdom. Both vocations have their place and their possibility only in this radical dimension. P. Benoit in *La Bible de Jerusalem* states in one of his few notes that "Jesus invites to perpetual continence those who are prepared to make this sacrifice to give them greater assurance of entrance into the kingdom of heaven and to serve it better."[6] Beare, on the other hand, states that "it is not suggested in the text that a voluntary celibacy gives one any greater assurance of entrance into the kingdom of heaven. 'For the sake of' (*dia*) is more naturally taken to mean 'to serve'."[7] That celibacy would give a greater assurance of entrance into the kingdom of God is implicit in traditional Roman Catholic spirituality and practice. Orthodoxy may have seemed to assume the same, but the fact that marriage is created by God indicates that comparisons are odious and assurances unwarranted. God's gifts are distributed as He may offer them. The fact that eunuchs were judged accursed by the Jewish law stands over against the eschatological hope enunciated by the Prophet Isaiah: "And let the eunuch not say: 'Behold, I am a dry tree.'For thus says the Lord: 'To the eunuchs who keep my sabbaths, who choose the things that please me and hold fast my covenant, I will give in my house and within my walls a monument and a name better than sons and daughters; I will give them an everlasting name which shall not be cut off'" (Is 56:3-5).

In conclusion, we may say that Jesus sets forth the aim and the fulfillment of creation both in terms of what God does and of what God will do. Heterosexuality is a created gift, as the gift of the other as a solace and a helpmate. The woman is given as an equal (the real meaning of Gn 2:21) and the union of man and woman create "one flesh." We read nothing whatsoever here about procreation. The call to leave the parents is again gift as well as vocation. This is the call to freedom from the oppressive bondage of dependence upon parents. "To cling" to one another is to be faithful and united. It is in the explication of the "one flesh" that St. Paul will spell out the fullness of Christ's teaching on marriage.

If one contrasts the gospels of Matthew and Luke with regard to their views on marriage and sexuality, a clear contrast emerges. Matthew is evidently a gospel which has come out of a Jewish milieu. For this reason we may also date it as earlier than Luke. Mark is from a Gentile milieu, sharing this characteristic with Luke. Nevertheless, that parts of Matthew would appear to be dependent upon Mark would seem to indicate an earlier and Jewish form of Mark's gospel. The contrasts between Luke and Matthew become clear when one compares the passage in Lk 20:34-35: "The sons of this age marry and are given in marriage; but those who are accounted worthy to attain to that age and to the resurrection from the dead neither marry nor are given in marriage." In Matthew the text reads: "For in the resurrection they neither marry nor are given in marriage" (Mt 22:30). The Marcan version is exactly the same as in Matthew. Clearly the meaning in Luke is different and would appear to make celibacy a condition for the resurrection from the dead and life in the new age. Similarly, Luke states: "If any one comes to me and does not hate his own father and mother and wife and children and brothers and sisters, yes, and even his own life, he cannot be my disciple" (Lk 14:26). In Matthew's version we read: "He who loves father or mother more than me is not worthy of me; and he who loves son or daughter more than me is not worthy of me"(Mt 10:37). In contrast stands Lk 18:29: "He (Jesus) said to them, 'Truly, I say to you, there is no man who has left house or wife or brothers or parents or children, for the sake ofthe kingdom of God, who will not receive manifold more in this time, and in the age to come eternal life."

It is abundantly evident that in Luke's gospel Jesus is presented as saying that the kingdom of God demands that only those who have abandoned all ties with family, including the tie to one's wife, can enter and receive eternal life. We have here an uncompromising call to leave the wife and family. None of this is evident in Matthew's gospel. There is no way that modern readers can avoid the question of what was the original form of the sayings of Jesus and to what extent the evangelists have reshaped the actual words of Jesus. These questions are far from being answered in contemporary scholarship, but the fact is plain that the historical, cultural, and theological milieus, Jewish in Matthew and Gentile in Luke-Acts, have strongly influenced the versions that we have in our Greek New Testament. Historically it is clear that Jesus was in his ministry and teaching deeply embedded in the Jewish context. The ascetic and anti-familial stance of Luke became full-blown within the Gentile churches at the end of the first century. We see in the work of St. Paul a struggle between the demands of the present and the demands of the age to come, the kingdom of God. Similarly, a similar tension exists, as I hope to show, between the Jewish acceptance of marriage and the ascetic, and probably Hellenistic tendency to reject the flesh in favor of an entirely spiritual life. Translated into the later concerns of the Orthodox Church these two poles become the domestic obligations of the married versus the radical disengagement of the monks.

The context of St. Paul's discussion of sexuality and marriage is primarily that of the Gentile church of Corinth. As a consequence of a certain understanding of what Paul was saying about the law and Christian freedom, some had begun to give a rather antinomian interpretation to St. Paul's teaching. Since St. Paul had taken the position that the legal taboos of Jewish law were no longer obligatory, some were concluding that nothing was forbidden. Paul's response was to reject antinomianism. Implicitly he sets forth a hierarchy of goods. Food is meant for the stomach, not the stomach for food, and God will do away with both. Consequently, the body is not meant for immorality, but "for the Lord, and the Lord for the body"(1 Cor 6:13). This statement is reinforced with two fundamental beliefs: God will raise up the dead as He raised the Lord from the dead, and the body is the temple of the Holy Spirit. The example is given of coitus with a prostitute. Since our bodies make up the body of Christ, they cannot be joined to a prostitute. To be joined in the Lord is to be one spirit with him (1 Cor 6:16). St. Paul's point is that coitus with a prostitute makes a man one body with her, but the body of the Christian cannot be so joined. A contradiction is involved: one cannot be one with the Lord and at the same time one with a prostitute. Fornication is a sin against one's own body which belongs to God, having been purchased by Christ (1 Cor 6:19-20). This paraphrase of St. Paul's teaching in makes it clear that his sexual ethic is built not on only on eschatological demands for abandoning all worldly ties but on the affirmation of the realities of union with Christ and the Holy Spirit now present in the lives of Christians. We find not a set of categorical imperatives telling us what we ought not to do but, rather, awareness of the profound inconsistency that would result from opposing and often contradictory ways of being: we cannot be one with God and one with the prostitute.

It is in response to the ascetic tendencies among the Gentile Christians that St. Paul answers their question, whether it is good for a man not to touch a woman. Many have taken this statement (1 Cor 7:1) as a simple affirmation that it is not good for a man to touch a woman. It appears, however, to concern a question posed to St. Paul by those among the Corinthians to whom he is writing. His response was that because of the danger of fornication, each man should have a wife and each woman a husband. This is, of course, the cornerstone of the rationale to be repeated by John Chrysostom and Augustine of Hippo as a primary *raison d'etre* of marriage. It exists to help us avoid sexual sin. However, St. Paul spells out the meaning of "one flesh" for the marital relationship: "The husband should give to his wife her conjugal rights, and likewise the wife to her husband. For the wife does not rule over her own body, but the husband does; likewise the husband does not rule over his own body, but the wife does. Do not refuse one another except perhaps by agreement for a season"(1 Cor 7:3-5). Sexual abstinence is recommended when by mutual consent time for prayer is desired. This time must be for a limited period since Satan might take advantage of weakness and tempt those abstaining. What St. Paul proposes he sets forth as a suggestion, not as a rule. Indeed, he states that "I wish that all were as I myself am. But each has his own special gift from God, one of one kind and one of another"(1 Cor 7:7). It is clear at this point that St. Paul conceives of the calling to marriage as a vocation and as a charisma. Again he invokes the argument that it is better to marry than to be burning with passion. Both widows and the unmarried are told that it is good to stay as they are, but marriage is better than torment by sexual urges.

In 1 Cor 7 St. Paul carefully distinguishes what is from himself and what is from the Lord. The word that he has from the Lord is that the wife must not leave her husband, or if she does, she must either remain unmarried or make up with her husband, and the husband must not send his wife away. This is directly in line with what we have read in the gospels of Matthew and Mark. St. Paul sets forth as his own opinion that if a Christian is married to an unbeliever and the unbeliever is content to remain married he must not send her away. He writes: "If any woman has a husband who is an unbeliever, and he consents to live with her, she should not divorce him. For the unbelieving husband is consecrated through his wife, and the unbelieving wife is consecrated through her husband. Otherwise, your children would be unclean, but as it is they are holy" (1 Cor 7:13-14). Indeed, the language of St. Paul is such that he speaks of a wife who is a Christian saving a non-Christian husband and a husband who is a Christian saving a wife who is a non-Christian. What is so astonishing here is the extent to which the realism of life in the body of Christ is taken. The logic of "one flesh" is pushed to the extreme. Since the body is the temple of the Holy Spirit, the partner is sanctified by the union with the Christian spouse.

Basically St. Paul is saying in 1 Cor 7 that one should remain in the condition that he was when he was called by the Lord, whether that be as an uncircumcised man or as a slave. This is because circumcision is nothing and because the slave becomes free in the Lord even when a slave socially. The norms of the earth and even of the law have become secondary because of this new relationship with Christ. As to remaining celibate, it is good to stay as one is because of the present distress. Presumably this distress is part of living in the last days and under the circumstances of turmoil and possible persecution. Yet St. Paul allows that if the celibate wishes to marry it is no sin (1 Cor 7:28). The married, on the other hand, are to stay as they are. It is the eschatological tension ("the appointed time has grown very short") which dictates that those who have wives should live as if they had none, and those who mourn live as if they had nothing to mourn for (1 Cor 7:29-30). The background here is surely the Beatitudes of Jesus with the contrast between the present age marked by mourning and the new age when they shall be comforted (Mt 5:4). The Apostle says explicitly: "For the form of this world is passing away" (1 Cor 7:31). So we are to live in the world as not involved with it. It is clear that St.

Paul thinks that under the circumstances being unmarried gives one freedom to devote oneself to the Lord and not be anxious about pleasing a spouse. He notes that the unmarried woman need worry only about being holy in body and spirit (1 Cor 7:34).

The general principle behind St. Paul's thinking is manifested when he addresses a person who marries because his passions are strong: "Let him do as he wishes: let hem marry - it is no sin" (1 Cor 7:36). Yet if desire is under control, he does well not to marry, for "he who refrains from marriage will do better" (1 Cor 7:38). The principle is one of freedom combined with the moral stance of what later ethicists call supererogation. Supererogation does not connote here any greater merit, but it does set forth a better way over against a lesser one which is nonetheless good and even praiseworthy. What is lesser is not any less worthwhile since the charisms that are given make comparisons pointless.

The entire passage in 1 Cor 7 is remarkable since it manages to retain the affirmation that marriage is good and holy in the Lord along with the sharp eschatological awareness which makes relative and secondary the concerns of this world. Business cannot go on as usual if the end is very near. Out of that relativity comes a freedom to marry without sin and yet a greater freedom to remain unmarried and devoted to the things of the Lord more directly. It is from this passage that monastic authors will make their claim for the better way (e.g., St. Gregory of Nyssa, *On Virginity*, and St. John Chrysostom, *On Virginity*).

What St. Paul says regarding the widow contains the essence of his teaching: "A wife is bound to her husband as long as he lives. If the husband dies, she is free to be married to whom she wishes, only in the Lord. But in my judgment she is happier if she remains as she is. And I think that I have the Spirit of God" (1 Cor 7:39). Moreover, the fidelity of the wife must be life-long. The widow has the freedom to remarry, and it is not sin as long as she marries in the Lord, but it is better not to marry, and for this St. Paul claims the inspiration of God. In the Apostle's statement stands a consistent ethic. Christian marriage is in the Lord, and the obligation to one another depends on a Word from the Lord.

Earlier we have seen that even the unbeliever may be saved since he is linked to the saints (that is, to the Church) by marriage with a Christian. As such, marriage in the Lord is holy and sanctifying. Yet a better and even easier way is to remain unmarried. Since this is an opinion inspired by the Holy Spirit, it has a warrant from God that cannot be pushed aside. Most commentators remark on how St. Paul moves between an asceticism which would have scorned all marriage and a Judaism which would have demanded marriage for everyone. Whereas the temptations within a Gnosticizing Gentile Christianity would be the simple identification of the flesh with what is evil, St. Paul is able to identify the body of the Christian with the temple of the Holy Spirit. Schillebeeckx argues that the so-called Pauline privilege allowing a separation and remarriage for the new convert to Christianity is not really present in St. Paul's thought.[8] In fact, it is only if non-Christian partner wishes to leave that such a marriage can be recognized as dissoluble. Marriage is not absolutized in itself since the union of the man and the woman stands within the eschatological horizon. The Spirit who has been given and who resides in the Christian is manifesting the first fruits of the kingdom to come. An interpretation of St. Paul's thought which reduces his theology to a new law or treats celibacy as so superior that marriage becomes in effect an evil would be radically unfaithful to the Pauline text. But equally the tendency to leave out the eschatological focus in marriage and to reduce it to a secular state is a betrayal of the peculiar and vocational charism of marriage.

There seems to have been a tendency of Gentile converts to the Christian faith to gravitate back to their pagan standards, as we see from Eph 5:3-5. In contrast with the evil ways of the pagans, St. Paul sets forth the Christian way which is to be wise, not acting like fools. He exhorts: "Therefore do not be foolish but understand what the will of the Lord is" (Eph 5:17).

At Eph 5:21 begins the classic passage in which St. Paul expounds his mature theology of marriage and the consequent ethic that follows from it. It is extremely important that we examine this text closely if we are to establish a marital ethic which is both biblical and Orthodox.

Eph 5:21-2: *Be subject to one another out of reverence for Christ. Wives be subject to your husbands, as to the Lord.*

The motive for subordination is given as the fear of Christ. As many commentators point out, this is the only example in the entire New Testament of fear of Christ being set forth as a motive for good action. There was indeed a legacy of the fear of God in the Old Testament. The eschatological elements found elsewhere in Ephesians (such as references to Christ's *parousia*, 4:13; to the last judgment, 6: 8-9; to the present and coming days of tribulation, 3:13; 5:16; 6:13) reveal the continuity of Paul's writing. Barth notes the significance of eschatology at this point: "It puts all ethical commands of the *Haustafel* under the sign of eschatological promise and hope, and calls for that conduct that heeds the crisis of the present, the last judgment, and the ultimate triumph of Christ."[9]

Subordination is urged in 1 Pt 2:13 to "every human institution," in Col 3:18 for wives to their husbands, and in 1 Tm 2:11 we read: "Let a woman learn in silence with all submissiveness." These texts are all part of what has come to be known as *Haustafeln* or sets of rules for the household where rules for households are set forth. But the context of subordination in Eph 5:21 is far from the Stoic formulas that provide apodictic norms for individual members of the household. The setting here makes the subordination depend as a participle attached to the imperative, "Be filled with the Spirit" (Eph 5:18). One may ask whether subordination is the last of a series of activities dependent upon the inspiration of the spirit (conversing with hymns, singing, praying, thanksgiving, and "giving way"), but it is clear from what follows that this is not the logic of the author's thought. Subordination leads on to a theological climax of which it is an essential part. It can hardly be said to be only one manifestation of spiritual inspiration.

One must note that in Eph 5:21 the phrase "be subject to one another" ("giving way" in the Jerusalem Bible) is mutual, for the man as well as the woman. Barth thinks that such subordination is neither "self-contradictory nor a call to chaos, but a challenge to the conservative and patriarchal concepts of social order which have often been attributed to Paul or derived from his teaching."[10] Barth's judgment is contrary to many feminist theologians and exegetes who have seen only the patriarchal structures and prejudices evident in the subjection of women to the authority and power of men. Yet even the most radical of feminist theologians, E. Schüssler Fiorenza, having stated that the injunction of St. Paul for subordination "reinforces the patriarchal marriage pattern and justifies it christologically" notes that the exhortation from St. Paul to the husband to love his wife (given three times, 5:25, 28, 33) modifies the traditional pattern (seen in Col 3:19) and presents a radical challenge to patriarchal domination.[11] Comparing the text of Eph 5:21 with Col 3:19 the most obvious difference is the lack of the verb "subordinate" (*hupotasso*) in addressing the wife. Stephen Francis Miletic has asked why this verb has not been used when addressing the wife at vv. 22 and 24b. Indeed, why does the verb only occur in connection with the Church at v. 24a? Miletic's answer is challenging and theologically important: "My contention has been that the construction...is best explained as the author's attempt to redefine the wife's subordination by linking it to the subordination of the eschatological community at v. 21 and v.24a. Such a link makes clear the ecclesiological nature of the wife's subordination."[12] One must also notice that in the Greek there is an ellipsis of the verb at v. 22. Miletic, after complex investigations into the linguistic meaning of this ellipsis concludes that it "represents the first illustration of how the lifestyle of individual members of the church has a direct impact on the wife's subordination."[13] He continues: "To what effect? The eschatological nature of the wife's subordination indicates that it is part of God's intent for *Endzeit* or redeemed humanity."[14] The claim made by many biblical exegetes that the *Haustafeln* represent the return of patriarchal ethics as against the radical ethic of St. Paul (as found earlier in texts such as Ga 3:28) is far too extreme a judgment in the light of Eph 5:21. It is the merit of John Yoder and Stanley Hauerwas, two Protestant scholars, to have restored the *Haustafeln* to a degree of moral authenticity by pointing out that subordination is meant to be mutual within the Christian community. All must be subordinate to all, but each in his or her particular calling.[15] This subordination is spelled out by the phrase, "wives to your husbands as to the Lord" (Eph 5:22). It is clearly an example intended to illustrate the meaning of subordination. Furthermore, it is wrong to conclude that St. Paul is speaking of the subjugation of all women to men. Stanley Hauerwas has specifically commented on v. 21:

> The command for wives to be subject to their husbands, for example, comes only after the admonition that everyone in the church must be subject to the other out of "reverence for Christ" (Eph 5:21). It does not say that wives should be subject to husbands as an end in itself, but rather as "to the Lord." So the manner of being "subject" cannot be read off the face of the text nor can it be made clear by exegesis alone. In fact, exegesis itself points us to recall the ways in which we as members of the church have learned to be subject to one another as faithful disciples of Christ. That direction should effectively restrain a contemporary reader from trying to understand "subordinate" from a perspective that assumes all moral relations which are not "autonomous" are morally suspect.[16]

Questions concerning the term of reference indicated by the phrase "as to the Lord" (Eph 5:22) have existed for centuries. Is the Lord here the husband or Christ? Markus Barth points to the fact that in Greek the text should read "'as to the(ir) lords' if it referred to the husband."[17] Clearly the reference is to Jesus Christ as *kyrios*, and only the verses that follow can enlighten us as to what is meant. Barth translates v. 23: "For (only) in the same way that the Messiah is the head of the church." It might be argued that for this phrase merely provides an illustration of a comparable headship, but this could not be possible since the references in Pauline thought never make Christ a confirmation of natural law or "an embellishment, a halo, or a mythological framework to an indisputable status quo."[18] In fact, Jesus Christ is the only cause and standard for the conduct of the saints. The logical structure of the next verse (5:24) confirms this interpretation, for the relationship between Christ and the Church is the archetype of the wife's subordination, not its illustration.

If we are to know what kind of authority the husband has over his wife, it is important to comprehend something of what is meant by Christ being the head of the Church, the savior of his body. The language of head and body is often used by St. Paul. The doctrine of the Church as the body of Christ is set forth in Rom 12:5, in 1 Cor 12:12-30 and in Col 1:18, 2:19, and 3:15. Interestingly, language of the head in relation to the body begins in Colossians and continues in Eph 1:23, 4:15, and 5:23. Insofar as Colossians and Ephesians are later Pauline epistles, this development of the doctrine of the Church as the body of Christ and yet under Christ as its head is quite remarkable. Indeed, in Col 2:19 the man described as having visions and worshiping angels (in all probability a Gnostic) is said to be "not holding fast to the Head, from whom the whole body, nourished and knit together through its joints and ligaments, grows with a growth that is from God."

Eph 5:23: *For the husband is the head of the wife as Christ is the head of the church, his body, and is himself its Savior.*

How did Christ save His body? The meaning only becomes apparent with the realization that the Church is His body. It is by His saving activity that He is the head of the body. One can compare Hosea 3:2 to this verse. Hosea the prophet was told by God to buy "for fifteen shekels of silver and a homer and bushel-and-a-half of barley" his wife who had become a prostitute. This forgiving love is a saving act. Even though the parallels and analogies between Eph 5:23-32 and the descriptions given by the prophets of the relation between Yahweh and Israel as a marital one are obvious and to be accepted, Barth states that there is "no evidence that Paul wanted to make the unique events in Hosea's marriage the model for all married couples. Gomer was Hosea's wife even before he had 'bought' her again for himself. Not every woman is a Gomer, nor each husband a Hosea."[19]

The reference to Christ as head of the Church "the savior of his body" can be understood through two exegetical options. The first would apply the headship and savior roles equally to the husband and to Christ. This would qualify the headship of the husband through Christ. Miletic states that this position must be clearly rejected in the light of the second option which interprets 5:23c as "an appositional phrase." As such, the "antecedent for *autos* at v.23c is normally the most proximate and definite (i.e., particular) noun."[20] The second option must be preferred because it corresponds with the grammar of the passage. In effect, Christ's role as "savior of the body" does not "impinge upon the husband/Christ analogy."[21] Accepting the analogical priority of the Christ/Church relationship necessitates our examination of what that relationship entails. There is more to the head/body link than might be immediately obvious since at 5:23b-c the term is qualified by Christ's role as savior. There is the act of God that creates the unity between Christ and the Church and the saving action of Christ who creates and saves the Church. Miletic refers to the New Creation theology present in this passage and already present in 2 Cor 5:17 and Col 1:15-20. Christ as head is connected to the reflections of St. Paul on Christ as the eschatological Adam. This is especially evident in Ephesians: "That is, the application of *kephale* to Christ expresses not only Christ's superior position in the cosmos, it also expresses his role as the first exponent of the New Creation. The mere association with Christ - she is his "body" - suggests that she also forms part of the New Creation. The depiction of the church as having been raised with Christ (cf. 2.6) confirms this suggestion."[22] Yet We cannot apply to the husband all the characteristics of Christ's relation to the Church. The husband and wife are analogically head/body, but the husband is not only not the savior, but the cosmological supremacy of Christ is entirely lacking for him.

Miletic has underscored this theology of the new Adam as basic to   this entire passage. As Christ is the new Adam, so the Church is the new Eve. Over against all the negative images of Eve found in the Pauline literature, we have here an entirely positive image, though the author of Ephesians does not directly refer to the Church as Eve. The idea is present, however, since the reference to Christ as head entails a theology of the Christ as the new Adam.

Moral theologians have increasingly seen scriptural admonition as based upon narrative and archetypical patterns. Some, like the eminent Catholic moral theologian Bruno Schüller have argued that all biblical ethics is parenesis and ultimately reducible to natural law.[23]   I would, on the contrary, argue that Christian morality, particularly that of the marital partners in this instance, is based upon God's revelation of the economy of His loving and saving acts. In Eph 5:21-33 we find an ethic built upon analogy with the paradigm of Christ and the Church, Christ as savior and the Church as subordinate and reconciling.

Many commentators take the pronoun "he" or in Greek *autos* which follows the two subject nouns "husband" and "Messiah" as referring to both, but if that were so, it would have to be *autoi* since *autos* must refer to the Messiah. Furthermore, *autos* introduces (as one can see from Eph 2:14 and 4:10) a laudatory utterance and should be read as "this is the One who is (the savior of his body)." Barth notes that neither in the Hebrew scriptures nor in any Jewish sources, do we see any association between "head" and "savior." Unless we consider Ephesians a Gnostic work (since the Gnosticized *Odes of Solomon* closely relates redemption and the title "head"), it is only in the case of Christ that we find these two functions joined. We may ask whether in the light of the immediate reference to the husband ("if the husband the head of his wife") a husband is not also the savior of his wife's body. St. John Chrysostom saw it as such, as did Theophylact. On the other hand, the phrase "he, the savior of his body" refers to Christ, and its extension to husbands is not based on the evidence at hand. Miletic concurs with this judgment: "Because the *autos* of v. 23c can only refer to

Christ at v. 23b, v. 23c is taken as an appositional phrase qualifying v. 23b. This line of argumentation simply points out that any link between the husband and Christ is based on the headship analogy and not on the headship/savior amalgam relevant to Christ."[24]   Clearly a husband could not be said to be the savior of his wife's soul, though it is plausible that he could be said to save her body - as Barth suggests, "by protecting her from improper personal conduct or from an intolerable yearning or suffering of her body (cf. Gen 3:16)."[25] Barth rejects such a parallel on linguistic evidence by claiming that the word "he" (*autos*) introduces an aretalogy, perhaps from an early Christian hymn.   Furthermore, he claims that if every married man were termed a "savior" of the body of his wife St. Paul would be suspected or even guilty of idolatry.   The fact is that there are no previous statements in either ancient or biblical literature speaking of headship as the role of the husband in relation to his wife. Thus the proposition "the husband is the head of his wife" is original with the author of Ephesians.   How we are to interpret this becomes clear when we realize that the husband's headship is entirely dependent upon the meaning of Christ's headship. What that dependence means is to be discerned from Mk 10:42-45: "The Son of Man also came not to be served but to serve and to give his life."   Headship is reinterpreted by Christ as serving, and from this perspective one could say that the husband is the head of the wife if he is her servant. There is clearly no unlimited role for being the *dominus* or *kyrios* on the part of the husband.

Eph 5:24: *As the church is subject to Christ, so let wives also be subject in everything to their husbands.*

The word usually translated as "but" (omitted in the RSV) and by Barth as "the difference notwithstanding" is in the original Greek *alla* which introduces a contrast, sufficiently strong to be translated as something more than the word "and." It introduces the phrase "just as the church subordinates herself to the Messiah so wives to their husbands." The way that the Church subordinates herself is by faith, love, unity, hope, confession, and testimony. In Eph 4:25-5:20 the Church and every member of Christ's body continuously seek to learn and do the will of the Lord. Such subordination is not an absolute. It is to be seen as like the Church's service before Christ. Barth gives three qualifications of the wife's subordination.[26] First, it is by an exhortation which calls for mutual subordination; secondly, it is by the statement that subordination is for the wife before the husband, not before all men; finally, it is by making quite specific the subordination which is called for. It is only to be a subordination like that which the Church has before Christ. It exists in freedom, and is a subordination to love, not to domination. Miletic agrees: "That the author wishes to stress the church's subordination as *the paradigm* for the wife is clear from the following. First, stated negatively, the verb *hupotasso* does not appear when the wife is being addressed. Both the absence of the verb in the context which surely demands its presence and the abundant witness of the tradition about the subordination of wives in New Testament and elsewhere suggests that the author is clearly modifying the address to the wife."[27]

Stated positively the verb *hupotasso* is used only with reference to the Church. Miletic notes that in 1 Cor 15:28 it was Christ who submitted Himself to God the Father, but in Ephesians it is the Church which is subordinated to God: "That is, in Ephesians the church is an important agent effecting the unity of (literally) everything with Christ...the subordination of the son at 1 Cor 15: 28, absent at Eph 1:19-23 is transferred to the church at Eph 5.24a."[28] The subordination of the Church to Christ is paradigmatic to the wife. The verb *hupotasso* is actually a military metaphor taken from secular Greek military language, but St. Paul's use of it is consistently in the middle or passive voices, and according to Barth this means that the action of subordination presupposes the activity of a morally free and responsible agent. There is a clear sense of order in the meaning of the word, but in Paul's thought this is taken up into the eschatological expectation.[29] The German biblical scholar Rudolf Schnackenburg notes the sense of order which the verb has but thinks that the wife's subordination is a loving response to her husband's love.[30]

Eph 5:25: *Husbands, love your wives, as Christ loved the church and gave himself up for her.*

The injunction, "husbands, love your wives," is correlated with subordination. Usually in St. Paul's thought love is self-sacrificing, other-directed, and creative. But marital love is here immediately taken up into the love of Christ. The love of Christ is not just a parallel to human love but a love modified in a particular way by the term "just as" (*kathos*) which gives it the force of being a quotation. Examples may be given from other passages in the Pauline literature (Eph 5:2, 25 and Gal 2:20) of formulas such as "he has loved...and has given himself for..." The analogy between the bridegroom and the bride and the relation of Christ to his Church is clear here. This analogy is carried so far by the German Catholic exegete Heinrich Schlier that marriage becomes a participation in the mystery of Christ's love for the pre-existent, the fallen, and then the redeemed Church. What is equally important in this passage is the radical recasting of sexual love by reference to the love and self-sacrifice of Christ for his Church. On the other hand, there is not here a spiritualization which would leave the physical behind and turn the relationship between husband and wife into an entirely Platonic or ascetic one. The language of "blood," "flesh,"and "body" (Eph 5:29-30) as well as the inclusion of the text from Genesis at Eph 5: 31 referring to "one flesh" avoids such spiritualization.

Eph 5:26-7: *That he might sanctify her, having cleansed her by the washing of water with the word, that he might present the church to himself in splendor, without spot or wrinkle or or any such thing, that she might be holy and without blemish.*

This passage refers to Christ's action upon his body the Church. Behind it lie several texts from the Old Testament such as Ezk 16:4,9, where the girl Jerusalem "," is pitied by God, chosen to be his bride, and joined to him in a covenant. There is another text of Ezk 36:25-27 which refers to the "clean water" which God will "sprinkle upon....you" so that "you shall be clean from all your uncleannesses," and He will give "a new heart" and put His "spirit within you." There was also the custom of the bath given a Jewish bride before her wedding. Almost all interpreters of this passage agree that the passage speaks of baptism. Water may signify the Spirit with whom the coming Messiah can baptize. Terms such as washing, purification and sanctification do not necessarily or exclusively mean or refer to baptism. Their reference can be the Spirit of God, the blood of Christ, or the word of Christ, or even faith.[31] They may include baptism as an illustration or application of their symbolic meaning. Schlier interprets v. 26 as referring to baptism but agrees that "elsewhere in Paul and the New Testament *katharizein* ("to purify, to make clean") does not occur in explicit connection with baptism. Later *loutron* ("bath") designates baptism relatively often."[32] The background to this sentence is the presentation of the bride to the bridegroom at the Jewish wedding. The best man did this, and the bride's friend has a counterpart in the "friend of the bridegroom." These assistants were indispensable and known as the *shoshbinin*. Each step in the process of match-making, betrothal, and the creation of the marriage contract and preparation of the wedding feast was carried out by them. God himself rendered this service to Eve when "He brought her to the man" (Gn 2:22). References to the "friend of the bridegroom" and the "sons of the bridal chamber" are made in Jn 3:29 and Mt 9:15. The bride's best man is mentioned in 2 Cor 11:2: "I betrothed you to Christ to present you as a pure bride to her one husband."

Barth notes that in Eph 5:25-27 two deviations are made from the customs of the Jews. One is that there is only one matchmaker, and this is the bridegroom himself: "The Messiah...presents (the bride) to himself."[33] This is paralleled in Ezk 16:3-14 where God is seen as both the fatherly friend and the bridegroom of Jerusalem. In 2 Cor 11:2 the apostle is the friend of the bride, not her bridegroom. Presentation implies a judgment. By presenting the church to himself Christ makes her perfect, without spot or wrinkle. He is pleased with the Church. In Eph 1:3-14 the people chosen and blessed are to stand before Him "holy and blame-less." Behind the word *endoxos* is the verb *doxazo* which is, in turn, derived from *doxa* having the meaning in Christian circles of "glory." In Eph 1:17 we read of the "Father of glory," who has promised rich glories for the saints to inherit (Eph 1:18). The Church is thus made "glorious" or "re-splendent."

The question has been asked by commentators over the ages as to whether the vision is the glorious Church without spot or wrinkle in the present or in the eschatological future, or perhaps a combination of the two. In favor of the future is the grammatical structure of verses 25-27. There we have three final clauses in the Greek beginning with *hina* ("in order to") with futuristic subjunctives. On the other hand, there are references in Ephesians which clearly speak of the present (2:6; 4:4-6; 5:8: "now you are light") as the time in which God is sanctifying his Church. The baptismal state of purity is preparation for the glorious transformation to be realized on the Last Day. The future fulfillment of the marital relation-ship is parallel in importance to the glorification of the Church at the last day. Theologically, Barth's stress on the future conveys the Neo-Protestant refusal to find present holiness in the Church. When we look to the Greek Fathers we discover a stress on a present, a realized eschatology, but one would be quite Orthodox in relating the holiness of the Church to the Kingdom of which Christ is the King and which He will bring. The combination of the present as participation in the future is evident in Eph 1:5-6. and reflected in the anaphora of St. John Chrysostom in the preface that precedes the Sanctus: "Thou it was who brought us from non-existence into being, and when we had fallen away didst raise us up again, and did not cease to do all things until Thou hadst brought us up to heaven and hadst endowed us with Thy kingdom which is to come."

Eph 5: 28: *Even so husbands should love their wives as their own bodies. He who loves his wife loves himself.*

The translation of verse 28 is crucial for an understanding

of marriage. The Vulg., the KJV, and the RSV leave ambiguous whether the words "as their own bodies" refer to the wives, who are the bodies of the husbands, or whether they are to be loved as the husbands love their own bodies. The Jerusalem Bible takes the latter option, but this is, as Barth suggests, quite arbitrary. Barth's own interpretation permits an analogy between the love of the husbands for their own bodies and the love of their wives' bodies. Aquinas found here a link between the natural law (loving one's own body) and the Christological (loving one's wife as Christ loves the Church). On the other hand, St. Paul links marriage to Christ's love for the Church as interdependent. The testimony of 1 Cor 6:16 shows that it is the link with Christ and the Holy Spirit that makes fornication the evil that it is. Gn 2:24 is given a clear Christological meaning in Eph 5:29-31. Thus both on contextual and on theological grounds we must follow Barth in verse 28 by translating "their wives for they are their bodies." The position of *kai* in the text indicates that the husband is compared with Christ and his love with Christ's. There is, therefore, no analogy between Christ's love for his Church and a man's love for his wife as modeled after his love for his own body. The analogy is between Christ's love for the Church as his own body and the husband's love for his wife as his own body. It is also interesting that the word "owe" (*opheilousin*) has nothing of the categorical imperative in it as the English word "ought" has. The term has its usual context in financial obligations, but sometimes in parental obligations, gratitude, or responsibility for the weak (Rom 15:1).

Eph 5:29-30: *For no man ever hates his own flesh, but nourishes and cherishes it, as Christ does the church, because we are members of his body.*

Various commentators have thought that the phrase "In loving his wife a man loves himself" is taken from a proverb and is a parenthetical insertion. There may well be here an allusion to Lv 19:18, an allusion which would be even more apparent in Eph 5:33 ("each one must love his wife as himself"). What is important is that there is no thought of devaluation of this love as mere "egoism." Self-love is recognized as good, but it is placed in a Christological context. We move not only from self-love to Christ but from Christ's love back to self-love. Only a love which is not selfish (1 Cor 13:5) and is gracious and self-giving will be appropriate here. The reference to one's own flesh refers to the wife, not to the man's appetites. Barth thinks that the transition from "body" to "flesh" is best explained by the use of the Genesis text in 5:31. What might appear to be a truism becomes a statement of theological depth, for if one understands the wife to be his own flesh this will exclude the hatred and enmity which arise in many marriages. Unity in the body of Christ also excludes the animosities of the nations which are overcome in the creation of the New Man (Eph 2:15). To "provide and care for it" would then refer not to the natural care of washing and grooming but to the provision and care given to a wife. Barth notes the various senses of providing and caring: that of a parent for a child, that promised in a Jewish or pagan marriage contract, the care that God the Father has for his body, the cosmos, or the sustenance (*epichoregeo*) that Christ provides for His Church (Eph 4:16b). The terms may have Eucharistic meanings since Christ nourishes the Church from the supper offered at His table (1 Cor 10:21;11:20).

The phrase "as Christ does the church, because we are members of his body" (Eph 5:29-30) gives us the foundational motive for our human action as husbands. The words "just as" in reference to the Messiah (Christ) are used for the third time (cf. verses 23 and 25). The deeds of the Messiah are the basis for our attitude toward our wives. The movement from the Church to the individual members reinforces the ethical and moral value given to this statement. An ecclesial ethic emerges far from modern individualism.

The phrase added in some manuscripts to Eph 5:30 "from his flesh and from his bones," is best taken as a later addition to the text. Various interpretations have been given to the words. John Chrysostom and Thomas Aquinas made them refer to the Incarnation, and others have suggested a reference to the Eucharist. Although the evidence for their exclusion from the original text is conclusive, this gloss is important in the history of the interpretation of Eph 5:21-33. If we accept the words "from his flesh and from his bones" as forming the end of 5:30, the reference may be to Gn 2:23. The Church as the body of Christ may allude to the creation of the woman from the rib of Adam. Again this gloss would give a clear reference for explaining the question of what *anti toutou* ("therefore," "for this reason") means. The gloss could, on the other hand, refer to the creation of the Church out of Christ's side, from his "flesh and bones." St. John Chrysostom believed that these words speak of the "substantial" unity of the church with Christ. He, Christ, shared our humanity so that we might share his divinity (2 Pt 1:4). We may also find here an anticipation of the recapitulation theory as set forth by St. Irenaeus. Chavasse has claimed that "as Eve was the continuation and projection of Adam's body...so the church, her antitype, is the continuation of Christ's incarnation."[34] Schlier pointed to the gloss as an "inauthentic anti-Gnostic gloss whereby the church is affirmed as still 'flesh,' not yet purely spiritual."[35]

Eph 5: 31: *For this reason a man shall leave his father and mother and be joined to his wife, and the two shall become one."*

Gn 2:24 is the source of the sentence quoted by St. Paul here. There are two changes in the text from the Hebrew. St. Paul follows the Septuagint in translating *'Ish* as *anthropos* rather than *aner,* which would have been more exact. He adds "The two" to the final phrase "will become one flesh." These changes are quite important in attempting an interpretation of the passage in Eph 5:31. It is well attested by modern biblical scholars that the creation narratives in Gn 1 and Gn 2 are widely variant and come from sources separate in historical origin and in the level of sophistication. The first (Gn 1:26-27) narrative speaks of simultaneous creation while the second (Gn 2:7-24) speaks of successive creation of the woman following the man. Philo faces this apparent contradiction by claiming that the man mentioned in Gn 1 was bisexual and androgynous and was later divided into the two when the woman was created from the rib of man. The two were later reunited (Gn 2:23-24). The conclusion drawn by Philo was that "he who has no wife is no man," that is, no complete man. Philo is dependent upon the Septuagint which uses *anthropos* to designate the male alone. The rabbis continue to follow this exegesis, which would demand that human wholeness depends upon the union of the male and the female. Philo, however, provides a Platonic interpretation whereby the female enters the male mind when he is asleep. The female brings the life of the senses and subverts the rationality of the male. More often he attributes to Adam joy at the sight of Eve.

The meaning of the text from Genesis in the context of Eph 5:21-33 is not at all obvious. Some critics have thought that it has no reference whatsoever to the husband and wife but refers only to Christ and the Church. This opinion is questionable at best. A more central concern is whether Eph 5:32 is connected to the address to wives at Eph 5:22-4. Miletic has urged, against the exegete A. T. Lincoln, that there is such a reference since the address to wives was guided by the theological agenda which the author of Ephesians took from the Pauline and Jewish theological reflection about the eschatological Adam.

Barth claims, on the other hand, that in Ephesians there are no traces of the ontological Jewish statements about the bisexual primal man.[36] He thinks that the teaching of St. Paul in 1 Cor 11:7, where man alone was made in the image of God and reflects his glory (the female only reflecting man's glory) has been forsaken in Ep 5. It is Christ alone who is the image of God in the later Pauline thought (2 Cor 4:6; Col 1:15; Heb 1:3). St. Paul's use of the creation story in Ephesians is consistently related to the new creation in Jesus Christ (Eph 2:15; 4:24; 5:25-27,32). Marriage is related not to a natural order but is an expression of the recreation of all things in Jesus Christ. Barth sees creation as an intimation of the new creation which was to be brought forth in Jesus Christ. It is clear that St. Paul quoted the Torah (Gn 2:24) rather than the prophets since the Torah has the highest authority in the Old Testament. The saying about union in "one flesh" is itself a prophecy and a directive. The directive is a command and interpreted as such. The ethical conclusions drawn from it in Eph 5:33 are that the man is to love his wife and the wife respect her husband. The language is stronger for the man: he ought to love his wife, and the woman is invited, as it were, that she may fear her husband: "and the wife...may she fear her husband." It is true that this softer tone may be contradicted by the verb "fear." Many have urged us to translate *phobetai* as "respect" to make it more palatable to modern readers, but this goes beyond the plain meaning of the words. Elsewhere St. Paul has no hesitation in calling us to the fear of Christ (Eph 5.21). Orthodox exegetes should have no problem with the fear of God.

When we compare the teaching of St. Paul regarding marriage in Eph 5 with what he says elsewhere in his letters we are amazed. In 1 Cor 7:1 we are told that it is a good thing not to touch a woman, but it is less evil to have a wife than to fall into sexual sin. Marriage binds us to the world and its care. It is better not to marry, so as to be free for the service of the kingdom of God. Paul allows that since not every Christian has a charisma to remain unmarried, there is the freedom to marry. Barth notes that the statements in 1 Cor 7:39 that speak of a marrying "in the Lord" and make the calling of the Lord available within any earthly setting "leave open and actually pave the way for the surprisingly positive statements on marriage in Ephesians."[37] St. John Chrysostom had long ago in his *Sermon on Marriage* linked 1 Cor 7:4 with Eph 5:21-33 when he said that in the earlier text St. Paul "introduces a great measure of equality." He notices that in other matters there needs to be a superior authority, but "where chastity and holiness are at stake, the husband has no greater privilege than the wife."[38]

If we look at another Pauline text dealing with women, 1 Tm 2:9-15, it is evident that the author, whom most biblical scholars think cannot be the Apostle himself, knew 1 Corinthians but not Ephesians. Being saved by child bearing is contrary to the thought of Eph 5:21-33. The clear inferiority of women in 1 Tm 2:11-15 is entirely lacking in Ephesians.

There is complementarity in Eph 5:21-33 which rejoices in the differences between the sexes when brought together in one flesh. At once that union is the union of the man and the woman and the union of Christ and the church. Whereas 1 Tm 2:9-15 looks to differences to establish the superiority of the man and posits childbirth as the way a woman may be saved, Eph 5:21-33 never mentions childbirth and promises sanctification and salvation through a union which shares in the union between Christ and the Church. This teaching about marriage is the highest to be found in the New Testament, hence our detailed study of the text. Marriage is not just a sign, among others, of the union of Christ and his Church, nor is it an allegory whereby the union of the earthly couple signifies the union of the heavenly couple (as the Gnostics would have it). The meaning of marriage is found in the saving, loving, cleansing, and recreative activity of Jesus Christ. It is true that some would claim that the identification of the man with Christ and the woman with the Church creates an unequal and undue male dominance. But the ethical injunctions, even if different, are such as to model the relationship on the loving care of Jesus and obedience of a faithful Church so that the outcome is "one flesh," not the battle of the sexes. The union of Christ and His Church is, indeed, a union of unequals, but insofar as Christ shared the human condition and came as the lover of mankind, His love is never enslaving but liberating. Mutual subordination is inevitably involved when the relationship between Christ and the Church ceases to be one of domination and subservience. Christ comes as a friend who saves and who serves. It is only the devils in their resistance to God who experience Him as a despot who forces His rule upon them.

The "one flesh" which is created speaks of sexual union, but that is undergirded by spiritual union. The reason that we cannot speak of the "one flesh" as a sign among others of Christ's union with the Church is that the union of Christ and the Church is not one feature among others which give the marital union its ground, validity, form, purpose, and blessing. In Eph 5:22-33, it is the sole basis upon which all statements of marriage are founded. The Old Testament scholar, von Rad has claimed that "one flesh" in Gn 2:24 referred to the child to be born of the united couple.[39] There are, however, no Jewish parallels for this interpretation, and it would appear to be utterly foreign to the context of Eph 5:21-33. Certainly the *henosis* which is the "one flesh" is not merely a sexual one, nor is it clearly legal. It is not a condition which comes only into existence upon the birth of offspring. It is a new being consisting of a man and a woman who have come to share in the union of Christ and His Church. It is an explication of what St. Paul meant by marriage "in the Lord." This is why the exegesis of Eph 5:21-33 is so very important for an understanding of the Orthodox doctrine of marriage as a sacrament.

The traditional questions posed in the Latin West about what makes marriage valid (consent or consummation) are foreign to the context of Eph 5:21-33. It is a union in the Lord which makes a marriage truly Christian and creates its authenticity. Outside that context marriages may exist but not in the Christian and sacramental sense. The originality of Eph 5: 21-33 is found in the statement that two unions are involved in marriage: that between the husband and the wife and that between Christ and the Church. It is not a mythic union of the heavenly man and the heavenly woman. It is the historical Jesus who revealed the love of God in his self-offering on the cross.

Whereas Heinrich Schlier gave Eph 5: 21-33 a mythical interpretation, it is clear that St. Paul is giving mythic thought a historical and concrete meaning, both in the life of Jesus Christ and in the sexual union of the earthly couple who share in Christ's love and saving action. Can we deduce from Eph 5:22-33 that marriage is a sacrament as Orthodox Christians believe it to be? Only the next verse can answer that.

Eph 5: 32-33: *This is a great mystery, and I take it to mean Christ and the church; however, let each one of you love his wife as himself, and let the wife see that she respects her husband.*

The word "this" (*touto*) may refer forward, but it is more

likely that it refers back to Gn 2:24. Barth thinks that all the previous references to "mystery" in Ephesians (1:9; 3:3,4,9; 6:19) "spoke of only one secret, that is, the incorportion of the Gentiles into God's people and house - a secret that was formerly hidden to all generations, but is now revealed through Christ to the apostles and prophets, and has to be made known to the world."[40]   Eph 5:32 speaks of one of several mysteries which were spoken of by St. Paul in 1 Cor 4:1; 13:2; 14:2. Barth thinks that *mysterion* can be translated in Eph 5:32 in the "original sense." This interpretation becomes clear when he translates *mysterion* as "secret meaning." This rather literal translation differs from three other translations. One sees *mysterion* as the Latin equivalent of *sacramentum*. From this originated the Roman Catholic view of marriage as a sacrament (though it is not clear that Augustine understood the term *sacramentum* primarily as an ecclesiastical rite conveying grace). Another way of translating *mysterion* is to give it the same meaning as mystery in English. This would involve a mystical reality with an unfathomable core. A third way is to understand *mysterion* as the equivalent of allegory or mythology. Thus a formerly secret meaning is brought to light by a revealed equivalent (either an antitype or an allegorical meaning). St. John Chrysostom understood Eph 5:32 in this sense. The "one flesh" of Gn 2:24 refers typologically to the union of Christ and his Church. We have good reason for accepting Chrysostom's interpretation of the word.

The words *ego de lego* appear elsewhere in Pauline texts to distinguish St. Paul's own opinion from the word of the Lord. Yet St. Paul believes that he has the Spirit of God. There is less authority here than in a word from the Lord, but more authority here than in a personal or private opinion. The words "I am saying" may also point to Paul's asserting the superiority of his interpretation over others which may have been current at the time. What is being said by St. Paul is that Gen 2:24 is speaking of Christ and the Church. One may ask whether St. Paul is indulging in allegory in Eph 5. I do not believe so. Although he uses the term "allegorize" in Gal 4:24, in Eph 5:21-33 his language is clearly typological.

The high doctrine of marriage revealed by St. Paul in Eph 5:21-33 is clearly sacramental in the sense that those married in the Lord share in the union between Christ and His Church. They share in that union not just by applying the ethical attitudes (mutual subordination, love from the man, and fear from the woman) appropriately drawn from Christ's relation to his Church and applied to the married couple. There is more than metaphor and parable here. There is real participation. The participation is not a *Nachvollzug* (Schlier's term) by which the earthly couple reenact and make flesh the spiritual union between Christ and the Church. Nor is it the entrance into an institution that works *ex opere operato* as a means of grace. Barth rejects the sacramental interpretation of marriage because his Western understanding of sacrament depends on criteria that cannot be met from Scripture. He lists the criteria for a sacrament in the Western churches: the institution by Christ, the use of the proper formula, the saving power of a "visible word" and the benefit available to believers. The "word" of Eph 5:26 can hardly qualify as such a dominical institution coming from Christ Himself, and the other criteria can be imposed only in the most artificial and arbitrary way on Eph 5:22-33.

Barth is aware that the Orthodox churches do not found their sacramental interpretation of marriage upon the supposed identity of *mysterion* with *sacramentum* in the legal, ritual, or ecclesiastical sense. He leaves the matter there. His attempted refutation of the Roman Catholic interpretation of marriage as a sacrament takes the form of claiming that a sacramental doctrine of marriage makes "every marriage between Christians equivalent to a *hieros gamos.*"[41] To Barth a sacralization of a structure and a mystification of an institution would occur if marriage obtained sacramental status. As such it could only be a new bondage. Barth's way of avoiding this "heavy yoke of bondage" is a union "created out of the dynamic of self-giving and voluntary subordination."[42] Indeed, he claims that the sacramental interpretation of Eph 5:32 "continues that pagan doctrine and practice of Eros in which the partners use one another in order to attain a good that lies far beyond the partner and his well-

being."[43] This Barth identifies as escapism and a "re-mythi-
fication of Christ's relationship to the church, or of the joint
life of a man and a woman, or both."[44] Instead of regarding
marriage as a sacrament, Barth prefers to designate it as a
covenant, but his evidence for this from Ephesians appears
slight indeed. All he can provide for this interpretation is
"what Paul says in 2:11-22 about the union of Jews and Gentiles who are joined in one covenant so as to have 'free'
access to God, is also reflected in the contents of 5:21-33;
both passages are strikingly similar."[45] By invoking the
notion of covenant rather than sacrament, Barth seeks to give
an ethical base to marriage rather than an institutional one.
Oddly, he thinks that a sacramental understanding of marriage
would consist primarily "in the benefits to be attained by each
individual partner."[46] Again, this view accepts all the presuppositions of Latin scholastic theology at the end of the
Middle Ages. The important thesis of Barth is that marriage
can be understood not from the perspective of creation alone
but only from that of Christology. Such a perspective is not
right if it reduces the mystery of Christ's union with the
Church to a secret now revealed proffering ethical wisdom to
us in our marriages. The typological significance of Gn 2:24
is a participation in the mystery of Christ, by the "one flesh"
which shares in the unity of Christ with His bride the Church.
To talk of sacrament as bondage and institution, as Barth
does, is only to reflect the obsession of Reformed Christians
with Roman Catholicism.

Barth is conscious of another view of marriage as sacrament. He quotes Joseph Ratzinger twice in ways that should
have opened to him a wider and less parochial understanding
of sacramental mystery. According to Ratzinger, Christ is the
proper sacrament between God and man so that "what the
church calls sacraments is strictly tied to one mystery only,
Christ's."[47] This is exactly what Orthodox theology would
say about marriage as a sacrament.

The joining of man and woman is not then a secular
phenomenon but a union "taken up" into the (new) covenant.
Ratzinger states: "In marriage sex and eros are accepted
inside the covenant."[48] Again, Ratzinger refers to the ratifi-

cation of the unity of creation and covenant, as well as the representation and confirmation of God's faithfulness in man's faithfulness. He writes: "In its capacity as order of the covenant this truthfulness is also the 'order of creation' and it enacts as order of the covenant the order of creation."[49] This is, I believe, an interpretation of the sacramental meaning of marriage which refuses to find marriage to be founded primarily in natural law or in the fallen created structures of human life (as among Protestants). It discovers the meaning, end, and fulfillment of creation only in Christ's saving action whereby the Church is cleansed, purified, and redeemed by His union with it. The ethics of marriage (love, mutual subordination, fearful respect) flow from the sacramental participation by the husband and wife in the great mystery of Christ and His Church. Insofar as they are baptized and made members of Christ's body, they share in a very particular way (in their vocation and relation to one another) the union of Christ and his Church, for they are members of the Church united with Christ. The husband is not Christ any more than the wife is exclusively the Church. Rather, as members of the Church, they relate to one another as Christ and the Church should relate to one another. How this is so, and how the husband can represent Christ and yet be a member of His body remains a mystery, the mystery of sanctification and salvation. The signs of this mystery become evident not in the couple's sexual union so much as in their love and respect for one another. But the sexual union both creates and expresses the couple as "one flesh" and as such it is holy and not unclean.

One must in the context of the modern discussion of gender roles and their links with power structures ask whether Eph 5:22-33 depends upon the acceptance of patriarchy. Those who would make the teaching of the author of Ephesians to be based on natural law would, in my opinion, come closer to the absolutizing of male supremacy than those who search the text for what God has revealed through the Christianization of ancient social and cultural forms. Paul Sampley in his book *And the Two Shall Become One Flesh* shows how the reference to Torah gives legitimation and support to the submission of women to men and underlies the use of the verb *upostassomai*.[50] Miletic is in agreement with this, noting that there is a basic exhortation to subordination and/or silence on the part of wives and/or women. In 1 Tm 2:11-15 there is an argument about the "order of being," in this instance regarding the inferiority of Eve. Along with this exhortation there is a reference to Torah, examples drawn from the past, either about Eve or about other women of the past. The contrast with Eph 5:21-33 is striking. Torah is brought forward at Eph 5:31, but the reference is positive and eschatological, about the *Endzeit* rather than the past.

One must ask whether Eph 5:21-33 is, as Schüssler Fiorenza claims, an example of patriarchal culture imposed on the Christian community. The answer is a qualified affirmative. But the qualification is even stronger than has been previously urged by either Barth or other exegetes. Miletic acknowledges that the text moves within an androcentric frame of reference. He urges, however, a radical revision of our reading of the text: "My proposal is that although the author thinks within an androcentric frame of reference, he nonetheless radically changes its orientation by changing the meaning of the language of subordination and headship. Thus while he maintains an androcentric conceptual structure he rejects its potential for domination, especially within husband and wife relationships."[51] The transformation of this structure takes place by the agapic love on which marriage is now focused. That love is not the result of an imperative but is to be patterned on the love of Christ for His Church and the response of the Church to that love. Marriage is now linked to the whole process of reconciliation and uniting which the letter to the Ephesians sets forth as the meaning of Christian faith and practice. The ethical significance of this is great indeed. Miletic puts it thus: "The wife/husband relationship also represents a re-creation of human dignity because Christian marriage now stands against the impulse to dominate and control. Now it must manifest how agapic love reconstitutes, recreates, reconciles and unifies."[52] Miletic knows that marriage is the most sensitive area in human life to sin and hurt. As he puts it, "It is precisely here where wife and husband might know the temptation to dominate, betray, destroy, or, to create, love and give the self to the other."[53]

Instead of talking of demythologizing the Gospel in terms of an philosophical reinterpretation, Miletic speaks of the "remythologizing process" which is called evangelization and conversion. He is correct in seeing this text as a vehicle for overcoming the bondage that exists within marriage between the stronger and the weaker, between the superiority of the male over the female, and any legitimation supporting this oppression of one sex by the other. The gospel is precisely the exclusion of the power struggle between the sexes and the invitation to an acceptance of one another in the mystery of Christ and His love for His Body. Maleness and femaleness are reconstructed in the significance of Christ as servant and savior, revealing in His cross the meaning of His love.

The ethic of marriage that emerges in Eph 5:22-33 is one of living eschatologically in the mystery of the new humanity. One is no longer living according to the rulers of this world who know only the resources of demonic power to realize their will. The realm of freedom and light is where Christians live in Jesus Christ. Their sexual lives and their lives as men and women must be rapt in this mystery to transcend the wounds inflicted by conflicts in the world. The Pauline text does not look to nature; it looks to the kingdom which is to come and in which we participate even now.

I have pursued the meaning of Eph 5:21-33 at such length and in such detail because it is the key to the entire theology of marriage as found in Orthodox tradition. John Meyendorff recognizes this when he writes: "Only in Ephesians is this negative view corrected (of Paul's preference of celibacy over marriage) by the doctrine of marriage as an image of the union between Christ and the Church--a doctrine which became the basis of the entire theology of marriage as found in Orthodox tradition."[54] It is noteworthy that the passage read for the liturgical Epistle in the marriage service of the Orthodox Church is precisely Eph 5:20-33.

Notes

(1) Edward Schillebeeckx, *Marriage: Human Reality and Saving Mystery* Vol. 1 (London: Sheed & Ward, 1965), p. 149.

(2) Eric Fuchs, *Sexual Desire and Love* (New York: Seabury Press, 1983), p. 65.

(3) Francis Beare, *The Gospel According to Matthew* (New York: Harper & Row, 1982), p. 388.

(4) Fuchs, p. 67.

(5) Beare, p. 391.

(6) The note is from *La Bible de Jerusalem* and is translated on p. 47 of the New Testament in the English version of the *Jerusalem Bible*.

(7) Beare, p. 392.

(8) Schillebeeckx, pp. 167-8.

(9) Markus Barth, *Ephesians 4-6*, in *The Anchor Bible*, Vol. 34A (Garden City, NY: Doubleday, 1974), p. 666.

(10) Ibid., pp. 666-7.

(11) E. Schüssler Fiorenza, *In Memory of Her, A Feminist Theological Reconstructidon of Christian Origins* (New York: Crossroad, 1985), p. 270.

(12) Stephen Francis Miletic, *"One Flesh": Eph. 5.22-24, 5.31, Marriage and the New Creation, Analecta Biblica* 115 (Rome: Editrice Pontificio Istituto Biblico, 1988), p. 99.

(13) Ibid., p. 99.

(14) Ibid.

(15) Stanley Hauerwas, *A Community of Character: Toward A Constructive Social Ethic* (Notre Dame, IN: University of Notre Dame Press, 1981), and John H. Yoder, *The Politics of Jesus* (Grand Rapids: Wm. B. Eerdmans, 1972).

(16) Hauerwas, pp. 70-1.

(17) Barth, p. 614.

(18) Ibid., p. 615

(19) Ibid., p. 615.

(20) Miletic, p. 102.

(21) Ibid., pp. 103-4.

(22) Ibid., p. 104.

(23) Bruno Schüller, *Die Begrundung sittlicher Urteile: Typen ethischer Argumentation in der Moraltheologie* (2nd edn Dusseldorf, 1980). Schüller's thought is available in English in *Wholly Human: Essays on the Theory and Language of Morality* (Washkington, DC: Georgetown University Press, 1986).

(24) Miletic, p. 102.

(25) Barth, p. 615.

(26) Ibid., p. 620.

(27) Miletic, pp. 105-6.

(28) Ibid., p. 93.

(29) Barth, p. 710.

(30) Rudolph Schnackenburg, *Der Brief an die Epheser* (Tubingen: J. B.C. Mohr, 1933), p. 254.

(31) Ibid., p. 689.

(32) H. Schlier, *Der Brief an die Epheser*, 2nd ed. (Dusseldorf: Patmos, 1958), pp. 256-7.

(33) Ibid., p. 679.

(34) Claude Chavasse, *The Bride of Christ* (London: Faber, 1940), p. 70.

(35) Schlier, p. 261, quoted by Barth, op. cit., p. 723.

(36) Barth, p. 730.

(37) Ibid., p. 733.

(38) John Chrysostom, *Sermon on Marriage*, trans. Catherine P. Roth and David Anderson in *St. John Chrysostom: On Marriage and Family Life* (Crestwood, NY: St. Vladimir's Seminary Press, 1986), p. 87.

(39) Barth, p. 727.

(40) Ibid., pp. 641-2.

(41) Ibid., p. 731.

(42) Ibid.

(43) Ibid.

(44) Ibid., p. 749.

(45) Ibid., p. 751.

(46) Ibid., p. 749.

(47) Joseph Ratzinger, in Greeven, et. al., *Theologie der Ehe* (Regensburg, Pustet, 1969), pp. 88-93, quoted by Barth, p. 746.

(48) Ibid., p. 746.

(49) Ibid., p. 92, quoted by Barth, p. 643.

(50) J. Paul Sampley, *'And the Two Shall Become One Flesh': A Study of Traditions in Ephesians 5:21-33* (Cambridge: Cambridge University Press, 1971), p. 97.

(51) Miletic, p. 116.

(52) Ibid., p. 117.

(53) Ibid.

(54) John Meyendorff, *Marriage: An Orthodox Perspective* (Crestwood, NY: St. Vladimir's Seminary Press, 1970), p. 17.

Chapter Two:

Marriage in the Patristic Tradition

In the aftermath of the apostolic age, we find an attempt within the emerging Church to deny the legitimacy of marriage for Christians. Already within the Pastoral Epistles we read of "those people who would forbid marriage and the use of particular foods" (1 Tm 4:1-5). This rigorism came to be known as "Encratism" (*enkrateia* meaning abstinence), and a sect composed of rigorists was called by this name. The assumption of the Encratites was that one could not be a baptized Christian and fail to practice sexual continence. Ultimately this view led to schismatic tendencies which the church had to oppose. The problem was posed by the fact that continence was upheld as a good as great as or even greater than marriage by vast numbers of Christians. This was particularly so within Syria and Mesopotamia. Indeed, in the early Syrian church celibacy was considered a requirement for admission to baptism.[1] We read in the Second Letter of Clement that only the "pure in body" may share in Christ's body the Church and that the kingdom of God will come only when all fleshly lusts and distinctions of sex shall have disappeared (2 Clem 14:3-5; 12:2 and 5). Encratism rejected "women, wine, and the eating of meat." In 170 A.D. Dionysios, bishop of Knossos, reproached a fellow-bishop in his area for "requiring the heavy yoke of virginity to be laid upon the faithful," and urged other bishops to be less demanding in regard to marriage.[2] Similarly, St. Ignatius of Antioch had asked Polycarp, bishop of Smyrna, not to require celibacy of Christians.[3] In the popular literature of the second century there is encountered the tendency to exalt sexual continence to such a degree that salvation is in grave doubt without it. Such tendencies continued into the third and fourth centuries, and it was under the influence of them that Origen castrated himself for the kingdom of God. The Church Fathers were called upon in conscience and in obedience to the biblical tradition to affirm both the goodness of marriage and the validity and value of celibacy. Edward Schillebeeckx notes, however, that this was not without qualification: "On the other hand, it cannot be denied that a patristic exposition of marriage more often supported the Christian advantages of complete continence than it presented a reflection on marriage itself. Time and again one finds the statement that marriage is good, but celibacy is better."[4]

Marriage was largely looked upon as a state of life for the weaker by many early Christian writers, a kind of second-rate Christianity. The justification of marriage was a rather difficult task in the mood of the times. The Orthodox resisted all attempts to call it evil, but it was often assumed that marriage was for those who could not be continent. The biblical affirmation that the Church was the bride of Christ was applied to individual believers. Such brides were not to be married to anyone other than Christ and the virginal state was the proper state for Christian "brides." Particularly in the Western Church the incompatibility of the priesthood with marriage was felt. Evidence of this is found in the writings of St. Jerome, St. Ambrose, Pope Innocent I, and Pope Siricius. Often spiritual literature presented a dark vision of marriage, in some ways just reflecting the profane literary themes of the age.

In many instances the Encratism encountered in the third century and even earlier was mixed with Gnostic dualism. The best evidence of this is given by Clement of Alexandria, who lived during the early portion of the third century. Clement is at a focal point in the battle between the Encratites and those who would indulge the flesh. In the third chapter of his *Stromateis* he names a large number of sects who had only scorn for marriage. He exposes their arguments from scripture in favor of perpetual continence. His basic reply is that creation is good and sexual intercourse as a contribution to creation is consequently good also. However, Clement is clearly in favor of avoiding any desire that would stimulate and indulge the appetites:

> But how is it possible to become like the Lord and have knowledge of God if one is subject to physical pleasures? Every pleasure is the consequence of an appetite, and an appetite is a certain pain and anxiety, caused by need, which requires some object...We must not live as if there were no difference between right and wrong, but, to the best of our power must purify ourselves from indulgence and lust and take care of our soul which must continually be devoted to the Deity alone. For when it is pure and set free from all evil the mind is somehow capable of receiving the power of God and the divine image is set up in it.[5]

For Clement nothing should be done from desire, whether it is eating or sexual intercourse. Rather, it is the will that should govern our actions, the will as directed only toward that which is necessary: "A man who marries for the sake of begetting children must practice continence so that he may beget children with a chaste and controlled will."[6] Clement points to some who have avoided marriage and have lapsed into a hatred of humanity, while others have married and ended as the beasts in their indulgence of the flesh. For Clement marriage for a person with mastery of his will is not harmful if it is done with self-control.

The strength of Clement's objections to sexual desire is fed by his adherence to the human ideal of continence set forth by Greek philosophy.[7] Ideally one should not experience desire at all, but as a Christian Clement thinks that this state is attainable only by the person who asks grace from God and receives it for this purpose. However, Clement does go along with the Pauline permission for a second marriage if a man burns with passion, but "he does not fulfill the heightened perfection of the gospel ethic." In fact, Clement is not at all certain of the salvation of the twice-married: "But he gains heavenly glory for himself if he remains as he is, and keeps undefiled the marriage yoke broken by death, and willingly accepts God's purpose for him, by which he has become free from distraction for the service of the Lord."[8] For Clement marriage is clearly for the begetting of children and "looking after domestic affairs."[9] He refers to marriage as holy and relates it to Eph 5:32, but in good Stoic fashion Clement thinks that the reason for marriage lies in the end of procreation. Indeed, John Noonan considers Clement the source of this rationale and calls it "the Alexandrian principle."[10] Earlier Athenagoras of Athens had taken a similar position when he wrote: "Since we hope for eternal life, we despise the things of this life, including even the pleasures of the soul. Thus each of us thinks of his wife, whom he married according to the laws that we have laid down, with a view to nothing more than procreation."[11] Clement did recognize, however, an ascetic dimension in marriage, and insofar as a man embraces marriage for such Stoic attitudes the married state is equal to the celibate life:

> And true manhood is shown not in the choice of a celibate life; on the contrary the prize in the contest of men is won by him who has trained himself by the discharge of the duties of husband and father and by the supervision of a household, regardless of pleasure and pain - by him, I say, who in the midst of his solic- itude for his family shows himself inseparable from the love of God and rises superior to every temptation which assails him through children and wife and servants and possessions. On the other hand he who has no family is in most respects untried. In any case, as he takes thought only for himself, he is inferior to one who falls short of him as regards his own salva- tion, but who has the advantage in the conduct of life, in as much as he actually preserves a faint image of the true Providence.[12]

Clearly many of the sects whose views Clement was rejecting considered the kingdom of God to have already come and
since there was no giving or taking in marriage in God's
kingdom (Mt 22:30-31), all should live in sexual continence.
Clement's response is that the Lord is not rejecting marriage
but "ridding their minds of the expectation that in the resurrection there will be carnal desire."[13] In fact, Clement interprets Jesus' statement about the age of the resurrection to
refer to life after death rather than the present life in this
world. Against the Gnostic sects Clement urges the goodness
of creation and the goodness of God's incarnation in Jesus
Christ. The flesh is not itself evil. Yet, Clement stands
against all indulgence of fleshly desire. Marriage is good, but
only for rational purposes, namely, the procreation of children. Again and again Clement quotes scripture about the
holiness of marriage, but what that holiness consists of is
never fully stated by him. Marriage was instituted by God
and thus it is holy. It is a participation in creation, which is
good. But, as Eric Fuchs discerns, Clement has moved from
a biblical morality based on the covenant between a man and
a woman to one based on the Stoic interpretation of natural
law.[14] This law had three meanings for Clement. One is that
it is a process not contaminated by sin or human error, another is that it is analogous to what animals do, and finally, there
is a structure found in the human body implicit in the purposes of organs which contributes to its moral meaning. Thus
the genital organs are for reproduction just as the human eye
is for seeing. This natural law ethic becomes a morality of
objective principles which assumed and legitimized the distinction and even separation of spiritual and bodily love. In
effect, physical love and sexual desire are excluded as not
Christian, though marriage is holy because of procreation and
its divine institution. Clement is explicit: "A man who
marries for the sake of begetting children must practice continence so that it is not desire he feels for his wife, whom he
ought to love."[15] Clement was a man who found inspiration
in the Stoic and other philosophical currents which stood
against the immorality of Roman society in his age. Gnosticism either rejected marriage as evil or allowed licentious

sexual behavior as having no significance in the light of the teaching that the divine spark in man is entirely immaterial and that consequently matter is irrelevant to spiritual matters. Clement affirmed the Christian doctrine of creation by having recourse to Stoic moral ideas as built into a doctrine of natural law. We can see a direct route from Clement of Alexandria to the encyclical of Pope Paul VI, *Humanae Vitae*. Yet he can allude to Eph 5.22-33 when he states that "as the Law is holy, so is marriage. This is why the Apostle compares this mystery with Christ and the Church."[16]

Encratism remained popular in monastic circles, and in the Western church there were many who sought to impose celibacy on the clergy. At the Council of Nicaea in 325 A.D. an attempt to do so was made by Hosius, the bishop of Cordoba (in what is now Spain) and other bishops. The move was rejected by the council. The bishop Paphnutius during the course of the council insisted that marriage was itself honorable and the marriage bed undefiled. He rejected the imposition of celibacy as too heavy a yoke for the clergy to bear. He is quoted by the church historian Socrates as saying: "For all men cannot bear the practice of rigid continence," and he termed the intercourse of a man with his lawful wife to be chaste.[17] Nevertheless, the council forbade marriage to the clergy upon receiving higher orders "according to an ancient tradition of the church."

The legitimacy and goodness of marriage was upheld at the regional council of Gangra in A.D. 340. Gangra was situated in Asia Minor, and the council was held in opposition to Eustathius and his disciples. Eustathius was the bishop of Sebasteia in Armenia and was a rigorist tending to Encratism. This regional council was confirmed by the fourth, sixth, and seventh ecumenical councils and thus have more than local authority. For the purpose of knowing what the teaching of the Orthodox Church is on marriage, the canons of the Council of Gangra are invaluable. The most important of them are as follows:

I. If anyone disparages marriage, or abominates or disparages a woman sleeping with her husband, notwithstanding that she is faithful and reverent, as though she could not enter the Kingdom, let him be anathema.

II. If anyone criticizes adversely a person eating meat (without blood, and such as is not meat that has been sacrificed to idols or strangled) with reverence and faith, as though he had no hope of partaking, let him be anathema.

IV. If anyone discriminates against a married Presbyter, on the ground that he ought not to partake of the offering when that Presbyter is conducting the liturgy, let him be anathema.

IX. If anyone should remain a virgin or observe continence as if, abominating marriage, he had become an anchorite, and not for the good standard and holy feature of virginity, let him be anathema.

X. If anyone leading a life of virginity for the Lord should regard married persons superciliously, let him be anathema.

XIV. If any woman should abandon her husband and wish to depart, because she abominates marriage, let her be anathema.[18]

The reverence for marriage that we discover in this council is deeply in accord with the biblical heritage. Once again we encounter the tension between the eschatological call to celibacy and the fact that one does not sin by marrying and certainly has the freedom to do so. This tension remains throughout the early history of the Church. One can see the tension in an eschatology whereby the kingdom of God having been realized required that we live as the angels and an eschatology which recognized in the church an existence between the times. The pressure exerted on the early Church by Gnostic dualism led to a scorn for the present world, for the flesh, for all institutions within this world. The eschatological call to an entirely spiritual life, based on the shortness and difficulties of the present age, slowly gave way to a dualism of the flesh versus the spirit in the present age. Marriage often suffered by being an institution of the present age and requiring a profound involvement in the bodily and the material through the procreation of children. Clearly marriage stood over against the Gnostic, Montanist, and monastic movements, which rejected the present age and sought to live entirely in the spirit. The resistance which the Orthodox offered to the rejection of the goodness of creation and the legitimacy of marriage lay in obedience to the incarnational principle. This is most evident in the work of St. Irenaeus of Lyons.

Monasticism had many sources. It was a development of eschatological life, that is, living entirely in the kingdom of God the life of the angels.[19] It involved a removal from worldly institutions in order to live only for God. It required, therefore, a perpetual battle against the flesh and its passions. By doing battle against the demonic powers, the monk became a witness (a martyr) who vindicated his allegiance to Christ, the victor over the Devil and all his forces. The tension between monasticism with its latent Encratist influence and the life of the ordinary Christian became very great. Bishop Kallistos Ware has explored the attitudes of monks toward married persons in an article which appeared in the *Eastern Churches Review* in 1974.[20] A wide spectrum of views is evident. For some it was necessary to lead the monastic life in order to be perfect as a Christian. We see this in the Gospel passage which acted as the call to St. Anthony of the Desert: "If you wish to be perfect, go, sell your possessions, and give to the poor...and come, follow me" (Mt 19:21). The admonitions given to St. Arsenius in the *Apophthegmata* and to Theodore's mother in the *Vita Prima* of St. Pachomius all demand flight from the world. As Bishop Kallistos notes, the difficulty lies in the call to monasticism of married people if they are to escape hell. Such a call is reported by St. John Cassian of Theonas.

Bishop Kallistos states clearly that none of these authors, Athnasius, Arsenius, Pachomius, and Cassian would have condemned marriage as evil. It is simply that monastic life is superior. The monastic tradition reveals an awareness that prayer and sanctity are possible to some who live in the world, and the tradition existed that some worldly people would be judged more favorably at the last judgment than many monks. But it turns out that those who are mentioned by name are ascetics under the cloak of worldly office. In an example from the *Apopththegmata*, the Emperor Theodosius, who is seen by God as on the same level as an old monk, becomes convincing in his humility, not for his ascetic endeavors, however great they may be. Throughout this story and another given in the *Apophthegmata* it turns out that the married men have long ceased to have sexual relations with their wives. Indeed, in the second case, that of Eucharistus, the marriage has never been sexually consummated. In three cases from the *Historia Monachorum in Aegypto*, Paphnutius comes across lay persons in the world who are living virtually as monks, and he admonishes them all to abandon the worldly life and enter the monastic. Perhaps no more could be expected of ascetic monks in assessing the spirituality of lay persons in the world, and yet the rare story does exist where higher examples of sanctity occur outside the monastic life. Bishop Kallistos calls to our attention a text from the *Apophthegmata* of Macarius of Egypt to whom it was shown that he had not reached the sanctity of two women who lived a normal sexual life with their husbands but had never quarreled. The conclusion is drawn that God gives His Holy Spirit to all "according to the intention of each."[21] Yet an alternative version of the story of Macarius exists which would make it the underlying intention of the two sisters to become nuns, though without the possibility of realizing this vocation because of their circumstances. In various stories (one from St. Antony and another from the *Pratum Spirituale* of John Moschus) it is evident that what matters is purity of heart, and if that can exist in a worldly setting, the holiness of such a person may well exceed that of the monks. It is this awareness that holiness can exist even in the midst of marriage or the singing of profane songs which breaks through the Encratist tendencies within monasticism in the early years of that movement. Bishop Kallistos quotes the words of St. Symeon the New Theologian as an outstanding example of this response:

Many regard the eremitic life as the most blessed,

> others the common or cenobitic life, and others the work of government, of teaching and instruction and church administration, for this provides many with nourishment of body and soul. For my part, however, I would not set any one of these above the rest, nor would I praise one and depreciate another. But in every situation, whatever the work or the task involved, it is the life lived for God and according to God which is wholly blessed.[22]

It has often been alleged that the spirit of the Desert Fathers is the result of a sharp dualism between spirit and body, the former being good and the latter being evil. This is not necessarily so, however. Peter Brown has focused his attention on this problem directly:

> In the desert tradition, vigilant attention to the body enjoyed an almost oppressive prominence. Yet to describe ascetic thought as "dualistic" and as motivated by hatred of the body, is to miss its most novel and its most poignant aspect. Seldom, in ancient thought, had the body been seen as more deeply implicated in the transformation of the soul; and never was it made to bear so heavy a burden.[23]

Indeed, the body is given a new importance that one would never find in the thought of Plotinus. Brown asserts this is based on the underlying value and significance given to the Incarnation of God in Jesus Christ, true man and true God. In the Western church clerical celibacy was eventually to prevail, partly because the clergy gathered around their bishops in semi-monastic settings during and after the barbarian invasions. In the Eastern Empire, the deacons and presbyters were much more closely integrated with the people, and the effect of the vast abyss between the barbarians and the Romans was not felt as acutely as in the West where barbarian invasions rent the fabric of society more deeply. The integration of Church and society was not only made more possible in the East by the victory of Constantine and his

60

successors, but it was assisted by the interpenetration of the married clergy in the whole of society.[24] On the other hand, the monks remain detached and lived out an implicit criticism of the established order.[25] In deciding to choose bishops only from among the monks, the Orthodox Church, in effect, rejected total assimilation into an imperial cult. The eschatological dimension was retained in the life of the church and remained vital through various periods when imperial control would have destroyed the orthodoxy of the Church. It is not without significance that the monks were the major force in avoiding not only heresies such as Nestorianism but also iconoclasm and the later attempt of the Emperor to impose the dogmas of the Latin church upon the Eastern patriarchates at the Council of Florence.

The fact that the greatest theologians of the Orthodox Church were all monks or aspirants for the monastic life did much to encourage the growth of respect for and recognition of the normative character of the unmarried state. We have only to recall St. Basil the Great, St. Gregory Nazianzus, and St. Gregory of Nyssa - the so-called Cappadocian Fathers. They created Orthodox theology in its definitive state and prepared for the great definitions and decisions of the Second Ecumenical Council at Constantinople. Only St. John Chrysostom stands as an equal to them. None of these Fathers wrote treatises on marriage but two of them wrote treatises on virginity (Gregory of Nyssa and John Chrysostom). Gregory of Nyssa was a married bishop who sought out monastic life without ever abandoning his wife and even lamented the loss of his virginity. In John Chrysostom we encounter a monk who was pressed into becoming the bishop of the capital city of the Roman Empire and was surrounded by a multitude of persons for whom he was responsible. The contrast between his early views on marriage in his treatise on virginity and those in his biblical homilies is striking. One can say that these biblical homilies come closer than any other theological works to presenting an Eastern Orthodox interpretation of marriage. Yet both men were monastically oriented and cannot be called advocates of marriage without qualification. It is the nature of the qualification that matters, however.

The contrast between St. Gregory of Nyssa and Augustine of Hippo is sharp indeed. Whereas Augustine held that sexuality existed prior to the fall of man, Gregory taught that sexual differentiation came by way of the garments of skin that were provided after the loss of the beatific vision of God in the paradise of Eden. Gregory conceives of virginity and incorruptibility as closely linked. It is the incorruptible nature which marks virginity. God grants virginity to those who in flesh and blood are to be set upright after the fall. The passions that caused the fall must be eliminated. Thus participation in God, both by the descent of the Holy Spirit and by the exaltation of man to a desire for heavenly things, brings with it a harmony which would eliminate the opposition between the flesh and the spirit. However, when Gregory sets out to enumerate the difficulties of marriage in his treatise *On Virginity* they emerge not as the evils of sexual pleasure but the existential consequences of trying to find the lasting in the ephemeral. Even if a marriage gives us what we hope for, namely, the joy of living with someone and a good family, wealth, harmony, affection, and even glory and power, all of these bring dire consequences in the end. Envy of the happiness of others arises, and death brings an end to the ties created by marriage. It is obvious that happiness cannot exist with such thoughts in one's mind. St. Gregory comes up with a host of dark possibilities. Parents are blamed by their offspring, charges are made against the divine economy. Tragedy stands ever at hand. Even if there are children one lives a life of fear lest some harm come to them. Women suffer both from oppression by their husbands and from the loss of them. Widowhood is an unfortunate state, where a woman suffers grievously at the hands of relatives and enemies. If such evils attend the happy ones, the unhappy will have multiple woe. Indeed, Gregory urges that "prosperous lives are marred by the expectancy, or the presence, of death; but the misery of these is that death delays his coming."[26] Marriage is fraught with miseries which the law courts reveal by their mass of marital cases. In fact, misery abounds for the married.

For St. Gregory of Nyssa every evil in life is such that it has no power over us unless we bring it upon ourselves: "A man who, seeing through the illusion with the eye of his spirit purged, lifts himself above the struggling world, and...slights it all as but dung, in a way exiling himself altogether from human life by his abstinence from marriage."[27] A wise person refrains from marriage and thus avoids the greed, envy, anger, and hatred which it brings. Indeed, Gregory traces the disease of pride to its original cause in marriage. Such a strong statement is justified insofar as the true good is higher than the things of this earth. Our goal is not in the meadows or the deserts but rather in heaven. It is plainly stupid to live only for the body and to be so alienated from the life of God. That is only to live in darkness with all the evils of greed and the unbridled passions. One passion leads to another, ending only in destruction. St. Gregory uses a most interesting metaphor of water which in a spring flows down in all directions. One must keep oneself out of these torrents, looking up to the light:

> Virginity of the body is devised to further such a disposition of the soul; it aims at creating in it a complete forgetfulness of natural emotions; it would prevent the necessity of ever descending to the call of fleshly needs. Once freed from such, the soul runs no risk of becoming, through a growing havit of indulging in that which seems to a certain extent conceded by nature's law, inattentive and ignorant of Divine and undefiled delights.[28]

The underlying Platonic theme is constant: to seek after and obtain the highest we must avoid the lower, which would ensnare us in its passionate darkness. In his discussion of the two saints of the virginal and ascetic life, Elias and John the Baptist, Gregory returns to the image of water. Water, when dissipated and let to flow everywhere, is useless and without force, but when it is directed and constrained in a pipe, its force even moves upward. Similarly, travelers who go on journeys and do not stay on the main highway do not arrive at their destination. Gregory sums this up by saying: "It is my baelief that they would not have reached to this loftiness of spirit, if marriage had softened them."[29]

Suddenly, in the body of his dissertation on virginity, Gregory turns aside and rather inconsistently enters into a defense of marriage as an institution. Marriage is not deprived of God's blessing. Gregory is reluctant to advocate marriage since our natural inclinations are to it because of its "indisputable inducement." Only if someone arises to dispute the teaching of the church on marriage would such a defense prove necessary. After restating the scriptural accusations against those who would detest God's creatures as abominations, Gregory states that those who scorn the creation do not comprehend the nature of evil. Evil consists in extremes. Gregory now sets forth a Greek, even Aristotelian doctrine of the mean as the basis of virtue, declaring: But our view of marriage is this; that, while the pursuit of heavenly things should be a man's first care, yet if he can use the advantages of marriage with sobriety and moderation, he need not despise this way of serving the state."[30] For him the ideal is found in Isaac who did not marry in his youth in order that marriage should not be a deed of passion but be entered into rationally. Isaac remained in marriage until the birth of twin sons and then withdrew into the realm of the unseen. It is clear that Gregory fears marriage may turn the soul away from the highest good: "What were we saying? That if it is possible, one should neither remain aloof from the more divine desires, not should one reject the idea of marriage. It is not reasonable to disregard the economy of nature or to slander what is honorable as disgusting."[31] Spiritual considerations have priority, but there is also the need in life for the succession of one thing from another, namely, reproduction. Gregory's concern is that the married person not lose the life of prayer by surrendering to the passions and becoming flesh and blood where the Spirit of God does not reside. He speaks of customary debts within the context of marriage. It would indeed be profitable to go through life without the experience of marriage, but our nature is weak and makes that difficult for many.

Gregory is very much aware that habit and a certain fantasy of beauty creates obsessions. Our whole understanding of the desirable is changed once the flesh is indulged. Consequently, it is for the weak most advantageous to flee to virginity for refuge. For a person who loves the world and involves himself in the things of this world, it becomes virtually impossible to love God with all his heart, soul, and mind. However difficult it may be to turn away from the pleasures of this world, the highest good is infinitely more pleasurable.

The remainder of Gregory's treatise becomes a Platonic dissertation on what is truly desirable and what is the nature of virtue. We have here a magnificent vision of the unity of the good, the true, and the beautiful as they exist in the Godhead. Gregory gathers all of this together when he says: "Indeed, the person who removes himself from all hatred and fleshly order and rises above all low and earthbound things, having ascended higher than the whole earth in his aforementioned flight, will find the only thing that is worth longing for, and having come close to beauty, will become beautiful himself."[32] Gregory describes this beauty in terms of light. The good is light, and the evil is dark. The fall of Adam brought about the shame and fear that followed upon the experience of pleasure and removed the first couple from the sight of God. Thus, human beings "were sent forth into this pestilential and exacting land where, as the compensation for having to die, marriage was instituted."[33]

Death is indeed the fate of all the fallen human race. If we are to avoid death, we must seek a life which does not have death as its consequence. This, Gregory states, is the life of virginity. As he puts it, "Everyone knows that the function of bodily union is the creation of mortal bodies, but life and incorruptibility are born, instead of children, to those who are united in their participation in the Spirit."[34] The logic of Gregory's argument is clear: death comes to be perpetuated by sexual reproduction. When marriage and sexual intercourse are abandoned, the march of death will be halted. Gregory even links the virgin birth of Jesus with his invulnerability to death. Oddly, the argument of Gregory depends upon the observation of the evils attendant upon marriage: widowhood, the orphans, the calamities of children. These bring an end to the pleasure of marriage. Employing a brilliant image, he writes: "For as the handle of the sword is smooth and well-fitted and polished and gleaming and adapted to the shape of the palm, but the rest of it is steel, an instrument of death, fearful to see, but more fearful to experience, such, also, is marriage holding out to us the smoothness and superficiality of pleasure like a handle which is adorned with skillful carving, but when it is in the hands of someone under attack, it brings pain with it and becomes the creator of grief and misfortune for men."[35]

Gregory proceeds to set forth a vision of two marriages, the one physical and the other spiritual. The spiritual is noted for self-control, mortification of the body and a disdain for everything connected with the flesh, while the physical is marked by the opposites of these virtues. The spiritual marriage is made with the divine and incorruptible Bridegroom; the physical is based on having a fine appearance, fitting adornment and sufficient wealth. The spiritual marriage requires restraint in regard to every bodily pleasure. Yet Gregory stops short of extreme asceticism and argues that both carnal indulgence and excessive mortification are opposed to the soul attaining perfection. There must be moderation in all things. The key to the Christian life becomes self-sacrifice, since Christians are priests anointed to offer themselves to God, indeed, to be crucified to the world, as was Christ Himself. This is the highest worship, to offer ourselves, and only the pure of heart are worthy to do so. Within this context of sacrifice Gregory urges that we follow Moses who ordered the people to abstain from the privileges of marriage in order to be present at the appearance of God: Wherefore we would that you too should become crucified with Christ, a holy priest standing before God, a pure offering in all chastity, preparing yourself by your own holiness for God's coming that you also may have a pure heart in which to see God, according to the promise of God."[36]

Gregory of Nyssa's theology may be read in various ways. The most radical way is that taken by Eric Fuchs and by John Bugge. Perhaps Bugge puts it most starkly: "In a word, man's first sin was somehow equivalent to sexual intercourse; its principal effects were death and sexuality itself...Nevertheless, the proposition that 'the original sin was sex' is a premise implicit in, and logically necessary to, the arguments these Fathers make over the nature of things."[37] Bugge thinks that these are essentially Gnostic ideas which, despite the Orthodox affirmation of marriage as soon have a simple logic of their own which is radically inconsistent with that affirmation. Sexuality is linked with death so that asexuality becomes associated with life. As he puts it: "Only a cessation of sexual activity can bring about a life without death: because where there is marriage there is death, when there is no marriage death will be no more."[38]

A more subtle reading of Gregory's treatise has been offered by Mark D. Hart, who notes that interpreters have failed to recognize Gregory's irony. True to the place of irony in the ancient philosophical tradition, we must discern that Gregory is providing us with a picture of marriage as built on selfishness and desire. Hart comments:

> While, on one level, the treatise attempts to persuade its readers to renounce marriage, on a deeper level it explains how the soul's desire for union with God may in fact be reconciled with the needs of family and community life that arise from the body, once the truer nature of spiritual development is understood. His negative portrayal of marriage, then, is not simply a foil for presenting the advantages of celibacy but constitutes also the foundation for a Christian understanding of marriage based upon the very quality of nonattachment Gregory calls "true virginity."[39]

The assumption that Gregory begins with is that a marriage built on pleasure ends in nothing but suffering and loss. True wisdom is to consider this before going blindly into such a marriage. Hart shows us how Gregory's "rhetorical venom is not marriage per se but the desire for pleasure and misguided expectations of happiness which are the basis of most marriages."[40] It is *symbiosis* (companionship) which leads to the greatest danger. Since human beings seek security, permanence, and immortality, they tend to seek it in companions.

Believing that we can live in and through others we weave a web of illusion around our lives. The opposite of *symbiosis* is to live according to oneself. This does not, according to Hart, mean that we must withdraw from others entirely but, rather, that we avoid passionate involvements with others out of anxiety.

Hart thinks that Gregory takes a different approach to marriage in chapters 7-9, a more positive stance: "There he considers marriage under the aspect of *leitourgia*, public service, rather than the search for gratifying companionship."[41] Gregory's attack on marriage in chapter 3 is not, therefore, an attack on marriage as such but on a particular experience of married life. Hart thinks that Gregory uses the term "marriage" with two meanings, as he does "virginity." Marriage "comes to be a metaphor for passionate attachment in general, just as virginity, in additional to its conventional meaning of celibacy, refers also to a general attitude of nonattachment possible also in marriage."[42] The polemic is against the passions, and the bodily passions in particular. But bodily passions are not to be viewed here as sexual (sex never appears in Gregory's treatise as an evil in marriage, as it does in John Chrysostom's similar treatise). Rather, the body is inclusive of the "body politic" - as in all Platonic thought - and thus refers to the social vices of envy, love of honor, greed, and the like. Gregory links the vices as in a chain, with vainglory at the top. Greed is linked to death, and it is the desire to be at the expense of others which joins the two. For Gregory celibacy converts erotic power from earthly things to spiritual things. But Gregory notes that the freedom from concerns for food and clothing would not have been forthcoming "if they had been made soft to the pleasure passions of the body by marriage."[43]

Hart notes that this is not Gregory's last word on marriage, which he considers positively in chapters 7-9. Celibacy is valuable because it allows one to focus the mind and to "dry out" the passions in order to experience purity of mind. However, Gregory defends marriage for two reasons: one is that the heretics reject it, and the other is that we all come from the marriage of our parents. Hart interprets this as meaning that the heretics do not understand moderation as a virtue between two vices. On the one hand, some deny the reality of the body, and others deny the reality of the spirit. Those who despise marriage live as if we were bodiless creatures. For Gregory the good of marriage lies in its *leitourgias*. He gives the example of the patriarch Isaac who did not enter into marriage because of passion but "because of the blessing of God upon his seed." Gregory, in fact, links marriage to the divine economy. God was called *choregos*, the provider, in chapter 2, and the Incarnation is seen as an act of *philanthropia*, a love for humanity. Hart links this all together:

> In the Christian economy of salvation God is not content to remain in the incorruptible state proper to the divine nature but accepts freely the physical corruptibility and vulnerability to suffering proper to human nature. By calling marriage *leitourgia* and God *choregos*, Gregory is suggesting that married life bears a greater resemblance to divine life than celibacy in its role as benefactor and provider for the community and its willingness to assume bodily burdens, even though celibacy may bear a greater resemblance to divine life in its freedom from the burdens of bodily existence.[44]

What is truly remarkable is that Gregory makes celibacy the option of the weak. It is for those who might not be able to restrain their passions rather than to live moderately in marriage. Celibates often lack courage since one must be able to stand up to the burden of nature courageously, "with manliness." Such courage is called for not only because of the troubles of married life but because of the loss, insecurity, and death that accompany life. Again, the originality of Gregory is clear when he interprets St. Paul's preference for celibacy as true only in the absence of true virtue. It is Gregory of Nyssa who unites the two ways, that of celibacy or virginity and that of marriage, since virtue in in the soul and the body brings the "partition-wall" of the vices to be removed so that "the two will become one and coalesce, because both are united to the good."[45] This dualism of body and soul is overcome by exposing the illusions about the body rather than waging war against the body. Hart suggests that the problem of how marriage and contemplation might be combined is resolved for Gregory "through a reconsideration of the passions and their origins, pointing to a freedom from passion which does not require the renunciation of marriage and worldly activity for its foundation."[46] Hart even suggests that for Gregory marriage may "be a higher realization of virtue than that generally found among celibates."[47] Hart thinks that Gregory's compaint in chapter 3 that his marriage separates him from the benefits of celibate life is really to be read as ironic. This does not mean that Gregory wishes to make of marriage a state higher than celibacy:

> Once again he would face the problem of two levels of Christianity and the danger of pride attached to the "higher." Chapter 9 suggests that an enlightaened marriage is superior to the virtue *generally* found among those who are married, but it is not clear that it is superior to the celibate life such as one finds in Gregory's brother Basil, whose activity in the community makes his life also a sort of *leitourgia* and whose virtue seems to be also based upon some sort of insight into nature beyond habit and perseverance against desire.

If we accept Hart's interpretation of Nyssa as correct, we discover that Gregory was not just covering his orthodoxy by espousing the paradoxical position that marriage is good but virginity is not only better but the only way of escaping death. Indeed, Gregory emerges as having not only a sophisticated view of marriage and celibacy but as prototypical of Orthodox theologians who link marriage and monastic vocation intimately with a common asceticism. Rather than denigrating marriage, Gregory sets forth a profound theology of marriage.

St. Gregory Nazianzus, the Theologian, opens the door to

his vision of marriage with a brief though profound comment.

> The two of them, say the Scriptures, shall be in one
> flesh. Then let this one flesh be accorded the one
> same honor. And it is by this example that Paul
> promulgates the law of chastity. How and in what
> way? "This is a great mystery; I refer to Christ and
> the Church." It is a beautiful thing for the wife to
> honor Christ through her husband; it is a beautiful
> thing also for the husband to not denigrate the Church
> through his wife. "Let the wife," says the Apostle,
> "honor her husband" - for this has to do with Christ.
> But the husband too, let him keep his wife in his care,
> for so does Christ with the Church.[48]

We see here an ethic built on something more than the
relationship of Christ and the Church as a normative example.
Indeed, there is a participation whereby Christ is honored in a
wife's love for her husband, and the Church is revered in the
husband's love for his wife. An incarnational mysticism
permeates Gregory's thought.

The treatise of St. John Chrysostom *On Virginity* was
written when the author was a young man pursuing the
monastic life. One can and must contrast his early teaching
on marriage with what he wrote later in life when he was a
priest in Antioch and then the bishop of Constantinople. The
young Chrysostom takes a route that may appear to many as
tortuous at best. Nevertheless, he owes a great deal to his
predecessors who had discussed virginity and its superiority to
marriage (most notably Methodius of Olympia and Gregory of
Nyssa). The first requirement of a Christian writer was to
deplore and repudiate the Encratite position that marriage was
of itself evil. Equally important in the minds of these authors
was their obligation to affirm that virginity was a higher state
than marriage. The intensity of Chrysostom's attack on the
Encratites is revealed in the first chapters of his treatise *On
Virginity*. In the light of the negative things he says about
marriage the opening pages of this treatise show an extraordinary concern, not simply to remain Orthodox, but to unfold

an argument which is at heart supererogatory. To remain a virgin because marriage is evil is to be condemned to eternal perdition. God has created marriage and procreation. Therefore to condemn them is to reject God and His providence. St. John writes: "For fasting and virginity are neither good nor evil in themselves but from the purpose of those who practice them comes each of these qualities. The practice of this virtue is unprofitable for the pagans; they earn no wage because they did not pursue it out of fear of God. As for you, because you fight with God and slander the objects of his creation, not only will you go unrewarded you will even be punished."[49]   Yet virginity is a good and better than marriage. Again St. John notes: "Virginity is as much superior to marriage as heaven is to earth, as the angels are to men, and, to use far stronger language, it is more superior still. For the angels, if they do not marry and are not given in marriage, are not a mixture of flesh and blood."[50]   The point is that we are made like the angels if we remain virgins. The argument of Chrysostom is not confused; it is at heart a statement of virginity as a supererogatory good:

> For I would call the woman who has the power to marry but chooses not to a virgin. By saying that marriage is forbidden, virtuous action becomes no longer a matter of deliberate choice but an obligation to obey the law. For this reason, we admire the Persians for not marrying their mothers, but not the Romans. Among the Romans such a marriage is thought to be a loathsome act by all, without exception; but in Persia, since people dared this practice with impunity, those abstaining from such intercourse deserved praise. To abstain from what has been forbidden is by no means the mark of a noble and generous soul. Perfect virtue does not consist of not doing these things for which we would think ourselves wicked before everyone. It consists of excelling in what does not entail reproach for those who do not choose it. It not only preserves those who have successfully elected this course from a bad reputation, but

also admits them into the rank of the good.[51]

St. John Chrysostom's *On Virginity* is actually a sustained commentary on St. Paul's First Letter to the Corinthians, Chapter 5. He asserts and pushes the ascetic element in St. Paul's thought to the furthest extent possible. He also denies that St. Paul is only giving a personal opinion in this chapter. St. Paul speaks by the Spirit, and we read in scripture that Christ had more to reveal to us in the future (Jn 16:12). Chrysostom traces the origins of marriage to the fall of mankind. Following the exegesis of St. Gregory of Nyssa, Chrysostom contends that there as no sexual intercourse before the fall. He states, furthermore, that man needed no helper:

> As long as they were uncorrupted by the devil and stood in awe of their master, virginity abided with them. It adorned them more than the diadem and golden raiments do kings. However, when they shed the princely raiment of virginity and laid aside their heavenly attire, they accepted the decay of death, ruin, pain, and a toilsome life. In their wake came marriage, a garment befitting mortals and slaves.[52]

Affirming the statement of St. Paul in 1 Cor 7:33 ("But the married man is busy with this world's demands"), Chrysostom expounds it thus: "Do you perceive the origin of marriage? Why it seems to be necessary: It springs from disobedience, from a curse, from death. For where death is, there is marriage. When one does not exist, the other is not about. But virginity does not have this companion. It is always useful, always beautiful and blessed, both before and after death, before and after marriage."[53]

In reply to those who think that marriage and sexual intercourse are necessary to the survival and the continuation of the human race, John Chrysostom declares that marriage did not produce Adam or Eve. God can create all the people whom the world needs:

Even as God at that time had provided from lifeless bodies the foundation and roots for so many thousands of descendants, so at the beginning too, if those about Adam had obeyed his commands and overcome their desire for the forbidden, they would not have needed a means of increasing the race of men. For marriage will not be able to produce many men if God is unwilling, nor will virginity destroy their number if he wishes there to be many of them. But he wanted it to be so, Scripture says, because of us and our disobedience.[54]

What then is God's purpose in providing marriage? The answer is that it is a concession to our own weakness. It is to guard us against fornication. Chrysostom does not, however, just leave the matter there. Following in the path laid by Methodius of Olympia, he believes that marriage was provided in the context not only of the fall of man but of our present call to a greater perfection. Marriage existed for children, but not for the perfect man coming to full stature:

Although the new commandments are superior to the old, the aim of the lawgiver is the same. What is it? To reduce the baseness of our soul and to lead it to perfect virtue. Therefore, if God had been anxious not to dictate obligations greater than the former ones but to leave things eternally the same and never to release men from that inferior state, he completely contradicted himself. If at the beginning, in fact, when the human race was more childlike, God had prescribed this regimented way of life, we would never have accepted it with moderation but would have completely jeopardized our salvation through immoderation. Similarly, if after a long period of training under the old law when the time called us to this heavenly philosophy, if then he had permitted us to remain on earth, we would have gained nothing much from his concession since we had no part in that perfection on account of which his indulgence arose.[55]

So after being nestlings we are led from the nest, we are called to fly higher. This is to leave marriage behind and move toward an angelic life. Again, in reply to those who honor marriage as providing continuation for our species, Chrysostom urges that it is sin and unnatural intercourse which threaten our species, not virginity. Even if marriage provided for procreation in the past, its sole purpose now is for the quenching of the fiery passions of our nature.[56]

In effect, St. John Chrysostom is carrying out his polemic against both the detractors of marriage and the detractors of virginity. Marriage is only for the weak, enabling them to avoid ruin through debauchery and licentiousness, and the strong had best avoid it: "For the man who learns that marriage is advised not because it is the height of virtue but because Paul has condemned him for having so much lust that without marriage he is incapable of restraining it, this man blushing with shame will hastily pursue virginity and be anxious to divest himself of such ill-repute."[57] Amazingly, St. John can take the words of St. Paul in 1 Cor 7:5, "Do not deprive one another ..." and turn them into an exhortation to virginity. Abstinence is called for during prayer, but the good of prayer is so great that abstinence should be the rule rather than the exception. In fact, Chrysostom thinks that Paul gives his advice in the form of a recommendation only in order to avoid offending the hearer by making commands. As he puts it , "in the case of virginity he has given his opinion but in the case of marriage he makes a concession. He orders neither the one nor the other but not for the same reason: in the one case, so that anyone who desires to rise above incontinence not be restrained, as he would be if bound by an injunction; but in the other case, so that someone capable of ascending to virginity not be condemned for having disobeyed a commandment."[58] In essence, St. John affirms St. Paul's simple statement, "I would like you to be as I am," as the will of God that all be continent.

The remainder of John Chrysostom's *On Virginity* is given to portraying marriage as darkly as possible. The invective is not against the indulgence of the flesh so much as the state of marriage which brings with it such suffering and unhappiness, and most especially second marriages. Marriage is bondage for both partners, but particularly for a woman. However, the major thrust of Chrysostom's thought is in asserting the primacy of the spiritual struggle for the Christian. The battle against the devil and victory over evil are the task of all Christians. Clearly a wife and children are impediments to virtue. In answer to the question of how a wife might be of help to a man, Chrysostom thinks that the benefit must be spiritual, not physical. He looks at marriage with its many cares, its worldly concerns, and considers them all obstacles to spiritual victory. Luxury is to be avoided, and if married one must live in detachment as if one were not. Virginity has no real drawbacks as does marriage. The Jews were offered temporal goods as motives for avoiding evil, but Christians are offered spiritual goods. Like St. Gregory of Nyssa, St. John Chrysostom toward the end of his treatise comes to regard virginity as virtually identical with a spiritual life. His conclusion is uncompromising:

> But it is inevitable that sinners be punished eternally, as the virtuous be honored. Christ has declared that there will be no end for either. There is eternal life, he says, and there is eternal punishment. For when he welcomed those on his right and condemned those on his left he added: "These will go to eternal punishment and the just to eternal life." We must therefore make every effort here. The man with a wife must be like him without one and the man who is in fact without one must practice every other virtue along with virginity, so that we do not in vain weep bitterly after our departure from this life.[59]

Herbert Musurillo has noted that John Chrysostom recognized three possible states of life: virginity, marriage with moderation, and marriage as the refuge of the weak, which could be considered a hypocritical form of fornication.[60]

St. John Chrysostom's early picture of marriage is a grim one, of a man tied to a woman who has a multitude of faults, who is wicked, talkative, wasteful, or of a woman tied to a man who is proud, impudent, or immoral. For him St. Paul's statement, "if you are tied to a wife, do not seek to break this bond" (1 Cor 7:27), is given the strictest and most negative interpretation. Indeed, for him marriage is precisely a bond, a tie, which enslaves and enchains the partners.

If we examine St. John Chrysostom's *Homily 19 on First Corinthians*, which is a commentary of 1 Cor 7, we find that the rather polemical tone against marriage has disappeared. This homily dates from his time in Antioch as a priest, some years later than the early treatise *On Virginity*. Whereas the earlier treatise revealed that he was firmly in favor of marital continence, he is less enthusiastic about it in the later homily. Marital intercourse was viewed as destructive of the duty of perpetual prayer in the earier treatise. Now we find that Chrysostom interprets 1 Cor 7:5 to mean that abstinence for the sake of prayer concerns an unusual earnestness of prayer, since the prayer that is recommended by St. Paul as "without ceasing" would seemingly deny all sexual intercourse. St. John has clearly come to think that prayer is compatible with sexual intercourse between married people. Again, St. John takes a less absolutist and rigid view of the phrase "because of your incontinence" (1 Cor 7:5) and likewise of St. Paul's recommendation of his own state of continence: "Howbeit each man has his own gift from God, one after this manner and another after that.'(1 Cor 7:8) Thus since he had heavily charged them saying 'for your own incontinence' he again comforts them by the words, 'each one has his own gift of God,' not declaring that towards that virtue there is no need of zeal on our part, but, as I was saying before, to comfort them."[61] Indeed, St. John Chrysostom can go so far as to recognize that abstinence from sexual intercourse is of no value if there is constant nagging, fighting, and discontent between the man and wife. Fasting and continence come to no good at all in such instances. Clearly no monastic spirituality is imposed on the marital state as it was earlier by the young Chrysostom. Even though St. John reaffirms that continence is better, he has shifted his uncompromising attitude toward continence and affirms that St. Paul "puts no force on the person who cannot attain to it, fearing lest some offense arise." [62] One also recognizes in his discussion of the Christian wife's sanctification of her non-Christian husband a subtle shift in emphasis. Whereas in his earlier treatise John Chrysostom had seen her redemptive and saving action as entirely spiritual, he puts it here in the context of being one flesh with her husband. [63]

That the mature St. John Chrysostom has changed his attitude toward marriage becomes even more evident in his homilies on other Pauline passages. The classic text is clearly Eph 5:22-24. The commentary provided by Chrysostom has become the *locus classicus* for the ethics of marriage. Chrysostom joins both the creation of woman from the flesh of man (Gn 2:23) and the consequent biblical affirmation of the union of husband and wife as "one flesh" with the Christian understanding that we become the body of Christ by virtue of the sacramental mysteries of baptism and the Eucharist. The biblical teaching regarding the creation of woman from the flesh of man assures us that by not fashioning woman independently from man God "would not think of her as essentially different from himself." [64] The husband must love his wife since the wife is of his own body. Using the variant text of Eph 5:30, St. John combines the truth of the Incarnation with our incorporation into Christ: "Because Christ was born from our matter, just as Eve was fashioned from Adam's flesh. Paul does well here to speak of flesh and bones, for the Lord has exalted our material substance by partaking of it Himself." [65] He continues: "We are truly members of Christ because through Him we were created, and we are truly members of His mysteries. There are some who affirm that He came by water and blood but will not accept that the Holy Spirit enables us to share His same essence through baptism. Foolish heretics! How can the children who confess His truth and are born again in the water not become His Body?" [66] Clearly St. John is setting forth a realistic view of the body which is profoundly sacramental and of which the union of man and woman as "one flesh" is only a further differentiation of unification. He considers the birth of a child to be a new creation of "three in one flesh" so that "our relationship to Christ is the same; we become one flesh with Him through communion, more truly one with Him than our children are one with us, because this has been His plan from the beginning."[67]

It is the union of the spirit and the flesh, following the pattern of incarnational theology which makes marriage like a spiritual birth. Sarah's marriage with Abraham was not one of fleshly passion but "wholly spiritual" like unto the union of the soul to God, but this is no cause to denigrate the physical. Using the example of Sarah and Abraham, St. John Chrysostom defends marriage and its physical union: "See how he does not despise physical unity, however, but uses spiritual unity to illustrate it! How foolish are those who belittle marriage. If marriage were something to be condemned, Paul would never call Christ a bridegroom and the Church a bride."[68] Marriage is not only upheld and not condemned, but Chrysostom speaks of marriage, following St. Paul, as "a great mystery." It is a mystery not only because of the "one flesh" of which Moses spoke but also because of Christ the higher mystery. The union of man and woman is like unto the union of Christ and the Church and even to the Trinitarian mystery. Quoting St. Paul in 1 Cor 11:3, "The head of Christ is God," John Chrysostom goes on to draw the conclusion that "husband and wife are one body in the same way as Christ and the Father are one."[69]

It is true that John Chrysostom follows St. Paul in designating the husband as the head and the wife as the body. But this headship is based on Christ's model of headship of the Church. Thus Christ gave Himself for the Church, a sinful and imperfect Church. As Chrysostom puts it, "So the Church was not pure. She had blemishes, she was ugly and cheap."[70] In fact, no woman could be more estranged from her husband or more corrupt than the Church had been before her purification by Christ. Husbands are thus called to love their wives as Christ loved the church and, indeed, even as they love their own bodies. Though the husband is the head, there is no cause for denigrating his wife's position. As Chrysostom says, "The wife is a second authority. She should not demand equality, for she is subject to the head;

neither should the husband belittle her subjection, for she is the body."[71] Again he asks: "So if you think that the wife is the loser because she is told to fear her husband, remember that the principal duty of love is assigned to the husband, and you will see that it is her gain."[72] The positive virtues of love and honor and the negative injunctions to avoid posses-siveness and nagging are not a simple application of "house-rules" taken from the popular maxims of the day. They follow, rather, from the profoundly realistic incarna-tionalism which is the source of Chrysostom's ethic. It is both Eucharistic and incarnational since the underlying assumption of John Chrysostom is that union in Christ is the basis of the Christian ethic. In this way the hierarchical thinking of Chrysostom is modfed not only by a mutual, though differentiated, subordination of the man and wife but by its integration into the organic metaphors and the consist-ent realism of Chrysostom's thought. It is unthinkable to him that democracy should exist within the household, "but the authority must necessarily rest in one person. The same is true for the Church: when men are led by the Spirit of Christ, then there is peace."[73] It is the Holy Spirit, not the authority of anyone, that brings peace, as Chrysostom recognizes when he notes how the five thousand members of the Jerusalem Church were united in one heart and soul. Similarly, for Chrysostom the family is a little Church.[74] Chrysostom's rigoristic tendencies have so disappeared that he is even ready to accept by concession a second marriage.[75] From this pre-sentation of the sacramental mystery of marriage, St. John deduces an ethic of mutual reverence, of respect, of avoid-ance of jealousy, of restraint of accusation and violence. All that is lascivious and lewd is to be avoided. Marriage has been removed in this homily from all the common and gross context of marriage in Roman life and has been transformed into a mystery whereby the union between Christ and His Church is made particularly present and evident.

The most mature thought of St. John Chrysostom on marriage is found in *Homily 12 on Colossians*. The homily was given in Constantinople and is set against the satanic pomp of aristocratic marriage in New Rome. Apparently harlots had participated in the celebration of marriage among many aristocrats. St. John finds nothing in common between Christian marriage and the pagan celebrations. "They ought to hide their faces when marriage is celebrated; they ought to be dug into the earth (for harlotry is the corruption of marriage) but we introduce them to our marriages...When you are preparing sweet ointment, you suffer nought ill-scented to be near. Marriage is sweet ointment. Why then introduce the foul stench of the dunghill into the preparation of your ointment?"[76]

In contrast to the Greek mysteries, not dancing but silence is appropriate to marriage. Chrysostom celebrates the wonder and greatness of marriage thus:

> A great mystery is being celebrated; away with harlots, away with the profane. How is it a mystery? They come together, and the two make one. Wherefore is it that at this entrance indeed, there was no dancing, no cymbals, but great silence, great stillness; but when they come together, making not a lifeless image, nor yet the image of everything upon earth, but of God Himself and after His likeness you introduce so great an uproar, and disturb those that are there, and put the soul to shame, and confound it? They come, about to be made one body. See again a mystery of love. If the two become not one, so long as they continue two, they make not many, but when they are come into one-ness, they then make many. What are we to learn from this? That great is the power of union.[77]

Indeed, marriage is an image of the presence of Christ. In the contrast between the ways of Christ and those of Satan, St.John clearly moves beyond marriage as a mere concession to the weakness of the flesh and our propensity to sin. Marriage is the mystery of Christ made evident in the union between husband and wife. A new ethic emerges: one of sobriety, temperance, endurance of the suffering that married life involves, and freedom from envy or jealousy. The priests are to be invited to the wedding, not the harlots. The union of "one flesh" is present even when there is no child to manifest the union. St John explicitly states that when there is no child forthcoming from the physical union of the man and woman, the two are still made one. As he says, "But suppose there is no child; do they then remain two and not one? No; their intercourse effects the joining of their bodies, and they are made one, just as when perfume is fixed with ointment."[78] Chrysostom urges the married couple not to be ashamed of this good thing that God has made:

> Some of you call my words immodest, because I speak of the nature of marriage, which is honorable; yet you show no modesty in your behavior at weddings. By calling my words immodest, you condemn God, who is the author of marriage. Shall I also tell you how marriage is a mystery of the Church? The Church was made from the side of Christ, and He united Himself to her in a spiritual intercourse ... Think about all this and stop treating such a great mystery so shamefully. Marriage is an image of the presence of Christ, and will you get drunk at a wedding? Tell me, if you saw a portrait of the emperor, would you insult it? By no means.[79]

Far from the grave hesitations that Chrysostom counselled in his early treatise *On Virginity*, as a pastor he urges parents to have their young sons married as early as possible. In his *Homily 5 on 1 Thessalonians* he writes: "Wherefore I exhort you first to regulate well their souls. If he finds his bride chaste, and know that body alone, then will both his desire be strong, and his fear of God the greater, and the marriage truly honorable, receiving bodies pure and undefiled, and the offspring will be full-charged with blessing, and the bride and bridegroom will comply with one another, for both being inexperienced in the manner of others, they will submit to one another."[80] The danger lies in young men learning indecency and dissoluteness from harlots. It is true that many young men remain in chastity and that refraining from sin is a matter of the will, but this will is exercised contrary to chastity by indulging in the spectacle of lewd women exhibiting themselves. Fantasies and dreams emerge to injure the soul. In the end, it is a matter of willing or unwilling chastity, and for that we will be punished or praised by God.

The mature John Chrysostom, the shepherd of souls, has moved far beyond the rather severely monastic stance of his youth to a biblical understanding of marriage as a holy participation in the mystery of Christ's union with his Church. He has furthermore come to recognize vocations for what they are, rather than putting down marriage as always due to weakness and "incontinence." In moving into the fuller Pauline vision, he can be said to have saved the church's vision of marriage as a sacrament from the Encratist tendencies and from the neo-Manicheism that influenced the mind of Augustine of Hippo. The Augustinian allowance for the permission of coitus only for the lawful purpose of creation is entirely lacking here. In fact, the tendencies toward a simple identification of the flesh with the sinful flesh have disappeared in the mature Chrysostom. The flesh has been sanctified by union with another, by the union of wills and spirit and by participation in the union between Christ and His Church. This ethic of marriage is built not on the natural law but the self-giving of Christ, even to the point of shedding his blood for his spouse, the Church. In his famous "Sermon on Marriage," Chrysostom makes the assertion, which has become famous, that "marriage is a remedy to eliminate fornication."[81] As such, marriage was instituted for chastity, not fornication or wantonness. On the other hand, the rather negative note found in that sermon is alleviated in the sermon "How to Choose a Wife." The grounds for loving a wife are found both in the law of God revealed in Holy Scripture and in the reasoning of human beings. John Chrysostom notes that God leads man to love of his wife by interchanging the divine laws and human reasoning.[82] We might well translate this by saying that we know the duty of love both from Scripture and natural law. But the mystery of marriage, whereby a girl leaves her own home for a man whom she scarcely knows, is not a human accomplishment: "It is God who sows these loves in men and women. He causes both those who give in marriage and those who are married to do this with joy."[83] Thus, though Chrysostom can in this very sermon come back to the theme of marriage to avoid fornication, he has already modified his position by affirming that it is God who causes and brings forth the love of men and women.

How far this early emphasis on the superiority of virginity and monastic life has been replaced by a new stress on the virtues of married life is apparent when Chrysostom affirmed in his Homily 7 on the Epistle to the Hebrews: "And if these beatitudes were spoken to solitaries only, and the secular person cannot fulfill them, yet He (Christ) permitted marriage, then He has destroyed all men. For if it be not possible, with marriage, to perform the duties of solitaries, all things have perished and are destroyed, and the functions of virtues are shut up in a strait."[84] On this text Vigen Guroian writes: "Chrysostom's argument is not just about the morality of Christians, married or celibate, either. It is an argument which dismisses all notions that the institution of marriage is inferior in God's plan of salvation or fails in its nature to serve his purpose.[85] Moreover, this judgment is confirmed by Chrysostom's conclusion: "And if persons have been hindered by the marriage state, let them know that marriage is not the hindrance, but their purpose which made an ill use of marriage. Since it is not wine which makes drunkenness, but the evil purpose, and the using it beyond due measure. Use marriage with moderation, and thou shalt be first in the kingdom."[86] Indeed, there was a noticeable reaction against rigorism in the second half of the fourth century. The link between rigorism and Encratism is clear, and there is evidence that baptized persons were not permitted to marry in certain areas, especially Syria. Earlier, about 179 A.D., Dionysius, the bishop of Corinth, admonished an episcopal colleague not to be too strict in this matter. The bishop had urged that young persons be permitted to marry rather than insisting upon continence. The reaction against rigorism is seen in St. Gregory Nazianzus who took up the task of acting as a marriage-broker for many Christian young people. Evidently the pastoral activities of John Chrysostom and his advice to the parents of young men to have them married earlier lest they fall into sin provided an entirely new orientation for him. Life as a bishop gave him a new awareness which the monastic life failed to do.

I have chosen these two great Fathers of the Orthodox church, St. Gregory of Nyssa and St. John Chrysostom, in order to focus attention on the tension that existed between the monastic vision which designated virginity as the highest Christian ideal (with the consequent tendency to play down the excellence of marriage) and the positive assessment of marriage as a sacramental mystery which sanctifies the union of man and wife. One continues to discern this tension among the Fathers of the Church. St. John of Damascus, writing in the eighth century, recognized the purposes of marriage as procreation and the prevention of fornication. Yet in his treatise dealing with moral problems (*Sacra Parallela*) we find him saying: "You have a wife. You have pleasure with impunity."[87] In the fourth century Syrian church we find both Ephrem and Aphrahat defending marriages as had the earlier *Didascalia* which also sprang from a Syrian milieu. In a scholarly work the English Jesuit Robert Murray has suggested that the defence of marriage by Ephrem and Aphrahat is carried out without much enthusiasm since both were committed to a life of consecration to Christ as a virgin (or as they put it a "single one"). There is clearly incipient monasticism here (which had been criticized earlier by the *Didascalia* as Encratite), but Murray cites the advocacy of purity by Aphrahat:

Dem.xviii, 837, mentions marriage among the good things God has created; Dem. vi, 260.1-261.1, repeating traditional warnings against the presumption of trying to live in virginity with one of the other sex, says it would be better to get married openly, which a true encratite would never have said. Ephrem, opposing the Marcionites, declares marriage, family, and possessions lawful, side by side with virginity and abstinenece in marriage (hcHaer. 45, 6-10; CSCO 169, Syr. 76, pp.179-80): even clearer in HVing. 5,14 (CSCO 223, Syr.94), p. 20:

> For to Him marriage is pure which is planted
> in the world like a vineshoot, and children are
> like fruit hanging from it.[88]

St. Ephrem also stated that "From Adam until the Lord true married love was the perfect sacrament."[89] Whereas St. Gregory of Nyssa thought that sexuality came into being only by reason of the fall of man, a contrary opinion was sometimes held in the Eastern Church, as we see from St. Ephrem. Interestingly, Augustine of Hippo wrote that "Christ confirms at Cana what he established in paradise."[90] Even St. John Climacus says:

> Some people living carelessly in the world have asked
> me: "We have wives and are beset with social cares,
> and how can we lead the solitary life?" I replied to
> them: "Do all the good you can; do not speak evil of
> anyone; do not steal from anyone; do not lie to an-
> yone; do not be arrogant toward anyone; do not hate
> anyone; do not be absent from the divine services; be
> compassionate to the needy; do not offend anyone; do
> not not wreck another man's domestic happiness; and
> be content with what your own wives can give you. If
> you behave in this way you will not be far from the
> Kingdom of Heaven.[91]

Two Byzantine theologians who brought differing and profound theological commentaries to marriage were St. Theodore the Studite and St. Symeon of Thessalonike. St. Theodore notes that the first conjugal blessing is that of Adam and Eve. From this he concludes that God's creation and the blessing of man and woman in marriage is the theological basis for the mystery of monogamous marriage. Insofar as Jesus refers to Gen 1:27 and 2.24 as the texts for a scriptural foundation of marriage, He has established the monogamous ideal. It is therefore in creation that marriage has its meaning. Theodore Stylianopoulos wisely comments that Orthodox theology, unlike the ancient Marcionites or the modern Lutherans, does not have inhibitions about the reality of salvation in the old covenant. The patriarchs and the righteous ones of the Old Testament knew communion with God and His grace.[92]

St. Symeon of Thessalonike brings a different perspective since he views marriage as a concession to fallen humanity. In contrast with St. Theodore he interprets the Old Testament couples mentioned in the marriage rite in a negative way: "that marriage really does not belong to the period of grace and was blessed by Christ only as an accomodation to human weakness. Symeon sets the perfect goal of the Gospel, virginity and incorruptibility, over against marriage. He, therefore, held that marriage is not a preeminent work (*prosegoumenon ergon*)."[93] It is clear that St. Symeon represents the other tendency found among the Fathers, upholding the superiority of virginity and linking it with incorruptibility.

Perhaps it is Peter Brown, the secular historian of late Roman antiquity, who provides us with the abiding recollection of what happened to human sexuality with the emergence of the monastic movement in the fourth century. Monasticism rose as a radical critique of the worldliness of the Church as it was being established under the aegis of the Roman Empire. So also, the city was deserted by the monks who wandered into the desert; there in a marginal zone, separated from all the supports of civilization, they "the lonely ones" had "recaptured a touch of the original glory of man."[94]

It was the encounter of the world and the desert that St. John Chrysostom's life reflected. Moving from a monastic life to episcopal responsibilities, John's sermons reflect a new awareness of the possibilities for sanctification of the people of God in the world. Since not everyone could go into the desert, the Word of God has to be addressed to those who were not monks and never would be. Brown notes that Chrysostom's lifelong dream was that the new age would one day dawn upon the city, but he died in exile "broken by the power of the world."

It was in the realm of sexuality that the mark of total

commitment to Christ was to be judged in the early Church. Whereas in the first two centuries of the Church apostasy was the sin that separated the sheep of Christ from the goats of the Devil, now it was separation from the sensuous, decadent, and immoral life of the city which was to be the criterion for fidelity to the Lord. This new awareness of sexual sin was felt most deeply and with vigilance by the monks, as we see particularly in St. John Cassian and Evagrius. Brown comments: "The doctrine of sexuality as a privileged symptom of personal transformation was the most consequential rendering ever achieved of the ancient Jewish and Christian yearning for the single heart."[95] But, whereas the monks would turn inward in their awareness of diabolically inspired thoughts, feelings, and passions, the monastic life was not extended to married persons. Particularly in the Eastern Church, without Augustine to focus attention on procreation as the only excuse for concupisence, sexuality remained much as it had been for centuries among the laity. Regarding this situation Brown comments: "In Eastern Christian morality the facts of sexuality were not communicated by the clergy as fraught with any particular sense of mystery. Either one lived with them, as a married person, in the world, or one abandoned them, in order to soak the body in the 'sweet smell of the desert.'"[96]

It is, therefore, as an escape from death through virginity that monasticism became a way of salvation for the desert fathers. But the Church, while accepting the heroic witness and the superiority of the monastic state, never allowed the sexual bond of marriage to be denegrated. At times simple loyalty to apostolic principles seemed enough in this defence of marriage against Encratism, zealous monks, and those who had nothing in common with the flesh or the opposite sex. But, gradually, a theology of marriage as holy and itself a way to salvation emerged. The fact that the priests and deacons of the Orthodox Church were married had, no doubt, an affect on this positive vision. That the Church still called married people to spend half the year fasting and abstaining from the marital embrace represented a compromise. If they could not be monks and nuns all the time, they must attempt a way of asceticism at least half of the time. Nevertheless, there were always those who knew that the joy of their married love was itself a mark of the Kingdom and a sign of God's grace. That their way of life remained one which was celebrated and recognized by the Church was not only a mark of the continuity of the biblical tradition but of the essential conservatism of the Church in the face of the experience of the monastic fathers.

Notes

(1) A. Voobus, *Celibacy. A Requirement for Admission to Baptism in the Early Syrian Church* (Stockholm, 1951).

(2) Edward Schillebeeckx, *Celibacy* (New York: Sheed and Ward, 1968), pp. 30-1.

(3) Ignatius of Antioch, *Letter to Polycarp* 5.

(4) Schillebeeckx, *Celibacy*, p. 32.

(5) Clement of Alexandria, "On Marriage" (*Stromateis* 3, 42), trans. J.E.L. Oulton and H. Chadwick, in *Alexandrian Christianity, Library of Christian Classics*, vol. 2, (Philadelphia: Westminster Press, 1954), p. 59.

(6) Ibid., 3, 7, 58, p. 67.

(7) Ibid., 3, 7, 5, p. 66.

(8) Ibid., 3, 5, 82, p. 79.

(9) Ibid., 3, 5, 82, p. 78.

(10) The term "Alexandrian principle" was first used by John T. Noonan in his book *Contraception: A History of Its Treatment by the Catholic Theologians and Canonists* (Cambridge, MA: Harvard University Press, 1965), p.105.

(11) Athenagoras, *A Plea for Christians* 33, in *Legatio and De Resurrectione*, ed. and trans. W. R. Schoedel (Oxford University Press, 1972), p. 81.

(12) Clement of Alexandria, "On Marriage" (*Stromateis*, 7, 12, 70), trans. Oulton and Chadwick, p. 138.

(13) Ibid., 3, 12, 87, p. 81.

(14) Eric Fuchs, *Sexual Desire & Love: Origins and History of the Christian Ethic of Sexuality and Marriage* (New York: Seabury, 1983), p. 92.

(15) Clement of Alexandria, "On Marriage" (*Stromateis* 3, 7, 58), trans. Oulton and Chadwick, p. 57.

(16) Ibid, p. 80.

(17) Socrates, *Ecclesiastical History* 1, 11, trans. A. C Zenos, ed., *Library of Nicene and Post-Nicene Fathers of the Christian Church*, ser. 2, vol. 2 (Grand Rapids, MI: W. B. Eerdmans, 1976); See also Sozomen, *Ecclesiastical History* 1, 23.

(18) St. Nicodemus the Agiorite and Agapius,*The Rudder* (*Pedalion*), trans. D. Cummings (Chicago: The Orthodox Christian Educational Society, 1957), pp. 523-32.

(19) Louis Bouyer, *The Meaning of the Monastic Life* (London: Burns & Oates, 1955), pp. 23-40.

(20) Kallistos Ware, "The Monk and the Married Christian: Some Comparisons in Early Monastic Sources," *Eastern Churches Review*, 7, 1 (1974), pp. 72-83.

(21) Ibid., p. 80.

(22) Symeon the New Theologian, *Theological and Practical Chapters*, 3, 65, ed. Darrouzes, in *Sources chrétiennes* 51, p. 100.

(23) Peter Brown, *The Body and Society: Men, Women, and Sexual Renunciation in Early Christianity* (New York: Columbia University Press, 1988), p. 235.

(24) Peter Brown, *The World of Late Antiquity* (London: Thames and Hudson, 1971), pp. 97-125.

(25) Alexander Schmemann, *Church, World, Mission* (Crestwood, NY: St. Vladimir's Seminary Press, 1979), pp. 45-51.

(26) Gregory of Nyssa, *On Virginity*, 3, trans. William Moore and Henry A. Wilson, in *Library of Nicene and Post-Nicene Fathers of the Christian Church,*, ser. 2, vol. 5 (Grand Rapids, MI: Wm. B. Eerdmans, 1972), p. 348.

(27) Ibid., 4, p. 348.

(28) Ibid., 5, p. 351.

(29) Ibid., 6, p. 351.

(30) Ibid., 7, p. 353.

(31) Ibid., 8, p. 33.

(32) Ibid., 11, in *St. Gregory: Ascetical Works*, trans. Virginia Woods Callahan, *The Fathers of the Church*, 58, (Washington, DC: Catholic University of America, 1967), p. 40.

(33) Ibid., 12, trans. Callahan, p. 46.

(34) Ibid., 13, p. 48.

(35) Ibid., 14, p. 49.

(36) Ibid., 23, trans. Moore and Wilson, p. 371.

(37) John Bugge, *Virginitas: An Essay in the History of a Medieval Ideal* (The Hague: Martinus Nijhoff, 1975), p. 19.

(38) Ibid., p. 20.

(39) Mark D. Hart, "Reconciliation of Body and Soul: Gregory of Nyssa's Deeper Theology of Marriage," *Theological Studies* 51, 3 (1990), p.451.

(40) Ibid., p. 455.

(41) Ibid., p. 456.

(42) Ibid., p. 458.

(43) Gregory of Nyssa, *On Virginity* 6.1.22-38, trans. Hart, p. 467.

(44) Hart, pp. 471-2.

(45) Gregory of Nyssa, *The Beatitudes* 7, in *St. Gregory of Nyssa*-trans. Hilda C. Graef in *Ancient Christian Writers*, 18 (Westminster, MA: The Newman Press, 1954), p. 165.

(46) Hart, p. 476.

(47) Ibid., p. 477.

(48) Gregory of Nazianzus, *Sermon on St. Matthew*, 12, trans. Theodore Mackin, *Marriage in the Catholic Church: Divorce and Remarriage*, (New York: Paulist Press, 1984), p. 150.

(49) John Chrysostom, *On Virginity* 4, 4, trans. Sally Rieger Shore, in *Studies in Women and Religion*, Vol. 9 (New York and Toronto: Edwin Mellen Press, 1983), p. 6.

(50) Ibid., 11, 3, p. 14.

(51) Ibid., 8, 3-4, pp. 11-12.

(52) Ibid., 14, 5, p. 21.

(53) Ibid., 14, 6, p. 22.

(54) Ibid., 15, 1, p. 23.

(55) Ibid., 16, 2, p. 24.

(56) Ibid., 19, 1, p. 27.

(57) Ibid., 27, 4, p. 38.

(58) Ibid., 34, 7, p. 48.

(59) Ibid., 84, 4, pp. 127-8.

(60) Jean Chrysostome, *La Virginité*, eds. H. Musurillo and B. Brillet, in *Sources Chrètiennes* 125 (Paris: Editions du Cerf, 1966), pp. 205-6, footnote 5.

(61) John Chrysostom, *Homily 19 on First Corinthians*, trans. David Anderson, in *St. John Chrysostom: On Marriage and Family Life* (Crestwood, NY: St. Vladimir's Seminary Press, 1986), p. 29.

(62) Ibid., p. 29.

(63) Ibid., p. 31.

(64) John Chrysostom, *Homily 20 on Ephesians 5:22-33*, trans. David Anderson in *St. John Chrysostom: On Marriage and Family Life*, p. 44.

(65) Ibid., pp. 50-1.

(66) Ibid., p. 51.

(67) Ibid.

(68) Ibid., p. 55.

(69) Ibid., p. 52.

(70) Ibid., p. 47.

(71) Ibid., p. 57.

(72) Ibid., p. 55.

(73) Ibid., p. 53.

(74) Ibid., p. 57.

(75) Ibid., p. 56.

(76) John Chrysostom, *Homily 12 on Colossians*, trans. John A. Broadus, in *Library of Nicene and Post-Nicene Fathers of the Christian Church*, ser 1, vol. 13 (Grand Rapids, MI: Wm. B. Eerdmans, 1956), p. 316.

(77) Ibid., p. 318.

(78) Ibid., p. 319.

(79) John Chrysostom, *Homily 12 on Colossians*, trans. David Anderson Anderson in *St. John Chrysostom: On Marriage and Family Life*, p. 77.

(80) John Chrysostom, *Homily 5 on Thessalonians*, trans. John A. Broadus, *Nicene and Post-Nicene Fathers of the Christian Church*, First Series, Vol. 13 (Grand Rapids, MI: Wm. B. Eerdmans, 1956), p. 346.

(81) John Chrysostom, *Sermon on Marriage*, trans. Catherine P. Roth in *St. John Chrysostom: On Marriage and Family Life*, p. 81.

(82) John Chrysostom, *How to Choose a Wife*, trans. Catherine P. Roth in *St. John Chrysostom: On Marriage and Family Life*, p. 94.

(83) Ibid., p. 95.

(84) John Chrysostom, *Homily 7 on the Hebrews*, trans. F. Gardner, *Library of Nicene and Post-Nicene Fathers of the Christian Church*, ser. 1, vol. 14 (Grand Rapids, MI: Wm. B. Eerdmans, 1956), p. 402.

(85) Vigen Guroian, *Incarnate Love: Essays in Orthodox Ethics* (Notre Dame, IN: University of Notre Dame Press, 1987), p. 101.

(86) John Chrysostom, *Homily 7 on the Hebrews*, p. 402.

(87) John of Damascus, *Sacra Parallela* 2.11.

(88) Robert Murray, *Symbols of Church and Kingdom* (Cambridge: Cambridge University Press, 1975), p. 12.

(89) Ephrem of Syria, *Commentary on Ephesians* 5:23.

(90) Augustine of Hippo, *Commentary on Ephesians 5:23*.

(91) St. John Climacus, *The Ladder of Divine Ascent*, Step 1.21, trans. Lazarus Moore (Boston, MA: Holy Transfiguration Monastery, 1979), p. 9.

(92) Theodore Stylianopoulos, "Toward a Theology of Marriage in the Orthodox Church,"*Greek Orthodox Theological Review*, 12,3 (1977), p. 270.

(93) Ibid., p. 270.

(94) Peter Brown, "Late Antiquity" in Paul Veyne, ed., *A History of Private Life*, Vol. 1 *From Pagan Rome to Byzantium* (Cambridge, MA, Belknap Press, 1987), p. 289.

(95) Ibid., p. 304.

(96) Ibid., p. 302.

Chapter Three:

Marriage in the Liturgical Tradition

The Roman Catholic theologian Edward Schillebeeckx has argued that the conception of marriage in the Eastern churches differs significantly from the preeminently secular and contractual perspective found in the Western church:

> The Pauline idea of the church as the bride of Christ exerted an earlier and greater influence in the East than in the West. The Syrian churches were the first to have a liturgical feast of the church as bride, and this feast was of very early date. To a greater extent too than in the West, the Eastern theology and liturgy of marriage were inspired by the idea of *henosis*, or communion of Christ with His church, in connection with Eph 5:22-32. The Western view of marriage, moreover, with its typically legal bias - marriage as a contract - played no part in the East, where more emphasis was placed on the mystical meaning of marriage and its spirituality. Finally, the theologians of the Eastern Church had a less pessimistic view of sex and sexuality than the Western Church Fathers and schoolmen. All these factors were bound to lead to marriage taking a different form in the East than it took in the West.[1]

It is the thesis of Schillebeeckx that the Western church

97

retained the early Christian view of marriage as "a straight-forward secular act."[2] In contrast, the Eastern church turned marriage into a sacred act. He admits that by the fourth century there is evidence of priestly prayer and blessing in connection with marriage, both in the East and in the West. He quotes Clement of Alexandria to the effect that "marriage that is concluded according to the *Logos* (the Word of God) is sanctified if the community of marriage is subject to God and contracted with a sincere heart in the fullness of faith by those who have purified themselves of guilt and have washed their bodies with pure water and agree in the same hope."[3] This is not, he would think, a reference to a priestly ceremony but to baptism, which Clement likens to the pagan marriage bath. Schillebeeckx says that "the liturgy of marriage was given an outward form of a Christian kind. The purpose of this liturgical framework was to demonstrate the holiness of the contract; it was prompted by motives of pastoral care and moral solicitude, and included prayers that God should 'harmonize' the marriage already concluded (Gregory Nazianzus, Epist. 231)"[4] But the prayers and the blessing that surrounded the Christian wedding did not constitute the marriage contract itself. As Schillebeeckx puts it, "Marriage 'in the Lord' in the first centuries of Christianity meant, as it did for Paul, marrying a fellow-Christian. It also implied, of course, that the marriage itself was, in the prevailing circumstances, to be experienced according to Christian principles."[5]

There is much dispute, however, concerning any liturgical setting for marriage in the early Church. Though Kenneth Stevenson finds no evidence for this in the works of Clement of Alexandria, he perceives references in the Cappadocian Fathers to liturgical blessings and even to the power of such blessings to constitute the marriage itself.[6] In St. Basil's treatise *On the Holy Spirit* marriage is described as "the bond of nature, the yoke (made) by the blessing, the uniting of those who are separate."[7] Stevenson says that "such a description can only mean that the institution of marriage is focused and completed in a liturgical rite, at the heart of which is a priestly blessing."[8] Basil's Canon 22 shows that two stages in marriage existed, the betrothal and then the marriage. Also in Canon 27 there is the condemnation of priests who have blessed marriages contrary to what is lawful. They are not to bestow blessings or distribute the Body of Christ (though they are not deposed from the presbyterate). St. Basil asks: "And how will he who does not have this blessing because of his transgression through ignorance communicate it to another?"[9] The clear implication is that it is the blessing of the priest which creates the marriage, though it cannot make right what is clearly unlawful.

The North African Christian Tertullian, writing in the third century, produced various works on marriage, one *De Monogamia,* another *Ad Uxorem* to his wife. Both anticipate the anti-sexual mentality which was to surface in St. Augustine of Hippo and seems to have distinguished North African Christianity. Since dating these works is difficult insofar as Tertullian left the Catholic Church to become a Montanist in his late period, controversy exists as to whether the customs that he describes are only Montanist or also Catholic. At various places he speaks of marriage "in the Lord." Schillebeeckx thinks that all this means is that the marriage of two Christians is sanctified by the fact that they are "in Christ" by virtue of their baptism. In Tertullian's treatise *To His Wife* we are given a classic picture of marriage: "Where can one find the strength to describe the fortune of those marriages which the church ratifies, the offering strengthens, the blessing seals, and angels publish, the Heavenly Father propitiously beholds?"[10] Schillebeeckx denies the presence of a priestly blessing or a nuptial Eucharist in this passage. He thinks that all we find in this text is the usual domestic service: "I do not accept the usual conclusion drawn from this text of Tertullian, but prefer to see it as a confirmation of the civil and family contract of marriage and of the secular character of marriage, which, however, has a special meaning for Christians by virtue of baptism and is sustained and nourished by Christian prayer and by the sacraments (especially the Eucharist)."[11] Indeed, Schillebeeckx claims that this text stands in the intermediate stage between the biblical affirmations and the later assertion of the sacramental nature of marriage between baptized persons. He admits that the nuptial mass appears in the West in the Roman Church between the fourth and fifth centuries, however. Though the patristic scholar Ritzler, whom Schillebeeckx follows, tries to diminish the significance of the above passage from Tertullian, Crouzel and Stevenson conclude that the words *conciliat, oblatio confirmat, obsignat benedictio* witness to a marital liturgy in the context of the Eucharist and in which a blessing is an important part. Stevenson comments:

> Since both the Graeco-Roman and Jewish practices involved betrothal and marriage, it would have been no difficult thing to adapt them to Christian rites, but it is hard to say *when* the rite becomes specifically Christian, and how far local communities distinguished a Christian marriage from a non-Christian one in the earlier part of our period. I would suggest that there *was* such a distinction early on, together with a recognized liturgical rite, at least for marriage itself, consisting of implicit consent, and a blessing, even though such an idea has been called into question. But it is essentially a rite merging out of a life, and not one that conveys sacramental "effect." Tertullian's discourse to his wife expresses this in tender and faithful terms, and captures something of the natural and supernatural aspects of experienced Christian wedlock. And why the blessing? Because Roman Law dictated that consent made marriage, but for the early Christians this was right, but insufficient.[12]

Ritzler's attempt to make Tertullian's testimony referable to a specifically Montanist setting for marriage goes too far and only shows his creative imagination.[13] Increasingly in the West, as well as in the East, the blessing of the priest was asked, but the first legislation of a priestly solemnization comes in requiring it for the lower orders of the clergy.[14]

Priestly blessings were not required in the West for marriages, nor were they always bestowed. It is to Ambrosiaster that we owe our first evidence for the marital blessing as a liturgical form. He contrasts it with Jewish practice and limits it to first marriages.[15] St. Ambrose of Milan often refers to marriage as a *vinculum* and a *jugum*. In his *Hexaemeron* he refers to the "link between separate persons", the "oath of love" and the "necks joined together by the same yoke of blessing of each."[16] Stevenson adds that in a letter to Vigilius, recently made a bishop, Ambrose spoke of the *fidei concordia*, which the blessing may contain and even be said to impart."[17] Ambrose was to allow that "although first marriages are made by God, second marriages are still permitted. The first marriages are celebrated under the blessing of God."[18] Stevenson thinks that this means that the nuptial blessing is what constitutes the liturgical rite of marriage, but this passage does not necessarily have a liturgical reference. Nevertheless, the implications for moral theology are great since the ambivalence of the Church toward second marriages is made clear in this passage. The place of the blessing in the Western liturgical tradition remained in an ambiguous relation to the consent of the married couple, so basic to the Roman legal tradition. The Western canonical tradition as it came into being fixed upon the validity of the marriage as lying within the consent and sealed by the consummation. The liturgical evidence is climaxed by Pope Nicholas I's *Responsum ad Bulgaros* (866 A.D.) which allowed the validity of marriages by mutual consent, even if other ceremonies were lacking.[19] Only in the eleventh century do we find further changes in the Western church. The Greek missionaries in Bulgaria had insisted upon a blessing if the marriage was to be legitimate. Roman curial officials sharply attacked this view.[20] Clearly the prevailing Western theology of marriage made its validity depend upon mutual consent, not upon any acts of the priest or his blessing. What may appear as an arid and historical technicality has profound importance for moral theology. If the celebrants of marriage are the man and the woman who are themselves the ministers of the sacrament, in theory (if not in practice) they may unite themselves (by vows and consummation) without the explicit blessing of a priest. The blessing would be a ceremonial gesture rather than the actual bestowal of the sacrament itself. Only after the Council of

Trent did the Latin Church set forth a canonical requirement (*Tametsi*) which threatened excommunication if a marriage was solemnized apart from the presence of a priest. Some liberal Roman Catholic moral theologians such as André Guindon are consequently enabled to argue that marriage may exist prior to any ceremonies that may occur in an ecclesiastical context.[21] The canonical requirement is only a matter of discipline, and prior to the Council of Trent few questioned the validity of marriages solemnized without a priest or his blessing. The issue of the legitimacy of "pre-ceremonial" marriages is one hotly debated by Catholic moral theologians and canonists.[22] At its base is the question of common-law marriages and their sacramental character as well as "marriages-in-the making," persons living together with a commitment, awaiting a ceremonial date which for external reasons must be postponed. If consent and consummation are present, one may ask what is lacking to their marriage. Outside the parameters of Latin discussions of validity it would be very difficult for such a question to emerge. Certainly it would not occur in an Orthodox context since it is the Church that creates the marriage, but on the basis of the relationship which has come into being and been ratified in the betrothal.

In the Eastern Church a liturgical service came to surround the occasional priestly blessing of a marriage toward the end of the fourth century, as we can see in St. John Chrysostom's references to it. Already in the time of St. Gregory Nazianzus garlands were sometimes placed on the heads of the couple by the bishop or priest. St. Gregory was not very happy about this being done by a priest, but the practice was taken up by St. John Chrysostom (*Homily 9 on 1 Timothy*) and transformed from a pagan act carried out by the father to a Christian one performed by the priest. This ceremony--the *stephanoma* --was the origin of the crowning ceremony in the Eastern church. The handing over of the bride to the groom was carried out more and more by clergy rather than by the father of the bride, the ritual ceasing to have the importance it once had according to Roman law. The most important passage in the writings of St. John Chrysostom regarding marriage rituals comes from his *Homilies on the Book of Genesis* 48, 6. From this homily Stevenson summarizes the information given by Chrysostom: "Marriages are conducted by priests, who 'through prayers and blessings bind (them) together in the same will and the same home,' in order that the groom's love may increase, and the 'shame' (*sophrosune*) of the girl may be stretched; he alludes to the 'works of virtue' in the home, banishing the schemes of the devil, a pleasurable life together, under the protection of God."[23] The clericalization of marriage may well have come about as a response to the secular and pagan character of many of the marriage ceremonies so decried by Chrysostom. In sum, Schillebeeckx writes: "We can say that the blessing by the priest was understood in the Greek Church, from the time of John Chrysostom onwards, as an 'honorary right'--and in the Church of Antioch, Alexandria, and Constantinople, from the fourth century priestly blessing appeared to be prescribed by the Church in the writings of St. John Chrysostom.[24] Ritzler presents similar conclusions about Chrysostom's role in the formation of marriage customs and ritual in the Eastern Church:

> In the homilies on the Epistle to the Colossians, where he presents to us the ideal of a Christian celebration of marriage opposed to immoral customs, he does not say a word about the blessing of a priest being present. On the other hand, he invites us to call a priest "for in him it is Christ himself who is invited." After one of the homilies on Genesis, which date from the time at Antioch, he says that it is "fitting" and that one "ought" to invite the priest for prayer and benediction.[25]

Second marriages were refused such blessings for many centuries, but in the end they could not be denied. Through the Roman practice of *consensus*, marriage by mutual consent was adopted by the legislation of the Emperor Justinian, though it did not prevail in practice. Betrothal by means of the *arrha* or earnest money came to be required and eventually was given liturgical form. Ritzler tells us the purpose of the betrothal with *arrha*: "Juridically the earnest money represents a real guarantee which, in the case of a unilateral rupture of the engaged couples by the party giving it, is lost for that one."[26]   He thinks that despite the solemn character of the betrothal prevailing in the East there was no benediction of the betrothed by a priest before the eighth century.

What established itself in the East was both a betrothal and marriage. A distinction emerged between betrothal with the blessing of a priest and a civil contract without the blessing. The former was legally indissoluble while the latter was dissoluble - though not in the eyes of the church. The Emperor Alexius (1081-1118 A.D.) made only ecclesiastical betrothal a contract of marriage in the civil sense and forbade the *arrha* to children. The betrothal without a blessing became merely an action without legal form, a mere promise.

On the other hand, from the eighth century the betrothal was brought closer and closer to the marriage rite, and from this time it was very rare for the two to be celebrated separately. Usually they took place on the same day.[27] There was imperial opposition to this joining of the two rites, since, in effect, the sacramentalizing of the betrothal created a duplicate marriage service. What had originally been a contract with an earnest had by the blessing become more and more assimilated to an ecclesiastical rite. Ritzler compares the relation of the betrothal to minor orders bestowed on a man destined to the priesthood. He has clerical duties but not the rights of the full order of priesthood. So the betrothed have duties to one another and are promised, not just in the weak modern sense of engagement, but by a bond which cannot be broken although in no way does it give them access to the full rights and joys of marriage.

A profound difference lies between East and West in the understanding of betrothal. Ritzler puts it thus: "If the Roman betrothals are basically a *pactum de contrahendo*, if they present themselves, in order to use an expression from Western canon law, as *sponsalia de futuro*, in the East on the other hand the bethrothed have the value of being *sponsalia de praesenti*."[28] Put very simply, the Eastern assimilation of the betrothal service to the crowning and blessing of matrimony is done by incorporating a blessing into it, thus making it virtually a marriage, though not quite. The historical attempt on the part of the Emperor Alexius Commenus to prohibit the celebration of the betrothal and the marriage on the same day did not succeed. An inner logic, derived from considering the betrothed as married, overcame such attempts. By the fifteenth century the two rites are joined so that the betrothal takes place just prior to the marriage in the narthex of the Temple. Attempts to separate them once more raise very serious questions which would be difficult to answer. Clearly the betrothal service is not an engagement to be married in the modern sense of the term. Since a blessing is given to the marriage, it cannot be broken without grave sin and canonical disabilities. Furthermore, the ambiguity created for those married according to a secular ceremony in many European countries, long before the sacramental crowning and blessing, brings great stress to the couple and presents a temptation to consummate a union which has come into being according to law and yet has not come into being sacramentally. It remains incomplete until the crowning, and the joys of sexual intimacy are not granted to those who have only been betrothed. With a theology of marriage which places a significant emphasis in marital union upon the blessing of the Church, it is clearly inappropriate for consummation to take place and be permitted until the crowning has taken place. This liturgical celebration is not only the earlier marital rite of the Orthodox Church, but it is only in this context that the sacramental union is achieved. Ritzler rightly points to the different beliefs of East and West in regard to the moment in which a sacrament is effected. As with the exact moment of Eucharistic consecration the Eastern rite of marriage has no moment at which the sacrament is validly received but, rather, looks to a series of actions culminating in crowning and consummation. Similarly Bishop Peter L'Huillier writes of the different ideas of East and West concerning marriage:

In the East, the ideas on marital bond formation, conveyed by Roman law, had a limited impact.

According to the views which were widely spread among Easterners, marriage comes into being by subsequent steps. Each of them are necessarily accompanied by rites of passage. In this process, the consent of the partners does not come into prominence. Settled in a Christian context, this conception tended to give a new significance to sacred blessing: a legitimate marriage does imply a religious solemnization. Nevertheless, it took a long time for this viewpoint to obtain official recognition.[29]

It has been the Church's sense of the sacral character of both the betrothal as well as the crowning that has brought these two services together, though the original purpose of the betrothal was to make a contract and arose out of the legal requirements of the state. The blessing of the priest at the crowning, originally within the context of the common cup, came, as we have seen, from the domestic rather than the juridical setting. Whether the marriage is celebrated in the setting of the pre-sanctified liturgy or, as in more recent times, in the shared cup of wine without Holy Communion, the ecclesiastical context has always taken priority in the Eastern Orthodox tradition. It is interesting to examine the various explanations which have been advanced regarding the betrothal service. Alexander Schmemann, reflecting on Russian use, viewed the betrothal in the narthex of the church as the blessing of "natural" marriage and the procession into the sanctuary as the entrance of marriage into the Kingdom of God.[30] This is a curious instance of extraneous and imaginative explanation. Not only do the Greeks not celebrate the betrothal in the narthex, but the prayers of the betrothal are just as Christian in their theology as those of the crowning in the body of the temple. The Greek Orthodox scholar Theodore Stylianopoulos notes how the second prayer, which is read just before the act of betrothal itself, "for the first time mentions *ta mnestra* (*sponsalia*, the 'betrothal') on which it invokes God's blessing. In this prayer the context is Christological: Christ's anticipated betrothal of the Gentile Church."[31] He continues by saying:

106

The term *arrabon* ('betrothal'; cf. also the verb *arra-bonizetai*) in the betrothal benediction is quite significant in this regard. An ancient Semitic loanword, it is used in Hellenistic times as a legal and commercial technical term meaning "earnest money," "down payment," or "first installment" validating a contract and securing a legal claim to something. Through St. Paul's decisive use of this term for the eschatological gift of the Spirit (II Cor 1:22; 5:5; cf. Eph 1:24), *arrabon* takes on predominant theological significance in the patristic tradition signifying the present blessings of salvation in the Holy Spirit, the new life in Christ, and the redeemed life of the Church. With regard to marriage, *arrabon* signifies the betrothal as a 'first pledge' or first guarantee toward marriage. Certainly this pledge is not simply legal and commercial, but above all personal and spiritual, sanctified by the Holy Spirit in the Service of the Betrothal. Against the theological meaning of marriage as an image of Christ's union with the Church, the betrothal *(arrabon)* is theologically suggestive as the image of Christ's betrothal of the Church by the gift of the Holy Spirit - the gift of the Holy Spirit as a token of each believer's salvation, anticipating the future fullness of salvation in the messianic Kingdom. This connection was in fact made in the patristic tradition by Symeon the New Theologian and Gennadios Scholarios, who compare the two-step event of betrothal and marriage to the two-installment experience of salvation.[32]

The theological elaboration and interpretation presented above provide many ways of reading the meaning of the present rites. The history of the rites indicate that what were originally two different phases in the process of marriage, a promise and then a giving in marriage came to be joined and in many respects this process duplicated the services. One sees this very clearly in the presence of two great litanies and the fact that the betrothal once administered by the Church is virtually indissoluble. It is thus with reason that the two have been joined, though a greater assimilation of the rites might have been beneficial in the interests of brevity.

The requirement for permission from the bishop for the marriage of two Christians appears as early as St. Ignatius the Godbearer in his Epistle to Polycarp. In contrast to the thesis of Schillebeeckx that the Eastern Church administered the sacrament of matrimony through her priests, Smirensky claims that the clericalization of the marriage service came through the imposition of legal duties by the Byzantine Empire upon the clergy. His view, similar to that held by John Meyendorff, is that the liturgy for marriage was the Eucharistic liturgy and that the separation of marriage from the Eucharist began precisely with the edict of Leo the Wise (893) which required all legal marriages to be performed in the Church. As this development came into being, the movement away from the Eucharist goes by way of receiving Holy Communion from the Presanctified Gifts and then, finally, to the substitution of a common cup which was only of blessed wine. Smirensky writes: "Today a marriage is understood to be a real marriage only if it is entered into by mutual consent and solemnized by the Church through the established ritual. The mandatory solemnization of the marriage by a ritual was not the idea of the Church, but of the State."[33] Since the links between Church and state have been broken in most Orthodox countries other than Greece, Smirensky urges Orthodox to return to matrimony in its more sacramental and less legal and juridical sense. By making ecclesiastical ritual the only legal form of entry into marriage, the state has gradually liberalized the canonical legislation, allowing for marriages after divorce and second and third marriages. Smirensky accuses the Russian Church of debasing Christian marriage by her link with the state under the Czars:

> The Church of Russia, receiving its faith from Byzantium, accepted the laws of the Empire together with the Canons of the Church. After the reform of Peter the Great and the introduction of the Synodal system, the Church became the agency of the State

which had jurisdiction over marriages and divorces. The discipline became even more relaxed. The old reluctance toward bigamous marriages went by the wayside and even second marriages came to be solemnized with the rite reserved only for the first marriage.[34]

It is entirely without foundation that for the Eastern Orthodox the essence of marriage lay in the crowning (*stephanoma*) as bestowed by the priest. Even when Novella 89 was issued under the Emperor Leo VI requiring the crowning for all Christian marriages, it was clear that those who did not or could not comply with this requirement were still considered to be validly married by the Church.[35] John Meyendorff makes this point also:

However, even the novella of Leo VI failed to suppress entirely the possibility for a particular category of Church members to marry sacramentally, through the Eucharist, without a separate - and often expensive - "crowning." The slaves, i.e., more than half of the Empire's population, were not touched by the new law. This discrepancy between marriage law for slaves and for free citizens was suppressed by Emperor Alexis I Comnenos (1081-1118) who issued another novella making "crowning" a legal obligation for slaves as well.[36]

Meyendorff suggests that the Church did not forget the original and normal link between marriage and the Eucharist. He points to the text of St. Symeon of Thessalonica as evidence for this. Ancient forms of the marriage rite instruct the bridal pair to receive Holy Communion "if they are worthy," and if not, only the gifts of antidoron at the end of the liturgy.

What the historical evidence shows is that Schillebeeckx's thesis is without foundation. He claims that the priest had a function in the East which "probably went back to the role assumed by the priest in the pagan marriage ceremonies."[37] Such a thesis owes much to Schillebeeckx's secularizing theology of marriage which, in turn, reflects a wider concern to secularize the totality of Christian life and thought.[38]   It is clear to me that no such assumption should be operative in our thought. The essence of the Eastern Orthodox view is that marriage is the taking of a created and natural union (referring back to Genesis 2:24 as the Lord did in the Gospels) into the sphere of the Kingdom, into the "transnatural" sphere of God's Spirit thus elevating the human by including it in the Incarnation of God in Jesus Christ. Such a position is neither secular nor supernatural; it is sacramental, based on the elevation of humanity into deity through *theosis*.   In many ways Smirensky is asserting that it was the Church's subjection to the often unchristian demands of the imperial state that led to the toleration not only of second marriages, but also of the vast abuse of divorce in pre-revolutionary Russia, carried out by proxy representation by lawyers before Church courts and granted with ease and frequency. There is no question that there were abuses. However, there are facts that need to be faced so as to place this entire discussion in a more critical light. The historical facts are that the blessing was regarded as the essential element in the marriage of two Christians from the fourth century on. It was presumed that everyone was Christian, and since most marriages were arranged by parents for spouses who were often unknown to one another and quite young the potential for disaster was great indeed.

The loss of a Eucharistic context may well imply the Church's hesitancy in giving Holy Communion to the less devout, but we must not jump to the simple conclusion that marriages were celebrated in the context of the Eucharist in the patristic Church. The Italian scholar G. I. Passarelli has reasons for thinking otherwise.[39]   He is followed in this by Stevenson when he writes about the third prayer that appears over the common cup in the Barberini 336 manuscript of the eighth century: "Traditionally this common cup has been interpreted as a eucharistic substitute; I would identify it as an example of Jewish influence, for the total decline of eucharistic participation at marriage was a later development; even if it is not Jewish, it may well be a throw-back to early domestic customs, as in the later medieval West."[40] The evidence is incomplete in the matter. Those who somehow make the Eucharist itself the uniting force creating a marriage for those who would receive it together as man and wife fail to recognize the pivotal point that the blessing has had over the centuries in both Orthodox liturgy and Orthodox theology informed by the patristic tradition. The Greek theologian Tremblas states the traditional Greek Orthodox position:

> The mutual consent of the betrothed expressed in full freedom constitutes the exterior aspect of the marriage as the natural bond; insofar as it is a sacrament, it is the sacred rite celebrated by the minister of the Church. By their mutual consent the betrothed do not contribute as principle ministers to the founding of the Christian marriage as it is thought by the Roman Catholic Church, for which the blessing conferred by the priest is a sacramental. The priest sanctifies the natural bond of the marriage, and it is he who joins the hands of the newly married and who by the prayers that he reads over them transmits   the invisible grace which elevates and consecrates the marriage to the dignity of being a sacrament."[41]

John Meyendorff is right to claim that none of the specific ceremonies, whether they be the *arrha* or the *stephanoma*, constitute the essential elements by which the sacrament of marriage is bestowed. What then are the essential elements in marriage? It is indeed the blessing which is essential: "If one considers that according to the most ancient manuscripts of the Byzantine Eulogia the codex Barberini, Coislin 957 and 1036 of Sinai, and others, the only consecratory prayer of the marriage is the third one in the contemporary Eulogion, where the minister joining together the hands of the betrothed address God with the prayers: 'Do Thou, the same Lord, stretch out now also Thy hand from Thy holy dwelling-place, and unite this Thy servant, N, and this Thy handmaiden, N.'"[42] Trembelas finds the attestation of this "form of the sacrament" in St. Gregory of Nazianzus, who wrote "I put the hands of the young persons in one another and both in that of God."[43]   But this blessing is not magic, and the attempt in Orthodox scholasticism to make a priest into the "minister of the sacrament" is, in my opinion, only taking a Latin understanding of sacraments (by such considerations as "validity" and "minister," "matter and form") and imposing it on a radically different tradition. The language of Trembelas, using terms such as "sacramental form" and "the ministers of the sacrament" also reveals too much of a legacy of scholasticism imported from the West.   In Eastern Orthodoxy there has been an attempt on the part of scholastics to make the priest a minister of the sacrament of matrimony rather than the man and woman as in the Latin tradition. When we let ourselves hear the words and gestures of the marital liturgies of the Eastern Church, we discover that what the Church is doing through her priests is approving, sanctifying, and giving thanks to God for the union made holy in love which is about to be crowned and consummated. The question by what ceremonies this may be done is secondary in my opinion.   Also I believe that we must reject all forms of clerical magic. It is not a question of any priest performing a blessing which is efficacious in itself. The priest is the agent of the bishop and stands as his representative. It is the bishop representing Christ and His Church who bestows the sacrament of matrimony. The priestly blessing is based on the assessment that a union has marks of thae love that promises to make it a way into the Kingdom of God. The crowns bestowed on the married couple point in this direction as well as the ritual journey during the singing of the troparion of the Holy Martyrs. Martyrdom through marriage, more visible in an age when women frequently died in childbirth, is a foundational theme within the Orthodox liturgical setting. Yet the fundamental liturgical meaning of the blessing is thanksgiving to God for the union of the couple and a public sign within the Church that it is a union approved of God. It is clear from the 27th canon of St. Basil that a priest may sometimes wrongly bless a marriage. One can interpret in a similar way the blessings that have been given to many marriages which were marriages in name only, in reality only fornication.

It is clear, as Bishop Peter L'Huillier has shown us, that consent is important to Byzantine jurists so that the lack of consent renders a marriage null and void, but "consent is regarded more as a prerequisite than the main factor in the process of marital bond formation...At any rate, Byzantine canonists did not perceive a dilemma, viz. consent versus priestly blessing."[44] It is important to note that only in the seventeenth century did the Russian Orthodox Church incorporate forms of consent into the betrothal service. This was done under the impact of the changes demanded by Rome of the Uniates and through the Latinizing influence of Peter Moghila incorporated into the Orthodox ritual. The rather intriguing fact is that prior to these changes made under Peter Moghila Orthodox betrothal rituals had no formulas of consent. As Stevenson remarks, however, these formulas "are fortunately singularly un-Latin in their style."[45] Eventually other Orthodox churches followed this tendency to produce formulas of consent, as Stevenson puts it, "according to local customs."[46] Oddly, even Stylianopoulos thinks that the Greek rites have inadequate formulas of consent and that this defect should be remedied.[47]

Stylianopoulos raises one of the most important questions in the Orthodox theology of marriage: Is marriage a sacrament which only the New Testament raises to a sacramental level? He is critical of John Karmires for making statements to that effect. We know that St. Theodore the Studite wrote that the first conjugal blessing is that of Adam and Eve by God.[48] Furthermore, the references to the ideal marriages blessed by God, those of Isaac and Rebecca, Jacob and Rachel, and others down to Zechariah and Elizabeth - all mentioned in the prayers of the marriage rite - give support to the thesis of St. Theodore. The Roman Catholic distinction between natural and sacramental marriage, based entirely on whether the married couple are baptized, would imply that something entirely new appears in the new covenant. Nevertheless, the Orthodox assumption is, as Stylianopoulos states, that "every marriage of persons who are in communion with God, even in the Old Testament, is sacramental in the essential sense of being a locus and vehicle of the holy presence of

the living God."[49]   He makes the point that Christ restores all
things, and this is especially so in marriage. The question of
whether the priest or the married couple are ministers of the
sacrament of marriage falls aside as a nonsensical one. Christian marriage begins with two baptized people who are living
a life in Christ, within the Christian community, and both are
disposed to live their marriage in this context. Stylianopoulos
speaks strongly against the ritualism which would make any
union Christian only by the rite performed over it. When the
inner dispositions are lacking, the outer rituals cannot make
up for them. This is already implicit in canon 27 of St. Basil.
It is God who creates a marriage, but God does not do this
solely by the sacramental rite. The life in Christ exists prior
to marriage, and if the life in Christ is absent, the ritual does
not necessarily create it. Thus both consent and priestly
blessing are involved, but more deeply it is the reality of love
lived as Christ lived it and as the Church received it which
makes for an authentic marriage. Stylianopoulos has some
profound words on this subject:

> The necessity of the external blessing heightened the
> theological value of the marriage rite in the
> consciousness of hierarchs, priests, theologians and
> the people to such an extent that marriage without it
> was gradually regarded as 'sinful.' This is the context
> of the tradition so strong among Orthodox people to
> this day that a marriage, even of Christians, without a
> Church blessing is to be shunned, and those involved
> in such a marriage were called "uncrowned"
> (*astephanotoi*). What is here involved is an almost
> complete externalization of the sacrament over many
> centuries, probably accentuated by the development of
> an excessively lengthy rite. The rite itself seem to
> become the sacrament because it is seen as conferring
> through the bishop or priest matrimonial grace uniting
> the couple in marriage. The extreme form of this
> externalization in modern times is the concern to find
> a particular moment during the marriage rite when the
> marriage is indissolubly sanctified by an external

blessing. The couple itself, two baptized Christians who are already leading inherently sacramental lives and are an essential part of the sacrament, is almost forgotten![50].

Stylianopoulos does not fall into the other extreme of thinking that the liturgical rite is unnecessary. In fact, he says that "it would be unthinkable that marriage should not be blessed by a rite in the Church expressing both the couple's integral participation in the life of the Church and the Church's (bishop's) authority overseeing the life of all members of Christ's mystical Body.[51]" In answer to the question posed by Roman Catholics as to who is the minister of the sacrament, Fr. Theodore responds that it is both the couple and the priest: "Both sides, of course, equally require mutual consent and the presence of a priest for an ecclesiastically valid marriage."[52]

The presence of the bishop or his deputy, the presbyter, is necessary in an Orthodox marriage insofar as it indicates the presence of the whole Church. Marriage is not lived out in a vacuum but in a community, and the Christian community blesses and receives the couple into its midst as blessed by God in their union. Therefore, there is no question of a legitimate, sacramental union apart from the Church, but, on the other hand, the external rite cannot make something loving where it is not. On the other hand, the support and blessing of the community is not unimportant. The Roman Catholic scholar, Michael Lawler, has stated that the Christian minister at marriage is more than a simple witness to their giving and receiving of consent: "If that was all there was to it, then all marriages of the faithful would not require a designated witness at all. No, the ordained minister is present to perform certain functions in the name of the Church."[53] Among these he includes blessing the couple. It is a need for a coherence of the private and the public that demands the celebration of the marriage before the whole assembly of the Church. The Church's response to the inner character of the couple's love and fidelity calls out for legitimation and blessing from the ecclesial community. Lawler moves closer to the Eastern

Orthodox position regarding the priest as the minister of the sacrament but hesitates in going the whole way:

> While I do not believe that we need to go all the way to the position of the Eastern Church, which views the priest as the sole minister of the sacrament of marriage, I do believe that we need to go beyond the established Western position, which sees the priest or deacon as merely a legal witness. We need to see him as a *co-minister* of the sacrament of Christian marriage.[54]

Finally, we can agree with Schillebeeckx that "the Eastern Church had, from the very beginning, a mystical and theological conception of marriage: The secular view of marriage which clearly prevailed in the West until the eleventh century (the idea of marriage as a secular reality to be experienced 'In the Lord') was apparently unknown in the East - although there too, and indeed centuries before it took place in the West, the Church's liturgy of betrothal and marriage came about by the Church's canonisation of the ancient family and civil marriage customs."[55]   Where Schillebeeckx has gone astray, I believe, lies in his assumption that the sacred is closer to paganism and the secular to early Christian norms of marriage. Contrary to Schillebeeckx, I would urge that there is no great distance between Eastern and Western liturgical customs during the first thousand years of the Church's life. Rather, the sanctification of marriage "in the Lord" is found in both traditions, not just in the presence of a priestly blessing but also in the covenant and promise made by the man and woman and often celebrated in the context of the Eucharist. Nevertheless, there were differences in the Eastern and Western theologies of marriage since the East exalted marriage as a sacrament and mystery of the presence of Christ in the union of the man and the woman as "one flesh." A difference lay also in the stress given in Western theology to the legal bond, to contractual thinking, and the reading of *sacramentum* as oath rather than as *mysterion*. The Western position, which made the man and woman the ministers of the

116

sacramentum rather than the Church as a whole (represented by the bishop or priest), was profoundly secular in its continuity with Roman law.   Schillebeeckx rejoices in this secularity. Others may lament it. Nevertheless, we may with with John Meyendorff recognize in the creation of a non-Eucharistic context for marriage an Eastern form of secularization created by conformity to secular norms. The fact that marriage ceased to be Eucharistic in context only accommodated the rites to the fact that less than fully Christian people were being married by the church and thus what had been celebrated at the heavenly banquet became more and more an affair only of this world. The paradox is, as Meyendorff notes, that the Western rites for marriage remained in the context of the Eucharist and the Eastern ones were separated from the Eucharist.[56] The Western theology of marriage remained secular and steeped in Augustinian gloom about the evils of concupiscence redeemed only by the natural functions of reproduction. Kenneth Stevenson, while examining the development of the Byzantine marriage liturgies, notes a progression of ideas as "address, creation of man and woman, marriage, supplication for the married couple, marital virtues, protection from evil, and children; and such themes can be illustrated by reference to biblical characters."[57] This structure, he thinks, is a standard one, something lacking in all Western liturgical expressions of marriage. He concludes:

But more important than this basic community of ideas is the strongly positive view of marriage, and the enjoyment of the things of the flesh when blessed by God; all this the   Byzantine marriage liturgy reinforces. You could never find a Troparion invoking the joy of the saints and martyrs at a wedding in any medieval Western rite! Moreover marriage is about *both*   partners, an insight given symbolic expression in that the   couple are crowned, instead of the bride alone being veiled. It   is not for nothing that even though the Byzantine rite makes   little fuss of the rings (when compared, say, with later medieval France or England), the fact that two rings first appear

117

in the   East shows that the Byzantine understanding
of the marriage relationship was not only highly
developed but given liturgical expression.[58]

Stevenson thinks that the choice of lections have
themselves influenced the Byzantine view of marriage. The
gospel reading was always Jn 2:1-11, the narrative of Christ
at the wedding of Cana, and the epistle was usually Eph 5.20-
33. The conclusions were a healthy happiness: "So instead of
hearing Jesus' pronouncement on indissolubility and Paul's
chauvinism on wifely obedience, Byzantine rite Christians
were married with a liturgy that did not encourage them to go
home to bed feeling slightly guilty."[59]   The assumption made
by so many Roman Catholic authors, even the most liberal,
that ecclesiastical influence led to oppression and legalism and
that a secular mentality was more natural and joyful is clearly
a reflection of their own Augustinianism, their own legalism,
and their own attempt to find a way out of this impasse.
From this past both Schillebeeckx and Guindon envisage a
natural marriage, administered by the couple themselves
rather than being subject to clerical control and ministrations.
Conflict between a priestly blessing and the free consent of
the couple has no place in the Orthodox world. Furthermore,
the sacred and the secular are not opposed. The body and the
spirit can be reconciled, and the community created in the
couple is itself a "little church" within the context of the
people of God who make up the whole Church. Perhaps the
posing of the question of the validity of a marriage is as
misplaced here as it is in the context of the validity of Holy
Orders. In the latter context the Orthodox view is that authenticity of ordination outside the Orthodox Church depends
not on some alleged validity but on the fullness of the ecclesial context, the rightness of faith and sacramental practice,
and the extent to which rituals used outside the Orthodox
Church communicate or fail to communicate the faith of the
Orthodox Church.[60]   The same principles may also apply to
the marriages which come within the purview of the Orthodox
Church. What matters is that the Church should recognize,
give thanks, and rejoice in a marriage which reflects the unity

118

of Christ with His Church and exists as a communion of two persons within the wider communion of the Eucharistic fellowship and a common faith. The reality of a marriage is not to be judged, as it is by Roman Catholics, on alleged validity. The hideous abuses brought in the back door in the system of annulments ignore and seek to cover up the evils attendant upon marital breakdown and the acknowledgement of sin in such instances. Validity has no place in the Orthodox assessment of marital reality. That reality is solely whether the marriage continues to reflect the union of Christ and His Church both in the love of the couple and in their willingness to walk in the way of the cross as an expression of their commitment to one another and to the Lord of their marriage.

The modern movement toward the recognition of common law marriages is unacceptable to the moral theology of the Orthodox tradition. Similarly the question of sexual activity outside of marriage, now widely accepted by many liberal Christians, is not even raised within the framework of the mystery of holy union which is a participation in Christ's love for His Church. Love, if authentic, is always a gift of God, but the expression of married love is necessarily a life-offering gift of self to another sanctified by the blessing of the Church. To move from the affirmation of the goodness of love to the affirmation of coitus as a legitimate expression of love is often fallacious. Coitus is a privileged sign of a relationship, which has not only become "one flesh" and thus moved beyond the merely passionate embrace, but is a social fact involving not only oneself and the beloved other but the potential children and the living out of a relationship beyond the immediate moment. People are deeply affected by coitus, and loving coitus brings with it a new status of being members of one another. As we are members of one another not only in families but in the Church, so this new union must be integrated within the whole. Otherwise, division and pain will ensue. What is felt to be love frequently becomes something quite other than love, an act of selfishness which divides people from one another. Individualism has no place in an Orthodox Christian context, and couples integrated apart from their communion with Christ in the Church are not only signs

119

of disunity but consequences of the brokenness of the world and divisions from the Church. This is not to say that they are always evil, but it is to say that they do not share in the unity which is the mark of the Kingdom of God and expressed in the Eucharistic mystery.

The history of marriage in the Byzantine era makes it clear that the norm increasingly became one in which the blessing of the Church designated the marriage as acceptable, canonical, and holy. That such a norm was not universally applied, even in novella 89 as issued by the Emperor Leo VI, is widely accepted. Bishop Peter L'Huillier states that "neither before the promulgation of the law nor after was crowning considered as a necessary condition for validity. To be sure, in the mind of the public at that time, crowning was closely associated with legitimate marriage."[61] That vast numbers of Orthodox people have over the centuries been married without crowning and that common law marriages lasted in Russia until the end of the seventeenth century are facts. The Church's task is to bring unions of its children into the sacramental context of Christ's love for the Church. The modern dilemma facing the Orthodox Church is precisely that vast numbers of her members are being married to non-Orthodox persons, often in non-Orthodox rites. Perhaps this parallel to common law marriages or of those not being crowned may be accepted. What cannot be accepted are those sexual arrangements made outside the context of the sacramental blessing and meaning given in the mystery of Christ and His Church. Persons committed to Christ and to His Church must seek that blessing, for it is a sign of the integration of their love with the love of God and their communion with the wider communion of all Orthodox Christians. The view that marriage is a secular enterprise, carried out by two people who become an integrated couple by their love, consent and carnal union, is false insofar as it isolates them from the Body of Christ and the communion of the Holy Spirit. Orthodoxy means the integration into wholeness and has no place for private unions based on individual initiative and choice. What may begin in the intimacy of a private space becomes integrated into the community by the blessing of the Church.

Orthodoxy depends not only on Holy Scripture and the writings of the Fathers for her theology but also upon the lived theology of the liturgy. His witness to this fact made of Fr. Alexander Schmemann a prophetic voice in our age. His successor, John Meyendorff has reinterated this fact. Orthodox liturgical theology witnesses as nowhere else to the goodness, the glory, and the excellence of marriage. Yet Orthodox practice leaves much to be desired, particularly in the loss of the Eucharistic context of the crowning and blessing of marriage. It is in recalling our practice to that fullness, to a greater awareness of what dispositions are necessary in those presenting themselves for marriage, and to conformity to the Gospel pattern that marriage will be restored to all the Lord wills it to be.

Notes

(1) Edward Schillebeeckx, *Marriage: Human Reality and Saving Mystery* (London: Sheed and Ward, 1965), Vol I., p. 344.

(2) Ibid., p. 248.

(3) Clement of Alexandria, *Stromata* 4.20, trans. Kenneth Stevenson, *Nuptial Blessing: A Study in Christian Marriage Rites* (New York: Oxford University Press, 1983), p. 16.

(4) Schillebeeckx, p. 251.

(5) Ibid., pp. 251-2.

(6) Kenneth Stevenson, pp. 21-3.

(7) Basil the Great, *On the Holy Spirit* 19, trans. Stevenson, p. 21.

(8) Stevenson, p. 21.

(9) Basil the Great, *Letter to Amphilochum* 188:199. in *St. Basil: Letters 186-368*, trans. Agnes Clare Way, in *The Fathers of the Church*, Vol. 28 (Washington DC: Catholic University of America, 1955), p. 54.

(10) Tertullian, *To His Wife* in *Treatises on Marriage and Remarriage*, trans. Le Saint, *Ancient Christian Writers*, (Westminster, MD: Newman Press, 1951), p. 35.

(11) Schillebeeckx, p. 353.

(12) Stevenson, p. 18.

(13) K. Ritzler, *Le Mariage dans les Eglises chrètiennes de ler au XIe siécle* (Paris: Editions du Cerf, 1970), pp. 110-120.

(14) Stevenson, p. 26.

(15) Ambrosiaster, *Book of Questions* 50.400; *On the First Epistle to the Corinthians* 7.40; *On the First Epistle to Timothy* 3.12.

(16) Ambrose of Milan, *Hexameron* 86.18, trans. Stevenson, p. 27.

(17) Stevenson, p. 27.

(18) Ambrose of Milan, *Letter* 19 (95).844.7, trans. Stevenson, p. 27.

(19) Stevenson, p. 44.

(20) Peter L'Huillier, "Novella 89 of Leo the Wise on Marriage: An Insight into its Theoretical and Practical Impact," *The Greek Orthodox Theological Review*, 32, 2 (Summer, 1987), p. 154.

(21) André Guindon, "Case for a 'Consummated' Sexual Bond before a 'Ratified" Marriage," *Eglise et Théologie* 8 (1977), pp. 137-181.

(22) André Guindon, *The Sexual Creators: An Ethical Proposal for Concerned Christians* (Lanham, MD: University Press of America, 1986), p. 110.

(23) Stevenson, p. 24.

(24) Stevenson, p. 24.

(25) Ritzler, pp. 139-40, translation my own).

(26) Ibid., p. 129.

(27) Stevenson, pp. 99-100.

(28) Ritzler, p. 180.

(29) L'Huillier, p. 157.

(30) Alexander Schmemann, *For the Life of the World* (Crestwood, NY: St. Vladimir's Seminary Press, 1973), pp. 88-9.

(31) Theodore Stylianopoulos, "Toward a Theology of Marriage in the Orthodox Church," *Greek Orthodox Theological Review*, 12, 3 (1977), p. 253.

(32) Ibid., pp. 256-7.

(33) Alvian N. Smirensky, "The Evolution of the Present Rite of Matrimony and Parallel Canonical Developments," *St. Vladimir's Seminary Quarterly*, 8, 2 (1964), pp. 39-40.

(34) Ibid., p. 43.

(35) Ibid., p. 44.

(36) John Meyendorff, *Marriage: An Orthodox Perspective* (Crestwood, NY: St. Vladimir's Seminary Press, 1970), pp. 30-1.

(37) Schillebeeckx, p. 355.

(38) Edward Schillebeeckx, *God and the Future of Mankind* (London: Sheed and Ward, 1969).

(39) G. I. Passarelli, "La cerimonia dello Stefanoma (Incoronazione) nei riti matrimoniali bizantini secondu il Codice Cryptense G. b. VII (X sec.)," *Ephremerides Liturgicae* 93 (1979), pp. 381-91

(40) Stevenson, p. 99.

(41) P. Trembelas, *Dogmatique de l'Eglise Catholique Orthodoxe*, Vol. III (Chevetogne, 1968), p. 363-4, translation my own.

(42) Ibid, p. 366.

(43) Ibid.

(44) L'Huillier, p. 159.

(45) Stevenson, p. 102.

(46) Ibid.

(47) Stylianopoulos, p. 283.

(48) Ibid., p. 269.

(49) Ibid, p. 270.

(50) Ibid., pp. 273-4.

(51) Ibid., p. 274.

(52) Ibid.

(53) Michael Lawler, *Secular Marriage, Christian Sacrament* (Mystic, CN: Twenty-Third Publications, 1985), p. 78.

(54) Ibid., pp. 78-9.

(55) Schillebeeckx, pp. 355-6.

(56) Meyendorff, p. 26.

(57) Stevenson, p. 103.

(58) Stevenson, p. 103.

(59) Ibid., pp. 103-4.

(60) C. J. N. Bailey, "Validity and Authenticity: The Difference between Western and Orthodox Views on Orders," *St. Vladimir's Seminary Quarterly*, 8 (1964), pp. 86-92.

(61) L'Huillier, p. 159.

Chapter Four:
Modern Approaches to Marriage

In the literature produced by modern Orthodox theologians on the subject of marriage, there are two quite distinct traditions. The older and more patristic is the Greek, and the younger and somewhat speculative is the Russian. If modern Greeks are sometimes tempted by the scholasticism that they have learned from Western Catholics, modern Russians have been deeply influenced by the strains of idealistic philosophy which have filtered through the borders from mainly German thinkers of the nineteenth century. Modern Orthodox theologians have, apart from those who eschewed all modern philosophy in favor of a return to the Fathers, been seeking a medium of philosophical discourse in which the faith might be presented in the modern world. As the Greek Fathers of the fourth and fifth centuries used forms of Platonism as a common hermeneutical basis for the dogmas of the faith, so with the loss of Platonism in the modern age theologians such as Sergei Bulgakov lived in the intellectual world offered by Soloviev, who, in turn had immersed himself in the thought of the German Schelling and in gnoseology. The same search for a philosophy is to be found in Christos Yannaras' use of Heidegger's ontology as a foundation for his personalism.

The Greek Tradition

It is best that we turn first to examples of the Greek tradition and then consider Yannaras' treatment of marriage. In our opinion the outstanding essay on the topic is that of Father Stephanos Charalambidis, first published in French and later in English as "Marriage in the Orthodox Church."[1] The Orthodox vision of marriage, he sets forth, is of "a special vocation by which people are called to achieve fullness of being in God and to transcend the state of separation and egocentric isolation, so prone to sin."[2] He envisages this kind of married love as pneumatophorous since it is a vehicle of the Holy Spirit. In advocating a personalist understanding of marriage, Fr. Stephanos contrasts the individualistic perspective in which the individual is seen as the product of biological processes and the personalist in which the person transcends the empirical ego: "The person is centered on the spirit and on the 'me' which lies infinitely deeper than the empirical one. The vocation of the person is to reunite created and uncreated nature through love by the acquiring of grace."[3] The human person is modeled upon the divine persons revealed in the dogma of the Holy Trinity. It is only in God that personhood can be said to exist, strictly speaking, but human beings are images of God insofar as there is a nostalgia to become fully a person. Thus human efforts are realized only insofar as the individual "participates in an Archetype, wholly directed toward the divine Other."[4]

The fall of humanity has perverted human sexuality, separating impaired masculinity and impaired femininity, giving rise to a constant oscillation between attraction and repulsion. Fr. Stephanos judges that the original dyadic unity existed in man *and* woman (not in man or woman). This unity reveals the fullness of the theanthropy, of God's image in man. Sexuality became tragic as a consequence of the Fall, and after the coming of God's kingdom, the sexual life of humanity regained its "perfect maturity of married love in a single being."[5] Fr. Stephanos quotes the second letter of Clement to the Corinthians 12:2: "When two become one and the outer is as the inner, and when male and female, reunited, are neither male nor female." This marriage restored the communion of male and female insofar as its sacramental bond is an expression of the power of the Holy Spirit within the new age of the Kingdom of God. Fr. Stephanos acknowledges that this union may appear difficult and impractical when conceived of an "an impossible ideal," but to this objection he replies: "The difference between 'sacrament' and 'ideal' is precisely that the sacrament is no imaginary abstraction but an experience in which it is not just man who acts but man in union with God."[6]

Theologically viewed humanity participates in the Holy Spirit, without ceasing to be "humanity." Here we have both the mystery of *theosis* and the mystery of synergy whereby the will must be used in freedom to receive what God gives. Without a life centered in Christ we cannot achieve the reconciliation between man and woman, nor the integration of *eros* and person. Without this integration we are driven by the impersonal play of erotic love. Marriage was established in paradise and is now restored to the grace in which love transcends the Fall and once again reveals the beauty of paradise. Indeed, the revelation of the glory of Christ at Cana was a witness to the presence of Christ at every wedding. Christ presides over every Christian wedding, and Fr. Stephanos identifies him as the true bridegroom: "He is the one and only Bridegroom whose voice is heard by his friend and makes him rejoice. This level of the mystical espousals of the soul and Christ, typified concretely in marriage and which occurs in every soul and in the whole Church, the Bride, gives St. John Chrysostom apt cause to say: 'Marriage is the mysterious icon of the Church.'"[7] Fr. Stephanos affirms the Eucharistic context of every marriage and asserts that the celebrant of the sacrament of marriage in the Orthodox Church can only be the bishop or priest, the celebrant of the Eucharist, who represents liturgically the whole Church. Wonderfully, the epiclesis is made by the priest when he prays: "Lord Our God, crown them with glory and honor." It was Christ's presence at the meal in Cana which provided the Eucharistic context of marriage within the Church's tradition.

In his splendid vision of marriage as an eschatological participation in the Kingdom of God present sacramentally in the married couple, Fr. Stephanos gives what can serve as the perfect response to an overly "spiritual" interpretation of marriage:

> A genuine love always comes back, wittingly or unwittingly, to that "ecstasy" of Christ's death on the Cross which gives birth to the new humanity. It begins to discover an ascesis which it draws from the inexhaustible ecstasy of Christ. From his pierced side flow the waters of baptism and the blood of the Eucharist. From his riven and tortured body springs the Spirit. So when human love seems to dry up, the answer is to penetrate to the deep and inexhaustible resources of that divine-human love. Through repentance, forgiveness, the unrequited trust of the "desert," the other person is suddenly restored to us, wonder and gratitude are deepened, and, in the Spirit, fidelity gives access to new life. In this way this "great mystery" is revealed among us again and again; unlike the exalted states of passion, its sure criteria should be peace, joy, and mutual trust. This is why, however paradoxical it seems, there is a link between marriage and martyrdom by virtue of the Cross which manifests love in its fulness.[8]

Thus the liturgical link of the bridal couple with the holy martyrs is not mere poetry or artificial piety since it is the cross of Christ which makes marriage possible. "All of this goes to show," says Fr. Stephanos, "that when the Church sets before people the absolute standards of the gospel she is not maintaining some abstract utopia but what is authentically human."[9] This is because the truth about fallen human nature and about the glorified human nature revealed in the person of Jesus Christ is the truth which is authentically human. The key to a Christian marriage, according to Fr. Stephanos, is that of repentance and grace. Instead of a gnostic flight to an elitist perfection of perfect love, we have here a vision of marriage as a participation in the cross of Christ, making up for our failures in love and yet uniting us to the love which God ever offers to His bride the Church.

Fr. Stephanos offers a link between celibacy and marriage as the two vocations within a single state of life, "two ways of responding to a single spiritual concern, sacramentally of equal value and which both possess the virtue of chastity or integrity, thus implying an equal submission to the gospel demand of perfection."[10] Chastity is the chief virtue of marriage, and by this virtue we refer to "a spiritual quality, the total 'wisdom' and power that comes with the integrity and integration of all that makes up human existence."[11] This integration may exist either in marriage or in celibacy in a virginal person. Fr. Stephanos views consecrated celibacy "not as a negation of sexual energy which is part of human reality, but in fact its legitimate transposition and necessary transfer to the eschatological level of God's Kingdom."[12]

Christianity has, according to Fr. Stephanos, "definitively established both the transcendence of the person and the fact that man and woman are both persons, more than equals, of absolute value."[13] So, also, the wholesome polarity of male and female has been restored to what it was in paradise. The sacramental nature of marriage follows from its relation to the Kingdom of God. But, as he notes, the sacraments are not magic. In the context of the Orthodox theology of freedom and grace this means that grace does not destroy human freedom: "The gift of the Spirit is always offered to free persons who retain the possibility of repulsing God's gift and of living merely 'according to the flesh.'"[14] What this means is that the marriage bonds which believers have contracted can be preserved even when the human elements are deficient. It is love which along with chastity, marks a Christian marriage, but this love has an ascesis "which it draws from the inexhaustible ecstasy of Christ."[15] When human love seems to dry up, the recourse lies in "the deep and inexhaustible resources of that divine-human love."[16]

Fr. Stephanos accepts the teaching of the Orthodox Church that only a first marriage has the fullness of sacramental meaning. This is why a second marriage is not allowed to priests. It is "an indulgence" when the Church allows a second marriage to lay people, but this is not something to be allowed the clergy who must uphold and teach the standards of the New Testament about the "unique character of marriage." Fr. Stephanos accepts the possibility of a second marriage after the disintegration of the first. However, he rejects any claim made as to the right to remarriage. The Church permits a remarriage out of her pastoral concern for the spiritual well being of her sons and daughters and from the principle of economy. The principles from which this permission is granted lie in the recognition that Christ taught that marriage ought not to be dissolved, not that it could not be. When a marriage has ceased to exist, then a bishop may permit a second marriage. Canonically this in no way makes economy into a form of indulgence which the faithful have a right to or may even come to expect. Rather, the theological foundation lies in the eschatological tension whereby we are between the time of the heavenly Kingdom and the present temporal conditions of the fallen world. As Fr. Stephanos puts it, "The Christian is not poised between two stools: he is not neutral but has a goal because despite his weaknesses and falls he is a citizen of heaven, an eschatological man, a prophet and a martyr."[17] The vision of marriage presented by Fr. Stephanos is one of a communion of two persons, of two sexes, without domination or contempt, living a life of celebration and tenderness as signs of the Kingdom of God. There is no mystical flight here, however, either from the natural or from the hard realities of life. Rather, we have the elevation of the ordinary through the transforming power of crucified love, making marriage conform not only to the Kingdom of God but to the Cross of Christ.

In my opinion, the theology of marriage set forth by Christos Yannaras in his book, *The Freedom of Morality*, is the most searching and profound created by an Orthodox theologian.[18] Yannaras shows how the natural *eros* of humanity is sanctified and transformed into "true *eros*." For Christians the mystery of marriage can never be a mere ceremonial blessing given to natural sexual relations, something imposed by religion to preserve the institution of the family.[19] These natural institutions have their place and their value in the life of fallen humanity since man is driven by desire. Nevertheless, this desire is for something more than sexual release and offspring. Following St. Maximus the Confessor, Yannaras writes: "In the objectified world of the fall, the world of safeguards for the subject and entrenched egocentric individuality, *eros* or sexual love remains one last possibility for a life of *relationship* and *knowledge*."[20] We are lifted out of our natural egoism by the revelation of the uniqueness and distinctiveness of a loved one.

Yannaras notes that lovers in mythology and in the classic prototypes formed by art perceive that love can scarcely last for a long period of time. Indeed, heroes often preferred to die in confirmation of their love. Yannaras find a profound mystery revealed in this preference: "Concealed in this preference is the truth that the only way of hypostatic existence and life 'in truth' is self-transcendence in love and loving self-offering as revealed by the cross of Christ."[21] In the Old Testament we see mankind moving beyond nature, beyond the cosmic participation in natural *eros* to a personal relation with God. From this personal or hypostatic relation comes the possibility of communion within the family. The joyful taste of personal love gives rise to an anticipation of transcendence of corruption and death. Yet it is precisely sexuality which makes us subject to the natural necessity of perpetuating death. The mystery which is Christian marriage is a bestowal of the fullest dimensions to sexual love. It frees love from its subjection to natural necessity and manifests it in the unity of man and woman, thus making it an image of the love of Christ for His Church.

Yannaras himself refers the transformation of *eros* to the great mystery concerning Christ and the Church. Natural *eros* is transfigured into 'true *eros* by an ascetic relinquishment of one's own will so that the will of the other can be accepted. This unity of man and wife is built, Yannaras urges, not on sexual impulses but on ecclesial communion, "which is self-transcendence and self-offering."[22]

This fullness of the personal and physical unity of the partners in the mystery of marriage is a dynamic event corresponding to Christ's assumption of humanity. For Yannaras *eros*, which is part of our fallen nature, is given hypostatic union in the relation between the two persons, husband and wife, who in turn are linked with the person of Christ since they are made members of His body the Church. There is an extension of the Incarnation here, a being taken up into the life of the Godhead. As Yannaras puts it: "In other words, the natural self-offering of sexual love is transfigured in church marriage, becoming a dynamic imitation of Christ's cross and conformity to His voluntary assumption of our nature's death - a conformity whose fruit is resurrection and incorruption."[23] Sexuality and the biological origins of marriage are not denied or scorned but fulfilled in the elevation of the natural into the hypostasis which is a unity of persons in freedom and love.

Yannaras maintains that long before Freud's discoveries of the profound implications of sexuality for our personality and our capacity for love, the Greek Fathers had connected man's existential problem with the orientation of his natural sexual impulse. That impulse turns one either towards sensual pleasure or toward living life in hypostatic reality as communion and relationship. He mentions St. Gregory of Nyssa's *On the Formation of Man* and St. Maximus the Confessor's *Theological Chapters* as examples of this patristic awareness. St. John Climacus also revealed a similar consciousness of these human options. After the assumption of natural *eros* into *hypostasis*, nature is inevitably subjected to an asceticism. That asceticism is not a hatred for the body or for *eros* (though, no doubt, it has become so for many). Rather, it is a taking of desire into a love like unto the love of Christ, who accepted crucifixion "for us men and for our salvation." This is, in fact, the Eucharistic mode of existence: self-offering. The giving of self stands as a necessity for hypostatic love. Like Fr. Stephanos Charalambidis, Christos Yannaras thinks that Christian marriage has little to do with the social institutionalization of the reproductive process.[24] It is most profoundly both an imitation of Christ and a participation in the mystery of His self-offering.

It is not for the indulgence of the flesh that the relationship between man and woman is exalted above the procreative ends of marriage. It is, rather, because the mystery of marriage is the mystery of freedom. Biological determinism stands opposed to freedom. Yannaras affirms that the mystery of marriage has more in common with the asceticism of monks than with the social institutionalization of the reproductive process. This is because both share a *true eros*. This is why the newly-wed couple are "martyrs" - witnesses to the truth which is being affirmed. The freedom of personal love has become no longer subject to natural necessity but has been taken up into the Eucharistic relationship. Indeed, Yannaras declares that the love of a man for his wife is in fact a love for all the members of Christ's body since she sums up the beauty and truth of the world, of all creation. Thus we begin to see why the virginity of monks and the *eros* which grafts marriage into the life of the Kingdom of God are basically the same. Virginity is *eros* free from the natural constraint of lust and pleasure, and it is the same *eros* which marks an Orthodox Christian marriage. Yannaras thinks that this is why there is no peculiar asceticism for married people but only the asceticism of the monks. If marriage is seen only within the context of the world, that would appear absurd or even scandalous. But if marriage demands an existential self-offering beyond this life and beyond our personal identity, beyond even corruption and death, one can indeed comprehend the overlap of monastic and marital asceticism. We also see why marriage is not allowed to a deacon or priest after ordination and why second marriages, even after the death of a spouse, are considered dubious and only concessions to weakness and sin. The marriage once taken into the Kingdom of God in the Eucharistic assembly must remain there. One can never go back, as it were.

Perhaps it is the prophetic stance of Yannaras which makes him stand out as one of the foremost contemporary Greek Orthodox theologians. Yannaras shows an awareness of the extent to which marriage has been debased by utilitarianism, auto-eroticism, and secularization. The mystery of marriage, with its cosmic and christological significance, is almost entirely lost in the modern world. Indeed, numbers of people come to Orthodox churches to be married and have not the slightest notion of what marriage might be apart from their sense that it gives legitimacy to their own self-centered desires. One might understand if the alienation of marriage occurred by reason of the weakness or immaturity of those who approach it. But the fact remains that many come forward, particularly in "mixed marriages" to receive a sacrament from the Church with only the most secular awareness of what marriage might be. It becomes incumbent on the Church to reject this secularization of marriage and the consequent debasement of the mystery. Only when Orthodox people understand that marriage gives the true freedom which is possible only by ascetic self-transcendence will marriage once more gain its integrity and mystery. Today, unfortunately, the bondage of marriage is contrasted with the "liberation of instinct" and the consecration of individualism - leading inevitably to a deep malaise in the married couple and often to divorce. The task for the Church will be to withhold the ceremonies requested and to bestow the sacrament only upon those who are ready and willing to enter into what is a death, a martyrdom, in preparation for resurrection. For Yannaras the debasement of marriage is closely linked with the loss of the communal sense of the Eucharist and the communion of the congregation. Externals become the norm when sacramental participation ceases. Being severed from the Body of Christ, the ceremonies of marriage cease to be meaningful to those who receive them.[25] The restoration of Holy Communion for the Eucharistic congregation and of marriage to the particular ethos of the Eucharist are the only ways toward a truly Christian married life. Ethics finds its ground, therefore, in sacramental life, not just in conscience.

Christos Yannaras has sought to unite patristic theology with the philosophy of Heidegger. This is not so evident in *The Freedom of Morality* (originally in Greek *I Eleftheria thou Ithous*) as in the second volume of this trilogy which he gave the title *To Prosopo kai o Eros* (*Person and Eros*). The Anglican critic Gerald Gray has asked why Yannaras speaks of *eros* rather than *agape*.[26] This is, I think, to miss the entire point of the cosmic dimension of Yannaras's vision of the transformation of the creaturely desire by the Holy Spirit. *Agape* is the transformation of *eros* to a higher commitment, but, nonetheless, it is desire which both gives energy to our lives and attracts us to one another. Of itself, desire ends in selfish lusts, domination of others, and inevitable conflict if it is not elevated and redeemed by God's grace. This is exactly the transformation of *eros* into *agape*. The example given by Yannaras from Tolstoi's story "Alyosha" refers to the cook falling in love with the ugly and wretched Alyosha. Yannaras' sentence "there is someone who needs poor Alyosha, not for what he does, but for what he is" contains "perhaps the most complete definition of the natural potentialities of *eros*.[27] We must note that he speaks of a human need and of a context having nothing religious or ecclesiastical about it. Yet for Yannaras the Church's task in marriage is to bless and offer a sacramental grace for human love to be transformed and perfected by the Holy Spirit. Individual loves are brought to the Eucharistic gathering of the saints to be integrated and celebrated as gifts of God. Creation is fulfilled, not obliterated, by the saving action of the Spirit of God.

The Russian Tradition

There are three outstanding works about sexuality and marriage coming from theologians writing in the Russian tradition. Two are by laymen: Paul Evdokimov's *Le sacrement de l'amour: le conjugale à la lumière de la tradition orthodoxe* (translated as *The Sacrament of Love* in 1985) and Philip Sherrard's *Eros and Christianity*. The other is Evgueny Lampert's *The Divine Realm*. Despite a lifetime devoted to Greek studies, Sherrard has written a book clearly in the Russian tradition, as he manifests his indebtedness again and again to Russian philosophers. Behind all of these works stands the figure of Vladimir Soloviev. His influence, explicitly recognized by Evdokimov and Sherrard, is pervasive throughout the Russian works on marriage.[28] It is perhaps best to return to an examination of Soloviev's little book *The Meaning of Love* if we are to discern the character of this distinctly Russian contribution to Orthodox teaching on marriage.

Soloviev's fundamental premise is that sexual love is radically distinct from the reproduction of the species. Indeed, he considers them to be *"in inverse ratio* to each other."[29] Soloviev entirely rejects the view that nature attains her aims for the preservation of the race by the allure of the feeling of love. In fact, the very intensity of love is often directly opposed to the continuation of life itself. Soloviev's example of Werther's passion for Charlotte in Goethe's novel of unrequited love and consequent suicide reveals the radically non-teleological character of sexual love. Indeed, one can take as a general rule that the intensity of such love either does not admit to posterity or, at best, admits only those whose importance does not correspond to the exceptional character of the relation which gave birth to that love. Furthermore, if we consider the Divine Providence's manner of generation, we find that there is no relation between love and procreation. The Bible testifies to this in the facts of the genealogy of Christ. There we discover that Jacob loved Rachel, but the Son of Jacob, Judah, was the offspring of Leah, the unloved wife. The birth of David depended upon the loveless union between Boaz and Ruth, and Solomon descended from David's sinful liaison with Bathsheba. Soloviev, in a rather post-Kantian fashion, insists that sexual love has no teleological designs. This may seem absurd to those who think of sexual love primarily as a biological drive resulting in coitus, but for Soloviev the sexual was in reference to the sexes, so that sexual love is viewed as an intensely idealized love between persons of the two sexes.

Sexual love is the "highest flowering of the individual life" for Soloviev.[30] This conviction does not follow from an adherence to a philosophy of individualism. Rather, it is consequent to Soloviev's conviction of the absolute worth of the human being. Rational consciousness takes absolute form in man. Not only is the human being rational, but the consciousness of rationality brings with it an understanding of truth and the ability to improve infinitely his existence while still remaining within the limits and boundaries of the human form. Consequently, human improvement lies primarily in developing ourselves, not in changing other beings. Individuals, however, are isolated in their egoism, and as a result, the truth is only an external illumination. It is love which frees us from our false self-assertion, which overcomes our egoism. What is unique to Soloviev is the stress that he puts on sexual love.[31] He is ready to recognize that all forms of love manifest the overcoming of egoism in favor of unity in the totality of being, but sexual love is a force which overcomes egoism both concretely and in relation to an "objectified subject like ourselves."[32] The fusion that results is not just a union of two creatures of the same nature and of equal significance, but it includes difference in both "capacity or mode of another form."[33] Soloviev discovers in sexual love both sameness and difference, two individuals, but also two sexes, yet in the same human nature. Soloviev is, in fact, presenting a philosophical version of the basic Orthodox belief that the sacramental love of man and woman is sanctifying and redeeming. He writes of the meaning and worth of love as consisting "in the fact that it makes us actually, with our whole being, recognize in *another* the absolute central significance which owing to egoism we feel in ourselves only."[34] He recognizes that this definition fits all kinds of love, but he thinks that sexual love "differs from other kinds of love by greater intensity, greater absorption and the possibility of a more complete and comprehensive reciprocity."[35] . Only in this way can two existences be fused into one. To confirm this truth he refers to Gn 2:24 in the Bible. The reference is odd since Soloviev does not include physical love as a normal or even legitimate expression of this sexual love. It is by feeling that this love is born, but the feeling is usually lost, and the result is often a sense of illusion. In a brilliant analogy, Soloviev compares love to speech. It is not the sounds themselves, any more than the feelings of love, that matter, but *what* is said. The absolute significance of the beloved must be communicated to her.[36]

At least by strong implication Soloviev has linked love with speaking to the loved one. This is what communicates feeling to another person and creates reciprocity. Soloviev rejects the notion that love is a "special idealization" of the beloved. He affirms that the special light in which the loved one is seen is not just a moral or intellectual estimation but a special sensuous reception: "The lover actually *sees*, visually receives, what others do not."[37] It is love which is the primary witness to an immortality which is more than the mere continuation of a dreary existence. Salvation thus takes place by love, which is the power of Being transforming us beyond the limitations imposed by death.

The perennial call of monasticism in the Eastern Orthodox tradition has been a promise of overcoming death by the rejection of sexual intercourse and its consequent offspring. As one can see from the arguments of St. Gregory of Nyssa, a holy virginity was a hope for immortality. Soloviev moves beyond this human protest against the inevitability of mortality by denying that virginity protects one from death.[38] Of course, monks and nuns have not regarded sexual abstinence as itself a deliverance from death; it was the participation in the eternal and timeless life of God who granted the gift of immortality by participation in his immortality. Nevertheless, Soloviev sees the separation of the sexes as itself a mark of the beginning of death.[39] Overcoming the dividedness of humanity in sexual separation is a way of restoring the wholeness of humanity. How, we may ask, can this restoration be achieved? For Soloviev spiritual love is the primary way in which human beings triumph over death.[40] Soloviev envisages a true spirituality as rescuing the flesh, not in denying it, raising it up by resurrection from the dead.[41]

In reality genuine love is built on faith, and faith lies in God, not in God abstractly but in God as giving the absolute and unconditional significance of the person. The worship of a human being would be idolatry, but the worship which is love for another becomes legitimate by the contemplation of the object of one's love in relation to the Divine. Soloviev is both philosopher and theologian at this point. The affirmation of another in God is equally dependent upon the affirmation of myself in God as the center and root of my existence. Theologically our faith is faith in the divine Trinity, which is both a subjective act on our part and yet recognition of differentiation within the unity of the Godhead.[42] For Soloviev the act of faith is prayer and the beginning of a true union with God. The union with another person of the other sex extends the life of prayer which is faith. Soloviev, the Orthodox theologian (though he would hesitate to call himself such) and Soloviev, the philosopher, are at one in seeing unity overcoming the separateness of beings as the basic affirmation of faith and the goal of our hope.

The latter portion of Soloviev's book *The Meaning of Love* is devoted to sophiology, the study of holy wisdom, the feminine ground of the Godhead. It is extremely difficult for modern people to grasp what the discussion of *sophia* in pre-revolutionary Russia was all about. However, its importance, in the light of rising awareness of feminine images of God cannot be overestimated. For Soloviev the other side of God, the ground distinct from the primordial divinity, is "a passive, feminine unity, seeing that in it the eternal void (pure potentiality) receives the fulness of the Divine existence."[43] Clearly the identification of pure nothing with God hearkens back to Gnosticism, perhaps as revisited through the Hegelianism which had triumphed in the thought of Schelling. This extraordinarily opaque language obscures rather than illuminates the phenomena of which Soloviev is referring. He seems to be saying that what is not God, namely, His creation, will become God, by its being perfected and unified. This eschatological vision, similar to that which was later to emerge in the thought of Teihard de Chardin, was an identification of pure potentiality with the feminine. Through the spiritual union of the masculine and the feminine the creatures of God who were two become one. As Soloviev puts it: "As God creates the universe, as Christ builds the Church, so must man create and build his feminine complement. It is, of course, an elementary truth that man stands for the active and woman for the passive principle and that he ought to have a formative influence upon her mind and character; we are concaerned, however, not with this superficial relation, but with the 'great mystery' of which St. Paul speaks."[44] This union is not just something that happens in our imagination, because objective transformation and regeneration take place.

The whole process becomes cosmic in its dimensions. Love therefore, has a mystical dimension which is cosmic. However, it is to experience rather than theory that Soloviev appeals. The Marxist axiom that our task is not so much to understand the world as to change it could well be applied to Soloviev's thought also. However, the change is from the physical to the spiritual, to overcome division and death by an experience of faith, which occurs through love between the sexes. From this union Soloviev takes the theme of syzeugetic relations (taken from the Greek *suzeusis* - to unite) whereby intimate union with another becomes the norm of social interaction rather than the domination of the superior over the inferior. A new form of social organism is coming into being, co-existent with each of its individual members. Thus, egoism is overcome by this union, as is patriarchy, despotism, and other forms of hierarchy. Finally, nature herself, the all-powerful matter, is overcome by its being raised into the personal and the spiritual. To enter the realm of the Divine and universal rational consciousness, one must do so *from within* so that all may be one.

There is in Soloviev's thought a love mysticism which initiates a union with God through the divine image revealed in the beloved other of the other sex. This is both ethical and mystical, understood rationally and by faith at the same time. The end is not a flight from the alone to the Alone but to a cosmic unity of all things in God. The union of the masculine and the feminine reveal not just a mingling of natures but of God Himself uniting Himself with *sophia*, the feminine ground of all being.

Vladimir Soloviev has been accused of heresy, of decadence, of dubious relationships with women, and of being lost in a sea of subjectivity. The theological assessment which is most critical of him is that offered by Father Georges Florovsky: "Solov'ev somehow internally left the Church. It was precisely at that time that he addressed to Rozanov that unexpected phrase about the religion of the Holy Spirit: 'The religion of the Holy Spirit, which I confess, is broader and more substantial than all the separate religions. It is neither their sum, nor an extract of them - just as the whole man is

neither the sum nor the extract of his separate organs.'"[45] In
this assessment of the whole movement of thought that pervaded *fin de siècle* Russia Florovsky writes:

> Solov'ev claimed to be not only a philosopher but also
> a "theurgist." He dreamed of a "religious act," and a
> religious act through art. Solov'ev must be judged not
> only on the basis of his philosophy but also on the
> merits of his religious life. After all, it is impossible
> to be a Christian solely by one's worldview...Tempta-
> tion yields to seduction. Sometimes it does not yield,
> but is conquered. Some enter the Church not to pray
> but to dream. And the religious life of those among
> the Russian intelligentsia who returned to the Church
> was stricken and poisoned by this temptation.[46]

Florovsky's opinions on Soloviev are associated with his
attack on all the currents in Russian theology other than those
received from the Eastern Fathers. His dislike for Soloviev's
personal mode of life comes, no doubt, from his ascetic and
unemotional personality, which stood in contrast to the
romantic and often unstable Soloviev.

From a different perspective Samuel D. Cioran has written
a devastating critique of Soloviev's public and personal life.
Soloviev's recourse to Gnostic mythology and mystical experience makes him very suspect because of his dependence
upon theosophy. It is not clear that Soloviev was so un-
Orthodox as Cioran would have us think, however. The
suggestion of sexual perversion and bizarre emotional involvements with women are rather lacking in substantial
evidence apart from the romanticism which Soloviev linked to
a hatred for the physical manifestations of sexuality. In my
opinion, N. O. Lossky was closer to the truth in his presentation of the many-sided Soloviev as primarily a philosopher,
writing in the milieu of romanticism and idealism, yet remaining an Orthodox Christian.[47] Certainly Soloviev was aware
of the dangers of his Sophianism when he wrote:

> Is not the feminine principle being introduced here into

Deity as such? Without discussing this theosophical problem on its merits, I must, in order to preserve the readers from temptation and myself from gratuitous reproaches, state the following: (1) the transposition of carnal, animally human relations into the realm of super-human is the greatest *abomination* and the cause of utter ruin (the Flood, Sodom and Gomorra, the "satanic depths" of the latest period); (2) the worship of the feminine nature as such - i.e., of the principle of ambiguity and indifference, sensitive to lie and evil in no lesser degree than to truth and good - is a great madness and the main reason of the now-prevailing sloppiness and weakness; (3) the true adoration of the eternal femininity as having from all eternity accepted the power of God head and truly embodied the fulness of good and truth and, through them, the undying glory of beauty, has nothing to do with this foolishness, nor with that abdomination.[48]

The reason for the extensive examination of Soloviev's views on sexuality and love is to support my claim that his ideas were widely accepted by many Orthodox theologians in Russia. This is the opinion of Olivier Clément in his foreword to the English translation of Evdokimov's book *Sacrement de l'amour* (*The Sacrament of Love*), where he includes Soloviev along with the influence of Bukharev, Bulgakov, Rozanov, Berdyaev, Vysheslavstev, and poets such as Pasternak.[49] It is my opinion that behind Evdokimov lies his assumption that spiritual love between the sexes is a way of salvation whereby God's saving grace is experienced through the "eternal feminine." Not only does Evdokimov take the ideas of Soloviev about sexual love and integrate them more fully into Orthodox theology, but he does this by way of an interpretation of marriage as a spiritual experience. Soloviev had rather obviously failed to do this, remaining himself unmarried and given to gnostic speculations about spiritual love unifying all beings in the One. The incorporation of sophiology by Sergei Bulgakov in the creation of his theological synthesis helped create the intellectual milieu in which

Paul Evdokimov moved during his life in the Russian émigré community of Paris after the Russian revolution. Clément may be given the last word regarding these Russian philosophers who gave so much to Evdokimov, Lampert, and Sherrard: "It appears to me that it is these Russian religious philosophers who were the first in the Christian world to have sensed the spiritual meaning of *eros* and who began to surmount the deadly schism that had inserted itself between human love and Christianity."[50]

Paul Evdokimov wrote two books on marriage. The first was *Le mariage: sacrement de l'amour*. In this work he set forth a mystical interpretation of marriage, setting it within the context of the relationship between matter and spirit. The mystery which is marriage was lifted from the natural into the realm of the Spirit so that it is transformed. The ethical core of the book lay in its interpretation of marital chastity as *sophrosune* which the author interpreted as the power of integration whereby all the forms of life may be united. Olivier Clément has stated that Paul Evdokimov needed a feminine presence to liberate his creative force. The first two books of Evdokimov, including his book on marriage, were written in the presence of his first wife, Natasha Bruel. After her death, Paul married again, this time a Japanese woman, Tomoko Sakai. His first book after his remarriage was *La femme et le salut du monde*, followed by a revised version of his book on marriage, now given the simple title of *Sacrement de l'amour*. It appeared in 1962 and was translated into English in 1985 as *The Sacrament of Love*.

In his introduction to his second work on marriage, Evdokimov draws a sharp contrast between the high dignity of marriage as a sacrament and the denigration of marriage and sexuality by Western Catholic theologians. For Evdokimov it is love which is elevated by the sacrament of marriage. In the cultural heritage of our civilization there is a conflict between the morality of the "superego" as prohibitive and the "contraint of repetition" based on the myths of virility and the subjection of the couple to the service of procreation.[51] Asceticism stands over against the indulgence of the flesh, and women were often the victims of such repression. The

Roman Catholic tradition of finalism in natural law made of woman a partner in the work of procreation. In that tradition marriage existed either for procreation or as a remedy for lust and concupiscence. Evdokimov speaks of this Augustinian tradition as "anthropological pessimism," something that diminishes the sacramental mystery in Roman Catholicism and negates the value of virginity and monasticism in Protestantism. Throughout the Western Christian tradition woman has been reduced to a status which is less than fully human. The world was thought to be essentially masculine, and woman existed as a boundary to be overstepped. For Evdokimov the negation of woman resulted in the negation of love. "Man has desecrated love," he states, "even before discovering its nature."[52]

Evdokimov discerns in the fall of humanity the division of man from woman and woman from man. Both become alien when separated from one another. He sees two possibilities: either man and woman are opposites who war against one another or they are complementaries who love each other. The fulness of humanity can only exist, he thinks, in "the sacrament of love," which he regards as a prophetic figure of the Kingdom of God, the ultimate unity of the masculine and the feminine in their totality in God. It is the woman as mother, virgin, and spouse who stands as a door to God.[53]

Evdokimov invokes the mystery of love that often escapes the religious. Love and religion have been torn from one another in much of the Christian world, particularly by the sentimentalism of modern society.[54] Over against such sentimentalism is the heroic stance of the Orthodox Church where the call to marriage is a call to a particular priestly ministry.

In what might appear to be a detour in his thought about marriage, Evdokimov embraces the thought of Soloviev with great enthusiasm. Marriage is not about the species humanity but about particular persons. Indeed, Evdokimov discerns in sexuality clear marks of the Fall, both in the selfishness of sexual pleasure sought as an end in itself and the reduction of women to mere tools for reproduction. Evdokimov recognizes a spiritual meaning in marriage which would elevate it "to perceive the countenance of the beloved in God, to the level of the one and only icon."[55] Evdokimov follows Soloviev in his vision of sexual love as distinct and separate from reproduction and its service to the species. The power of the species over the individual would reduce persons to mere functions. It is interesting, however, to see how he focuses his attention on the Fall and the restoration of paradise rather than on *sophia* and her union with the male principle. It is love which rescues humanity from the Fall and its consequences in concupiscence. The personalism of Evdokimov turns him away from the Gnostic mythology and its consequent mysticism. He is equally distant from Augustinian pessimism about human nature. He, in turn, moves to Christian anthropology, where the effects of the Fall are overcome, particularly the alienation of the sexes and the distance from God created by Adam and Eve. Mary as the new Eve reverses the alienation of God and humanity and of men and women in her obedience and in her supreme holiness. The institution of monasticism is the affirmation of the value of the individual above the social, and married love "proceeds from spiritual interiority and gazes toward the inside."[56] The kenosis of love is part of the nuptial and the monastic tradition. The love of the spouses in marriage manifests this interiority, and Evdokimov calls to witness the Fathers of the Church, particularly Theodoret and St. John Chrysostom. *eros* in marriage is thus a means of sanctification. Evdokimov's use of patristic quotations, as we have noted, often reads in more than the Fathers intended. When faced with this criticism, he replied that he was a dogmatic theologian, not a historian of dogma.[57] This is hardly an adequate response since Evdokimov uses patristic sources to justify theological interpretations of marriage of which few of the Fathers were aware. Moreover, he claims that a similar tradition of spiritual love is to be found among Western Franciscans and that there exists "an unbroken tradition" in both East and West to support "the personal meaning by showing the lovers being one for the other, one toward the other."[58] Thus marriage does not have to be "pardoned," for it is "a value in itself."[59] The emergence of personalist perspectives was widespread in France during this particular period. Mounier and Marcel are examples of this movement. The change of direction among modern Roman Catholic theologians who identified love as the chief end of marriage is welcomed by Evdokimov, and the popularity of his books in Catholic circles is a witness to the convergence of Eastern and Western viewpoints around the time of the Second Vatican Council.

Love has an eschatological character. To this end he interprets the agraphon found in the chapter 23 of 2 Clement:

> When will the Kingdom of God come? When you will destroy the vestment of shame, when the two shall be one, and the male with the female neither male nor female.

Evdokimov fails to note that this quotation is not an authentic statement of St. Clement of Rome but comes from a Gnostic text masked by a pseudonym. The contradictions in human nature are overcome not by a shameless sexuality but in the sexual modesty which is revealed in the Virgin Theotokos. The end of time, the *eschaton*, will be the restoration of Adam-Eve. Love is an anticipation of the Parousia. Over against the functional ends of marriage as procreative, we have in Evdokimov's interpretation of marriage as priestly something ontological, a new creation that fills time with eternity. The self-offering of the spouses to one another is indeed an offering to God, a reverence of the image of God revealed in the other of the other sex. Reading Evdokimov one discerns not only a new and vital rethinking of the Orthodox tradition but an extraordinary (should one say "innovative?") exegesis of passages such as 1 Tm 2:15. Critics would say that we are not far from Gnosticism when this passage ("Woman will be saved by childbearing") comes to refer to the bringing to birth of a new aeon beyond all biological fertility.

I shall not make an effort to expound Evdokimov's anthropology. It owes most to the Greek Fathers in the importance given to freedom, the person, and the restoration of the likeness to God in the human image. Evdokimov applies the monastic vows to marriage, following his friend Boukharev. An inner poverty, chastity, and obedience are found in the sacramental transformation of human nature in marriage. Evdokimov rejects the Western, bourgeois understanding of marriage as permission of sexual pleasure which is otherwise forbidden. A spirituality of the married state is set forth as a special charism, a form of service, a way of existing without dominating the other. Marriage does not stand as contrary to monasticism but, rather, as a parallel form of monastic life providing inner transformative power. The priestly meaning of marriage lies in the self-offering made by one spouse to the other, before God and in God. The anointing of the lay person with the Holy Chrism is a form of ordination, distinct from the ministerial priesthood which is functional rather than ontological. Marriage exists within this framework and becomes the "image of heaven" - as St. John Chrysostom put it. For Evdokimov, this unifying of the sexes brings a proximity to the Kingdom where we shall be as the angels, neither giving nor taking in marriage.

Perhaps the richest vision of marriage is based on Evdokimov's view that love is the purpose of life. To be in love is to be fulfilled, satisfied, and to partake of the grace of God. Love, he urges, is not a generality or a psychological fact within the immediate reach of human nature. Love is the gift of grace, and it remains ever concrete, unique, and particular. Love reflects the Trinitarian wholeness of three divine persons, yet one in nature. The theology of marriage enunciated by St. John Chrysostom, according to Evdokimov, compares the union of the man and woman in marriage to the union of persons in the Godhead. This union involves a grafting of humanity into the renewed image of the One who has created mankind. Loneliness is overcome by the intimate union with the person of the other sex and the creation of the nuptial community. The union reflects the archetype whereby the love of Christ for the Church is reflected.

Having taken us to the heights of spiritual love in the context of marriage, Evdokimov passes on to consider some rather specific areas of concern. In a brief commentary on the rite of marriage in the Russian Orthodox ritual, he observes: "The prayer for nuptial chastity is the opposite of every concept advancing 'a remedy for concupiscence;' it asks for something entirely different, the miracle of the transfiguration of Eros."[60] This vision is in stark contrast with the sexual freedom posed by the modern world where the indulgence of the flesh is not so much a sin of the flesh as a sin against the flesh. The boredom of sexual laxity masks the yearning for love. Marriage is not only a mystery but the matter of marriage "is not only a 'visible sign,' but the natural substratum that is changed into the place where the energies of God are present."[61] Using the language of the scholastics, Evdokimov concludes that the matter of the sacrament of marriage is "the love of man and woman."[62] Within the eschatological perspective preserved by Orthodox sacramental theology, marriage becomes a restoration of paradise. Evdokimov brings a host of witnesses to this affirmation, but the most effective affirmation is made by the Orthodox Ritual itself: "Neither original sin nor the flood has in the least damaged the sacredness of the nuptial union."[63]

In his discussion of the minister of the sacrament of marriage, Evdokimov provides us with a collection of texts from which he infers that it is the priest who administers the sacrament. Many of the patristic references, including the famous text from the Letter to Polycarp of St. Ignatius the Godbearer (5:5) and texts from St. Gregory of Nazianzus and St. John Chrysostom, in no way require the interpretation given them by Evdokimov. The later texts from the seventeenth and eighteenth centuries do indeed teach that the priest (or bishop) administers the sacrament. However others (e.g., Novella 89) need only imply that marriage without the presence of a priest is invalid.

Evdokimov appears to ignore the tension between his romantic vision of marriage as built on the love between a man and a woman and a very clerical and somewhat scholastic understanding of the priest as the minister of matrimony. He reserves his discussion of sexuality for a final chapter. He attempts to move between the "angelism" of many monastic authors who had no place for the body in their vision of salvation and the pansexualism of many modern authors who reduce men and women down to their bodies. Evdokimov perceives in the modern bourgeois understanding of sex and marriage only the "licentiousness of legalized mating."[64] There is a dismal banality in the obsession with sexuality which results from the universal loss of the sacred. Love is lost in favor of a physical eroticism, "devoid of spirit or finesse."[65] Psychoanalysis put an end to the great passions. What is evident in modernity is not only the loss of the sacred but the absence of any archetype for the nuptial reality. On the one hand, in traditional Roman Catholicism the marriage of St. Joseph and St. Mary appears as archetypical - meaning that sexuality has no intrinsic value in a Christian marriage - and on the other hand, in the post-Christian world, unrestrained sexual indulgence has become the norm. For Evdokimov the loss of asceticism and chastity in marriage destroys the spiritual dimension, whereas the Roman Catholic model disallows the transformation of *eros* from the natural and physical level to the spiritual dimension He agrees with Dr. Carl Jung that *eros* is to be distinguished from sexual energy. Only a spiritual *eros* can transform sexual energy, since the physical leads only to the imprisoning of the human being when the spiritual is lost. After orgasm one finds only a void, whereas love unites through its orientation "toward the chaste integrity of being."[66] For Evdokimov chastity is essential for a married couple since by chastity he means "the integration of all the elements of the human being toward a whole that is virginal."[67] He believes that sexuality transcends itself in a symbolic movement toward the spiritual integration of two persons into one. Here is where marriage rejoins monasticism, both raising human life into the Kingdom of God.

Chastity as a key virtue is Evdokimov's translation of *sophrosyne*, a word we find in 1 Tm 2:15. There it has little of the meaning which Evdokimov gives it by his peculiar eisegesis. For him *sophrosyne* does not mean sobriety so much as knowledge, the power of integrity, and the integration of all the elements in life. Rather than interpreting chastity as purity, Evdokimov gives to it an integrative function. *Sophrosune* is a spiritual quality, and it is only possible because of the androgynous character of the human being. One can discern the influence of Soloviev in this spiritual vision. Included in Evdokimov's use of the word is the underlying sense of *sophia*, a virtue bringing the feminine power of the intuitive and esthetic knowledge over the rational, male intellect. For Evdokimov the transformation of the sexual energies is not by repression or denial; it is rather by the integration into the spiritual life of love.

Perhaps the perspective of Paul Evdokimov is made most clear in his discussion of the practical issues of contraception. He objects, quoting the priest Vladimir Palachkovsky, to clerical interference in the intimate domain of the husband and wife. There is not only a legitimate autonomy in the right of the spouses to make decisions about contraception, but Evdokimov strongly objects to arguments which would make artificial contraception wrong in order to permit a "natural" form of birth control. Either way the intention is the same, namely, the exclusion of offspring. Evdokimov insists that marital love is in no way dependent upon natural forces and to make it so dependent is to risk disaster. Speaking of what is clearly the official stand of the Roman Catholic Church's position on contraception, Evdokimov thinks that it lowers the human race to a bestial understanding of sexuality. Clearly voluntary procreation is more noble than procreation which is left to chance, and Evdokimov argues that if we accept painless childbirth, there is no reason to refuse a time of temporary sterility. Nevertheless one cannot recommend contraceptive techniques since the solution lies in spiritual mastery. He affirms that "man must uplift himself progressively toward this mastery and do it *freely*.[68]

One cannot overestimate the work of Paul Evdokimov in his beautiful construction of a theology of marriage. However, his agenda is clear. It is the integration of the romantic view of spiritual and sexual love (largely taken from the thought of Soloviev and, of course, Evdokimov's own experience) with the Orthodox teaching about the sacramentality of marriage. In the later work of Evdokimov there also emerges his reading and adoption of Jungian depth psychology. Not only did Jung's theory of archetypes appeal to him, but his doctrine of the *coincidentia oppositorum* resonated deeply with Evdokimov's experience. His enthusiasm for Jung's *Answer to Job* put him on the fringes of Orthodoxy by the search to incorporate the woman into the doctrine of the Trinity by positing a fourth hypostasis. What is clear, however, is that the stress on the spiritual in marriage not only goes back to Soloviev but interprets the passages of the Fathers on love in a context for which they never intended their thoughts on the subject. The incorporation of monastic spirituality into his theology of marriage is, as Clément notes, a reversal of monastic misogyny. The love which creates the union between the man and the woman in marriage is so veiled and so spiritual that Evdokimov is hesitant to enter into its inner sanctity. One notes, however, his devotion to the hieromonk F. Bukharev, who asked to be reduced to the lay state to pursue a life of service to the Kingdom of God and to marry. He accepted the disdain of Church officials as part of a *kenosis* in his conformity to the way of Christ in the context of the world. Evdokimov saw in Bukharev an authentic image of Christ though he had turned aside from the celibate way of monasticism. If many Orthodox people regarded the laicization of Bukharev as a scandal or a tragedy, Evdokimov saw it as a sign that the way of marriage was a spiritual odyssey equal to the monastic way. One may question the extent to which Evdokimov took seriously the incarnation and the doctrine of the "one flesh" set forth by St. Paul. His christology, like his theology of marriage, tends to become docetic at places. This was to remedied by Father Evgueny Lampert, whose failed career was to prevent his thought from having the impact that one would have hoped it might have had.[69] His book *The Divine Realm: Towards a Theology of Sacraments*, the substance of his doctoral dissertation at Oxford, presents a theology of sexuality along with considerations of other theological themes.

If we examine carefully the *The Divine Realm*, we find a remarkable realism which identifies Neo-Platonic asceticism as a blasphemy against the body and against the world. Lampert admits that Neo-Platonic tendencies had a profound impact upon certain forms of historic Christianity, and he identifies Origen as teaching that both the creation of the world and the clothing of the soul with flesh were a "falling away" from light to darkness. For Origen the basic human task became one of reestablishing the world in its original, spiritual condition. Lampert considers much Christian ascetic literature to reflect these tendencies, to be an admonition against the body rather than a struggle for the body. Central, however, to Christian faith is the dogma of the Incarnation, which gives a positive evaluation of the body.

For Lampert the classic text regarding marriage is Eph 5:23-32, which he refuses to allegorize. It is the transformation of the flesh, not the destruction of it, which is God's purpose. Rather than scorning the sensual, Lampert rejoices in its reality, which is not only the ideal made flesh but the revelation of the beautiful since the Incarnation is an event which is not "un-natural," either for God's being or that of the world.[70] Lampert considers the *kenosis* (or self-emptying) of the divine Word to be in accord with the very nature of the Word, which was primordially human. It is God's corporeality which emerges here. Thus Christianity is neither pure spiritualism nor a naive-realistic materialism. It is the indwelling of the Lord's divinity in His human body that sanctifies and glorifies human corporeal existence. The body becomes not just an instrument of the spirit but the expression and revelation of the divine-human being.

In a short chapter on sexuality, Lampert breaks new ground in the history of Orthodox thinking on the subject. He affirms the bisexual creation of humanity as male and female, following Gn 1: 27. He rejects the contention of Origen, St. Gregory of Nyssa, St. Maximus the Confessor, John Scotus Erigena, and Jacob Boehme that the creation of woman was the beginning of the fall of humanity. This would be to make redemption into a liberation from sexuality. At heart their way of thinking is Gnostic. The consequent hatred for woman profanes and degrades sexual life. In a most interesting footnote Lampert speaks of Berdyaev and Charles Williams as moving toward a romantic and erotic spiritualism which leaves out the place of the body and the goodness of the bisexual creation. Lampert thinks that much later Christian practice separated marriage from *eros* in favor of pro-creation, driving sex into a kind of prison of domesticity unless one escaped into irreligious forms of life.[71]

Lampert insists that sex must be established not just as a biological factor nor as an accidental phenomenon:

> Sex is a transcendent reality. Sexual life has transcendent significance, and the union of the sexes in love is a witness to the fulness of being and life eternal. The creation of woman is the acknowledgement of the reality of sex as the *fulfillment* of creation. It is, therefore, essential to bring the fulness of the image of God in man into line with his bi-sexuality.[72]

Refering to Eph 5:32 Lampert affirms that the relation of the sexes is symbolized by the relation of Christ and the Church. A Christian understanding of sexuality must affirm the mystery of the true antinomy for human reason of the two in one:

> In this sense sex is not only the prototype of the union of all into an integral community. The unfathomed secret of Christian love consists in that it unites men not only in virtue of altruistic charity and agape, but perhaps also of wedded love and eros. Sexual love is not merely the power of personal life, but also of life universal, of *catholicity* - no more and no less."[73]

Lampert stands against all spiritualism which would omit the concrete, fleshly reality whereby the created beauty of the cosmos is sensually perceived in the woman: "In the person of Eve Adam found the undefiled sensuality of the world, which up to now was something illusionary, abstract and unreal to him."[74] Even the woman can be made fully aware of her femininity only by her perception of herself in the eyes of her lover. The differentiation of the sexes is required by the necessity of the sensual element in life. Lampert discerns in the sexual union an overcoming of the division and differentiation of the sexes insofar as the couple becomes one flesh.[75] From this perception Lampert draws a bold conclusion: "It is therefore also in the bodily union of sexes that the true spiritual nature of sex is revealed. Moreover, nowhere more than here do we realize the *positive, ontological relation of flesh and spirit* - the spirit-bearing nature of the body and the 'incarnational' meaning of the spirit."[76] This leads to the most astonishing conclusion of all: "In sex and sexual experience man grows into the mystery of God-manhood and is present at the eternal fulfilment of life."[77] Lampert is perhaps the first Orthodox theologian to state that it is in sexual union that the Spirit of God touches human flesh:

> It is the mystery of a sudden merging and union into a single indivisible being of flesh and spirit, of heaven and earth, of human divine love. The divine Spirit touches human flesh, since it is transparent to Him in its primeval depth, and indeed received Him in the burning moment of erotic ecstacy. We are witnessing to a true sacrament: the Spirit of God invades the cosmic element, without ceasing to be Spirit, and the flesh widens into the transcendence of the Spirit without ceasing to be flesh.[78]

The fact remains that this limited and fallen nature of human beings cannot contain erotic experience, with the consequence that a tension is perceived between the temporal and the eternal. Indeed, this is why, Lampert argues, "the attempt to oppose and evaluate eros and sex on purely moral grounds is one of the futile undertakings."[79] He protests strongly against the separation of marriage and love (as found in Dante, for example). Christian marriage has failed precisely because it has denied this transcendental meaning of sex, leaving us with only the alternatives of fornication or convenience. Fornication may be found even in marriage, but it is "non-existent when man and wife become aware of heavenly flames in the fire of their wedded love, and come to know the transcendent source of this seemingly 'animal' relation."[80] Lampert asks whether this is not a "debasement of heaven" or "Can we rise to heaven in this way?" The answer is clear, for it is "the fiery element of sex and the eros of life which above all thirsts for illumination of the Holy Spirit."[81]

Lampert recognizes the importance of sophiology in Russian theology and in particular in that of Fr. Sergei Bulgakov. He links himself with these sophiologists saying, "I am indebted to them, and in particular to S. Bulgakov, in many ways, and most of all in the general *leitmotif* and underlying inspiration of their thought."[82] Lampert's contribution was not found in sophiology, however, but in his exposition of the Incarnation as the foundation for the "one flesh" of marital union. What is in question is the particular openness of the creative processes of nature to the presence of the Holy Spirit.

Perhaps the most tragic aspect of Lampert's career lay in the dismissal of his work in the theological discussion which has ensued since the publication of *The Divine Realm* in 1944. In my opinion, the movement from Gnostic mythology and mystical romantic flights to the centrality of Holy Scripture and the centrality of the Incarnation was one of signal importance. Too often the discussions of the Eternal Feminine neglected the importance of the concrete, historical woman to whom a man is married. It is a testimony of Lampert's spiritual experience that he dedicated his book to his wife. The sad outcome of the whole affair at Oxford - whatever may be the merits of the case for or against Lampert's scholarly integrity - was Lampert's removal from the theological discussion of the place of women in the economy of salvation and the legitimacy of marital intercourse as a privileged sign of the union of Christ with His Church. It was Lampert who modified the excessive influence of Soloviev in Russian Orthodox thinking about sexual love as an entirely spiritual and ascetic form of domestic monasticism. Unfortunately the theological significance of Lampert has been minimal because of the embarrassment over what happened at Oxford.

A more recent book is Philip Sherrard's *Eros and Christianity*, written not only from an Orthodox perspective but more polemical in tone than the previous works that we have discussed. Boldly Sherrard contrasts the views of St. Gregory of Nyssa and St. Maximus the Confessor with those of Augustine of Hippo. The former held that no sexuality existed before the Fall, and restoration to the state of incorruptibility and immortality requires a radical transcendence of sexuality, to the extent that it must be extirpated altogether. In contrast, Augustine associated concupiscence with sexuality and considered only procreation to provide a rationale to justify sexual relations. Augustine allowed that sexual intercourse took place in Paradise between Adam and Eve but that they had total control over their desires, not being subject to the disorder of concupiscence. Sexual desire came to have an entirely negative connotation for Augustine. The medieval controversy over what makes a marriage valid involved the contradiction between the spiritual union of the couple and the requirement of physical consummation for the marriage to be truly a marriage. That physical act was thought of as evil, because of the powerful desires of the sexual appetite, yet somehow the act had to be carried out. The evil was thought to be erased by the intent of coitus as a procreative act. The whole weight of the Augustinian solution lay in procreation as the chief end of marriage, not in the loving relationship. As Sherrard puts it, "To copulate for any motive other than procreation, or with any intention of frustrating procreation, is simply abominable debauchery and cancels that exemption from the venial sin which is accorded to married couples who perform the shameful deed because they cannot encompass the good work of begetting children in any other manner."[83]

Augustine's theology failed most surely, Sherrard contends, in its assumption that coitus was carried out (or ought to be carried out) only for the sake of begetting children. The sacramental sign which marriage possessed became something quite external to the inner and intimate life of the couple: "In the case in point, if the symbolism of Christ and the Church applied to marriage is to have a creative or spiritualizing influence on marriage, it must be recognized that the relationship between man and woman is capable of being transformed into an eternal and metaphysical bond of the kind that exists between Christ and the Church."[84] This relationship is unknown in the thought of Augustine or of the later scholastics. There is no sense of the "unique personal relationship" in Augustinian or Thomistic theology. In fact, in Roman Catholic theology the sacramental character "is still regarded as conferred, effective, and binding quite apart from the interior harmony and reciprocity of qualities in the man and the woman who are meant to embody it."[85]

According to Sherrard, the Roman Catholic natural law philosophy assumes that the present world is the normal one and the one willed by God. The Eastern Orthodox tradition assumes to the contrary that this life is abnormal and only to the return to the state of paradise before the Fall can be normal for human beings.[86] the assumptions that the human race must continue to procreate in the natural world and that this world is that willed by God are both put in question by Sherrard. The further assumption that the unitive function of coitus must be yielded up to the primacy of the procreative involves the questionable premise that sexual union and communion are identified "in a more or less exclusive manner with the act of coition."[87] In fact, Sherrard claims, the theologians who have identified sexual communion almost exclusively with coition laid the intellectual groundwork for the "dislocation and debasement of man's sexual life of which the consequences are only too evident today."[88]

Despite the fact that Christians have affirmed the resurrection of the flesh (Apostles Creed) and the resurrection of the dead (Nicene Creed), Christian attitudes toward the body have been notoriously negative. If we allow, as we must theologically, that we are incarnate selves, we must not only be more aware of our sexuality but of the mysterious link between sexuality and the sense of beauty. Sherrard notes that he does not speak of sex in a prurient way but of sexuality in the deepest sense as a form of energy closely related to intuitive spirituality. There is, indeed, a "subtle, intimate correspondence between them"[89] Sexuality is often a matter of desire, and Christ Himself is quite explicit about sexual desire when He said: "But I say to you that every one who looks at a woman lustfully has already committed adultery with her in his heart" (Mt 5:28). Sherrard thinks that much of the Christian hostility toward the body and the efforts to escape from it come from the awareness of how easy it is to commit adultery in the heart. Lust is the desire for the body of another for one's own selfish satisfaction. Lust is clearly not love since love is centered on the value and importance of the other as other. Love centers itself on the divine image in bodily form. The union in which one offers himself or herself to the sacred being of the other is an offering of oneself to God. Such a union is not carried out for pleasure but in order to "participate in the transparent metaphysical reality of each other's being."[90] Sherrard compares this form of sexual union with the Orthodox use of icons where the spiritual is mediated through matter.

Sherrard recognizes the dangers that are present with sexual love and himself disavows any plea for sexual promiscuity. Rather, the dangers are analogous to the idolatry that can ensue from the use of icons. But the abuse does not take away the use, and it is clear that "suicidal asceticism is to be replaced by a positive and transfiguring attitude."[91] Lust results when love is detached from its spiritual source. Modern life is filled with lust since the separation of sexuality from spirituality is the outcome of the Augustinian heritage.

Sherrard is of the opinion that Christian attitudes toward sexuality have taken three forms: the ascetic, the marital, and the moral condemnation of all expressions of human sexuality outside of marriage. The marital has been closely tied to the procreation of children and the family. Sherrard's own opinion is that "the love in which the sexual relationship between man and woman is felt to be endowed with a sacramental holiness is not really embraced by any of these three forms to which the Christian attitude to human sexuality is, generally speaking, limited."[92] Christian attitudes have neglected and found incomprehensible the loves of Abelard and Heloise, of Tristan and Iseult, as well as many others. Three Russian philosophers have sought to move beyond the limitations of Christian thought toward sexual love.

These are Vladimir Soloviev, Dimitri Merezhkovsky, and Nicholas Berdyaev All three writers discern the presence of the mysterious androgyne in sexual love. The animal instincts are purified and elevated by *eros* so that a spiritual communion between the two separated halves of the human being are once more united. Merezhkovsky anticipated the work of C. G. Jung by ascribing to each person, both male and female, a presence in the self of the other sex. Prior to the male-female division stands the androgyny, the man-woman. Marriage becomes a union of persons and of the genders in a way that restores the wholeness of two persons. Throughout nature there is the polarity of the masculine and the feminine, the passive and the active, the attraction and the repulsion of opposites. Similarly, Berdyaev has two poles in his thought: sexual continence and the idea of the androgyne. The sexual act is transcended, and only by that transcendence can sexual life reach its highest levels of expression. None of these philosophers find in coitus the end and purpose of sexuality, any more than they identify them with procreation. Sexual love is a finding of the other side of one's being in the beloved other. It involves a reintegration of the self that was divided as a consequence of the Fall.

Sherrard notes how none of these thinkers embrace the three forms to which Christian attitudes have limited sex. One even questions whether the Russian philosophers can be reconciled with Christian thought at this point. Sherrard does point to the fact that they build on the Christian base set by St. Gregory of Nyssa who found in virginity the return to the primal state of humanity before the Fall (and the consequent clothing with flesh and the coming into being of two sexes). To move beyond fleshly indulgence would be to regain paradise. The other pole of the thought of Soloviev, Merezhkovsky, and Berdiaev is the awareness that the ultimate meaning of love is found in androgyny. Love between the sexes restored the androgynous personality, but this is only possible if love is freed from animal sexuality.

Sherrard is aware of the dangers inherent in this way of thinking. Woman is either reduced, as in Augustinian theology, to her reproductive role and identified with the flesh, or woman becomes superfluous when the original man regains and reunites the masculine and feminine principles in his own being. The real woman is lost in this debasement of woman to finding her identity and vocation in childbearing or to her exaltation as entirely spiritual and indeed, the eternal archetype of the feminine. Sherrard thinks that we can begin with another reading of Genesis (and one quite different from that of Gregory of Nyssa) whereby woman was not inferior to man but taken from his innermost being. As he puts it, "On the contrary, it may be regarded as a creation in which the image of God is further and more fully made manifest on the human plane, so that woman - Eve - stands with man - Adam - not as part or portion of an original androgyny, as Plato or the Gnostics or the Kabbala or the authors under discussion would have it, but as one pole of the archetypal, ideal, and potentially eternal human relationship."[93] Indeed. as an alternative reading of creation, the primary significance of Eve is that she is the "I" to the "Thou" of Adam. Communion is thus the end and goal of the fulfilled sacramental relationship between man and woman. The Russian thinkers under consideration fail to affirm the independent and equal significance of woman in relation to man. Sherrard thinks that this may be endemic to Christianity, but he finds a way out, and a profoundly Eastern Orthodox way. God need not be exclusively viewed as masculine (and if He is, there is no way that woman can be affirmed as in God's image). Within the Godhead is not only the divine Light but the divine Darkness. The *ex nihilo* from which all was created is not as the Thomists think only a privation of God (a mere nothingness). Sherrard finds in the apophatic theology of the Orthodox tradition "the idea of a pre-ontological reality - of the pure potentiality of God's unknowable essence."[94] He concludes that "Its importance in the present context is that it is precisely this principle which may be recognized as constituting the feminine principle or pole of the divine nature."[95] In a very adventuresome exegesis, Sherrard even thinks that St. Paul (in 1 Cor 11:3) need not assume that man is woman's superior or her master by calling man her head. She may rather be seen as the heart of man. The spiritual tradition of the Hesychasts would witness to the importance of the heart in prayer, and in this we would "have an analogy not only to these two aspects of the divine under discussion but also to how these two aspects of the divinity are reflected in man and woman."[96] Sherrard does not think that the idea of the androgyne need necessarily be abandoned, but "it must no longer be taken to imply the reabsorption of his estranged feminine element by man and the consequent suppression of the woman as an independent creature. It must be taken to signify the full and reciprocal co-partnership of man and woman as a single whole in God."[97]

At this point we may well be impressed by the theological acumen of Philip Sherrard. Instead of seeing Orthodoxy as a patriarchal religion which would put women down as inferior and scarcely created in the image of God, Orthodox Christianity is to be contrasted with both Roman Catholicism and Protestantism by its refusal of the primacy of a procreative role for women. Just as Orthodoxy has exalted the New Eve, the ever Virgin Theotokos, so Orthodoxy delights in sexual love when mutual self-giving reflect the Trinitarian relations of the divine persons. However, the question remains of how this highly spiritualized sexual love relates to Christian marriage. Clearly sexual love exists prior to and distinct from marriage, which has unfortunately been closely related to a contract to insure the reproduction of the species. It is the yeast without which no marriage can be said to be possible:

> It possesses, or can possess, a sacramental quality and function. It also has to be recognized that though the purpose of marriage is achieved when the relationship between the man and the woman is such that the sacrament becomes an effective existential reality in the manner indicated above, this reality is by no means conferred automatically through the exchange of marriage vows and a priestly blessing. At the most, what is conferred on the relationship at the marriage ceremony is a potentiality for the relationship to become a sacramental reality provided certain conditions are fulfilled.[98]

Sherrard defines a sacrament as the revelation of divine life to the creature that participates in it. He concludes that the sacramental quality is not derived from any purposes such as the procreation of children but is derived "from the fact that its own origin is divine and its own nature is sacred."[99] Not every manifestation of sexual power is sacred, only that which is creative and divinizing. Since this energy is "capable of functioning as a creative, divinizing power in man it must be recognized that, far from being identified exclusively with the biological procreative impulse, it is the energy that lies behind and within whatever positive expression or form man may give it in his life."[100] One finds in human beings levels with their capacities and their own mode of functioning, from the physical to the spiritual. Sexuality is evident at both lower and higher levels. It is only by the energies flowing to the higher levels that the integral relationship between man and woman can be fulfilled. If this does occur, no man can put asunder their spiritual union, but if such higher levels of union are not achieved, their marriage will have no lasting, sacramental significance. "It remains confined to their moral selves, and their union is put asunder if not by man, then by death."[101]

It is evident that most people do not arrive at this spiritual union. It is possible, however, that solitary saints and sages arrive at an inner transformation within the context of their single life. Prayer and invocation become vehicles of sacred energy and can allow this energy to rise to higher levels without being wasted or dispersed. In conclusion, Sherrard sets forth five conditions for the coming into being of a sacramental reality in marriage:

It is imperative that the man and woman be aware of the task which they have undertaken. They are to look upon each as in the image of God and as having received the call to be perfect "through bringing this image into full and active radiation at the centre of their beings."[102] No other purpose may be allowed to enter which would subvert the other person to a lesser end. "Their love for each other must be a personal love, concentrated on the particular soul-body reality which each affirms."[103]

The love between the man and woman must be a sexual love. Without this the inner dynamic of tensions will be lacking, and there will be no polarity. What Sherrard says here is important: "A non-sexualized love may be full of devotion and self-sacrifice. But it is incapable of setting into motion that transforming process which is the key to the purpose of marriage."[104] Without this sacred reality of the "other" we find only adultery, whether in or out of the institution of marriage.

The third condition requires that if the sexual union is to become a full sacramental reality all aspects of the two persons must be involved. Sherrard claims that a marriage remains "outside the sphere of a fully achieved sacramental union, a union sealed by the spirit and indissoluble" if a full degree of accord between the man and the woman has not been achieved spiritually.[105] He concludes: "This in itself will give an idea of how few marriages, whether blessed by the Church or not, are sacramental. The Church may be right in asking that those who enter into marriage should intend that their relationship become sacramental; and she would be right to give her blessing only to those who express this intention and understand what it involves."[106]

The Church's blessing may consecrate the intention of the couple, but it cannot make a marriage a full sacramental reality since this is only possible by the joining of the man and woman at all levels of their spiritual being. Physical consummation does not make the marriage since it is only one expression of union.

The fourth condition is that the sexual forces become active only to the extent to which the higher levels are developed in a person. Not only does this mean a coming into being of the various levels of a person but the actual functioning of those levels so that reciprocity between corresponding levels takes place. It means that partners must grow together since the transforming process will be denied if one stays behind the other. Then one will seek out another relationship, leading to conflicting interests and different spiritual qualities.

If the previous conditions are met, the fifth condition becomes possible. The realization of a polarity within sexual love and its transformative power lead to a demand for the totality and continuity of the commitment of the man and the woman to one another. By the very nature of the depth of the relationship any short-term affair is excluded. Fidelity is called for at a far deeper level than that of genital intercourse. Without fidelity, Sherrard says, "either or both of the partners

will be led to break the totality or continuity of their companionship in ways which may gratify their superficial egos, but
which will frustrate their own ultimate union. "[107]   That
union is sacramental by the benediction offered by the Creator
to the man and woman "who have run the course of their love
through whatever it may have led them and have entered,
transfigured at last, the holy ground of their being. "[108]

I have examined Sherrard's argument very closely since he
is, in my opinion, the most theologically astute of the authors
whom we have examined. He walks into the discussion of
marriage with enormous courage, unwilling to compromise
his own experience, to satisfy the demands of doctrinal conformity. He shows us how marriage can be a holy estate,
sanctifying, precisely as a form of sacrificial love, at base
sexual and blessed by God. But he makes no compromise by
yielding to externals to insure the legitimacy of the union or
to the other ends of marriage, whether social or reproductive,
to excuse the personal defects in love. One may think that
Sherrard's vision of marriage is indeed elitist and involving a
seemingly inevitable conclusion that there are vast numbers of
people who have been married in Church with the blessing of
a priest but whose lives in no way reflect the realities of a
sacramental marriage. One sees why the Church of Rome has
sought external signs to guarantee the validity of marriages,
the exchange of vows and physical consummation. Nevertheless, Sherrard will give not an inch to the reproductive purposes of marriage as somehow legitimizing less than holy
unions. His personalism remains one with the mystical theology of the Greek Fathers, but he has extended, as they never
did, the same transformative process to the marital union
itself. Marriage as a sacrament has never been so clearly and
beautifully revealed as in the thought of Philip Sherrard.
However, one may have grave questions about the conditions
that Sherrard imposes if a marriage is to count as a sacramental marriage. It seems to me that he has inverted the order to
make the goals of marriage into conditions for marriage. Not
only would Sherrard's criteria rule out vast numbers of marriages as truly sacramental (however blessed and celebrated in
Church), but he creates a romantic elite comparable to the

holiness that is the end and goal of the monastic life. Marriage, like monastic vows, may have its authenticity as a way to perfection, even if that goal has not yet been achieved. Indeed, Sherrard is correct in seeing the perils that ensue if the couple does not achieve the *henosis* to which they have been called, but in putting such a strong emphasis upon the love of the couple and the absolute necessity of its authenticity, Sherrard has failed to grasp the significance of the sacramental as such. The Church's blessing is both a thanksgiving and a ratification "in the name of God" of a life together that shows promise of a love inspired by the Spirit of God. The prayers of nuptial blessing are indeed epicleses of the Spirit since only the Spirit can bestow and energize the charisms necessary for married love as an ecclesial reality.

The development of a theology of marriage within the Russian Orthodox tradition takes for granted the primacy of love (even romantic love in the aftermath of Soloviev's influence) over any procreative ends of marriage. The sympathetic acceptance of the saving power of the woman and of marriage as a form of salvation springs from the profound empathy Soloviev, Evdokimov, Lampert, and Sherrard experience in their relationships with significant women. Many, particularly those following Father Georges Florovsky in his disdain for the sophiological currents in Russian theology, have no use for what they consider this gnostic and non-patristic influence of Soloviev. Nevertheless, the personalism and the speculations about the Eternal Feminine in sophiology were contributions to Russian theology of profound impact. Olivier Clément recognizes this when he writes of those Russian religious philosophers who "were the first in the Christian world to have sensed the spiritual meaning of Eros and who began to surmount the deadly schism that had inserted itself between human love and Christianity."[109] The discussion of androgyne, of the sexual images that one may or may not predicate of God, of the status of woman vis-à-vis man, of the personal meaning of marriage as a dialogue of duality within unity, all are prominent concerns of the modern world. The reevaluation of sexuality did not begin with the so-called "sexual revolution" but with nineteenth century

Russian philosophy. There are those Orthodox Christians who find only permissiveness, hedonism, and the exaltation of lust in the modern obsession with sexuality. One has only to read the 1983 Encyclical Letter of Metropolitan Philaret of the Russian Orthodox Church Abroad to encounter this tendency.[110] An alternative response lies in the openness of a book issued in 1980 by the Department of Religious Education of the Orthodox Church in America. This study, *Women and Men in the Church* undertakes a reconsideration of the canons refusing Holy Communion to women who were menstruating. Rather than an integrist approach which accepts the canons without any possible critique, this study undertakes a discrimination based on the holy Fathers and their theological principles. This is, I believe, the only way that one may evaluate those canons and customs which have grown like barnacles upon the body of the Church.

The Church is weighed down and made unmovable if the valid ethical and spiritual insights of human experience are excluded. Just as the Greek Fathers used Platonic philosophy (mostly Middle Platonism) to make the dogmas of the faith intelligible to the intellectual milieu in which they lived, so Yannaras has used Heidegger's thought and Evdokimov and Sherrard have used Soloviev's interpretation of sexual love as a dialogue between two sexes and two persons within a circle of androgynous unity. However, just as neither Gregory of Nazianzus nor Gregory of Nyssa fell into the abyss of Origenism but made radical revisions of Platonism, so Evdokimov and Sherrard have rescued what they learned from Soloviev and saved it from the vicissitudes of romanticism, Gnosticism, and flights of emotion. Both have founded their discussions of sexual love in marriage. Both have seen the dialogue of the sexes rather than androgyne as the goal. And then, Lampert has brought forth the centrality of the incarnation to make concrete the woman who happens to be one's spouse rather than an abstraction of the Eternal Feminine. Lampert has gone so far as to accept love-making or coitus as itself a sacramental experience of the grace of God since the body is included in human love, just as the body was taken up into the *Logos* when He took flesh of the virgin Mary.

168

In Sherrard's critique of Christian reductions of marriage to the procreative purposes of reproduction and of ecclesiastical externalism there is an attempt to arrive at a truly Christian doctrine of marriage. His inclusion of woman as a creature, fully made in the image of God, and, indeed, reflecting the femininity of God the Creator, is in line with the whole development of sophiology. That Sherrard is ready to take this last dangerous step when others fiercely reject any sexual predications of God only points to a courage that understands created wholeness as reflecting the Being of God. If we allow gender predications of God, who is without limitation and beyond everything we can say of Him, we must allow that the masculine gender implied in calling God "Father" and "Son" would also allow us to call God "Mother."

The affirmation of God as feminine as well as masculine is further strengthened if we take seriously the Syriac affirmation that the Holy Spirit is indeed our Mother. The logic of this inclusion of a feminine aspect of deity comes not just from a wish to include other than Byzantine traditions within the Holy Tradition of Orthodoxy. It follows as a necessary conclusion if all that is distinct in the creation and its goodness has its source in God the Creator. A consistent apophatic theology may go so far as to disallow any gender predications of the Godhead - indeed, all predications must be negated. The Orthodox tradition has affirmed both the kataphatic and the apophatic. Roman Catholic Thomism deals with this paradox by positing the way of analogy which both affirmed and denied what was said. Orthodoxy has been more content to live with the paradox. However, it will not do to accept a scriptural positivism and say that only masculine gender attributions can be made of God since He has only revealed those particular ones in the revelation of the Trinity. What is revealed in the Trinity is not fatherhood as such but the source of the Godhead as like unto a father, the Logos as like unto a son, and the gift of God to the Church immanent in her being as a new life, sent by the Word as He departs into glory. This is the Holy Spirit. The Spirit has been given in the Orthodox tradition both masculine and feminine language, and the fact that the Spirit descended upon the Holy Virgin and upon the Church speaks of the revelation of the Spirit in and through the feminine.

Language from creation, mother, father, son, are all predicated of God, not literally but symbolically. As Paul Ricoeur has urged, the language of the family becomes the language of symbol and thus loses its oedipal connotations.[111] The implications of this for the economy of salvation is that the Holy Theotokos is a particular revelation of divine wisdom in the feminine mode, not hypostatically as in Christ her Son, but by participation in the Spirit. It is only by a rediscovery of the apophatic implications of our use of language about God and the viability of feminine language about God that we can escape from the particular trap which identifies the power relations between men and women in patriarchal societies with the internal relations of the Godhead. Men and women stand as equal before God, not only because they are both made in the image of God and share a common union in the body of Christ and in the power of the Holy Spirit, but because the hypostases of the Holy Trinity are equal and share both masculine and feminine language. Strictly speaking they are entirely without gender since gender is part of creation. It could be argued that masculine gender is privileged since God became incarnate in a man. However, there are two objections to such a claim. One is that God took human nature in Christ, not masculinity as such. If we are to be saved, both men and women, it must be the wholeness of humanity, not just a male humanity which was taken by the Logos. The other objection lies in the particular Orthodox affirmation that our salvation was achieved by Mary as well as by her divine Son. Her consent and her cooperation, under the influence of the Holy Spirit who descended upon her, were an intrinsic part of salvation history, as are her prayers for us today.

The meaning of all this for human creation as man and woman is that man is not whole without woman, and woman is not whole without man. This is the affirmation that the Russian theologians have proclaimed. It is a rich heritage and one that is not incompatible with the Greek, particularly the work of Christos Yannaras, who has similarly approached the Orthodox tradition from a personalist perspective. Both affirm that *eros* is a force and energy created by God and moving humanity toward its greater fulfillment and sanctification. Yet each would recognize the *eros* is incomplete without the grace of God which forms it as *philia* and *agape*.

Notes

(1) Stephanos Charalambidis, "Marriage in the Orthodox Church," *One in Christ* 13, 3 (1979), p. 204. French original in *Contacts* 101 (1978), pp. 52-76.

(2) Ibid., p. 205.

(3) Ibid., p. 208.

(4) Ibid., p. 210.

(5) Ibid., p. 214.

(6) Ibid.

(7) Ibid., p. 210.

(8) Ibid., p. 214

(9) Ibid.

(10) Ibid., p. 215

(11) Ibid., p. 208, ftn. 9.

(12) Ibid.

(13) Ibid., p. 209.

(14) Ibid., p. 214.

(15) Ibid.

(16) Ibid.

(17) Ibid., p. 221.

(18) Christos Yannaras, *The Freedom of Morality* (Crestwood, NY., St. Vladimir's Seminary Press, 1984).

(19) Ibid., p. 158.

(20) Ibid., p. 158.

(21) Ibid., p. 158, ft. 20.

(22) Ibid., p. 162.

(23) Ibid., p. 164.

(24) Ibid., p. 165.

(25) Ibid., p. 167.

(26) Gerald Bray, *Sobornost* 5, 2 (1983), p. 99.

(27) Ibid., pp. 158-9, ft. 20.

(28) Paul Evdokimov, *The Sacrament of Love*, trans. Anthony P. Gythiel and Victoria Steadman (Crestwood, NY: St. Vladimir's Seminary Press, 1985), pp. 42-3, and Philip Sherrard, *Eros and Christianity* (London: S.P.C.K., 1976), p. 53.

(29) Vladimir Soloviev, *The Meaning of Love*, trans Jane Marshall (New York: International Universities Press, 1947), pp. 6-7.

(30) Ibid., p. 17.

(31) Ibid., p. 25.

(32) Ibid., p. 26.

(33) Ibid., p. 26.

(34) Ibid., translation by Natalie Dunnington, in S. L. Frank, ed., *A Solovyov Anthology* (New York: Scribners, 1950), p. 162.

(35) Ibid., p. 162.

(36) Vladimir Soloviev, *The Meaning of Love*, trans. Jane Marshall, p. 36.

(37) Ibid., p. 37.

(38) Ibid., p. 44.

(39) Ibid., p. 46.

(40) Ibid., p. 55

(41) Ibid.

(42) Ibid., p. 60.

(43) Ibid., pp. 161-2.

(44) Ibid., trans. Natalie Duddington, p. 171.

(45) Georges Florovsky, *The Ways of Russian Theology: Part Two* (Vaduz: Buchervertriebsanstalt, 1987), p. 245.

(46) Ibid. p. 251.

(47) Nicholas O. Lossky, *History of Russian Philosophy* (New York: International Universities Press, 1952), p. 132.

(48) Vladimir Soloviev, "Preface to Collected Poems," quoted by Lossky, pp. 131-2.

(49) Olivier Clément, Foreward to *The Sacrament of Love*, p. 9.

(50) Ibid., p. 16.

(51) Evdokimov, *The Sacrament of Love*, p. 31.

(52) Ibid., p. 31.

(53) Ibid., pp. 34-41.

(54) Ibid., pp. 42-3.

(55) Ibid., p. 43.

(56) Ibid., p. 43.

(57) Peter C. Phan, *Culture and Eschatology* (New York: Peter Lang Publishing Company, 1985), p. 50.

(58) Evdokimov, p. 44.

(59) Ibid., p. 44.

(60) Ibid., p. 155.

(61) Ibid., p. 125.

(62) Ibid., p. 126.

(63) Ibid., p. 126.

(64) Ibid., p. 164.

(65) Ibid., p. 164.

(66) Ibid., p. 168.

(67) Ibid., p. 169.

(68) Ibid., p. 178.

(69) The tragedy of Father Evgueny Lampert resulted from the allegations that portions of his doctoral dissertation at Oxford were plagiarized from the writings of Father Sergei Bulgakov. Subsequently his D. Phil. was withdrawn. Whether these allegations were true is unclear.

(70) Evgueny Lampert, *The Divine Realm: Towards a Theology of*

Sacraments (London: Faber and Faber, 1944), p. 88.

(71) Ibid., 94.

(72) Ibid., p. 94.

(73) Ibid., p. 96.

(74) Ibid., p. 96.

(75) Ibid., p. 96.

(76) Ibid., p. 97.

(77) Ibid., p. 98.

(78) Ibid., p. 98.

(79) Ibid., p. 98.

(80) Ibid., pp. 98-9.

(81) Ibid., p. 99.

(82) Ibid., pp. 27-8.

(83) Philip Sherrard, *Christianity and Eros* (London: SPCK, 1976), p. 10.

(84) Ibid., pp. 13-4.

(85) Ibid., p. 16.

(86) Ibid., p. 26.

(87) Ibid., p. 28.

(88) Ibid., p. 29.

(89) Ibid., p. 42.

(90) Ibid., p. 47.

(91) Ibid., p. 48.

(92) Ibid., p. 52.

(93) Ibid., pp. 70-1.

(94) Ibid., p. 72.

(95) Ibid., p. 72.

(96) Ibid., p. 74.

(97) Ibid, p. 74.

(98) Ibid., p. 76.

(99) Ibid., p. 77.

(100) Ibid., p. 77.

(101) Ibid., p. 81.

(102) Ibid., p. 87.

(103) Ibid., p. 87.

(104) Ibid., p. 88.

(105) Ibid., p. 90.

(106) Ibid., p. 90.

(107) Ibid., p. 93.

(108) Ibid., p.93.

(109) Clément, Foreword to Evdokimov, *The Sacrament of Love*, p. 8.

(110) Metropolitan Philaret, "An Encyclical Letter of the Chairman of the Council of Bishops of the Russian Orthodox Church Outside Russia," *Orthodox Life* 6 (1983), pp. 19-24.

(111) Paul Ricoeur, *Conflict of Interpretations: Essays in Hermeneutics* (Evanston: Northwestern University Press, 1974).

Chapter Five:

Divorce and Remarriage in Orthodox Faith

The New Testament Tradition

It is important to discuss the marriage discipline of the Orthodox Church, not just to defend it but to use it as a means of understanding the principles on which it is based. There are various approaches to that discipline as it has developed over the years. One is that which has been taken by many Roman Catholics. Traditionalist Roman Catholics have usually claimed that the Orthodox have fallen into error in both the theory and the practice of divorce and remarriage. The Jesuit G.H. Joyce in his book *Christian Marriage* maintained a sustained polemic against the "errors of the Greeks" on the matter of the indissolubility of marriage and their alleged capitulation to the lax standards and laws of the Byzantine emperors. Even a theologian as sympathetic to the Orthodox as Louis Bouyer considers the canonical obstacles to stand in the way of reconciliation between Orthodox and Roman Catholics.[1] Yet, on the other hand, many Roman Catholic theologians seeking revision of their own rigorous practice regarding divorce and remarriage have sympathetically approached the Orthodox on this matter. One has only to recall the names of Victor Pospishil and Bernard Häring and the proposals which they have made for a revision of the practices of the Roman Church in favor of Orthodox proce-

dures involving a use of "economy." The firm line traditionally held by the see of Rome has been reiterated by Henri
Crouzel in his the claim that the Fathers with only one exception believed remarriage after divorce to be a grave sin of
adultery.[2] This position has also been upheld in a new book
by two English Protestants.[3] The authors, W.A. Heth and
G.J. Wenham, attempt to show not only that the Fathers did
not allow divorce and remarriage but that the Lord himself
excluded both. Inevitably we must examine the correctness,
both at a theological and biblical level, of the Orthodox practice and its rationale.

It is a truism of biblical exegesis that two passages from
Mark (10:1-12) and Matthew (19:3-12) give a context which
places Jesus in a discussion with the Pharisees over the debated question taken up by the followers of Shammai and Hillel
as to the grounds on which divorce may be permitted. The
former considered divorce and remarriage (for the non-guilty
partner) possible only if the woman had committed adultery.
The latter allowed divorce and remarriage for various other
reasons including simply dismissal. The Marcan version is
uncompromising: dismissal was allowed by Moses only
because of hardness of heart. Therefore, no separation is
possible since the man and the woman have become one flesh,
and what God has joined man must not separate. Any dismissal involving remarriage is adultery. Commentators point
to the fact that Mark (unlike Matthew) includes dismissal by
the woman of her husband, something allowed in Roman law
but not in Jewish. The implications of this fact are quite
simply that a revision of the oral tradition (presumably within
the context of Jewish law) has been made by Mark. However, despite the modification of the text, many, perhaps most,
commentators consider the Marcan version the earlier one
insofar as there is no exception clause (as there is none in
Luke either). It is also important to note that Mark separates
the teaching of Jesus into the public teaching (chapter 10:1-9)
and the private teaching given only to his own disciples
(chapter 10:10-12).

What is most important in both versions of Matthew's ac-
counts of Jesus' teaching on divorce and remarriage is the

exception clause, "except for *porneia.*" We cannot translate exactly the Greek word *porneia* since its meaning is unclear and highly controverted. The two Greek phrases *parektos logou porneias* (Mt 5:32) and *me epi porneia* (Mt 19:9) are generally regarded as having the same meaning. It is note-worthy that according to Matthew, the Pharisees asked Jesus if it was "lawful for a man to divorce his wife *for any cause at all* (Mt 19:3)." In Mark this this phrase is missing while in Matthew it becomes a key to the meaning of the modified passage, "except for *porneia.*" I shall follow Theodore Mackin in his book *Marriage in the Catholic Church: Divorce and Remarriage* by specifying six different interpretations of this phrase:

1. *Porneia* refers to a legal disability which was noted by rabbis in the *erwat dabar.* This category was used in Rabbinic law to designate uncleanness in marriage: sexual impotence, Gentile parentage, infertility, consanguinity or affinity within a forbidden degree, etc. Jews would already be aware that such uncleanness provided a reason for dissolving the mar-riage. If the phrase *me epi porneia* is a simple Greek transla-tion of *erwat dabar* then it only translates what was obvious to Jews since no marriage could exist if such "impediments" existed. This would not give any cause for alarm, and yet it is alarm which the disciples express by their response: "If this is the way it is with a man and wife it is better not to marry (Mt 19:10)." This rather radical response stands as the major obstacle against a simple translation of *porneia* as *erwat dabar.* Clearly the disciples thought that Jesus was saying something very strong, quite out of line with normative Juda-ism in this period of time.

2. The second interpretation is that put forth by Van Tilborg, who would relate the exception clause to Mt 1:18-19. If the man who marries a woman finds her not to be a virgin, he may put her away. Mackin thinks, however, that this would be very rare since Jewish girls married between the ages of twelve and thirteen. More importantly he thinks that Jesus would scarcely allow such an exception in the light of his teaching on forgiveness. If Van Tilborg's interpreta-tion were correct, it would provide only a reason for Mat-

thew's insertion of the exception. It could hardly come from the lips of Jesus himself.

3. The third interpretation takes *porneia* to designate an incestuous union. This view had been set forth originally by J. Bonsirven who considered the Matthaean texts in relation to Acts 25:20-29 and Acts 21:25, in which Christians were urged to refrain from all "unchastity." Bonsirven interpreted *porneia* as meaning a marriage in conflict with the Jewish prohibitions of marriage. He narrows the meaning, however, so that *parektos logou porneias* is a literal translation of *erwat dabhar*. Following Dupont he judges that "*porneia* referred to those cases of fornication or unchastity for which divorce was permitted according to the school of Shammai (i.e., adultery or moral misconduct on the part of the wife). In considering this interpretation, it is important to note that Bonsirven's view has been reasserted by Joseph Fitzmyer on the basis of the *Damascus Document*, an Essene text which refers to the *zenut* or unchastity of certain Jews. Two examples are given: the taking of two wives during a lifetime, whether by polygamy or by divorce and remarriage, and the practice of taking nieces and nephews in marriage. Such an interpretation remains tentative. since we do not have the evidence to show that Matthew used the *Damascus Document*.

4. The most traditional interpretation in the Western world has been that which assumes *porneia* to refer to adultery. This identification became standard with St. Jerome who upheld it. The leading exponent of this view in the modern world has been Jacques Dupont in his book *Mariage et divorce dans l'évangile*, published in 1959. Dupont points to the fact that in Matthew's gospel the Pharisees asked Jesus if it was "lawful for a man to divorce his wife *for any cause at all.*" The underlined phrase is absent from Mark's gospel. This makes it evident that Mark is concerned with the general legitimacy of divorce, whereas Matthew is more specific in his concerns. The context in 19:3-9 (like that of Mk 10:11-12) is the dispute between the adherents of Shammai and the followers of Hillel. The Pharisees are asking for Jesus' opinion. In contrast to both schools Jesus goes behind Moses to Genesis and the divine law for the new age, which is the restoration of

the law of paradise. In reference to the rejection of the law of Moses, the Pharisees refer to Dt 24:7. Jesus replies that this law was given because of the hardness of their hearts, but originally there was no such permission to divorce. The apodictic character of the statement of Jesus is apparent inasmuch as he says that "Whoever divorced his wife and marries another commits adultery." As Heth and Wenham put it, "If divorce is against God's creative will, then remarriage after divorce is even worse, namely, adultery."[4]

The situation of the divorced husband is comparable but differs in various ways. It is not the divorce itself but remarriage which is the basis of Jesus' statement that the second marriage is adulterous. Furthermore, a man who marries a divorced woman by that very fact commits adultery. In effect, polygamy is condemned here. Dupont comments: "This short sentence...therefore constitutes a profound revolution in relationship to the Jewish conceptions of marriage. In the eyes of Jesus, the indissolubility of marriage is absolute. Not only does he forbid divorce, but he denies the power to break the marriage bond. Moreover, he conceives marriage as only monogamous, granting the same rights and powers to the husband and the wife."[5]

Dupont's basic position is that the interpretation of Jesus' sayings as it is found in the early Church, permitting separation but never remarriage, is less complex than the other views. Other views create more problems than they solve. He notes how in Matthew's gospel there is a pattern of quoting a saying twice. The two passages about divorce in chapters 5 and 19 are characteristic of this pattern. If we take the position that Mt 5:32 involves complete dissolution of the marriage (by reason of adultery), the logic of the statements becomes very obscure and even contradictory. Jesus said: "Every one who divorces his wife, except for the cause of unchastity, makes her commit adultery (Mt 5:32)." It would appear that adulterous wives (if we allow *porneia* as the basis for the divorce) have more freedom to remarry than those divorced for lesser grounds. Dupont considers it absurd to permit remarriage to the divorced adulteress but not to a woman divorced for other reasons. Dupont thinks that the absurdity may be mitigated if the innocent husband is allowed the right of remarriage though not the adulterous wife. Jesus permits nothing of the sort. A man who puts away his wife for her adultery and remarries another woman is said by Jesus to be committing adultery (Mt 19:9). There is, Dupont urges, no contradiction if separation is permitted from a wife who has committed adultery. It is remarriage which is condemned as adultery, not separation. Dupont interprets 19:9 as a double conditional clause. The exception clause is stating an exception to the first condition, "if a man puts away his wife." The next step is to ask whether the exception modifies the second clause, "and marries another." R. H. Guntry thinks this is most unlikely.[6] Dupont allows, however, that it might be possible for the exception to qualify the second clause, "and marries another." It is unlikely, however, because of the question posed at the beginning of the passage, "what reason justifies divorce?" as put by the Pharisees. The answer is clearly that only *porneia* justifies divorce, but even then remarriage is adultery. The advantages of this interpretation are many, but one is that the verb "put away" (*apolyo*) which is used in Mt 5:31-32 and in Mt 19:3, can in each instance mean to separate, not to break the marriage bond.

Much of the strength of Dupont's interpretation comes from his integration of Mt 19:10-12 with the previous passage on divorce and remarriage. The traditional interpretation of these verses been that they present a call to celibacy. Mt 5:9 makes it clear that whatever *porneia* meant it did not mean any lessening of the bonds of marriage. Indeed, the response of the disciples was to a view of marriage much more demanding and stronger than anything previously held within Judaism. From one point of view the following verses (Mt 19:11-12) might be interpreted as a lightening of the radical demands made by marriage. This interpretation would even make their acceptance of those demands optional or obligatory only for those "who are able to stand it" or to "those to whom it is given to be so." W.D. Davies, perhaps the most outstanding exegete of the Sermon on the Mount, uses them to excuse us from the observance of the new law which is fixed for all of Jesus' disciples.[7] Some commentators have compared the words of Jesus with those of St. Paul in 1 Cor 7:7, "I wish that all were as I myself am. But each has his own special gift from God, one of one kind and one of another." This special gift (*charisma*) would apply to those who decided not to marry, to remain celibates. Consequently, the verse about eunuchs (Mt 19:12) would refer to celibates.

To interpret the sayings of Jesus about divorce and remarriage as being only for those who have the charism to accept them is a gross misinterpretation. This brings us to ask to what "this statement" (*ton logon touton*) in Mt 19:11 may refer. Heth and Wenham assert that its reference must be Mt 19:12, the statement that the disciples have just made about the inadvisability of marriage.[8] Dupont answers the difficulties that emerge in this exegesis by stating that the eunuch-saying in verse 12 refers back to the indissoluble character of marriage rather than carrying the discussion forward to the subject of eunuchs. Several exegetes find a parallel between Jesus' reaction to his disciples' response to the rigor of his teaching and the reaction revealed in Mt 19:26. The context there is the meeting with the rich young man. The word "this" (*touto*) in vs. 26 does not allude to the question of the disciples but to the statement that it would appear to be impossible for a rich man to enter the kingdom of God. The pattern is clear. We have a "harsh word" from Jesus, a shocked reaction from his disciples, and then a response from Jesus: "With men this is impossible, but with God all things are possible."

It is clear that the verse Mt 19:11, "But he said to them, 'Not all men can receive this precept, but only those to whom it is given'" is not intended to set up two categories of disciples. Nothing could be more inconceivable. We are not in the world of liberal agreement to accept or not accept the teachings of Jesus. Rather, in the context of Matthew's gospel we may relate verse 11 to Mt 13:11: "To you to it has been granted to know the mysteries of the kingdom of heaven, but to them it has not been granted." To understand or comprehend is a privilege granted only to the disciples. In Matthew the disciples comprehend, while in Mark's Gospel they fail again and again to comprehend. There are not two categories

185

of believers but rather the category of the Pharisees and other believers contrasted with the disciples of Jesus who hear the word, who accept his teachings and apply them. Obviously "this statement" of Mt 19:11 refers only to the hard saying of Jesus on divorce and remarriage as adultery. To depend upon St. Paul to provide a key by referring it to optional celibacy is misleading and depends upon reading Mt 19:12 as belonging to an entirely different context.

That the exception clauses in Matthew refer to adultery has been reinforced by several modern scholars. J. J. Kilgallen's recent treatment of Mt 5:31-2 as a continuation of Jesus' discussion of the seventh commandment, which begins in Mt 5:27, is to be noted.[9] The prohibition of adultery would be violated either by divorce (unless for reasons of *porneia*) or remarriage after divorce for whatever cause. Divorce is permitted when the woman has committed adultery, but not remarriage. Divorce for other reasons is not allowed. These rulings are part of the original teachings of Jesus. The recovery of the original order of Genesis is the recovery of the condition of paradise before the Fall and man's hardness of heart. The rulings comprise a new law, a law not based on legalism but established by a new age, the inbreaking of the reign of God. The contrast between the way of the kingdom and the way of the world becomes sharp indeed, but to know and to keep the teachings of Jesus depends entirely upon receiving them and keeping them. Upon entering the kingdom those called to feast at the banquet of the Lord will have garments worthy of the feast by their obedience to this new law.

5. The interpretation which has been most widely accepted outside of Roman Catholicism is that *porneia* not only means adultery but that in the case of the adultery of the woman (and in some circles of the man also) divorce and remarriage are open to the innocent partner. Mackin rejects the view that the exception clause permits divorce by reason of adultery and presumably remarriage by urging that the entire tone of the discussion in Mt 19:3-12 indicates that Jesus is refusing to take sides in the dispute between Hillel and Shammai.[10] To have allowed the exception for adultery would have been to

side with the followers of Shammai. He goes on to claim that even if the exception clause comes from Matthew alone, the interpretation that divorce is legitimate on account of adultery, creates an inconsistency within Jesus' own thought. Furthermore, Matthew had a perfectly good word for adultery in *moicheia* and *moicheuein,* so why should the vague term *porneia* be used? Even if *porneia* is a catch-all term the consternation revealed in the disciples' response to what Jesus had said is unaccounted for. But perhaps more decisive is the fact that Jesus' teaching made forgiveness so central that putting a wife away for adultery would violate that injunction.

The Australian Roman Catholic theologian, Brian Byron, has explored an interesting parallel to the exception clauses in Mt 5:32 and 19:9 in 1 Cor 7:15. Byron argues that they are exceptions sharing much with St. Paul's permission for remarriage after a non-believing partner has departed from the marriage. He claims that *porneia* is a generic term, less explicit than adultery (*moicheia*) in its meaning but nonetheless a word that would indicate that a marriage has in fact become irreparably damaged and destroyed.[11] Byron notes that Jesus said that the marital union should not be dissolved, not that it could not be dissolved: "Nor does He speak of indissolubility, which means literally 'impossibility of being dissolved.' Jesus does not say the union cannot be dissolved; He says "What God has joined, *let* no man separate.' Indeed, the prohibition itself implies that it *can* be sundered. So Jesus does not speak of an indissoluble bond but of a union which man may not destroy."[12] Byron thinks that Jesus made no ruling on the case of a partner abandoned by the other, who has remarried (according to Roman law). Matthew brings in the exception to refer to those who have been abandoned by a spouse who has entered into another marriage. This is directly parallel to the case that St. Paul discussed in 1 Cor 7:15.

Byron is also able to accept Quesnell's argument, namely, that Mt 19:12 is not about voluntary celibacy but about remarriage after separation from an adulterous or impure wife. The Christian may have a duty (following *The Shepherd of Hermas*) to separate himself from an adulterous wife, but he must always be ready to receive her back, and thus may not remarry. However, if she remarries, which would be outside the context of Christian faith and lead to apostasy, the case would be comparable to that given by St. Paul in 1 Cor 7:15. The second marriage of the unfaithful partner would not be termed "adultery" in ordinary speech according to Byron but would come under the category of Jesus' prophetic denunciation of "adultery" of the heart (Mt 5:28).

Byron's argument is important since it is consistent with an interpretation which will become vital in the Eastern Orthodox understanding of divorce and remarriage. This is not the easy identification of *porneia* and adultery, which, as we have seen, is bad exegesis and unwarranted. It is, on the contrary, the view that *porneia* implies a marital breakdown which may destroy the marriage in exactly the same way as St. Paul says, a marriage ceases to be when the unbelieving partner leaves. A new marriage becomes possible because the old marriage has ceased to be. The sinful character of *porneia* is evident in this breakdown. The false assumption, however, is that marriage continues even when the union has been broken and one partner has moved into another marriage through infidelity and *porneia*. Both partners as Christians were obliged to do everything possible, by repentance and forgiveness, to restore the marriage. Byron takes very seriously the exception clauses in Mt 5:32 and 19:9 and gives them a force which other authors fail to do. His discussion of 1 Cor 7:15, which I shall present below, will further enlighten us on his exegetical and theological interpretation.

6. A final interpretation is based on the disciples' response to the saying of Jesus about adultery as the result of putting one's wife away. In Mt 19:11 Jesus says: "Not all men can receive this precept, but only those to whom it is given." Mackin interprets this as a demand that one can fulfill only with the help of God's grace.[13] The key is found in the final statement of the passage: "For there are eunuchs who have been so from birth, and there are eunuchs who have been made eunuchs by men, and there are eunuchs who have made themselves eunuchs for the sake of the kingdom of heaven. He who is able to receive this, let him receive it." Mackin perceives the key here to be the term "eunuch" which

refs to a man who has been unable to produce children. After his examination of the possible interpretations of the Matthew's exception clause, Mackin is skeptical about any clear evidence to make a definitive interpretation. He does think that we can come to "the solidly probable conclusion that the phrase is not Jesus' but a device within Matthew's attempt to interpret Jesus' mind."[14] The meaning is, I believe, not to be found by pursuing the absolute law of indissolubility based on Jesus' sayings taken as a new law. Rather, it is by realizing that the presence of the kingdom of God as the *eschaton* makes possible what is ordinarily impossible. The contrast between the old age with its hardness of heart and the new brought by Jesus is abundantly clear. The new age restores the plan of creation whereby man and woman become one flesh. But the new age also brings grace and fulfillment of what is impossible for ordinary mortals. To be a eunuch for the kingdom of God is not only to be a celibate but also to be a married man without offspring. Divorce and remarriage have no place in the kingdom. But since the kingdom has not yet come the difficulties of living in the world allow for exceptions. Whatever Matthew's exceptions may mean they are exceptions made for the human community. The tension is between then and now, between kingdom and historical community. Lisa Cahill has commented on this exegesis:

> Scholarly consensus solidly supports the inferences that not only an absolute prohibition of divorce is closest to the - original saying of Jesus but also that some primitive Christian communities interpreted responsibility to that command as including some sort of "exception" to its literal force. The implication for normative Christian ethics is that authoritative moral norms ought to be based on the essential insights and concrete injunctions of the Bible (e.g., Genesis, Mark, and Luke); but that the authoritative and canonical collection itself constitutes a model for the developmental "handing on" (*paradosis-traditio*) and modification of specific moral norms.[15]

It is wrong, I believe, to reduce the norms of Jesus to ideals, and yet they are not categorical imperatives. The tension between the two can be resolved only by the eschatological context. Dominic Crossan has noted that exegetes have always been ready to distinguish between ideal and program in applying the teachings of Jesus in the Sermon on the Mount but there has been greater reluctance to do this with regard to divorce and marriage:

> Commentators were much more ready to sanction the possibility of self-defense and war, despite Jesus, than to permit divorce and remarriage, despite that same Jesus. Both divorce and war are tragic human failure, but once they have irrevocably happened no apodictic condemnation of their possibility tells us how to handle their actuality...The categorical imperative of Jesus can never be used as a casuistic absolute but only as a catechetical idea. The New Testament itself recorded two exceptions as its experience of life progressed. There will be unfortunately many more exceptions, many more cases where divorce and remarriage must be sorrowfully accepted as part of our human weakness and our failure to form community, before Christ is all in all.[16]

In response to those who would seek to reduce the obligatory character of Jesus' teaching on remarriage after divorce, Joseph Fitzmyer has written of the various fashions of exegetical interpretation of the Sermon on the Mount. To view Jesus' teachings as ideals versus legal norms is to impose considerations extrinsic to the texts themselves. He states: "The history of the exegesis of that Sermon has gone through an entire gamut of interpretations, and one of them is the Theory of the Impossible Ideal--a blueprint for utopia. And the question has always been whether that theory measures up to the radical program of Christian morality proposed by the Matthean Jesus."[17]

St. Paul in 1 Cor 7:10 gives us the most important non-synoptic source in the New Testament regarding separation, divorce and remarriage: "To the married I give charge, not I but the Lord, that the wife should not separate from her husband (but if she does, let her remain single or else be reconciled to her husband) - and that the husband should not divorce his wife." One can relate this passage to both Roman and Rabbinical law. Roman law allowed for three ways of divorcing One, which had become obsolete, was simple dismissal. The second was repudiation, and this was available under Roman law to both husband and wife. The third mode was by common consent. Divorce was also permitted by reason of the penal deportation of one of the spouses into exile, the enslavement of one or both of them, separation by captivity and prolonged absence of either spouse. These circumstances were unusual and often tied to upheavals in society as a whole. Rabbinical law allowed a dismissal on the part of the husband. No such action was available for the wife, though she could urge her husband to dismiss her. Clearly in 1 Cor 7:10-11 we have the context and background of Rabbinical law. This is odd, of course, since the Christian community in Corinth would have been presumably Gentile. In the light of the passages following (1 Cor 7:12-13) we must presume that the prohibition of remarriage and the exhortation to reconciliation apply to the marriage of two Christians. It is important to note that the admonition based on the word of the Lord - Mackin thinks it is based on Mk 10:1-12 - that no separation ought to occur - has not, in fact, prevented a separation. St. Paul allows that the separation may continue if reconciliation is sought and no remarriage takes place. St. Paul continues his discussion of marriage in 1 Cor 7:12-16:

> To the rest I say, not the Lord, that if any brother has a wife who is an unbeliever, and she consents to live with him, he should not divorce her. If any woman has a husband who is an unbeliever, and he consents to live with her, she should not divorce him. For the unbelieving husband is consecreated through his wife, and the unbelieving wife is consecrated through her husband. Otherwise, your children would be unclean,

191

> but as it is, they are holy. But if the unbelieving
> partner desires to separate, let it be so; in such a case
> the brother or sister is not bound. For God has called
> us to peace. Wife, how do you know whether you will
> save your husband? Husband, how do you know
> whether you will save your wife?

This text would provide an exception to the absolute prohibition of divorce in 1 Cor 7:10-11. They were the basis on which the so-called Pauline Privilege was to be constructed by later canonists, but a careful examination of them reveals that the permission to let the unbelieving partner go is based on the lack of peace between them. It is not a simple matter of permission to part. Indeed, neither spouse is to part unless one chooses to do so. The union between them is sanctified by the presence of the Christian spouse. The norm is not legal but eschatological: whether the Christian can save the partner and the couple live in peace together are the basic considerations in the matter. Marriage had itself been placed within the context of the kingdom of God by Jesus in Mt 5:31-32, which is part of the Sermon on the Mount. It is true that marriage has a provisional character in the New Testament as we see in Mk 12:25: "For when they rise from the dead, they neither marry nor are given in marriage, but are like angels in heaven." But in St. Paul's thought it is either in celibacy or in a life-long fidelity to a spouse that we discern signs of the kingdom. Again, the tension exists between the heroic stance taken in the light of the end-time and the necessities of life in community, a tension that lies at the heart of New Testament ethics. Marriage "in the Lord" is a criterion that relates marriage to the kingdom of God and the end-time.

Brian Byron has urged that the reason behind St. Paul's position in 1 Cor 7:15 has nothing to do with baptism or the lack of the same (as the Pauline Privilege has alleged), nor does it have to do with a privilege concerned with exclusively helping converts to Christianity. Most certainly it is not a dispensation from the law of Christ. It is, rather, a "statement concerning the party whose marital status was not discussed by Jesus, viz., the definitely abandoned partner."[18]

According to Byron, St. Paul's ruling in 1 Cor 7:15 is a universal principle which the Church may use for the benefit of all: "That principle is this: when a person who is himself prepared to remain faithful to his marriage commitment is abandoned by the other party in a way that can realistically be understood as definitive and absolute, such a person is free of commitment to the union, because in fact it no longer exists."[19] The importance of this statement is that St. Paul's teaching is explained neither as an exception to an absolute rule which is built on an indissoluble norm nor as a legal option to give converts the freedom to enter the Church without reluctant and non-believing partners. It is what we claim the Orthodox principle to be: marriage has an absolute obligation as an ideal and a sacramental reality as long as it exists, but when the relationship is no longer in Christ (as the sanctification of the non-believing spouse must be seen to be according to 1 Cor 7) the marriage simply does not exist. Thus the Christian partner is free to choose another spouse in the Lord. The stance that sacramental marriage differs *de toto genere* from non-sacramental marriage is not found in 1 Cor 7. The norms of all forms of marriage in the Lord (whether one or both partners are baptized) are that the marriage is indissoluble in the sense that neither partner should abandon the other, but if one does then the abandoned one has freedom to remarry. One must ask how this avoids violating the principles of 1 Cor 7:10-11. The difference between the two passages lies in the fact that 7:10-11 involves believing Christians, while 12-16 involve an unbelieving spouse and a believer.

The Patristic Tradition

The patristic evidence about divorce and remarriage is highly controverted. Because of the appearance of a challenging book by Victor J. Pospishil, *Divorce and Remarriage: Towards a New Catholic Teaching* in 1967 various Roman Catholic scholars conducted a close and critical examination

193

of what was alleged to be evidence for remarriage after divorce during the early Christian period.[20]Pospishil's thesis was controverted by Prof. Henri Crouzel, whose book *L'Eglise primitive face au divorce*, showed Pospishil's thesis to be entirely unfounded. In fact, Crouzel claimed that only Ambrosiaster interpreted the texts of the New Testament regarding divorce and remarriage so as to allow remarriage for the innocent party after separation for adultery. Crouzel urged that this was only a personal view of Ambrosiaster (actually a pseudonym for an unknown author formerly confused with St. Ambrose) and in no way reflected evidence of the practice of remarriage after divorce.[21] In turn, Crouzel was challenged by his former student Giovanni Cereti, whose book *Divorzio, Nuove Nozze E Penitenza Nella Chiesa Primitiva* examined the patristic evidence and came up with quite different conclusions.[22]

Of the earliest recorded instances of patristic comments on marriage and divorce, we have material from the Shepherd of Hermas, St. Justin Martyr, Athanagoras, Theophilus, Clement of Alexandria, and Origen. These authors date from the second century, except for Origen who lived from A.D. 185 to 254. *The Shepherd of Hermas* is a work dating either from the end of the first century or from about 140-50. Many of the Fathers, including Irenaeus, Clement of Alexandria, Tertullian, and Athanasius (in his earlier years) considered *The Shepherd of Hermas* to be canonical or at least quasi-canonical. What is intriguing about the discussion of divorce in this work is that Hermas asks his guardian angel what a man should do if he discovers the adultery of his wife and she continues in her adultery. The angel strongly insists that he must depart from a wife who is entirely unrepentant and continues in adultery. But the husband is to remain single, and should he marry again he would be committing adultery himself. It is for the sake of repentance that the husband must remain single: "'But, if, sir,' I said, 'after the divorce the wife repents and wishes to return to her husband, will he refuse to receive her?' 'No, indeed,' he said. 'If the husband does not receive her, he sins. He incurs a great sin. The sinner who has repented must be received. However, not often, for there is only one repentance for the servants of God. To bring about her repentance, then, the husband should not marry."[23] It is clear that Hermas is following Roman law in this passage since that law commanded that the husband send his wife away within sixty days if she is guilty of adultery. Indeed, to keep the wife is to be guilty of cooperating with her adultery. Hermas stands opposed to the practice of Roman law, however, in forbidding remarriage and commanding that the wife be received back if repentant. What makes the passage odd from the secular standpoint is that the same would apply to the guilty husband. The shepherd, the angel of repentance, continued to dictate:

'This is the course of action required for husband and wife. Not only is it adultery,' he said, 'for a man to pollute his flesh, but it is likewise adultery for anyone to act in imitation of the pagans. So, if anyone persists in acts of this kind and does not repent, keep away from him, do not live with him; otherwise you also have a part in his sin. This is the reason why you were commanded to live by yourselves, whether husband or wife be guilty. For, under these circumstances, repentance is possible.[24]

Hermas has gone beyond Matthew's teaching and adapted his own to the Marcan in which equal rights and duties are set forth for husband and wife. Hermas moved far from the commands of the New Testament by making it a Christian duty for the husband to separate from an adulterous wife and a wife from an adulterous husband. He has also ignored the evangelical duty of forgiving over and over again by allowing only one repentance. Crouzel is followed by Heth and Wenham in thinking that Hermas absolutely opposes remarriage for the man who has divorced an adulterous wife who has persisted in her sin. Other scholars are not so convinced, however. In an extended critique in *Theological Studies* of Crouzel's book, J. Alex Sherlock has assessed the evidence to show that Crouzel has assumed the indissolubility of the marriage and read this into his interpretation. As he puts it,

"Hermas may well have opposed remarriage, even forbidden it, for the husband of a recidivist adulteress, but if he did so we simply have no such evidence."[25] In fact, we may well assume that Hermas infers toleration since he does not mention remarriage for the innocent spouse. Foremost in Hermas' statement is the assertion of only one forgiveness. If the other partner does not repent, one might well assume freedom to remarry.

St. Justin Martyr sets the norm which appears in all of the early Fathers other than Origen: "Those who, according to human law, contract double marriages (*digamias*), are sinners against our master (*didaskalo*)."[26] In this passage we must ask what is the forbidden and sinful second marriage to which St. Justin is referring. There are four possible meanings: bigamy, successive remarriage after the death of a spouse, remarriage after divorce, and remarriage of any kind whatsoever. Heth and Wenham think that the best case can be made for the third option since St. Justin has just quoted Mt 5:32b and Lk 16:18b.[27] Furthermore Justin focuses on the inner lust which is in the teaching of Jesus the equivalent of adultery. The strongest ground for this option, however, is the reference to the legality of the second marriage according to the human law. In the *Second Apology* (2:1-7) Justin repeats the teaching that Christians must separate from adulterous spouses. He provides a case of two pagans, one of whom, the wife, became a Christian. She tried to reform her husband, but ultimately he departed and fell into immoral behavior. She presented him with a bill of divorce so as to leave him, but not a word is said about her marrying again. Crouzel thinks that Justin simply assumes that marriage is indissoluble and indeed, in the text from the *First Apology* Justin has deliberately suppressed part of Mt 5:32. Nevertheless, we have no certainty that Justin had the full text of Mt 5:32. Furthermore, his admonitions regarding second marriage, civil obedience, swearing, and impatience are dealt with in the same manner. Christians are presented in ideal fashion, not in a concrete pastoral context.

Athanagoras wrote his *A Plea for Christians* about 177, addressing it to the emperors Marcus Aurelius Antonius and

Lucius Aurelius Commodus. Chapter 33 has become a most important text for the discussion of divorce and remarriage in the early Church:[28]

> We are not concerned with the exercise of eloquence but with the performance and teaching of deeds - either to stay in the state in which a man was born or to remain satisfied with one marriage; for a second marriage is gilded adultery. For "whoever divorces his wife," it says, "and marries another, commits adultery." Neither does it allow a man to divorce a woman whose maidenhead he has taken, nor does it allow him to marry again. For he who detaches himself from his previous wife, even if she has died, is a covert adulterer. He thwarts the hand of God (because in the beginning God formed one man and one woman), and he destroys the communion of flesh with flesh in the unity characteristic of the intercourse of the sexes.[29]

The quotation from the NT is either Mt 19:9 as abbreviated and without the exception clause or Mk 10:11, omitting the last two words (*ep' auten* - against her). Heth and Wenham speculate that he omitted it thinking that it applied only to dismissal of a wife, not to a divorce and a decision to marry again.[30] Yet Athanagoras would appear to go further than this when he writes "He who detaches himself from his previous wife, even if she has died, is a covert adulterer." Seemingly he objects to any second marriage at all. Crouzel interprets this phrase to be only against remarriage after divorce, not against remarriage after the death of a spouse. Some think that this text of Athanagoras reflects Eastern asceticism, even Encratism, which was widespread in A.D. 177. Yet the meaning of the text reflects the importance of the "one flesh" doctrine rather than a form of asceticism. Athenagoras may well refer to second marriage after the death of a spouse. His opinion as to remarriage would then represent what was to be a minority opinion and one rejected by the Catholic Church in both the East and the West.

197

Theophilus was, according to Eusebius's history of the Church, the sixth bishop of Antioch. He is the first Father of the Church to quote the exception clause of Mt 5:32: "The gospel voice provides a stricter teaching about purity when it says, 'Everyone who looks upon another person's wife to desire her has already committed adultery with her in his heart.' 'And he who marries,' it says, 'a woman divorced by her husband commits adultery, and whoever divorces his wife except for fornication makes her a partner in adultery.'"[31] One may note that he inverts the two clauses of the sentence in quoting Mt 5:32. On the other hand, he may be quoting Luke 16:18b and then placing Mt 5:32a beside it. Theophilus would appear to embrace indissolubility without qualification, but the exception clause is entered here without any explanation of its meaning. We may also note that the word translated as "fornication" refers to *porneias* in the Greek. Again the interpretation is not clear. Crouzel largely ignores the witness of Theophilus, but his critic Sherlock draws more drastic conclusions:

> Why, since Theophilus knows and accepts Mt 5.32 with the exception phrase as a "holy, divine word," does he not comment on the innocent husband's right or denial of remarriage. Perhaps everyone in the Church knew what was to be done in such a case? Perhaps innocent husbands never wanted to remarry? The second century world allowed such a remarriage, with only Athenagoras (a contemporary in Egypt, quite unlike Theophilus) forbidding it. If we must assume anything, it should be that the husband could remarry.[32]

Clement of Alexandria, as we have seen previously, is the theologian who may well be said to be the chief advocate of marriage in the Patristic age. He stands a generation before the greatest of the Alexandrian theologians, Origen. Clement is a clear witness to the indissolubility of marriage: " Now that the Scripture counsels marriage, and allows no release from the union, it is expressly contained in the law, 'Thou shalt not put away thy wife, except for the cause of fornication;' and it regards as fornication, the marriage of those separated while the other is alive."[33] Clement is quite explicit: separation is only permissible by reason of *porneia*, and all subsequent remarriage is excluded as adultery. It is particularly interesting in the light of Quentin Quesnell's interpretation of Mt 19:12 to find that Clement relates this passage to the previous verses about divorce and remarriage. He writes that the Gnostics "do not realize the context of this passage: After his word about divorce some asked him whether, if that is the position in relation to woman, it is better not to marry; and it was then that the Lord said: 'Not all can receive this saying, but those to whom it is granted.' What the questioners wanted to know was whether, when a man's wife has been condemned for fornication, it is allowable for him to marry another."[34] Clement views the Lord as linking those left single by a broken marriage with those who have embraced continence for the kingdom of God. It is assumed by Crouzel that Clement regards all remarriage after divorce as adultery, but Sherlock once again questions this interpretation: "'Those separated' seems to include him 'putting aside his wife,' but what then of those who have put aside an adulteress? Crouzel assumes that 'those separated' includes the man putting aside an adulterous wife - which assumption is unproved. There appears to be some real doubt as to whether or not Clement considers the case of the innocent husband with a repeatedly unfaithful wife."[35]

It is with Origen that we have the first rays of light about Church practice. Since Origen is discussing the Gospel of Matthew allegorically, it is extremely difficult in a brief space to explore the complexities of his argument concerning Mt 19:3-12. Scholars such as Crouzel and Cereti differ considerably about the significance of Origen's discourse in regard to current fourth century practice among Christians. However, it would appear that Origen does give evidence that remarriages were allowed to certain persons:

> But now contrary to what was written, some even of
> the rulers of the church have permitted a woman to

marry, even when her husband was living, doing contrary to what was written, where it is said, "A wife is bound for so long time as her husband liveth," and "So then if while her husband liveth, she shall be joined to another man she shall be called an adulteress," not indeed altogether without reason, for it is probable this concession was permitted in comparison with worse things, contrary to what was from the beginning ordained by law, and written.[36]

Cereti makes the point that Origen witnesses to the practice of remarriage and that if this was permitted to women, it was surely permitted to men. He thinks it likely that some bishops wished to apply to women what was previously granted only to men.[37] The texts of St. Paul had stood in the way since they had been interpreted literally and consequently applied only to women. Origen elsewhere had stated that all remarriage was adultery as long as one's former spouse is alive. Separation from the adulterous spouse is, however, obligatory. We can see in the passage quoted above that Origen felt the conflict between the scriptural absolutes and an accommodation which was worked out on the lesser of evils by spouses abandoned by a partner. Origen held, furthermore, that Moses allowed marriage to be dissolved because of "something unclean" whereas Jesus allows it to be dissolved (the Greek is *dialuein*) only for adultery.[38]

The patristic teaching of the fourth century shows more awareness of the complexities and difficulties which occur in attempting to reconcile the norms of Christian doctrine regarding the indissolubility of marriage with the practical complications arising within the Christian community upon the breakdown of a marriage. The lesser Basil, the bishop of Ancyra, in Galatia provides us with a parallel between the mystical marriage of a virgin with Christ and the marriage of a woman to a man. Just as there is no way the virgin espoused to Christ can be released since Christ is immortal, so the woman who has been dismissed by her husband must not deepen her sin by marrying another. He discusses the case of a man who marries a woman who has been dismissed by her husband. Clearly to marry her is to commit adultery: "But you, before even understanding the fault that has merited her dismissal, and wanting the right to live with her, in an absurd way you render her even more shameless in her sin. In continuing to commit adultery with her as with a stranger, and while her husband still lives, you absurdly stimulate her tendency to sin within her married life."[39] Again, there is nothing about the freedom of a man who dismisses an adulterous wife in order to marry once more.

St. Basil of Caesarea makes a similar point in his *Moralia* that a husband must not separate from his wife nor a wife form her husband unless one of them has been taken in the act of adultery or else one desires to enter the monastic life. We may well ask what happens to the spouse who has been dismissed for adultery or the one left behind when the other enters the monastic life. The answer to the first question is given in Rule 73 where he says that it is not permitted to him who has dismissed his spouse to marry another. Neither is it permitted to a woman who has been dismissed by her husband to marry another man.[40]. The answer to the second question is never given. St. Basil provides us with a somewhat different picture when he reports on the canonical practices in the Church of Cappadocia. As Mackin states, "These canons have been made a kind of primary source of the Eastern churches' marriage law."[41] In Canon 9 Basil insists that men and women be subjected equally to the law of Christ but recognizes that men have often been given a liberty not available to women. What is most important here is the refusal to condemn the abandoned spouse for remarriage. The condemnation for adultery is directed against the spouse who abandoned the other and remarried, the man who married a woman who had been dismissed, and the woman who dismissed her husband and then remarried.

In canon 35 St. Basil expresses his own opinion in the case of a husband who has been abandoned by his wife:

> In the case of a husband who has been deserted by his wife, the reason for the abandonment must be looked into. If it appear that she has departed without a

proportionate cause, the husband is to be deemed to deserve pardon, and she is to deserve a punitive sentence. This pardon shall be given to him for the purpose of enabling him to commune with the Church.[42]

The context of this canon would appear to be that of a second marriage. It makes no sense at all to speak of pardoning the husband unless it is a question of his remarriage. Similarly, Canon 46 gives us further knowledge about the demands made on those who have entered upon a second marriage after being abandoned by a spouse:

A woman who unwittingly marries a man abandoned by his wife for a time and who has afterwards been left by him on account of his former wife's returning, has committed fornication, albeit unwittingly. She shall not, therefore, be denied marriage, though it were better that she remain single.[43]

In Canon 77 Basil gives us a statement of mitigation of penance granted by his local traditions to husbands who have abandoned their wives and remarried:

A man, however, who abandons his legally wedded wife, and marries another woman, according to the Lord's decision, is liable to the judgment of adultery. But it has been ruled and regulated by our Fathers that such persons are to weep for a year, listen on the side for two years, kneel for three years, in the seventh year co-stand together with the faithful, and then be deemed worthy to participate in the offering, provided they repent with remorseful tears."[44]

What is important here is the implicit acceptance of the second marriage. The penance assigned is a condition for returning to communion, not for continuing in the second marriage.

A similar tension about remarriage is clearly evident in St.

Gregory of Nazianzus. His exalted view of marriage is something that we have previously noted. Yet, as the bishop of Constantinople he was requested to assist in obtaining a writ of dismissal for a daughter of the civil governer Verian. Gregory simply states: [It] is simply contrary to our laws, even if the Romans judge the matter otherwise."[45] One may note that Verian was the civil governer. Later Gregory wrote to Verian stating that if he wanted his daughter to be given a writ of dismissal he must find someone else to do it.

St. Gregory of Nyssa made two contributions to the theology of marriage and divorce. He allows the distinction between fornication and adultery on the part of a married man - the former is with an unmarried woman, the latter is with a married woman.[46] Gregory was not lax in his theology of marriage, however. He records how his sister would not marry again after the death of her husband since she was bound to him even beyond death in hope of the resurrection. Apparently he stated this with sympathy and agreement with the position that she had taken.

If we compare the views of Theodore Mopsuestia and St. John Chrysostom we see two traditions in tension and even in conflict with one another. Theodore states that even if a woman is dismissed by her husband and becomes a stranger to him, the spiritual reality of their being one flesh remains even when appearances are contrary.[47] Indeed, the language used here conveys the contrast between the *noumenon* and the *phenomenon*. Since the former is the spiritual reality, a remarriage is impossible after a separation. No matter how alienated the married partners may become, their inner reality is that of being one flesh. St. John Chrysostom, however, states that to try and dissolve a marriage is to act against nature insofar as the husband and wife form one body, and it is against nature to divide them. Yet, having said this, St. John states that a husband must separate himself by dismissal from an adulterous wife, and he concludes that after the wife's fornication her husband is no longer her husband.[48] St. John in his Homily 19 on I Cor 7:1-40 uses the Greek word *dialuein* to indicate the division which has resulted from a marriage which has been dissolved by adultery. He comments:

> Once an unfaithful wife has dishonored and wronged her husband by becoming another man's, and ignoring the duties of marriage, how can she win him back, especially if they remain as strangers to each other? A husband is no longer a husband after such infidelity, but in the other case, even if a wife is not a believer, it does not destroy the husband's marriage rights.[49]

In 398 A.D. St. John Chrysostom delivered three homilies on marriage in which he set the divine law over against the human law. In the second homily he clearly stated that a dismissed wife must not take another husband as long as her first husband should continue to live. Indeed, in the first sermon on marriage St. John urged that a wife with faults be retained but that an adulterous wife be dismissed. This is clearly stated also in *Homily 29 on 1 Corinthians*, which has been delivered in Antioch in 392. The adulterous wife must be dismissed. St. John clearly identified *porneia* with adultery. In a letter to a young widow whose husband had died, Chrysostom urged that they remain united and joined in their love for one another. Though John would not allow the remarriage of a wife dismissed for adultery, he never stated whether the remarriage was possible for the husband who was innocent in the matter. We are left in silence on the question.

In the West St. Ambrose of Milan stood as uncompromising in his belief that since marriage was indissoluble, remarriage of a spouse, even after the dismissal of the guilty party, is only another adultery. St. Ambrose states this in several of his writings, but perhaps the clearest example is to be found in his treatise *On Abraham* where Ambrose writes: "You are forbidden to take another wife as long as your first wife lives."[50] There is clearly no recognition here of any exception in cases of adultery. Exactly the contrary is stated in Ambrosiaster's commentary on 1 Corinthians 7:

> The woman is not permitted to remarry when she has left her husband because of his adultery or aposta-

sy...because the inferior cannot live by the same law as the suprior. But if the husband apostasizes or tries to use his wife perversely, she can neither marry another man nor return to her husband. And a man must not dismiss his wife: but here is understood implicitly "except in case of her fornication." For this reason Paul does not add, as he does when instructing the wife, "If he leaves her, he must remain unmarried." For a husband is allowed to take a second wife when he has dismissed a sinful first wife. For the man is not to be held to the law in the same way as the wife. He is indeed the head of the wife.[51]

A scholarly debate about the significance of this passage has ensued so that Crouzel, on the one hand, finds the passage a solitary exception to the universal norm of the Fathers that no second marriage is permitted to a Christian whose first wife is still alive.[52] On the other hand, Careti accepts the exception as representative of widespread practice, not as a solitary example of dissent. A moderate opinion exists with Mackin who notes that there is no evidence of this statement as an expression of debate on marriage. It is only an opinion of an unknown author who interestingly brings in the excepive clause from Matthew in his discussion of St. Paul's teaching on marriage.[53] The dominant Western opinion regarding divorce and remarriage was formed by St. Jerome and St. Augustine. Both stood solidly against remarriage under any circumstances other than the death of a spouse. The *sacramentum* remained intact despite separation and even hatred, and reconciliation was the only option for a Christian married couple. The development of an alternative opinion and practice was to prevail in the East, forming a major difference and source of potential conflict between the two traditions of the Church. Perhaps the most significant differences were not so much in to be found in a doctrinal debate as in the fact that in the East Roman law remained intact with its fundamental assumption that marriage could be dissolved. The Western experience was radically altered by the barbarian invasions. With the emergence of Augustine as the primary theologian in the Western Church, his opinions were to prevail. Western practice was to be conformed to his views only with the emergence of a canon law enforced by secular authority. Since an effective and unified canon law largely depended upon Roman authority, the suppression of local deviance would be a long and painful undertaking, but one which was ultimately successful. The experience of the Eastern Orthodox Church was essentially different, depending upon its conforming to the direction of a Roman Emperor through all of its life until the fall of Byzantium to the Turks.

Notes

(1) Louis Bouyer, "Réflexions sur le rétablissement possible de la communion entre les Eglises orthodoxe et catholique, Perspectives actuelles," *Istina*, (1975), 2, pp. 112-115.

(2) Henri Crouzel, *L'Eglise primitive face au divorce* (Paris: Beauchesne, 1970).

(3) W. A. Heth and G. J. Wenham, *Jesus and Divorce: Toward an Evangelical Understanding of New Testament Teaching* (London: Hodder and Stoughton, 1984).

(4) Heth and Wenham, p. 47.

(5) Jean Dupont, *Mariage et divorce dans l'évangile: Matthieu 19, 3-12 et paralleles* (Bruges: Désclee, 1959), p. 69.

(6) W. R. Gundry, *Matthew: A Commentary on His Literary and Theological Art* (Grand Rapids: Eerdmans, 1982), p. 20.

(7) W. D. Davies, *The Setting of the Sermon on the Mount* (Cambridge: University Press, 1964), p. 393.

(8) Heth and Wenham, p. 57.

(9) J. J. Kilgallen, "To What Are the Matthean Exception-Texts (5,32 and 19,9) an Exception?" *Biblica* 62 (1980), pp. 102-5.

(10) Theodore Mackin, *Marriage in the Catholic Church: Divorce and Remarriage* (New York: Paulist Press, 1984), pp. 60-1.

(11) Brian Byron, "1 Cor 7:10-15: A Basis for Future Catholic Discipline on Marriage and Divorce?," *Theological Studies* 34, 3 (1973), p. 438.

(12) Ibid., p. 436.

(13) Mackin, p. 66.

(14) Ibid, p. 66.

(15) Lisa Cahill, *Between the Sexes: Foundations for a Christian Ethics of Sexuality* (Philadelphia: Fortress Press, 1985), p. 76.

(16) Dominic Crossan, "Divorce and Remarriage in the New Testament" *The Bond of Marriage: An Ecumenical and Interdisciplinary Study* (Notre Dame: University Press, 1968), pp. 30-3.

(17) J. A. Fitzmyer, "Matthean Divorce Texts," *Theological Studies* 37, 2 (1976), p. 225.

(18) Byron, p. 440.

(19) Ibid., p. 445.

(20) Victor J. Pospishil, *Divorce and Remarriage: Towards a New Catholic Teaching* (New York: Herder and Herder, 1967).

(21) Crouzel, p. 359.

(22) G. Cereti, *Divorzio, Nuove Nozee et Penitenza Nella Chiesa Primitiva* (Bolognia: Edizioni Dehoniane Bologna, 1977).

(23) *The Shepherd of Hermas*, trans. J. M.-F. Marique, in *The Apostolic Fathers, The Fathers of the Church*, 1 (Washington, DC: Catholic University of America, 1947), p. 262.

(24) Ibid., pp. 262-3.

(25) J. Alex Sherlock, "Review of *L'Eglise primitive face au divorce: Du Premier au cinquième siécle* by H. Crouzel," *Theological Studies* 33, 2 (1972), p. 335.

(26) Justin Martyr, *First Apology* 15, trans. C. C. Richardson, in *Early Christian Fathers, Library of Christian Classics*, vol. 1 (Philadelphia: Westminster Press, 1954).

(27) Heth and Wenham, p. 27.

(28) Athanagoras, *A Plea for Christians* 33 in *Legatio and De Resurrectione*, trans. and ed. W. R. Schoedel (Oxford: Oxford University Press), p. 33.

(29) Heth and Wenham, p. 29.

(30) Theophilus, *Ad Autolycum* 3.13, in *Theophiulus of Antioch: Ad Autolycum*, trans. R. M. Grant, (Oxford: Clarendon Press, 1970), p. 119.

(31) Sherlock, p. 336.

(32) Clement of Alexandria, *Stromata* 2, 13, in *Library of The Ante-Nicene Fathers*, ser. 1, vol. 2 (Wm. B. Eerdmans: Grand Rapids, MI, 1977, p. 379.

(33) Clement of Alexandria, "On Marriage," (*Stromateis* 3.5.50), trans. J. E. L. Oulton, and H. Chadwick, in *Alexandrian Christianity*, *The Library of Christian Classics*, vol. 2 (Philadelphia: Westminster Press, 1954), p. 63.

(34) Sherlock, p. 336.

(35) Origen, *Commentary on St. Matthew* 14:23, trans. John Patrick, in *The Library of Ante-Nicene Fathers*, ser. 1, vol. 10 (Grand Rapids, MI: Wm. B. Eerdmans Publishing Co., 1974), p. 510.

(36) Careti, pp. 207-15.

(37) Origen, *Commentary on St. Matthew, 24*, trans. Mackin, p. 140, ftn. 21.

(38) Basil of Ancyra, *On the True Integrity of Virginity*, trans. Mackin, p. 145.

(39) Basil of Caesarea, *The Long Rules*, Rule 73, Ch. 2, in *St. Basil: Ascetical Works*, trans. M. Monica Wagner in *The Fathers of the Church*, 9 (Washington: Catholic University of America, 1950),

p. 189.

(40) Mackin, p. 147.

(41) Basil of Caesarea, Canon 35, *The Rudder (Pedalion)*, p. 818.

(42) Basil of Caesarea, Canon 46, *The Rudder (Pedalion)*, p. 823.

(43) Basil of Caesarea, Canon 77, *The Rudder (Pedalion)*, p. 837.

(44) Gregory of Nazianzus, *Letter 44 to Olympios*.

(45) Gregory of Nyssa, Canon 4, *The Rudder (Pedalion)*, pp. 871-2.

(46) Theodore of Mopsuestia, *Commentary on St. Matthew's Gospel*, quoted by Crouzel, pp. 171-2.

(47) John Chrysostom, *Homily 62 on St. Matthew's Gospel*.

(48) John Chrysostom, *Homily 19 on First Corinthians 7:1-40*, trans. David Anderson in *St. John Chrysostom: On Marriage and Family Life* (Crestwood, NY: St. Vladimir's Seminary Press, 1985), p. 32.

(49) Ambrose of Milan, *On Abraham*, 1, 7, trans. Mackin, p. 160.

(50) Ambrosiaster, *Commentary on 1 Corinthians*, trans. Mackin, p. 160.

(51) Crouzel, pp. 267-74.

(52) Mackin, pp. 161-2.

Chapter Six:

Divorce and Remarriage in Orthodox Practice

Many Fathers often contrasted God's law with man's law, St. John Chrysostom being a notable example.[1] A second marriage was considered to be a violation of God's law and indeed adulterous. They firmly rejected a double standard for men and women, as was reflected in Roman law which allowed a husband to have extra-marital affairs which were not considered to be adulterous as long as they were with unmarried women. But what is especially surprising and even shocking to modern Roman Catholics, notes Mackin, is the fact that the Christian spouse was not required to give up a spouse taken in a second marriage. Only with Jerome and Augustine do we see the rigorist position beginning to emerge which will deny the possibility of forgiveness to persons in second marriages while the first wife is living.[2] Mackin notes one text that clearly prescribes a kind of penance for the husband who has dismissed his unfaithful wife. That is the 23rd canon as attributed to St. Gregory the Illuminator, the apostle of Armenia, and dating from perhaps 365 A.D.: "A husband is permitted to dismiss his wife by reason of her adultery, but he must abstain from the marriage bed a year after doing so."[3]

We have already examined the canons of St. Basil the Great for what they show us regarding the Church's practice of divorce and remarriage. However, the older canons are those that are now called "Apostolic" - though scholars assure us that they do not actually date to the time of the Apostles. Canon 48 from the Apostolic Canons reads: "If any layman who has divorced his wife takes another, or one divorced by another man, let him be excommunicated."[4] Many of those interpreting this canon do so on the basis of later assumptions, often making the obvious exception for adultery, but as the canon stands there are no qualifications. The statement is as bold and direct as can be. Nevertheless, the interpretation that was given this canon in later Byzantine canon law provided a proviso "unless for reasons foreseen by the law (*ton nenomothetemenon aition*)."

Canon 8 of the first ecumenical council of Nicaea tells us a great deal about the practice of fourth-century Christians regarding marriage and divorce. The canon refers to the requirements for readmission into the Catholic Church of the Novatianists. Why this canon is so important for our purpose is that the Novatianists were required to receive Holy Communion with those twice-married persons who had carried out their penance and had been restored to communion with the Church. We may ask who the twice-married (the *digamoi*) were. The term *digamoi* was used in Christian writings in the late second and third centuries. It usually referred to persons living in a second marriage, whether men or women, after their spouse had died, or those remarrying after dismissing a spouse either without just cause or on the part of men after dismissing an adulterous wife. It had been stated in the *Apostolic Constitutions* that *digamoi* could not be clerics, though Hippolytus of Rome criticized Pope Callistus for allowing this. It is true that some critics claim that the *digamoi* consisted only of those who remarried after the death of a spouse. The objection against this view is that the followers of Novatian had never objected to the practice of remarriage after the death of a spouse. The battle which ensued in the third century between rigorists and Catholics was over the forgiveness of such grave sins as fornication and adultery. The Novatianists and the Montanists thought forgiveness of such sins impossible after baptism. St. Cyprian of Carthage began his episcopal career as a rigorist but changed his mind after the Novatianists infiltrated his community. By the middle of the third century, despite the protests of Tertullian, Hippolytus, and Novatian, adultery was being forgiven after due penance. For us the central question becomes one of asking whether a repentant but remarried Christian could remain withinh his or her marriage. The modern Roman Catholic assumption would be that the second marriage must be abandoned, but this proves not always to have been so in the early Church. First, we must realize that there was no concept of marriage maintaining the existence of the bond apart from the relationship of the married couple. Both law and custom were lacking which might sustain such a fiction. Mackin argues that early Christians recognized that it was gravely sinful to destroy a marriage, but, he says, "they took for granted that what was forbidden could be done, that they could annihilate their marriages."[5] The bishops did not insist that the second marriage be abandoned. What was sinful was the destruction of the first marriage, not continuation in the second. There is no evidence that penitents were required to return to the former marriage. In fact, the Church accepted as normative the Deuteronomic law requiring wives to be dismissed for adultery. They were not to be taken back. There is evidence of this from Origen's *Commentary of St. Matthew* (XIV:2), Basil's Canon 9 (for Amphylochius), Jerome's *Letter to Amanda*, and Cyril of Alexandria's essay "On Adoration and Worship in Spirit and in Truth." Only Augustine held the contrary position.

The later canonical tradition of the Eastern Church became quite explicit about Christians remarried after divorce. We can set forth examples of this awareness: the Council of Neocaesarea in Cappadocia (held between A.D. 314 and 325) in its Canon 3 stated: "As for those who have married more than once, the period established (for their penance) is known, although their conduct and their fidelity may shorten in time."[6] Canon 7 stated: "Priests are not to take part in the nuptial banquets of those marrying for the second time. For if a man who has remarried later asks to do penance what will a priest say who has already consented to his marriage by taking part in the wedding feast."[7] The Council of Laodicea (meeting between A.D. 343 and 380) decreed in Canon 1:

"In conformity with ecclesiastical law we have decreed that communion must be given with forgiveness to those who entered legally and freely into a second marriage (without having contracted a clandestine marriage), but after an established period and once they have given themselves to prayer and fasting."[8]

It is in the canons of the Quinisext Council (*in Trullo*) that we encounter the classical norm of the Orthodox Catholic Church regarding divorce and remarriage. This council (A.D. 692) was known to Byzantine writers as the "Sixth Council" because, as John Meyendorff has put it, "its entire canonical corpus was given post factum an 'ecumenical' status in being procedurally attributed to the ecumenical councils of 553 and 680 - - 102 canons."[9] It is true that the council took place long after the legislation of Justinian, but that legislation does not appear in the content of the canons of 692. Canon 87 from the 102 canons is concerned with divorce and remarriage and is composed of three canons from St. Basil the Great. It imposed penances for those women who leave their husbands without good reason but imposed none on the husband. The husband who abandons his lawful wife and takes another is placed under penance as having committed adultery, but after seven years may be restored to the company of the faithful. It is not stated whether a man who takes another wife must give her up during and after the execution of the penance. From the same council we have a canon (93) stating that a woman who cohabits with another man after her husband has departed and vanished is committing adultery. Yet when it is a case of husbands who have been soldiers, "there is room for condoning their conduct because there is more suspicion of death."[10] Since the soldier might return, he may reclaim his wife even if she has married another. The significance of the canonical legislation of the Quinisext Council is summarized by R. C. Gerest: "The right to remarry was not denied to the husband victimized by adultery or abandoned for no reason, according to Origen, Lactantius, Basil, or Chrysostom. They interpret Matthew's famous interpolation as support for this concession and like adultery or the death of a spouse. That opinion becomes canonized in

214

the East by the Council at Trullo in 692."[11] Even in the West the rigid position defended by Jerome and Augustine was not established as definitive until the ninth century. Jerome could say: "A husband may be an adulterer or a sodomite, he may be stained with every crime and may have been left by his wife because of his sins, yet he is still her husband, and, so long as he lives, she may not marry another."[12] This viewpoint remained only an opinion, however. The differing stand taken by Ambrosiaster confirms this fact.

The close relation between Church and state which existed in Byzantium was to be of profound significance in the formulation of marital practice and the possibility of remarriage after divorce in the Eastern Church. This was particularly the result of the legislation of the Emperor Justinian I. He was particularly eager to provide new legislation for marriage which he did in his new codex of law issued in 535 A.D. To the provisions of the previous laws created by Theodosius and Anastasius, Justinian added new grounds for divorce: the wife's procuring of an abortion, bathing in common with men for lascivious purposes, and attempting marriage to another man. In addition, the husband was allowed to choose "a solitary life" and a wife to choose "monastic practice." The choice of monastic life was treated as the equivalent of death. Theodosius had allowed divorce for adultery, homicide, the practice of medicine and burial violation. These had been retained from the laws of Constantine I, and to them were added the grounds of either husband or wife plotting against the empire or kidnaping. Wives were permitted to divorce their husbands if the husbands rustled cattle, or were guilty of counterfeiting, robbing or receiving robbers. Criminal acts were included, such as for a husband to beat his wife if she was a freewoman. A husband could divorce a wife who struck him. The assumption of adultery was made in the case of a wife who frequented the theatre, circus, or arena against her husband's wish. The emperor Anastasius had allowed divorce: "if a libel of repudiation was given with mutual consent, the wife did not have to wait five years, she could pass to a second marriage after a year's wait."[13]

Justinian's legislation on marriage in Novel 22 became the most important in the history of Byzantine civilization. Justinian, who was trained as a theologian, sought to provide a Christian basis for his law since by 535 the majority of his citizens were Christians. In this legislation two basic assertions are made: one that mutual affection makes marriage, the other that marriage can be dissolved, with or without penalty. Indeed, he states: "for, of those things which occur among men, whatever is bound is soluble" (n.22.3). It was on the basis of marriage as soluble that Justinian was to erect his entire juridical edifice. Justinian affirms four ways in which dissolution is effected during the life of the marriage partners: by the consent of both; for rational ground which is called "good grace;" without cause; and with rational cause, which is not good grace. Nothing is said of the first, for the partners would arrange that as it pleased them. The divorce for rational cause followed what Justinian had already provided in his previous legislation. The woman was refused marriage rights and the man was granted them immediately. This was, according to Noonan, because the law assumed the man would be incontinent and would have intercourse whether married or not. Thus immediate remarriage after marital dissolution was discouraged and it was stated that not to marry was a blessed and happy decision. Yet remarriage was allowed, as all Roman law assumed it, if a divorce was granted. However, the admonition to refrain from another marriage was based on the property rights of the children, not, as Noonan says, "because of its severing of a natural or indissoluble bond."[14]

Additional legislation was implemented in 542 A.D. with Novel 117 which tightened up the good grace clauses . Impotence was ruled as a cause of divorce only if present from the beginning of a marriage. Divorce to provide for entry into religious life was stated to require the assent of the other marriage partner. Consensual divorce was limited to entry into the life of perpetual chastity. There was, indeed, an increase penalty for unjustified divorce, and severe penalties were set forth so that a woman lost her dowry, with two-thirds of her property going to the children and one-third to a monastery if a woman divorced without cause. Indeed, Novel 117 set forth the procedures whereby a husband might legitimately kill an adulteress. It was only in 548 A.D. that equal penalties were provided for men and women. Adultery as a cause for divorce was not to be an easy way to another marriage. The woman, if convicted, was to be beaten and placed in a monastery. Her husband had two years in which he might allow her return. If this did not occur, she had to receive the monastic habit, and apparently the husband was then free to marry once more. This was reversed, however, by Justinian's successor, Justin II, who claimed that many had sought a change in the law.

Justinian's marriage legislation affirmed that marriage was dissoluble. The reasons were manifold. Some have claimed that the intention was to take account of the religious pluralism existing within the Roman Empire, but John Noonan thinks that this explanation does not stand up. It goes contrary to the explicit Christian purposes adopted by Justinian. Moreover, the law concerning remarriage was used to discourage some divorces and to allow others. Sanctions against non-Christians were enacted under both Theodosius II and Justinian. The key to Justinian's legislation would appear to lie in comparable legislation regarding slavery, the theatre, and prostitution. All were subject to Christian disapproval, but laws were made to govern them, nonetheless. As to prostitution, we discover that laws were in existence to protect Christian women from being sold into brothels. No one accepted prostitution as a good, and the laws set forth were not part of a legislation designed to distinguish between good and evil prostitution. The law stated that acting on the stage was indecent but necessary. It even went so far as to conclude that persons who were actors on the stage were not capable of being Christians or receiving the sacraments. Once a woman had been separated from the stage she could never go back, and if she did, she could not receive absolution. Slavery was accepted by Christian theologians, and hundreds of laws existed to regulate it. This does not mean that we may consider slavery as moral today - few do - but it means that from a certain "other-worldly" perspective Christians in the sixth century accepted it as a social condition.

Many Roman Catholic scholars wonder how the Church could have accepted the code of Justinian. The Jesuit G. W. Joyce went so far as to contend that the Church in the Eastern Empire capitulated before the pagan laws of the state.[15] John Noonan decidedly rejected this view. His position is that Christians "in good faith could believe that marriage was dissoluble or indissoluble without anyone's calling his opponent a heretic."[16] He states, furthermore, that whatever evidence of Christian belief might be afforded by the law is of an ideal character. The law applied only to the upper classes in any case. We have no knowledge of the extent to which the provisions can be taken as descriptive of the practices of the common people. All we may discern is that the emperors and their administrations had "no principle which existed to prohibit divorce and remarriage."[17] Noonan thinks one can make a case that Justinian's laws reflected a tendency to move against divorce. Grounds for divorce were restricted to cases where "juridical fiction would assimilate to death and to cases, such as plotting against the empire, where death would be the penalty if the grounds were criminally proved."[18] Adultery remained grounds for divorce, but adultery itself did not dissolve the marriage. The way out of the impasse was through monastic profession which was required of an adulterous woman if not reconciled to her husband after being put away for two years. By the time of the last legislation, in Novel 556, divorce by consent was permitted, for certain grave crimes, and then for monastic profession. Again, as Noonan insists, Justinian's own positions are based on his belief that marriage could be dissolved.

What is the significance of this legislation on divorce by Christian emperors? Mackin thinks it part of the Caesaro-Papism which prevailed during the reign of Justinian. His is close to Joyce's view, but Mackin is more nuanced since he recognizes that in the East all jurisdiction lay in the hands of the empire, and the Church and the empire were so intimately linked in the minds of emperors such as Theodosius and Justinian that no one even entertained the possibility of separate ecclesiastical courts. Only when the empire crumbled did the bishops begin to exercise any jurisdiction over divorce and remarriage, and that was to be the pattern in the West, not in the East.[19]

Joyce, writing before the days of Roman Catholic ecumenism, suggests that the very nature of the Greek schism lay in this abandonment of the norms of Christ for the laws of the emperors. For Joyce it is a simple case of the popes standing for Christ's position on divorce and remarriage and the Eastern Church surrendering to secular and ultimately pagan norms. Furthermore, he claims that the Church "long refrained from giving canonical approval to the system prescribed by Justinian."[20] Joyce attempts to estimate the Church's "measure of protest in the face of this glaring violation of Christian law" - particularly the return of divorce by mutual consent under Justin II.[21] He points to the Trullan Council of 692 as manifesting a weak effort at restoration of Church discipline. However, the canon of this council only repeat the canons of St. Basil, allowing the husband whose wife is caught in adultery not to be debarred from communion. Joyce notes that the canon does not refer to a remarriage but that it may be presumed. Joyce also calls our attention to the Patriarch St. Tarasius who opposed the Emperor Constantine VI in 795 in his attempt to marry Theodota after having put his previous wife into a monastery.[22]

The legislation of the Isaurian Emperors of the eighth century attempted to restrict divorce so that by 740 divorce by consent was removed from the law. Joyce claims that this new legislation was ignored so that Leo IV and his son Constantine VI had to issue a new law to prohibit divorce by mutual consent. The eventual victory of Justinian's legislation as amended by Leo meant that the Eastern Orthodox Church accepted the legal norms of the Byzantine State rather than adhering to the norms of strict indissolubility. The fact remains that the exception for divorce by reason of adultery has been a tradition within Eastern Christianity from at least the fourth century. The present discipline of the Orthodox Church dates back to the Council of Constantinople held in 920 A.D. It was called under Patriarch Nicholas the Mystic and recognized without canonical punishment second marriages concluded with the blessing of the Church, canonical sanction for third marriages, and the absolute interdiction of fourth marriages. The canonical sanction of divorce was finally given by Patriarch Alexius (whose time as Patriarch was from 1025 to 1043 A.D.). This extends to allowing a priest to bless the marriage of a divorced woman, where the husband's conduct gave cause for divorce. Those women who were victims of their husbands' evil conduct were allowed new marriages without blame for them or for the officiating priest. No man may marry a woman divorced for adultery, and no priest may bless the second marriage of those who have procured a divorce by mutual consent. If he does this, he must be deposed. Further grounds for divorce were granted, including not only madness but abortion, prenuptial unchastity on the part of the wife, unnatural vice on the part of the husband, implacable hatred on both sides, and apostasy from the Christian faith or entry into heresy. Joyce notes that since the fall of Constantinople in 1453 A.D. even wider grounds have been given for divorce and remarriage in the Greek Church. These grounds include (1) a serious malady on the part of the partners; (2) complete incompatibility of temper; (3) desertion of one partner by the other for a period of three years or even less; (4) the commission of a crime by one of the partners; followed by a sentence involving disgrace; and (5) mutual consent in special cases approved by the Patriarch.

It is curious that two students of Eastern Orthodox marital discipline should come to such different conclusions as do the Jesuit G. H. Joyce and the Orthodox priest and canonist Jerome Kotsonis. Joyce writes:

> It is perfectly plain that in the Greek Church marriage has completely lost that character of indissolubility which, according to our Lord's express teaching, belongs to it by a divine law, and which the fathers and the councils regarded as an essential property of marriage within the Church of Christ. To all intents and purposes it is dissoluble at will. We have here a signal illustration of the truth that unless the law of

indissolubility is maintained in all its strictness, it will be swept away altogether.[23]

This may be contrasted with the opinion of Fr. Jerome Kotsonis:

> The Orthodox Church, distinguishing between law and ethics, indeed teaches the indissolubility of marriage and looks adversely upon any act of separation. But, condescending to human weakness, and basing itself upon our Lord's words about the exception which allows the possibility of dissolving a marriage when it is in reality already broken, the Church confines itself to simply confirming a fact. That the Orthodox Church has never reconciled itself to the position of the state on the dissolution of marriage is demonstrated by the fact that even civil legislation from the ninth century onward has gradually demanded certain conditions for divorce before the dissolution of the marriage is recognized.[24]

One may wonder how these two statements can be reconciled in view of the fact that Kotsonis and Joyce give essentially the same grounds for which the Greek Church allowed divorce and remarriage. The core of the difference lies, I would suggest, in Joyce's view that the bond of marriage continues to exist even when the partners are totally alienated from one another. It is the extension of the dissolution of a marriage by death to the death of a marriage by adultery which provides the inner logic of this development. Later other forms of the "death of a marriage" were permitted as grounds for a second marriage. Bishop Peter L'Huillier makes the same point:

> Clearly the Church deplores divorce, and it is the role of pastors to dissuade couples as much as possible from the recourse to divorce. But once the conjugal union has been broken and this rupture has been legally ratified, it is difficult to pretend that the marriage

continues to subsist in the abstract. Such an affirmation does not even withstand a serious philosophical analysis of the notion of bond, as was recently shown by Ladislas Orsy.[25]

This paradox is stated most boldly by Alexander Schmemann in his brief article, "The Indissolubility of Marriage: The Theological Tradition of the East":

On the one hand, the Orthodox Church explicitly affirms the indissolubility of marriage; yet, on the other hand, she seems to accept divorce and has in her canonical tradition several regulations concerning it. How can these apparently contradictory positions be reconciled? And, first of all, what does this paradox mean? Is it an uneasy compromise between the maximalism of theory and the minimalism of practice, that famous "economy" which the Orthodox seem to invoke so often in order to solve all kinds of difficulties?[26]

Schmemann notes that Orthodox theology, canon law, and liturgy have never taken on a consistent and systematic character. This does not mean that there is no Orthodox teaching, but rather that it has been given no "juridical" formulation. Insofar as marriage is a sacrament, it is a transformation from the old to the new age initiated by Christ. As a sacrament marriage is indissoluble since it is a sign of the Kingdom of God for whom a man and a woman are crowned in matrimony.

Divorce and remarriage belong to human weakness and failure. The liturgical expression of a second marriage in the Orthodox Church is that of a penitential service. Many scholars have recognized that the context of the sayings of Jesus on marriage and divorce lies in the eschatological character of the Sermon on the Mount. They have also urged that the exceptions to this absolute demand lie in the pastoral problems of a community not yet fully integrated into the eschatological Kingdom of God. So Schmemann affirms that there is not only the *theoria* or vision of marriage as belonging to the "early, maximalistic and eschatological period of the Church," but also a "second dimension" which "is the fruit and the result of the long and painful pilgrimage of the Church through history."[27] He explicates this paradox in a most interesting fashion:

> The whole point therefore is that this is not a "compromise" but the very antinomy of the Church's life in this world. The marriage *is* indissoluble, yet it *is* being dissolved all the time by sin and ignorance, passion and selfishness, lack of faith and lack of love. Yes, the Church acknowledges the divorcer, but she *does not divorce*. She only acknowledge that here, in this concrete situation, this marriage has been broken, has come to an end, and in her compassion she gives permission to the innocent party to marry again. It is sufficient, however, to study only once the text of the rite of the second marriage to realize immediately the radical difference of its whole "ethos." It is indeed a penitential service, it is intercession, it is love, but nothing of the glory and joy of that which has been broken remains.[28]

Fr. Alexander admits that the Church by reason of her organic connection with Christian states, has had to accept many functions and duties alien to her nature. Nevertheless, the tension that exists between marriage as indissoluble and the realities of human frailty and ambiguity must be lived out. Here is the source of the paradox that Joyce found so incomprehensible. For him the law of Christ was simply an absolute law to be obeyed under all circumstances. For Schmemann the law of Christ is the ideal of the Kingdom to be kept through grace but often broken by human sin. The Church allows a second marriage out of mercy and for the salvation of the man or woman whose first marriage has died. Schmemann speaks of the "condescending" of the Church "to the unfathomable tragedies of human existence."[29]

A similar but even stronger protest against the abuses that

have crept into Orthodox practice is set forth by Father Elie
Melia, a priest in the Greek Orthodox tradition.   Fr. Elie
thinks that the Church ought not to celebrate second marriages except in the case of the innocent victim of an adulterous spouse and then only by using the penitential service.
Indeed, he takes a very strong stand: "But once a union in
fact is established in a durable fashion (as so evaluated),
rather than having recourse to the formal canonical fiction of
the dissolution of the marriage legitimately celebrated by her,
it would be better that the Church open the way for Holy
Communion, employing the canonically sanctioned penance,
all the while granting no sacramental guarantee to a matrimonial bond contracted in these conditions where she will have
taken no part."[30]   Divorce is not religious and has no place in
the Church which is one and holy. The grounds on which the
Church may tolerate divorce are found in the fundamental fact
that the Kingdom of God has come yet is not fully realized in
this world. As he puts it: "The Christian does not sit between
two chairs: he is not neutral but oriented, a citizen of heaven,
despite his weaknesses and falls, an eschatological man,
prophet and martyr."[31]   Melia invokes the principle of
economy at this point, noting that economy takes two forms:
the pastoral and the canonical. The former implies concretely
the non-application of disciplinary sanctions for an infraction
of the law. Melia gives as an example the readmission to
Holy Communion after grave sin and the imposition of a
penance, "even in the case where a valid obstacle has not yet
been lifted, but not in view of a slight of hand removing the
obstacle but from a certain medicinal relaxation in the effort
or again, in order to provoke a responsive shock."[32] Pastoral economy would take into account the milieu in which
Christian people live today, surrounded by erotic propaganda,
urbanization, uprootedness and a culture at odds with the
values of the faith.   Fr. Elie cautions against indulgence as a
norm. The pastor must insist upon "greatness of man rather
than on his weakness." He is aware that economy has never
been formally explicated and cautions us that his approach is
personal, especially its terminology. Having stated this,
however, he thinks that "the principle of economy witnesses

to an experience lived by all of Christianity, with a wisdom which it does not pretend to be the only one possible in this area but which has the advantage of presenting an attempt at a solution if not to the problem of divorce, at least to that of divorced persons."[33]

Two episcopal voices may be heard in their witness to Eastern Orthodox teaching on divorce and remarriage. Peter L'Huillier claims that while "Jesus clearly teaches that marriage should not be dissolved, he does not say that it cannot be."[34] Bishop Peter rejects outright the placing of divorce entirely within the sphere of economy.[35] His explanation is stated thus: "On the contrary, in declaring 'Let not man separate what God has united' (Mt 19:6 and Mk 10:5), he shows that this eventuality, which assuredly constitutes on the part of man a transgression of the divine will, is not impossible."[36] In a similar fashion, the Greek Bishop Athenagoras Kokkinakis spells out the moral and spiritual grounds which may destroy a marriage. He refers to *fornicatio spiritualis* which incites to evil deeds as do heresy and apostasy. Mutual trust, love and faith may be broken by conjugal infidelity. Thus the marriage may be destroyed by sin just as the marriage is dissolved by death.[37] What we find quite extraordinary is Bishop Athanagoras' espousal (in 1958) of the view that a second marriage after the failure of the first marriage may be accepted as the lesser of evils:

> Would it be better to leave souls of innocent children, as often occurs in such cases, exposed to an environment of life with immorality, psychological dangers, perverted manifestations of living, and thus to contribute to their moral laxness and lurking criminality; or would it be preferable to safeguard these tender souls from the consuming flame of parental failure? The truth is that there is no alternative, except choosing the lesser evil. And in the case of broken families the lesser evil is divorce, which the Church, following the example of Moses, grants, not easily and gladly, but hesitantly and sorrowfully, to those who because of "the hardness" of their hearts, feel unable to continue

living their married life "in two bodies as in one."[38]

Bishop Athanagoras rejects the idea that the Orthodox Church is wrong in allowing divorce and remarriage. A certain laxity, which needs correction, may be present in its practice. Yet the system of the Roman Church, whereby annulments are easy and frequent, is, he claims, no better than the Orthodox practice. Rome simply denies the reality of the first marriage and the sin that brought about its demise. Legalism is made to prevail in the Roman system rather than mercy and a willingness to grant a second marriage as the lesser of evils.

We can enumerate four fundamental reasons for which divorce and remarriage have been justified by Orthodox theologians: (1) the tension between the ideals of the Kingdom of God and the fallen condition of our present life in history, (2) mercy extended by economy for saving the person or persons who have failed in their first marriage, (3) the non-existence of the first marriage which had been bestowed upon an Orthodox Christian couple by the Church but which has disintegrated, (4) divorce and remarriage as the lesser of evils under the circumstances. It should be obvious that these four reasons (quite distinct from divorce itself, which can be distinguished as divorce *cum damno*, by reason of sin, and divorce *bona gratia*, not by reason of sin) are distinct, although they may overlap. Economy may be exercised, for example, so that a lesser evil may be lived out when persons approach the Church for remarriage after a broken marriage. The invocation of economy as a solution to every canonical difficulty must be regarded as spurious at best, however, and it may be a connivance with evil in some instances. We must remember what Georges Florovsky had to say on the topic. The "economical" interpretation of the canons might be convincing and probable only in the presence of direct and perfectly clear proofs, whereas it is customarily supported by indirect data and most of all by indirect intentions and conclusions. The "economical" interpretation is not the teaching of the church. It is only a private "theological opinion," very late and very controversial, having arisen in a period of theological confusion and decadence in a hasty endeavour to dis associate oneself as sharply as possible from Roman theology.[39].Florovsky's opinion is confirmed by the multitude of conflicting opinions presented by Orthodox writers on the nature of economy.[40] There are those who would prefer a strict application of the doctrine of indissolubility within Orthodox practice. It is correct that the Church has no business granting divorces, and in fact, it does not do so. When, due to the union of Church and state, it has involved itself in divorces, it has officially only certified that a marriage has broken down. As Bishop Peter L'Huillier has said: "The ecclesiastical procedure is quite simple. It consists in identifying the applicant, the religious status of the previous marriage, and the legal proof of the civil divorce."[41] This does not grant a right to another marriage, and permission must be granted by the bishop before such a marriage can be bestowed. Bishop Peter asks whether the gap between the professed doctrine of the Church and actual practices may not be "somewhat old-fashioned." His answer is that from a strict point of view this may be true, but, he responds, "reality is more complex: In the first place, the Orthodox Church must proclaim the holiness and the unity of marriage between Christians; in the second place, the Church does not think that, in the domain of marriage as in many others, it is necessary to systematically exclude compassion, as long as this pastoral tendency does not lead to official laxity."[42]Similar grounds for divorce and remarriage have been set forth by various contemporary Roman Catholic moral theologians. In 1973 Bernard Häring wrote an article which undertook a critique of the Roman system of marriage tribunals and nullifications.[43] In fact, Häring sought a rapprochement with the Orthodox Churches on the question of divorce and remarriage.

In his theological study of marriage Häring prefers the model of covenant over that of contract. A contract may be made between two families for a marriage that may benefit them both, but a sacramental covenant reflects the union between Christ and his Church. If one's concern is to determine the validity of a marriage by examining it as a contract, marriage tribunals concerned with juridical evidence will take priority, but if one's concern is with the visibility of the presence of Christ in a marriage then the concern of the Church will be redemption from infidelity by forgiveness and reconciliation. His conclusion is that no marriage should be declared null and void if it has any hope of working out as a salvific sign and event. Häring would extend the notion of consummation so that not a merely physical act is involved but a sign and realization of mutual love and respect becomes evident in the spiritual and physical union of the couple.

Häring notes that we are no longer living in the age of paternalism but in an age where we are called to mature responsibility. The presumption should be, he thinks, in favor of a marriage where the partners seek ratification for their marriage by the Church and have a deep sense that the first marriage was invalid since it has had not the slightest sign of hope for stability. This is a moral certainty on the part of a couple. To treat that couple to a tutiorism which made the norm an absolute *favor juris* (an absolute presumption of the law) is to betray that moral certainty and make the couple subject to a humiliating paternalism and externalism. The tribunal seeks to be absolutely sure that there are not two marriage contracts, both of which "could perhaps have the character of contract-sacrament."[44] Häring would propose adopting the principle of probabalism in this matter, allowing one to act on a solid doubt against the law at hand. At this point he is clearly within the Latin tradition of moral theology and moving far from Orthodox thinking. However, in his final paragraphs, Häring approaches the possibility of adopting the position of the Eastern Orthodox tradition since it is not concerned with questions of validity but with the reality or non-reality of a particular marriage. Häring notes that the Eastern tradition does not favor a second marriage, even after the death of a spouse. The command "What God has joined together man must not separate" is interpreted as forbidding a separation because it means a real death of the marriage. The call of the Orthodox tradition is to forgiveness and reconciliation, not the declaration that a marriage has never existed because of the alleged invalidity of the sacrament. Even if a marriage is hopelessly dead, the spouse is urged to choose celibacy for the kingdom of God. Yet, he claims, the scripture (cf. 1 Tm 5: 14) would suggest a marriage rather than the danger of burning with wrongful desires or even adultery. Where a spouse is deserted the Orthodox have allowed economy, which Häring compares with *epikeia* in the Western moral theological tradition. He makes the rather bold initiative of urging the reintegration of the Orthodox tradition of divorce and remarriage into the Latin Church. This would reverse the *favor juris*, always assuming the validity of the previous marriage. He writes: "While there is no exception about the norm of saving a marriage as long as it can be saved, the Orthodox spirituality and practice allow exceptions after the total 'death' of a marriage, in view of God's economy of salvation and in trust in God's mercy."[45] The reason for this suggestion is not in order to deny the indissolubility of a sacramental marriage but, rather, to allow the principle of economy to be exercised for the good of the person.

Another Roman Catholic witness to the authenticity and evangelical necessity of taking the Orthodox stand regarding divorce and remarriage is J. P. Jossua, a French Dominican theologian. After upholding indissolubility as a demand and a sign, Jossua embraces the view of Fr. Moingt: "Christ does not say that man has not the power to destroy the bond forged by God; he says that man has not the right to separate the couple united by God...Man *should* not undo what God has built, but that does not prevent its being undone in fact.[46] Jossua explicitly invokes the Orthodox approach to divorce and remarriage:

> The councils of the fifth and sixth centuries thought marriage to be dissolved by persistent adultery, which destroyed the community of rights and duties between the spouses. Furthermore, plenty of testimony is available that re-marriage, without being a right or appearing fully legitimate, was tolerated for the "innocent" party in cases where dismissal was allowed. Admittedly, this toleration which is continued in Orthodox Christianity seems to have appeared only

about the second century; but the same is true of quite a few other things (the sacrament of penance, re-marriage after a partner's death) - and the celebrated "pauline privilege" came in at a much later date.[47]

Jossua also advocates taking the notion of economy as a point of departure. In reply to those who would consider such changes as an apostasy and a diminishment of the standards of Christ, Jossua states clearly and firmly that "the present state of affairs is intolerable, that tradition gives us the authority to extricate ourselves from it and that canonical solutions, be they good or abominable, will never allow us to do so." Indeed, he says, "the Holy Spirit is urging us, not to lower our standards, but to place them on the truly human level which is that of the mercy of Jesus Christ."[48]

In conclusion, the move to integrate Orthodox practice regarding divorce and remarriage into the Latin Church has not only been a bold initiative on the part of Häring and Jossua but stands as a significant ecumenical gesture. The differences in theory and practice which have emerged between the Eastern and Western Churches have stood as obstacles in their *rapprochement*. In the face of criticisms such as Joyce's, Orthodox have sometimes felt apologetic in their seeming abandonment of patristic principles regarding divorce and remarriage. In fact, the initiative of Häring is a recognition of the profoundly Christian character of the Orthodox exercise of economy in regard to those whose lives have been damaged by marriages which have failed through no fault of their own. The Orthodox approach to divorce and remarriage cannot be put down to Caesaro-papism or the abandonment of the evangelical teaching of the Lord about remarriage as adultery. Indissolubility is not a legal absolute but a note of marriage as a sharing in the grace of the kingdom of God and the union of Christ and his Church. The absolute moral norm demands two things: (1) the married couple must not allow their marriage to die, and (2) they must do everything they can to resuscitate it if it appears to be dying. The second marriage must not be made easy or be made available without awareness of the consequences for the entire community. No one can decide for the partners in a failed marriage that the marriage has died. Only the spouses can determine this. On this delicate issue the Jesuit Richard McCormick has written:

> When marriage is truly dead, then it seems meaning-less to speak of the moral ought of not letting the marriage die. If indissolubility is conceived in highly juridical fashion, the unbreakable *vinculum* continues and subsequent remarriage is in violation of this *vinculum*, is an objective state of sin, must not be allowed, etc. If, however, indissolubility is viewed as an obligation, an ought on the couple, the obligation continues to urge resuscitation of the relationship as long as this is possible.[49]

We have a testimony here from the outstanding Roman Catholic moral theologian in the United States that marriage can be recognized as indissoluble without that involving a refusal to accept the fact that marriages can and do die. McCormick certainly espouses the possibility of the second marriage when a first marriage has definitively died.

One of the issues at stake in the discussion regarding divorce and remarriage is whether there are any norms which admit of no exception. Latin moral theology has traditionally claimed that the natural law makes certain norms exceptionless, including the prohibition of masturbation and contraception. Certain other norms were exceptionless because of revelation, remarriage after a valid sacramental marriage being always impossible. What the new moral theology of the Catholic proportionalists has urged is that exceptionless norms are not nearly so many as once believed to be. They are either exhortative and have within them the negative judgment (such as murder is always wrong but not necessarily all killing, murder being the form of killing which is always wrong and thus to be rejected from its very nature), or they are intrinsically evil insofar as the malice is always present to such a degree that no good consequences are conceivable and no circumstances possible to allow the deed to become right. An example of this would be genocide, torture, or slavery. What

231

an increasing number of Roman Catholic moral theologians are arguing is that even if divorce is a premoral evil, it may not be a moral evil if it is the lesser of evils. Equally one may assert that remarriage after divorce may be the lesser of evils if promiscuity or financial ruin would result from remaining single. When a marriage is destroyed, a person may not be able to bear the burden of isolation, economic deprivation, or sexual starvation. The principle of acting on the lesser of evils has often been taken by Roman Catholic revisionists as not only legitimating actions that of themselves would be taken to be evil but as having no moral evil about them whatsoever.

The Orthodox moral theologian would not so quickly absolve the person choosing what is now a lesser evil from all moral responsibility and sin. The liturgical text for a second marriage in Orthodoxy is a penitential service, not the proclamation of joy as was the first marriage. Nonetheless, the principle of choosing the lesser of evils in circumstances where not to do so would necessarily bring much greater evils is, we believe, one that Orthodox have sometimes applied in the case of divorce and remarriage. This principle is that which Catholic proportionalist moral theologians have used for allowing masturbation for adolescents, sexual coupling for homosexuals who cannot live a chaste and celibate life, and abortion in cases where the mother would die if the abortion were not to be carried out. Similarly, a host of Catholic revisionist moral theologians have built their rationale for contraception on this basis as did the entire French Catholic hierarchy after the appearance of *Humanae Vitae*. Such evils would include economic ruin for the family if another child were to be added, the possible destruction of the health of a weak and sick woman, or the collapse of the sexual relationship of the husband and wife. The principle invoked is known as "proportionalism" which is usually linked with a contextual weighing of goods and evils and the conditions for realizing them. It is clear that this principle was applied in the case of divorce and remarriage by Bishop Athenagoras Kokkinakis, former Dean of Holy Cross Greek Orthodox Theological School in Brookline, Mass. It is interesting that

Bishop Athenagoras was unwilling or unready to apply the same principles to contraception. His reasons, however, are nowhere given. It is clear that Orthodox moral theologians have often been selective in their application of proportional judgments without giving clear grounds for admitting it in one case and not in the other. The Latin Church was ready to compromise on the matter of oaths and usury (both condemned in the New Testament) but not on the matter of divorce and remarriage since marriage was seen as indissoluble and an absolute good no matter what personal horrors existed in the life of the couple. Only recently a document produced by the Quebec Assembly of Catholic bishops circulated a document which stated that the Church has often contributed to wife-battering as it "sacrificed people to maintain the marriage bond."[50] Orthodox theologians, on the other hand, have allowed compromise in matters of divorce and remarriage, but most have refused it for masturbation and homosexual relations between committed couples of the same sex. Once the principle is admitted, however, its use can hardly be refused elsewhere. This does not mean that Orthodox moral theologians should invoke the principle to allow for a casuistry quite foreign to the Holy Tradition. The tradition which has allowed for various reasons and grounds for divorce and remarriage invoked principles more complex and plural than those of simple proportionate judgment. But the Orthodox approach to marriage and divorce invoked a realism beyond the legalism of an absolute moral norm which could be invoked to save a "marriage" no matter what the personal relationship of the couple might be. A moral theology of absolute law is foreign to the Orthodox ethos, just as a moral theology built on the individual's situation is equally foreign.

A contextual ethic built on proportional judgments can be extremely dangerous since the objective grounds for such judgments are difficult to establish. Individual judgment becomes selective at best. Proportionalism would imply that in some instances an evil must be carried out, not as a means to an end but as a lesser evil. Clearly, permission for a second marriage involves something of this sort, not just on the principle of economy but as a necessity if certain evils are not to follow. The future of an Orthodox moral theology which is more than a mere repetition of past judgments lies in examining the underlying method by which moral judgments are to be made and the theological principles which are their basis. This is what we have tried to do in setting forth Orthodox theory and practice on divorce and remarriage.

Notes

(1) Mackin, p. 171.

(2) Mackin, p. 171.

(3) Ibid., p. 171.

(4) St. Nicodemus the Hagiorite and Agapius,*The Rudder* (*Pedalion*), trans. D. Cummings, (West Brookfield, MA: The Orthodox Christian Educational Society, 1957), p. 76.

(5) Mackin, p. 180.

(6) *The Rudder* (*Pedalion*), p. 509.

(7) Ibid., p. 512.

(8) Ibid., p. 552.

(9) John Meyendorff, *Byzantine Theology* (New York: Fordham University Press, 1974), p. 81.

(10) *The Rudder* (*Pedalion*), p. 509.

(11) R. C. Gerest, "Quand les chrétiens ne se marient pas à l'église: histoire des cinq premiers siècles," *Lumière et Vie* 82 (1967), p. 244.

(12) Jerome, Letter 55:3.

(13) John T. Noonan, "Novel 22," in W. W. Bassett, *The Bond of Marriage* (Notre Dame, IN: University of Notre Dame Press, 1969, p. 53.

(14) Ibid., p. 87.

(15) Joyce, G. W., *Christian Marriage* (New York: Sheed and Ward, 1933).

(16) Noonan, "Novel 22" in Bassett, p. 89.

(17) Ibid., p. 88.

(18) Ibid., p. 89.

(19) Mackin, p. 109.

(20) Joyce, p. 367.

(21) Ibid., p. 367.

(22) Ibid., p. 370.

(23) Ibid., p. 375.

(24) Jerome Kotsonis, "Fundamental Principles of Orthodox Morality," in *The Orthodox Ethos: Studies in Orthodoxy*, Vol. 1 (Oxford: Holywell Press, 1964), p. 246.

(25) Peter L'Huillier, "The Indissolubility of Marriage in Orthodox Law and Practice,"*St. Vladimir's Theological Quarterly*, 32, 3 (1988), p. 218.

(26) Alexander Schmemann, "The Indissolubility of Marriage: The Theological Tradition of the East," in Bassett, p. 97.

(27) Ibid., pp. 100-1.

(28) Ibid., p. 104.

(29) Ibid., p. 103.

(30) Elie Melia, "Le lien matrimonial à la lumière de la théologie sacramentaire et de la théologie morale de l'église orthodoxe," in *Hommes et l'Eglise* (Strasbourg, 1970), p. 104.

(31) Ibid., p. 185.

(32) Ibid., p. 190-1.

(33) Ibid., p. 194.

(34) Pierre L'Huillier, "Le divorce selon la théologie et le droit canon de l'Eglise Orthodoxe," *Le Messager Orthodoxe de l'Exarchat du Patriarche Russe en Europe* (1969), no. 65, pp. 26-36.

(35) Ibid., pp. 26-36.

(36) Pierre L'Huillier, "Un point de vue orthodoxe à propos du divorce," Congrès de l'Association de théologiens pour l'étude de la morale, *Divorce et Indissolubilité du Mariage* (Paris: Editions du Cerf, 1971), p. 122.

(37) Athananagoras Kokkinakis, *Parents and Priests as Servants of Redemption: An Interpretation of the Doctrines of the Eastern Orthodox Church on the Sacraments of Matrimony and Priesthood* (New York: Morehouse-Gorham Co., 1958), pp. 47-8.

(38) Ibid., p. 50.

(39) Georges Florovsky, "The Limits of the Church," *Church Quarterly Review* 117 (1933), p. 125.

(40) Cf. F. J. Thomson, "Economy: An Examination of the Various Theories of Economy Held Within the Orthodox Church, with Special Reference to the Economical Recognition of the Validity of Non-Orthodox Sacraments," *The Journal of Theological Studies* 16 (1965), pp. 368-420.

(41) L'Huillier, "The Indissolubility of Marriage," p. 220.

(42) Ibid.

(43) Bernard Häring, "A Theological Appraisal of Marriage Tribunals," in L. G. Wrenn, *Divorce and Remarriage in the Catholic Church* (Paramus, NJ, Newman Press, 1973), pp. 16-28.

(44) Ibid., p. 18.

(45) Ibid., pp. 19-20.

(46) J. P. Jossua, "Moral Theology Forum: The Fidelity of Love and the Indissolubility of Christian Marriage," *The Clergy Review*, 56 (1971), p. 177, originally published in *Divorce et Indissolubilité du Mariage* (Paris: Editions du Cerf, 1971), pp. 110-20.

(47) Ibid., p. 180.

(48) Ibid., p. 181.

(49) Richard McCormick, "Notes on Moral Theology," *Theological Studies*, 36, 1 (1975), p. 114.

(50) *The Montreal Gazette*, Wednesday, Nov. 22, 1989, p. A-5.

Chapter Seven:

Orthodoxy and Contraception

What has the Orthodox Church taught regarding the morality or immorality of contraception? On first examination, it would appear that her position is identical with that enunciated by Pope Paul VI in his encyclical *Humanae Vitae*. This is certainly what the late Patriarch Athanagoras of Constantinople thought.[1] On the other hand, there are many voices within the Orthodox Church favoring the morality of contraception.

The first rule of Orthodox theology is to look to the Holy Scriptures and to the Fathers before making a theological judgment. Holy Scripture, however, has nothing to say on the subject of contraception. The possible exception is the story of Onan in Genesis 38:8-10. St. Epiphanius, alone among the Greek Fathers, identifies the sin of Onan as contraception. His interpretation is set within the context of an attack against the Gnostics, who scorned both creation and procreation. St. John Chrysostom speaks of Onan as evil without making his sin that of contraception. It was the Latin Father St. Jerome who translated Gn 38:8-10 in a manner which would make it "a powerful text in later times against contraception."[2] When one compares the Old Latin text with that of Jerome, it becomes clear that the introduction of the word *semen* as the object of the term "spilled" and the assertion that God killed him because he did a detestable thing (*rem detestabilem*) makes his sin one of coitus interruptus and/or one of contraception. This is clearly contrary to the Hebrew text where the sin lay in Onan's refusal of his duty to impregnate his dead brother's wife and thus fulfill the levirate law.

It is within the context of the Gnostic crisis that the fundamental objections of early Christian theologians to contraception emerge. They take the form of adopting Stoic concepts of nature and physical teleology in a response to the Gnostics. Gnostic dualism gave no place to the material world in the design of God for the salvation of human souls. Both St.Justin and the Greek Christian philosopher Athenagoras had argued that sexual intercourse is permitted only if for the sake of procreation. Athenagoras wrote in his book *A Plea for Christians*: "For as the farmer casts seed into the ground and awaits the harvest without further planting, so also procreation is the limit that we set for the indulgence of our lust."[3] Clement of Alexandria reflects both Philo and Stoicism in his opposition to Gnosticism. His basic position was that "the law intended husbands to cohabit with their wives with self-control and only for the purpose of begetting children"[4] John Noonan notes that for Clement sexual desire was viewed as evil. Clement was very clear about this: "A man who marries for the sake of begetting children must practice continence so that it is not desire he feels for his wife, whom he ought to love, and so that he may beget children with a chaste and controlled will."[5] He goes on to say: "Because of its divine institution for the propagation of man the seed is not to be vainly ejaculated, nor is it to be damaged, nor is it to be wasted"[6] Indeed, Clement thought the ideal was to experience no desire at all. Origen, living in the same milieu as Clement, but in a later generation, taught that those who were spiritually circumcised would not commit adultery and would have intercourse with their wives "only for the sake of a posterity."[7] Both Clement and Origen rejected sexual intercourse in pregnancy. It was argued that a man may sow seed only where the soil admits seed. Further evidence of this norm exists in the *Didascalia*, a collection of canons from Syria about 220-250. There we find all forms of sterile sex condemned: sodomy, bestiality, fornication, adultery, and intercourse with a pregnant wife.[8]

John Noonan asserts that there are only two dissenters from the Alexandrian rule among the Fathers: Lactantius and St. John Chrysostom. Lactantius allows that intercourse may be permitted within pregnancy to keep a man from seeking satisfaction of his lust elsewhere.[9] Lactantius makes this assertion without compromising his claim that sexuality ("this most burning desire") was given by God so that all animals can "propagate and multiply the species."[10] The other dissenter was St. John Chrysostom, far more important for Orthodox theology. In his work *On Those Words of the Apostle: "On Account of Fornication"* he formulated the basic principle: "Marriage was instituted, that we may live chastely and that we may become parents."[11] Since it is quite possible, according to Chrysostom, that we may become parents spiritually, only the former reason for marriage remains. Thus, as he puts it: "So there is one occasion for marriage, that we may not commit fornication."[12] It is on this basis that St. John Chrysostom was able to admit that intercourse in old age is without blame. By analogy intercourse could be admitted during the time of pregnancy. However, contraception is ruled out by St. John insofar as it violates the laws of God:

> Why do you sow where the field is eager to destroy the fruit? Where there are medicines of sterility? Where there is murder before birth? You do not even let a harlot remain only a harlot, but you make her a burderess as well. Do you see that from drunkenness comes fornication, from fornication, adultery, from adultery murder? Indeed, it is something worse than murder and I do not know what to call it; for she does not kill what is formed but prevents its formation. What then? Do you condemn the gift of God, and fight with His laws?[13]

In a sermon on avarice, Chrysostom also speaks of contraception. Men who are avaricious and desirous of avoiding children "mutilate nature, not only killing the newborn, but even acting to prevent their beginning to live."[14] Noonan

241

states that he held the generative act to be sacred and consequently any interference with it would be an attack on the work of God.[15] It is also clear that Chrysostom placed his focus on motivation when he interprets the text of Matthew 5 in Homily 28. Contraception is sinful insofar as its evil lies in avarice as well as in the mutilation of nature. It is not entirely clear, moreover, as to whether St. John differentiates between abortion and contraception. However, he condemns those who castrate themselves and calls them "homicides." We find a similar ambiguity in the strictures of St. Ambrose against the rich "lest their patrimony be divided among several, deny their own fetus in their uterus and by a parricidal potion extinguish the pledges of their womb in their genital belly, and life is taken away before it is transmitted."[16] With St. Cyril of Alexandria there is a return to the Alexandrian rule since he insists that the only good of marriage is procreation. Indeed, St. Cyril urges that the seeking of pleasure in coitus is sinful. Of Onan St. Cyril states that "he broke the law of coitus."[17]

It is not enough to repeat the opinions and teachings of the Fathers of the Church. These teachings must be interpreted by the Church in each generation. If we examine the reasons given by typical Fathers such as St. John Chrysostom for his opposition to contraception, we discern his opposition to lie in three areas: the method of contraception was perceived as involving an abortifacient, the motives were base and selfish, and the interference with nature was perverse. A modern study can easily show that methods now exist which involve no harm to a fertilized egg since none has come into being. Similarly, the motives remain perennially in question and must ever be critically examined by married couples. Base motives invalidate any intention to contracept if such motives are evident. But the crucial issue remains that of whether nature is violated by sowing seed where it cannot be fruitful and multiply. The theological question is whether the natural law argument will stand. Insofar as sexual intercourse is allowed to older people who are sterile, a similar logic might allow the use of contraceptives when there is good reason for their use. There is a rhetoric of natural law in St. John

Chrysostom, but there is no theology of natural law, only an incorporation of Stoical common sense arguments.

In modern Orthodoxy there exist side by side two traditions. One allows contraception, and the other forbids it. Perhaps it is best to examine a case of Orthodox opposition to contraception. Bishop Athenagoras Kokkinakis had taught theology in Boston for many years and returned to Greece to become a bishop. His position is very clear: "Since the purpose of matrimony is clearly explained in the sources of the Orthodox doctrines, no measures and devices against the realization of its purpose can be justified."[18] He sets forth the judgment of the Sixth Ecumenical Council in the 91st canon against those who commit abortion and moves on to create a rule:

> Planned parenthood, or birth control and birth prevention, is another practice which disturbs the peace and endangers the health and the lifelong unity of the spouses. That this practice violates the sacred purpose of matrimony, letting the sexual functions of the spouses dominate their shared life and replace all other objectives of their unity, is beyond doubt.[19]

He very quickly admits that others in the Christian world disagree with this judgment. However, his judgment is that both physical and psychological defects follow from the use of birth control and birth prevention. The moral consequences are even worse. Reducing sexuality to the gratification of the senses often leads to conjugal infidelity by setting up hedonism as a norm. This can, in turn, lead to adultery and divorce. He admits that priests may hear other arguments, particularly rising from the financial condition of the family, but he urges priests to allow no compromise except when a physician's advice has been given to the contrary. Christians must be taught to trust God rather the world. Living by the Holy Spirit married people will learn temperance. Only prayer, Holy Communion, fasting, or reading the Bible and religious books can be of assistance here. In conclusion, Bishop Athenagoras wishes to invoke the authority of the encyclical letter issued by the bishops of the Greek Church in 1937. This letter not only condemned contraception, birth control, and planned parenthood but invoked alleged statistics and scientific sources in doing so. It strongly castigated the clergy for their laxity on the question of birth control. All endorsements of contraception create "great and criminal scandals for which the responsibility of the priest is tremendous."[20]

The encyclical letter of Pope Paul VI, *Humanae Vitae*, issued in 1968, has been the crucial example of natural law thinking about marriage and procreation. The Pope was ready to recognize that marriage had two purposes, the exchange of love on the part of the husband and wife and the creation of offspring through the genital act of love. Previous discussions in Roman Catholic theology had failed to resolve the priorities among the ends of marriage, but the dominant position had been that procreation was foremost. Both the Second Vatican Council and Pope Paul VI were ready to accept as an end of marriage the love of the couple as long as it never excluded the end of procreation. The conclusion drawn by the Pope was that "each and every marriage act must remain open to the transmission of life."[21] The reason for this injunction lay in the fact that man did not have unlimited dominion over his body in general, and particularly over his generative faculties. These faculties are governed by the natural law. The Pope allowed recourse to the natural rhythms "immanent in the generative functions" but forbad impeding "the development of natural processes." What this means is that one may not exclude "any and every action which, either in anticipation of the conjugal act, or in its accomplishment, or in the development of its natural consequences, proposes, whether as an end or as a means, to render procreation impossible."[22]

The sharpest Orthodox rejoinder to Pope Paul's encyclical has been an article by the English theologian Philip Sherrard. In an article originally published in *Sobornost*, Sherrard claims that the Pope has subordinated marriage and the positive image of married love to the production of children. He shows no awareness of marriage as a participation in the

244

divine life and the restoration of fallen human beings to paradise. Rather, marriage is a relationship limited to this mortal life whose purpose is that we cooperate with God in the procreation of children. As Sherrard puts it: "God appears as the master of a great human stud in which married couples are 'ordained to the procreation and bringing up of children,' so that these presumably in their turn may marry and beget, perpetuating in this way the history of man's disgrace into an indefinite and empty future."[23] He notes various other objections to the arguments of Paul VI which make the Encyclical internally inconsistent and self-contradictory:

> If it is repugnant to the nature of man and woman, and also contrary to God's plan and holy will, to use the divine gift of the generative function while depriving it, even if only partially, of its meaning and purpose - the begetting of children - how is it not equally repugnant to man and woman and equally contrary to God's plan and holy will to use it with the specific intention of depriving it of its meaning and purpose, when, that is to say, one knows as certainly as one can know that it will not beget children? To say that the vital qualitative difference in each case is whether it is God or man who has deprived the generative act of its natural potential to create human life, and that provided man sticks to the facility instituted by God (the infertile period) then he is not violating the purpose and meaning of this act even when he deliberately intends to avoid having children, and means to make sure none will be born, may pass as an adroit piece of legalistic or moral quibbling, but it is surely a very pathetic argument with which to present the mature Christian intelligence and conscience.[24]

Philip Sherrard not only finds the papal argument inconsistent but he regards the argument of *Humanae Vitae* to be radically insufficient because of three interconnected assumptions. The first is that man should go on endlessly begetting children within the mortal and corrupt conditions of the materialized universe which results from the fallen existence of humankind. Man only perpetuates "his condition of slavery to a process in which his own personal created dignity is sacrificed to the abstract common good of a hypothetical future human society."[25] There is no awareness in the encyclical that men and women are called to participate in the Kingdom "not of this world." The second assumption is that what happens in nature is what is God's will for humankind. Sherrard wisely comments that how one regards natural processes depends upon what significance one gives to the Fall of Man:

> But if it is understood that it is not the state of this fallen world which is natural, but that of nature, and of man in nature, as it is in Paradise, and that it is this paradisaic state of man and nature which expresses the will of God, then there is likely to be quite another attitude to things. For then what is regarded as man's natural life, and so as the norm providing the basis for the moral law, will be that of this original creation; and man's life as it is now, in this world, and the biological processes to which he is subject, will not be regarded as natural, but as a consequence of a breach in nature, a declension from the natural state, and an entering into conditions that are abnormal and corrupt.[26]

Here the currents of Christian theology merge and reveal their true directions. The commitment of the Roman Church to natural law as normative is both a rejection of the profound pessimism of Augustine and of the recovery of paradise by a sacramental mystery which is the essence of orthodox spirituality. The third assumption of the Pope is equally revealing. It is that "the unitive significance of the sexual relationship between man and woman is inseparably connected with the procreative significance, and hence with the physical generative act."[27] This means that for the Pope it is copulation which must thrive since there is a clear identification of the sexual relationship and sexual love with the procreative sexual act. Sherrard goes to the heart of the matter:

> It seems not to take into account that this relationship
> of love - this sexual relationship or love - extends far
> beyond this expression, and reaches into the deepest
> strata of human life and even perhaps further; and
> that to identify its significance so inseparably with
> biological procreation is to ignore and hence to stultify
> its potentiality as one of the divinely-given means
> whereby man and woman in this world may so de-
> velop that they grow with God's grace into the trans-
> figured life of Paradise.[28]

In the Genesis narrative children and their conception only
are spoken of after the expulsion from paradise. Sherrard
asks what this might mean:

> Whatver the answer, it may be said that until the
> possibility, involving a belief in miracles, of the
> personal love between man and woman continuing
> beyond the limits of this mortal and corrupt existence
> is placed squarely and firmly at the centre of the
> Christian understanding of marriage as its ultimate
> purpose; and until something of what its realisation
> entails, in terms of transcending all biological procrea-
> tive considerations and even the physical sex act itself,
> is clearly stated: until this is done, the Christian
> doctrine of marriage will continue to be presented in
> that truncated, uninspiring form, weakened by evasion
> and compromise, which it is given in so many official
> pronouncements purporting to speak of what is after
> all one of the most profound of all the Mysteries.[29]

It is clear that Sherrard is not writing a defense of contraception. He is, rather, exploring in its assumptions the papal
encyclical and its reasons for excluding "artificial" contraception as immoral. The issue of contraception is inevitably
dependent upon one's doctrine of marriage and its purposes.
If we are true to a sacramental vision of marriage as a partici-

pation in the mystery of Christ's love for his church, then such a natural understanding of coitus and its inherent teleological norms subverts the mystery of love. The procreation of children should not be the condition to making love. As Sherrard notes, the distinctions between natural rhythms by which we avoid having children and the artificial barriers to conception do not address the intention, which in both instances would be to exclude conception. By basing his prohibition of human manipulation of physical processes upon natural law, the pope, and any who would follow him in this, fails to see that children must be the consequence of love. Without love the presence of children becomes destructive for everyone. It is interesting to note that the duty to procreate if we copulate is recognized by the Catholic moral theologian André Guindon as itself an evil premise since our offspring must be invited into life, not just arrive as a natural consequence.[30] Thus, Guindon follows the same line of argument as we see in Philip Sherrard's article, though it is in no way dependent upon Sherrard's article.

The second theological discussion dealing with the problem of contraception is that of Father Chrysostom Zaphiris, an Orthodox theologian who has taught both at Holy Cross School of Theology in Brookline, Mass. and at the Ecumenical Institute for Advanced Theological Studies, Tantur, Jerusalem. He holds a doctorate from the University of Strassbourg. His discussion is, in our opinion, the most nuanced and persuasive found in contemporary Orthodoxy. He addresses himself to three questions: (1) what is the purpose of marriage as we find it in the Holy Scriptures and in the writings of the Fathers; (2) what is the official teaching of the orthodox Church on contraception; and (3) what moral legitimacy can be given contraception from an Orthodox theological stance?

From our reading of the Bible it is clear that contraception was never addressed as such. Moreover, modern means of contraception were unknown in the ancient world. What chemical means existed were abortifacients. To answer the question of the morality of contraception we must first ask what place children have within the theology of marriage set forth in the Bible. What confronts us is that the procreation of children has little place in the biblical teaching on marriage. It is assumed that a sexual bond exists within the context of marriage. For St. Paul marriage is a sign of the union between Christ and the Church. The couple participates in the sanctifying power of this union. St. Paul also views marriage as an antidote or outlet for normal human sexual passions. Indeed , his sensitivity to limiting abstinence to a specific and limited period of time shows his awareness of the force of sexual instinct as well as what Zaphiris calls "his elasticity of judgment in giving moral counsel."[31] Zaphiris asserts that both from the text of Genesis (1:28; 2:18) and the writings of St. Paul, the procreation of children is either ignored or secondary.

In his discussion of the patristic texts Zaphiris points out that Clement of Alexandria gave a literal exegesis of 1 Cor 7:23 and recommended marriage to prevent fornication.[32] Zaphiris tends to ignore the centrality of procreation in the totality of Clement's moral theology. In fact, no author in antiquity can be said to have opposed contraception so strongly. The point of Zaphiris is that both Clement and Origen viewed marriage as a legitimate concession to human weakness. Methodius of Olympus is brought forth as another witness of marriage as a legitimate way of avoiding fornication. He applies the same principle to second marriages.[33] It was the great St. John Chrysostom who affirmed that marriage does not have any other goal than that of hindering fornication. Procreation does not even enter the discussion as a goal or purpose of marriage. In his portrayal of the official teaching of the Orthodox Church Zaphiris sets forth the following as authoritative: The Church rejects the option of excluding all children from a marriage as well as being opposed to all forms of abortion. Equally infanticide is rejected as immoral and evil. But the Orthodox Church has not promulgated any solemn statement from its highest synods on the contemporary methods of contraception. Zaphiris is of the opinion that "it is accurate to say that, as long as a married couple is living in fidelity to one another and not allowing an immoral egotism to dominate their sexual relations, the particularities of their sexual life are left to the freedom of the spouses to decide."[34] It is, rather, the motives of pride and egotism which are condemned by the Church, not the use of contraceptives in themselves.

Zaphiris sets up the dilemma of the couple who have several children and feel that they cannot provide adequately for more. Their alternatives are sexual abstinence or the begetting of a child who "ceases to be a sign of their shared love, but risks being a burden which causes only anxiety and even hostility."[35] Abstinence from intercourse leaves one exposed to the temptation to some form of adultery. The only alternative which Zaphiris can personally advocate in this dilemma is the use of contraceptives. He does not see any moral significance in the various methods, whether they are natural or artificial. The use of contraceptives would allow for a controlled sexual life within marriage which would allow for a harmony between the husband and the wife. Indeed, Zaphiris invokes the teaching of St. Paul here (1 Cor 7:4-5) by urging married people to abstain only for a limited time lest Satan tempt them to sin.

Theologically Zaphiris grounds his stand on contraception in the teaching of the Greek Fathers whereby human reason is a participation in the divine revelation. Participation in the Logos does not suppress human freedom and, indeed, it gives us the liberty to employ the discoveries and interventions of humankind. Furthermore, Zaphiris urges that temporary infertility in women would indicate that God did not intend every act of human sexual intercourse to result in a pregnancy. Zaphiris holds that physical union mediates a spiritual union insofar as matter and spirit are united in the incarnation of the Logos. Continence is permitted only for spiritual reasons within the intimacy and freedom of the couple's inner life together, not by reason of fear of pregnancy. Zaphiris insists that he does not propose "a complete and unqualified endorsement of the practice of contraception."[36] He explicitly rejects the "new morality" which would allow sexual activity outside of matrimony when backed up by universal contraception.

Zaphiris expounds a high doctrine of marriage as founded

on St. Paul's teaching in Ephesians 5:21-33. Marriage unites human love to a sacrament which mediates salvation to human beings. Fidelity expresses an aspect of God's covenant with humankind, and relationship between God and humans is a "creative collaboration."[37] This is the doctrine of synergism as set forth by the Greek Fathers. The heart of the conflict with the Church of Rome on the matter of contraception must be discerned at a deeper level than usually has been done by controversialists. Roman Catholic theology in its slavish obedience to natural law leaves out the role of men and women as co-creators and co-legislators with God. Zaphiris writes on this matter:

> The Eastern Orthodox view of contraception, unlike that of the Latin Church, is that our capacity to control procreation is an expression of our powers of freedom and reason to collaborate with God in the moral order. A human being is viewed not only as a subject which receives passively the "natural law," but also as a person who plays an active role in its formulation. Thus natural law, according to Eastern Orthodox thinkers, is not a code imposed by God on human beings, but rather a rule of life set forth by divine inspiration and by our responses to it in freedom and reason. This view does not permit the Eastern Orthodox Church to conclude that the pill, and artificial contraceptives generally, are in violation of human law.[38]

Indeed, Zaphiris holds that the conception of natural law in *Humanae Vitae* "contains a deterministic understanding of human marital and sexual life."[39] Behind this determinism lie the doctrines of Aristotle taken up by Thomas Aquinas in his teleological philosophy of nature. Aquinas' philosophy of nature combines Aristotle's means-end logic with the biblical doctrine of God as creator. Consequently, if one disobeys the inherent purposes of the natural law, God's own creation is undermined. For Zaphiris this determinism is a bondage which ignores the free, rational, and spiritual place of human-

251

kind in creation. From this anthropology Orthodox theologians can say that there are three aspects of contraception to be distinguished and considered. Psychologically one must say that contraceptives are permissible only when their use is based on a common decision reached by both partners. Medically it is imperative that contraception be distinct from any abortifacient, which remains always gravely evil. Furthermore, it must be medically assured that contraception is only temporary, not permanent. Such temporary sterility is not morally contrary to the natural law. The morality of contraception must always be set within the context of the purposes of marriage: the creation of a new life together for the man and woman and the expression of a deeply felt love. The strength of an Orthodox permission of contraception lies not in its permissiveness but in its assertion that all procreation must have a moral decision behind it. *Humanae Vitae* is lacking precisely by its attempt to distinguish procreative power from all the other powers that make human beings human. Its deep inconsistency lies in allowing sexual intercourse during the woman's safe period if conjugality has as its goal an aptitude for procreation. Orthodox theologians do not believe that we are subjects bound to a law of nature but persons living and acting freely in the natural world.

The Eastern Orthodox Church has not, and Zaphiris believes that it will not, legislate the prohibition of contraception. Not only is the entire discussion of the morality of contraception in the area of *theologoumena*, that of theological opinion, but it involves human freedom and responsibility, not just obedience. As Zaphiris puts it: "The Eastern church's refusal to provide specific answers to some concrete moral questions is based on a fundamental theological principle - the belief that no one can specify where human freedom ends and divine will begins. Synergism means the collaboration of human beings with God in the continuing creation of the world."[40] This implies that no theologian can state specifically what finally constitutes the divine-human collaboration. Orthodoxy sets forth the faith that God's love (his *maniakos eros*) has divinized all creation. We play a part in God's creation moving all beings toward God. Both the legislative and creative actions of men and women are, Zaphiris urges, a liturgy of the church. This liturgy is a harmonious cooperation between God and human beings. Contraception must be viewed within this context or it will inevitably be distorted, either toward antinomianism or toward situation ethics. Both tendencies are false since they supply a false context for the ethical life.

It is this theocentric movement which is the primary interpretation of the sacrament of marriage in the theology of the great Russian Orthodox writer Paul Evdokimov. In touching on the question of contraception, he agrees that priests should not make enquiries into the private sexual life of spouses.[41] His entire understanding of the Church differs from that of the Roman magisterium, which issues rules for the temporal life of its subjects. For Evdokimov the Orthodox Church is eschatological in spirit, leading us by repentance to a new life in the Kingdom of God. The Church both discerns spirits and bestows spiritual gifts. She has infinite respect for the image of God in mankind and thus for human freedom to take responsible decisions.[42] The clergy may indeed provide counsel, but it remains at the personal level, not a matter of universal directives with the force of law. Orthodoxy not only recognizes the freedom of persons to decide about such matters as contraception but poses the question of the spiritual age. A couple matures "and finds an appropriate solution at each 'age' of the nuptial life."[43] Thus, a different answer may be appropriate to a different age of development. For Evdokimov, reducing the married life to the material ends of procreation lowers sexuality to the animal world, introducing into a marriage a sense of fear and panic. He thinks that once the principle of limitations of birth is permitted the means is irrelevant. Once we accept painless childbirth, there is no reason to reject temporary sterility. Yet, one cannot "purely and simply recommend contraceptive techniques; the most deserving solution lies in spiritual mastery."[44] There is no easy way according to Evdokimov since even painless childbirth does not diminish the total gift and even includes the risk of losing one's life. He concludes his reflections on contraception with words of profound wisdom: "At the hour of its maturity, love transcends all regulation, every technique, all prescription imposed from without and reaches the crucial plane; faithful to its vocation, it cannot avoid the summit of love crucified."[45]

The development of theological opinion favoring contraception within the context of marriage by Orthodox theologians is a fact of vital importance to our investigation. The opinions of the ancient Fathers against contraception as a moral procedure were largely based on confusions between methods thought to be abortifacients and other methods of contraception. There was also a confusion between the motives behind contraception and the moral status of the procedure itself. The most forceful attitudes against contraception lay with those (particularly Clement of Alexandria and St. Cyril of Alexandria) who thought that procreation alone justified sexual relations between husband and wife. This was not an opinion which was to become the dominant or exclusive one within the Eastern Orthodox Church. Rather, it was the views of St. John Chrysostom which prevailed. Marriage was justified as a sacramental bond in which sexual intercourse stood as a remedy for concupiscence. Nevertheless, St. John Chrysostom rejected contraception because he assumed it to be unnatural. It is this opinion that modern authors have forcefully challenged. Twentieth century historians know that a Stoic philosophy of nature was introduced into Christian theology with an assumption of its truth which can no longer be allowed by modern philosophers, particularly since the advent of modern science. Not only are the alleged purposes of organs not to be given a normative status in an ethic built on natural law, but any attempt to do so leaves out the manifold complexity of meaning inherent in both human and animal behavior. The Stoic natural law philosophy simply cannot stand up under the critique posed by the philosophy of science. The attempt by Pope Paul VI to justify natural law foundations for the ban on artificial contraception either rules out all technology by implication (once the stress is placed on the artificial as prohibited) or bases the prohibition on ecclesiastical authority. This violates the very foundations of natural law since its truth must self-evident to all reasonable persons if it is universally true. If we can know that reasoning only by faith, then the natural law is so transformed that we know it only by the authority of a magisterium which is available only to Roman Catholics. Such an argument is, of course, unacceptable to Orthodoxy. We are convinced that Zaphiris is correct in affirming the human freedom to form nature to our purposes while at the same time recognizing the created goods that God has given us in nature.

Already there are in circulation two books arguing in favor of contraception and published by clergy of the Greek Orthodox Church in North America.[46] They, together with Zaphiris, affirm that the intention to marry and to conceive children within the sacramental context of marriage does not prohibit the regulation of births. Such regulation, accord with reason and health, united with a generous spirit of the married couple, is part of the responsibility by which we have been invited by God to cooperate with the divine will in procreation. This is increasingly a concensus in Orthodox theology, and in this we may rejoice.

We may, therefore, draw certain conclusions about contraception from Orthodox moral theology:

1. The interpretation of the natural law as a teleological ordering of our bodies to fulfil the purposes of God and setting up laws to prohibit use of the reproductive organs apart from that finality stands contrary to an Orthodox understanding of grace and nature and of human freedom. Physiological teleology is based on a biology which is entirely outdated by modern science and has no place in theological ethics. Traditional Orthodoxy has concerned itself more with human motives and intentions than with some alleged purposes of the sexual organs.

2. The human ordering of nature is legitimate in accord with the principles of synergism. Natural goods may or may not be realized in accord with whatever vocation we may be given by God. Just as the good of reproduction is not incumbent upon all, so the marital union need not in every instance be open to procreation. This is clearly the case in "un-aided" nature so that to "aid" natural processes to assist our realiza-

255

tion of a good under optimum circumstances is fully in accord with Orthodox theology. The processes of nature are clearly not inherently sacred and beyond human intervention. Medically there is little difference between processes which interfere to sustain life and those which would interfere to postpone pregnancies or for sufficient reason suppress them entirely.

3. No form of contraception may be employed which acts to destroy a conceptus. This would be abortion, and abortion is gravely evil as a sin against human life. Such forms of contraception would quite obviously be the interuterine device and the so-called "morning after" pill which acts by destroying a fertilized egg in a woman's body. It is clear that the steroid pill does not inflict such damage insofar as it prevents ovulation.[47]

4. Contraception may not be a permanent policy and practice between married couples unless there is a proportionate reason such as the presence of unavoidable genetic disease or conditions of life which would make the raising of children impossible. Children are clearly to be welcomed into the life of those who have become "one flesh" and indeed, express the "one flesh" in a unique and wonderful way. Generosity and self-sacrifice are fundamental to the couple united in Christ. Such ethical attitudes are expressions of the union of Christ with His Church which marriage sacramentally shares. Contraception is a temporary measure to be undertaken with good motives, usually in consultation with one's spiritual father, and only on a temporary basis.

5. Permanent sterilization of either the man or the woman in the context of marriage is not morally acceptable unless it is to prevent a likely and probable evil. Such an evil would be a succession of dangerous births where the medical judgment is that a woman must not conceive another child since such would pose grave risk to her life and health. The same principles that we invoke here would be equally applicable to a woman's mental health or an extremely unstable marital union. There is a basic requirement of a stable and secure marriage if conception is to occur. One may, on the other hand, raise the question of whether sexual intercourse should

take place where the marriage itself is at risk, but pronouncing on such delicate issues is very difficult and should be undertaken with much caution.

6. The contraceptive mentality, which excludes children on principle, should find no place in an Orthodox home. It is one that rises from hedonism and from a form of modern liberalism that takes individuals as the absolute norm. In law it has become normative in some countries (such as the United States) where the right to privacy is foremost even to prevail over the right of the fetus to life. Such individualism is completely contrary to the Orthodox mind where interdependence is fundamental and makes of the home a "little church" (St. John Chrysostom). In fact, the contraceptive mentality is only selfishness in the form of individualism which takes pleasure as the first and highest good and dismisses the purposes of the Creator as irrelevant to one's own will and control of one's body and environment. Under such ideology the family becomes a site for conflict which seeks only power and having one's will at the expense of others. Openness to one another and to God's purposes in giving us new life in the context of the family is part of the divine plan of salvation whereby we are saved by becoming members of one another in the Body of Christ.

Notes

(1) Joannes, Fernando Victorino, ed., *The Bitter Pill* (Philadelphia: Pilgrim Press, 1970), p. 247.

(2) John T. Noonan, *Contraception: A History of Its Treatment by Catholic Theologians and Canonists* (Cambridge, MA: Harvard University Press, 1967), p. 102.

(3) Athenagoras, *A Plea for Christians* 33, in *Legatio and De Resurrectione*, ed. and trans. William R. Schoedel (Oxford: Oxford University Press, p. 81.

(4) Clement of Alexandria, "On Marriage," (Stromateis 3.11.71.4), trans. John Ernest Leonard Oulton and Henry Chadwick, in *Alexandrian Christianity, The Library of Christian Classics*, Vol. 2 (Philadelphia: The Westminster Press, 1954), p. 73.

(5) Ibid., 3.7.58, p. 67.

(6) Clement of Alexandria, *Paedagogus* 2.10.91.2, trans. Noonan, p. 93.

(7) Origen, *Third Homily on Genesis*, 6, trans. Noonan, p. 77.

(8) *Didascalia* 6.28

(9) Lactantius, *Divine Institutes* 6.23.2.26.

(10) Ibid., 6.23.2, trans. Noonan, p. 103.

(11) John Chrysostom, *On Those Words of the Apostle, On Account of Fornication*, trans. Noonan, p. 78.

(12) Ibid.

(13) John Chrysostom, *Homily 24 on the Epistle to the Romans*, trans. Noonan, p. 98.

(14) John Chrysostom, *Homily 28 on Matthew 5*, trans. Noonan, p. 99.

(15) Noonan, p. 79.

(16) Ambrose of Milan, *Hexameron* 5.18.58, trans. Noonan, p. 99.

(17) Cyril of Alexandria, *Critical Comments on Genesis 6* 15, trans. Noonan, p. 139.

(18) Athenagoras Kokkinakis, *Parents and Priests as Servants of Redemption* (New York: Morehouse-Gorham Co., 1958), p. 55.

(19) Ibid., p. 156.

(20) Ibid., p. 60.

(21) Pope Paul VI, *Humanae Vitae (On Human Life)*, 11.

(22) Ibid, 14.

(23) Philip Sherrard, "Humanae Vitae: Notes on the Encyclical Letter of Pope Paul VI," *Sobornost*, 5, 8 (1969), p. 575.

(24) Ibid., pp. 576-7.

(25) Ibid., p. 577.

(26) Ibid., p. 578.

(27) Ibid., p. 579.

(28) Ibid., p. 579.

(29) Ibid., p. 580.

(30) André Guindon, *The Sexual Creators: An Ethical Proposal for Concerned Christians* (Lanham, MD, University Press of America, 1986), p. 46.

(31) Chrysostomos Zaphiris, "The Morality of Contraception: An Eastern Orthodox Opinion," *The Journal of Ecumenical Studies* 11, 4 (1974), p. 679.

(32) Ibid., p. 679.

(33) Methodius of Olympus, *The Banquet of Virgins*, 3 12.

(34) Zaphiris, p. 682.

(35) Ibid., p. 684.

(36) Ibid., p. 685.

(37) Ibid., p. 685.

(38) Ibid., p. 685.

(39) Ibid., p. 688.

(40) Ibid., p. 688

(41) Paul Evdokimov, *The Sacrament of Love* (Crestwood, NY: St. Vladimir's Seminary Press, 1985), p. 175.

(42) Ibid., p. 175.

(43) Ibid., p. 176.

(44) Ibid., p. 178.

(45) Ibid., p. 179.

(46) D. J. Constantelos, *Marriage, Sexuality and Celibacy: A Greek Orthodox Perspective* (Minneapolis: Life and Light, 1975); N. D. Patrinacos, *The Orthodox Church on Birth Control* (Graphic Arts Press, 1975).

(47) The effects of oral contraceptives currently in use are set forth, together with an ethical analysis, by James W. Knight and Joan C. Callahan in *Preventing Birth: Contemporary Methods and Related Moral Controversies*, Vol. 3, *Ethics in a Changing World* (Salt Lake City: University of Utah Press, 1989). The evidence for multagenicity and teratogenicity is entirely negative.

Chapter Eight:

Masturbation and Moral Theology

One of the most obvious cultural changes brought about by the sexual revolution in North America is that masturbation is treated as legitimate and respectable, indeed, normal and moral by the majority of sex educators. The Kinsey data prepared this shift of opinion by reporting that 40% of all females in the United States have masturbated: 63% of female college graduates; 59% of the high school group; and 34% of the grade school group. Contrary to the pattern of males, masturbation among women increases until middle age and subsequently remains fairly constant. Of the male population in the United States, 92% are involved in masturbation which leads to orgasm; 96% of college graduates; 95% of the high school group; and 89% of the grade school group. Though masturbation among men decreases after marriage, Kinsey reports that 70% of married men with a college education find 9% of their total sexual outlet in masturbation. Other sources confirm the findings of Kinsey both in America and Europe.[1] Indeed, an article appeared by Jane E. Brody in the *New York Times* on November 4, 1987, reporting the change of opinion and practice with regard to masturbation in the United States. What was once considered pathogenic or gravely evil is increasingly accepted as normal for most human beings.

Despite efforts on the part of progressive Catholics to have masturbation accepted as normal and not gravely evil, the position taken by the Vatican in the *Declaration on Certain*

Questions Concerning Sexual Ethics (*Persona Humana*) is that masturbation is a grave moral evil insofar as it violates the principle of finality. The natural law dictates that sexual organs are to be used only for procreative sex within the bonds of matrimony. The Congregation did allow that the "immaturity of adolescence (which can sometimes persist after that age), psychological imbalance or habit can influence behavior, diminishing the deliberate character of the act and bringing about a situation whereby subjectively there may not always be serious fault."[2] It asserts that such a lack of deliberation is not to be assumed but must be shown to be present. Furthermore, the Congregation states, "In the pastoral ministry, in order to form an adequate judgment in concrete cases, the habitual behavior of people will be considered in its totality, not only with regard to the individual's practice of charity and of justice but also with regard to the individual's care in observing the particular precepts of chastity."[3] The Congregation also asserts that the opinion whereby masturbation was condemned as morally evil only insofar as the subject deliberately indulges in solitary pleasure closed in on self ("ipsation") is an opinion contradictory to the teaching and practice of the Roman Catholic Church. Masturbation remains an intrinsically disordered act because the deliberate use of the sexual faculty outside normal conjugal relations violates the finality of that faculty. Protestant opinion on the morality of masturbation varies between the traditional taboo and the increasingly widespread toleration of masturbation as harmless.

We must ask where an Orthodox moral theology stands on this question. That, of course, involves our looking to Holy Scripture and to the patristic tradition. First of all, it is difficult to know what to look for. The modern word for masturbation dates only from Montaigne (Essays, II, 12). Prior to that we find the use of the words in Latin *pollutio* and *mollitia*, both of which appear in the works of Thomas Aquinas. The word *mollitia* is a Latin translation of the Greek word *malakos* which appears in the New Testament, specifically in 1 Cor 6:9. It has been wrongly translated as "homosexual" in many modern translations. The term appears elsewhere (Mt

11:8, 9:35, 10:1) to mean "sick." Aristotle used the word in the *Nichomachean Ethics* (7.4.4) to mean "unrestraint" in regard to bodily pleasures. The word *malakos* came to be applied to masturbation by later authors.[4] The word "onanism," which until very recently referred to masturbation, is a misinterpretation of Gn 38:9-10 where Onan spilled his semen and evaded the Levirate law to raise up offspring from his deceased brother wife. The sin of Onan lay in a refusal to do his duty to his brother's wife. It was, in fact, a case of *coitus interruptus* rather than of masturbation. Nevertheless, from early days (cf. St. John Cassian's Conferences V, II) we see the use of the example of Onan to refer to a sexual act without a partner.

Just as biblical scholars point out that Onan's sin had nothing to do with masturbation, so scholars point to the fact that *malakos* in no way refers to masturbation in the use given to it in the New Testament where it appears in 1 Cor 6:9. The word did come to have this meaning in some of the Fathers of the Church, and clearly is used in this sense in the canons (falsely) attributed to St. John the Faster (d. 595). Masturbation is *malakia* which is interpreted as a sin which is against nature (*para phusin*). The canons reflect a monastic rather than a Eucharistic setting. John Erikson says, "Above all, these penances are viewed as medicinal, rather than vindictive. The forensic element, present in Western and to an extent in early Christian penitential discipline, disappears beneath a barrage of medicinal imagery."[5] In these penances there is an extraordinary differentiation of sexual sin which anticipates all the complexity of the Latin manuals. In the Akolouthia for Confession ascribed to John the Faster the questions addressed to the penitent begin with the confessor asking: "Tell me, my son, how did you first lose your virginity?" If the penitent is unable to convey this information, the confessor mentions various possibilities. Masturbation is mentioned along with other fleshly sins, and masturbation by the hand of another is suggested as a complicating factor. Needless to say, such suggestions were dangerous in the extreme, making the penitent aware of practices which otherwise might have remained unknown to him. The penances imposed upon masturbators by John the Faster are quite mild in comparison with those for fornication. The penance for fornication is two years' exclusion from Holy Communion while for masturbation there is a penance of forty days absence from Communion. This doubled if masturbation was by the hand of another. On the other hand, the priest who has masturbated is given a penance of a year's suspension from his holy functions. If he masturbates two or three times after that he is to be dismissed from the priesthood and become a reader. Erikson notes with regard to the Akolouthia that "the format provided for confession closely follows that for a novice entering upon that life of permanent penance which is monasticism, in which his entire life is reviewed."[6]   He also points to the loss of the ecclesial context of penance and the Eucharistic orientation of the early Church's penitential system. In the texts ascribed to John the Faster "reconciliation to the eucharist becomes only partial. After a certain period of penance, one may receive communion on specified days, like Easter and the Dormition, but in the interval penance must be resumed."[7]

St. John of the Ladder, in his chapter on purity and chastity in *The Ladder of Divine Ascent*, writes:

> The devil often has the habit, especially in warring against ascetics and those leading the solitary life, of using all his force, all his zeal, all his cunning, all his intrigue, all his ingenuity and purpose, to assail them by means of what is unnatural, and not by what is natural. Therefore, ascetics coming into contact with women, and not in any way tempted either by desire or thought, have sometimes regarded themselves as already blessed, not knowing, poor things, that where a worse downfall had been prepared for them, there is no need of the lesser one.[8]

He writes of a man of whom St. Anthony grieved, saying "A great pillar has fallen." St. Anthony had hidden the manner of his fall, "for he knew that bodily fornication is possible without intercourse with another body."[9]   John

Climacus speaks of this sin as a kind of death and as a devastating sin, "which is ever borne about with us, but especially in youth." This is, indeed, the secret sin of which St. Paul wrote in his letter to the Ephesians and of which he wrote that "it is a shame even to speak of, or to write or to hear." God is, nevertheless, ready to forgive even unnatural sins. St. John continues:

And our merciless foe, teacher of fornication, says that our man-befriending God is very merciful towards this passion as it is a natural one. But if we observe the guile of the demons we shall find that after sin has been committed they say that God is a just and inexorfable Judge. They said the former in order to lead us into sin, and now the latter to drown us in despair. As long as sorrow and despair are present, we do not so easily abandon ourselves to further sin. But when sorrow and despair are quenched, the tyrant speaks to us again of God's mercy.[10]

St. John makes it clear that the reason for purity lies in our putting on the likeness of God, as far as it is humanly possible (Step 15:36) Thus it is evident that for St. John masturbation is a constant and dangerous temptation for the solitary monk, that it is unnatural, and that it brings the monk down into the flesh and separates him from the likeness of God. "Unnatural" means, I would judge, that it is the embracing of a phantom rather than the real body of a woman. Michel Foucault notes that masturbation had in pre-Christian antiquity been considered "an act of Nature herself, one that, without recourse to passions and artifices and in complete independence, corresponds strictly to need."[11] Furthermore, he makes the point that "in Western literature - beginning with Christian monasticism - masturbation remains associated with the chimera of the imagination and its dangers. It is the very form of unnatural pleasure that humans invented in order to exceed the limits assigned to them."[12] Indeed, Foucault has argued that masturbation becomes *the* sin for monks and takes on an importance never previously known. A new inward-

ness in human consciousness is constructed by the interioriza-
tion of lust on the part of celibates.[13]

If we look at modern Orthodox literature which deals with
masturbation, we become aware that many of the arguments
advanced there were based on no scientific evidence. The
Greek commentator in the *Pedalion* could write:

> Masturbation causes damage also to the body and to
> the health of the body; for, as all authorities in
> common assert, including both old and modern physi-
> cians, masturbators are wretched and miserable be-
> cause: 1. they have a yellowish complexion; 2. their
> stomach is weak, and they cannot digest their food
> properly; 3. their eyesight is poor; 4. they lose their
> voice; 5. they lose the quick wittedness and acuity of
> their mind; 6. they lose their memory; 7. they lose
> sleep, owing to disturbing dreams; 8. their body
> experiences tremors; 9. they lose all the manliness of
> their body and soul, and become cowardly like
> women; 10. they are liable to apoplexy, or what is
> commonly known as "a stroke"; 11. they are liable to
> frequent emissions in their sleep, and many times even
> when they are awake, owing to their seminal passages
> being wide open; and finally 12. they age quickly and
> die badly.[14]

These commentators appeal to the common knowledge of
physicians, but today the common knowledge of physicians is
that none of this is true. Nevertheless, Metropolitan Antony
Khrapovitsky in his book *Confession: A Series of Lectures on
the Mystery of Repentance* speaks of the secret sins of children and adolescents (masturbation) which ruin their health
and lead them to greater sexual sins. He writes: "The sin will
gain in strength, falls will become more frequent, and God's
punishment will not be slow in coming, in the form of tuber-
culosis or neurasthenia, incapability of leading a married life
or even idiocy and epilepsy."[15]

The Orthodox reader who is acquainted with modern
sexual literature emanating from sexologists and physicians

will be aware that masturbation is now accepted in secular society as normal for adolescents and even for adults, married and unmarried. Modern advocates of masturbation discern none of the terrifying consequences of physical and mental degeneracy, but rather a normal and acceptable practice. Yet, instead of being seen as a passing phenomenon of adolescence, it is now hailed by many secular authors as a positive good, more satisfying than married sexual intercourse and something never to be abandoned. A Protestant author, William E. Phipps, has claimed that masturbation is even a virtue, a true good, and certainly no vice.[16] The Catholic James Cameron has claimed that modern secular ideologies of sex have made masturbation the archetypical form of sexual experience.[17]

The basic supposition in Catholic moral theology has been that masturbation is gravely sinful because it violates the principle of the finality of the sexual faculties in procreative, heterosexual intercourse. This may well be objectively true, but subjectively masturbatory acts often lack imputability as grave sin since deliberation is frequently imperfect.[18] Adolescent masturbation, in particular, is failing in both evaluative knowledge and the personal freedom necessary to make of it a mortal sin. The traditional Catholic position has been attacked by two moral theologians, Charles Curran and André Guindon. In their opinion masturbation has wrongly been categorized as grave sin, since there is parvity (lightness) of matter, despite the traditional claim to the contrary. Viewing it as an inability or failure to speak the language of love adequately, Guindon has held that masturbation is normal among adolescents and young people. He and Curran have urged that masturbation rarely becomes a fundamental option for a person. Only fundamental options involve grave sin, cutting one off from the grace of God. To make of masturbation such an option one would have to embrace it as one's good in place of the vocational good which lies ahead of one, either in marriage or in a monastic life. For Guindon adult masturbation reveals a failure to develop maturely. It may be pathological, or it may involve a refusal of the other with a consequent turning in upon oneself and one's fantasies.

Perhaps the most discerning study of masturbation from a Roman Catholic standpoint is that of the Indian Capuchin priest Felix M. Podimattam, *A Difficult Problem in Chastity, Masturbation.* His study of the psychology of masturbation is sophisticated in exploring the obsessive and compulsive drives that may emerge and lead to masturbatory acts. The instability of the adolescent frequently prevents him from maintaining self-control. Factors such as habit, the pressure of unconscious drives, the intensity of sexual temptation, and the vehemence of sexual propaganda all deprive the masturbating person of full freedom and knowledge. Podimattam even puts forth as a possible, probable opinion the view that sexual relief provided by oneself may not be masturbation in the traditional sense:

> It can therefore safely be concluded that not every self- induction of semen or self-relief is necessarily masturbation. Generally it is, but there are circumstances in which it need not be masturbation. Self-relief is masturbation when it is unreasonable, that is, when there are no proportionate reasons for it. It is not masturbation when there are adequate reasons for it. To my mind, self-relief is of the same category as killing a man, taking the goods of another, excising an organ, etc. Just as there can be reasonable and licit killing, licit and reasonable taking of another's goods, reasonable and licit excising of organs, etc., so there can be reasonable and licit self-relief. Killing, taking of another's goods, excising of organs, etc. are generally evil but they cease to be evil in a conflict situation. Similarly self-relief is generally evil but not so in a conflict situation.[19]

The same reasons are found acceptable by many Roman Catholic moral theologians, for example, when ejaculation of semen is allowed for purposes of sperm testing, usually to discern the sources of infertility in a couple.[20] Such reasons are acceptable for revisionist moral theologians who refuse to allow that a physical act is of itself the norm of what is natural and what is unnatural. The sufficient reason alone reveals to us the morality or immorality of the act.

How then can an Orthodox moral theology deal with the morality or immorality of masturbation? The first point to be made is that the Orthodox tradition has not put its stress on the unnaturalness of the masturbatory act as violating the purpose of the sexual faculties. Rather, the emphasis has been placed on the fact that masturbation is a yielding to fleshly passions. It stands in conflict with the spiritual life which means a conformity of the whole person body and soul to the Spirit of God. The raging passions, whether they be sexual in nature or those of irascibility, harm the soul by disturbing the serene inner peace given by the Holy Spirit. Insofar as masturbation is the making flesh of a fantasy (so discerningly portrayed by the psychiatrist R.D. Laing), it is the creation of an illusion incarnate. [21] This is particularly dangerous to the monk who is called to perpetual prayer. The fundamental option of the monk is spiritual and thus mastur-bation threatens that option.

There are other vocations for Orthodox Christian people. The vocation of each involves a different developmental scheme. Sexuality must be developed as a language of love. What emerges in the male at puberty is a powerful drive which often has no personal direction and by definition is lacking in integration. That integration can only occur in the love for the significant other. This task of love is a move-ment from narcissistic and self-centered libido to the focusing of libido onto the other sex in the union of "one flesh." This is the task which culminates in the mystery of marriage. The later marriage occurs in our society the greater the difficulty and the more likely a tendency to masturbation as a form of substitute satisfaction and release. Masturbation cannot be accepted as a good in itself because it is a failure to achieve the union of "one flesh." It is a sign of an unfocused sexuali-ty. It is sinful in the sense that it misses the mark, the fulfill-ment of the sexual project. If we view marriage as a dialogue, a form of expression in self-giving and love, we can see that it is akin to attaining the usage of a language. Learning to speak is never easy, but it is even more difficult to learn a foreign language. Learning to speak the sexual language begins with fantasy, and fantasy often activates the sexual organs to high intensity. Furthermore, modern people are surrounded by a multitude of erotic stimuli and tension-producing factors making restraint of sexual excitement very difficult and very rare. The Orthodox moral theologian cannot accept this dilemma with ease. That would be to accept an evil as inevitable or even as good. Yet we cannot expect the novice to speak the sexual language immediately without mistakes. The awakening of one's sexuality without the possibility of satisfaction in marriage leads to a dangerous and awkward situation. Mistakes are inevitable. The priest who acts as confessor must lead the young person toward the goal that is his or her fundamental option. Two such goals exist, marriage and monastic life. The single life may exist as a legitimate option only when one's personality, condition, or history makes it necessary. Such an option would clearly be by way of a *faute de mieux*, by way of an obstacle (physical, mental, or social) to a vocation more sacramentally appropriate to the Kingdom of God.

Masturbation is often a sign of a failure in relatedness. If viewed as a failure in communication, as a failure of dialogue, it may be said to be a way of talking to oneself. Such autistic speech usually has an inner object, sometimes unconscious, sometimes conscious. This object is an image of the imagination or at best a symbol. The object may be a project for the future (as with an adolescent envisaging union with a loved one) or a substitute image in a lack of any prospective union. One may psychologically speak of object relations here or of part objects (such as a breast or a phallos). A full object is the image of a whole person, whereas a part object is concerned only with a symbolic part. Masturbation often occurs as a reaction to a rebuff or a defeat. Under such conditions the ego regresses to an earlier and even infantile state where object relations are abandoned for a purely narcissistic self-love. As a way of consoling oneself masturbation is often a compulsive reaction offering both a pleasure and a release of painful tension. Such masturbation may occur not only in youth but in adult life. The married person may masturbate in the absence of a beloved spouse with the image of the spouse being entertained as a full object. After a dispute involving anger and disturbance, masturbation may be carried out as an act of revenge or of consolation. A deeply disturbed marriage may give rise to masturbation by either partner with erotic images of a partner other than one's own spouse. Again, there may be no image but only a consolation of one's self. Such comfort as the practice provides, however transitory and insufficient, stands over against the acute pain a person may be feeling.

Traditional Roman Catholics have argued that the comprehension of the psychodynamics of motives and drives leading to masturbation is relevant only insofar as freedom and knowledge may be curtailed leading to an imperfect act. They argue that the masturbatory act is *ex objecto*, by its physical nature and structure, *malum in se*. I believe that this is not a position fully consonant with Orthodox theology. Masturbation is wrong because of the influx of the passions which disrupt spiritual integration. It is true that traditional fathers and mothers of the spiritual life have viewed the invitations and temptations of the flesh as coming from the demons that seek to destroy souls.

To state this, however, does not mean that we must necessarily ignore the dynamics of the psyche. We must ask whether masturbatory acts result from a breakdown in the basic dynamisms of love and other-directedness or whether such acts are inadequate but essentially directed movements toward that love which is celebrated in marriage. One whose love will be realized in marriage must take a different route from those whose love will be realized in a monastic vocation. However, a large number of those who masturbate fall into neither of these categories. Such persons indulge in masturbation by reason of pathological impulses which disturb their self-control. One cannot make an accurate moral assessment of acts that are carried out compulsively or obsessively, often as expressions of acute anxiety. Masturbation is a means by which ease is sought from such anxiety or of depression. One does not have to resort to Freudianism to conclude that much human behavior is motivated by fear or anger directed against the self. Pathological tension partially expresses itself by regression and by an intense need for release and consolation. Masturbation is an easy resource in defending oneself against internal disintegration. Dr. Hans Kohut has urged that masturbatory acts of this sort are not so much regressive and infantile erotic phenomena as defenses against submergence of the ego.[22] One has only to see a sick and disturbed infant to observe that he or she seeks out the genitals for consolation and comfort in the face of adversity. The adolescent, the distraught adult, or the aged may act in similar fashion. This is no case of moral wantonness. There is no indulgence here in a world of pornography for the sake of lewdness, though fantasy may provide a magic escape from the suffering that a person experiences.

One often discovers that masturbation is a way of reacting to failure. Paradoxically both consolation and the incorporation of defeat are felt in the masturbatory act. This form of masochism unites a self-punishing act (which will only be reinforced by moral condemnation) with a self-pleasuring act. Such pathological masturbation is not unusual. Indeed, the evidence among depressives indicates that masturbation may be the one thing that is felt to provide relief when suffering becomes most intense. The problem is that the aftermath of masturbation is often only a deeper depression, particularly if the act is laden with guilt feelings. The experience of psychoanalyis as it is practiced today is not that masturbation is a good but that it is a sign of something else. It is as much a symbol as an expression, often as much a pain as a pleasure. Dr. Edrita Fried has suggested that the disturbance felt after masturbation results from the fact that the sexual drive which by its nature seeks another has been expressed with a phantom image, and since the self must identify both with the active doer as well as the passive recipient, a deep inner divide is experienced in the ego, giving rise to a sense of anxiety and disturbance.[23]

If we look upon masturbation as a sign and a symptom rather than seeing it as a primary evil, we discover the complexity of the phenomenon. Robert Solomon is most illuminating in his perception:

> If sexuality is essentially a language, it follows that masturbation, while not a perversion, is a deviation and not, as Freud thought, the primary case. Masturbation is essentially speaking to oneself. But not only children, lunatics, and herits speak to themselves; so do poets and philosophers. And so masturbation might, in different contexts, count as wholly different extensions of language. With Freud, we would have to distinguish masturbation as autoeroticism from masturbation as narcissism - the first being more like muttering to oneself, the latter more like self-praise; the first being innocent and childlike, the latter potentially either pathetic or selfish and self-indulgent.[24]

There is clearly more to masturbation than either the autoerotic or the narcissistic. Its masochistic and self-punitive aspects must not be ignored. For the moral theologian the primary criterion in making a moral evaluation of masturbation would, I think, be whether the subject embraced masturbation as a good or as an evil. The evil of masturbation is not perceived if it is conceived entirely as a satanic temptation to illegitimate pleasure. It is, rather, a false move in the self's search for love. It becomes an act of despair if it means that one rejects the love of the other or the love of God in favor of such reparative and defensive self-love. To seek masturbation as an end in itself would be to take an option in its favor. This is clearly the aim of the books published by Sharon Hite who urges masturbation as a preferable form of sexual pleasure for both men and women.[25] That is clearly wrong and contrary to the created purposes of our sexuality. However, masturbation as a temporary form of sexual growth when a person is not yet able to become integrated with another person as a couple is quite another matter. Similarly, masturbation as an expression of underlying illness or distress must not identified as immoral. One ought not to condemn the lonely and isolated person who can speak no language of love. God's purpose for that person remains one of dialogue with Himself in the communion of saints. That discourse may fail by reason of illness or anxiety or depression and the resulting behavior differs from the hedonism of the masturbator who buys pornography with which to entertain himself. The nature of pornography is that it portrays the flesh without the person. The identity of the pornographic image is not revealed. The body is given as only flesh, in turn, to arouse the flesh. The Orthodox understanding of the image (the icon) is that the person must radiate through the visual image. Nudity outside the context of personal intimacy is often subhuman, revealing the flesh without the person. Thus it degrades the sanctity of human persons and the human body, which is the temple of the Holy Spirit.

The teaching of the Orthodox Church is that we are subject to passions from which we must be saved if we are to be shaped into the likeness of God. The physical act of masturbation incarnates the passion of lust in the absence of a desired person. As such, the passion is not only embraced but made flesh. We can never accept the gnostic view so widespread today that the activities of the body have little or nothing to do with the soul. Yet a physical act may on occasion be not an expression of a passion but merely a release of tension or built up excesses of semen in the male. The fact that clear and careful distinctions are made in the penitential literature between seminal emissions in sleep and those of men who are awake is indicative of this vital difference. In the canons attributed to John the Faster the important point is made that consent is the "origin and cause of penances."[26] Masturbation is differentiated from emissions of both the sleeper and the man awake in the *Penitential*. My point is that masturbation carried out by one's own willing touch may, nonetheless, have more in common with seminal emissions than lustful passions. That depends upon not only the extent to which the will and the intellect are involved but also whether the act is carried out for pleasure or from relief of tension, loneliness, or anxiety. However, pathology is what one suffers, and pathological masturbation is a response to suffering, even if the person involved acts consciously. The sin which exists in this form of masturbation should probably to be judged as involuntary. The judgment of a confessor or counselor on masturbatory activity must also assess whether a person has opted for fantasy in place of a genuine relating to another person. An intentional relation to an image of an unknown woman in a centerfold is quite different from that directed to one's absent spouse. This is not to say that we should support masturbation as a good in itself, but one can differentiate the forms it may take and the motives that inspire it. Masturbation in those who are legitimately oriented toward married love can be a yearning for that which is absent. Masturbation in those who have no legitimate orientation toward marriage is far more grievous since it invites fantasy into one's life where spiritual reality is the good to be embraced. Thus the concern about masturbation among monks must be greater than about the same practice among adolescents who in a traditional society would be married but in modern society are deprived of marriage because of economic and educational factors.

The traditional language of Orthodoxy regarding the passions is the language of the demonic. That modern people perceive of their passions from the viewpoint of a dynamic psychology makes for a difference in perspective. Whereas traditional ascesis views sensual images as inspired by the devil, a psychology of drives draws them from the appetites or instincts. We are far from being able to integrate the two perspectives. To attribute the imagination of sensual fantasy to the devil is basically to say that such images are evil and not good for the soul. Therefore the question of fantasy and its morality becomes the primary question when we investigate the morality of masturbation, for once we abandon the position that masturbation is evil because of its unnatural character we are forced back to a consideration of the fantasies that entice one to masturbation.

The fact is that masturbation has a multitude of causes, some pathological, some hedonistic, and some anticipatory. I have argued above that the spiritual and penitential investigation of masturbation will be concerned with discovering the causes of masturbation, the degree of assent, and the vocational direction of the person involved. For the monk who is moving toward the imageless prayer of the heart, masturbation, by invoking destructive, distracting and indeed diabolical images can bring about great harm in the practice of prayer. The young person moving toward marriage, however, may be mobilizing a sexuality toward a significant other to whom he or she may one days be joined in marriage. The married person deprived of the normal expression of sexual union may fall into masturbation as a substitute for a beloved partner. Again, the disturbed person may masturbate to find assurance and escape from a loneliness of terrible proportions. In all these cases masturbation is an inadequate solution and less than good. The desire of the self for the other is such that there is a latent intentionality whereby tumescence in the male or lubrication in the female usually results from the entertaining of sensual images. Such images create an inner reflection of the external reality. In our world of television the mind is cluttered with sensual images. In fact, one may ask whether the soul can survive the onslaught of sensual images portrayed and given "reality" from the television screen. Kinsey discovered that masturbation increased notably in the college-educated and those with a rich imagination.[27] One can even say that our age may become known (as noted by James Cameron) as the age of masturbation since ours is a culture built on artificial, enticing, and stimulating images. More than one sexologist has noted the harm done by pornography to married sexuality. The normal is subverted by the abnormal, the prosaic by the fantastic. The psyche and the glands are put in constant state of hyperactivity by the barrage of stimuli.

If we cannot adequately comprehend the nature of masturbatory activity by reference to the alleged purposes of the sexual organs, equally we must not focus entirely upon the individual person and his or her pathologies. In fact, masturbation emerged in Christian consciousness from within the monastic movement with its intense rejection of all sexual imagery as satanic and its search for interior solitude. [28] The sociologist Richard Sennett has written of the varieties of solitude:

We know a solitude imposed by power. This is the solitude of isolation, the solitude of anomie. We know a solitude that arouses fear in those who are powerful. This is the solitude of the dreamer, of the *homme revolte*, the solitude of rebellion. Finally, there is a solitude that transcends the terms of power. It is a solitude based on the idea of Epictetus that there is a difference between being lonely and being alone. This is the sense of being one among many, of having an inner life that is more than a reflection of the lives of others. It is the solitude of difference.[29]

The third type of solitude is clearly the solitude sought by monks. Both Sennett and Foucault recognize the crisis of solitude as it confronted those modern sexologists who created "sexuality" as a problem. As Sennett puts it, "The first modern researchers on sexuality believed they were opening up a terrifying Pandora's box of unrestrained lust."[30] The person alone was faced with terrifying forces without the civilizing restraints that social life imposed. From the early Augustinian horror of sexuality to the obsession with fantasy and masturbation evident in St. John Cassian's writings masturbation has become a major problem for solitary persons. Foucault claims that a script of expectations was formed and later translated into the obsessions of confessors and the manuals for confessors with "solitary vice".[31] From the treatise of Tissot published in 1710 under the name of *Onania, or the Heinous Sin of Self-pollution* to the guides for young persons published throughout the nineteenth and early twentieth centuries a link was drawn between sexual behavior and character. The modern view that we are what we do with our sexuality and our solitude was well on the way to realization. Clearly the exaggeration of the evils of masturbation created an obsession as well as a context in which sexuality had become all important. Both the negative reading of masturbation as self-damnation and the positive evaluation of it as the fundamental pleasure before all others assume a disconnected solitude which is painful for modern people.

Masturbation is, therefore, not just a symptom of interior disorder but of a social disorder. Sennett calls this disorder the fall of public man and discerns a direct relationship between solitude and sociability:

> Unless a human being can be comfortable alone, he or she cannot be comfortable with others. There is a rhythm between the solitude of difference and sociability that ought to obtain in society, and it is a rhythm we do not feel because, in part, the experience of being alone with ourselves is so troubled. This rhythm is possible for us to experience in a way that it was not in the past, because an immense opportunity was opened up in Western bourgeois society, which is to live in a fragmented society.[32]

The fact is that solitude has become extremely painful and difficult for the majority of people in our society. Some retreat to drugs and dreams. Others act out rebellion, even by masturbation perceived as an act of defiance. Few are able to attain to real solitude since the continuity between withdrawal and participation has disintegrated. Being alone is felt to be a way of alienation, a way of being cut off. The vacuum which is experienced invites us to fill it up with noise or fantasies provided by video-tapes, television, or pornography. The arousal of the body is a way of feeling alive rather than experiencing the deadly loneliness which is so extremely painful to so many people today. Masturbation is a way of dealing with loneliness for many people, and the resolution of the loneliness must come through the creation of community, of interdependence, not through threats of damnation. Such threats would only increase the obsession and anxiety which lead to the need to escape through masturbation in the first place.

If we are seriously to evaluate masturbation from the viewpoint of Christian life, it is not enough to invoke terms such as "obscene" or "diabolic" in reference to the images that stimulate it. It is not enough because once we commit ourselves to unraveling the complex symbolic meaning of sexuality we must learn to read the script of behavior. This is not to deny that obscene thoughts or diabolic inspiration may lie behind masturbatory behavior. It is to say that all behavior is symbolic and sexual behavior is especially so. Insofar as married love expresses a union which is itself a sign of and participation in the union of Christ with his Church, all actions that convey that love, whether in the bed or in the daily household chores, are good. Masturbation is always a sign of a lack, but it may point to the resolution of the lack, either through marriage or through the recovery of the beloved partner who may be absent for reasons of necessity or illness. Masturbation is fundamentally a making do with the state of absence. This is why it is often so unhappy. One is not happily self-sufficient when it comes to love. To call masturbation self-love is a mistake because the underlying wish which comes forth in the fantasies is for the other, to be loved by the other and to love the other.

Ideologically the "gospel of masturbation" as an unmitigated good is closely linked with the assaults against the family and the assertion of radical independence of the individual. Sharon Hite provides many quotations from men who find in masturbation the independence of not having to depend on anyone else for sexual satisfaction. Similarly, she advocates masturbation for women so that they will not have to depend on men for sexual satisfaction. Such attitudes are strongly contrary to the interdependence which is fundamental to the reality of life as perceived by Orthodox theology. We are members of one another, and we need one another. Masturbation becomes the temptation of doing without the other at the sexual level of relating. Edrita Fried describes masturbation as a haven for forbidden desires, sometimes infantile, sometimes incestuous, sometimes homosexual. Insofar as such desires are felt as forbidden, their indulgence and acceptance in masturbation leaves a person feeling guilty, alienated, and often bizarre.[33] As an act which invokes the forbidden and expresses regression, masturbation can hardly be the healthy act proposed by authors such as Hite, Masters and Johnson. It is only in discerning the motivation of masturbation that we can determine something of its morality.

The modern attempt to bless masturbation as self-love is inadequate and misleading. Masturbation is solitary by nature (mutual masturbation may be either homosexual or heterosexual but by involving another person it becomes a form of dialogue, even if minimally so). By its very exercise it invokes a fantasy most of the time since the arousal of the sexual organ (both in males and females) usually depends on fantasy. Consequently, the moral evaluation of masturbation must include a moral assessment of fantasy. The question is whether the fantasy is an avenue to reality or a substitute for reality. The reality of female masturbation also tells us that discussion of the phenonmenon in terms of finalities or emissions tell us nothing of its moral significance.[34]

It is, I believe, wrong to castigate those who fall into masturbation to relieve their anxiety, isolation, or depression. The act remains reparative, symptomatic, and usually dysfunctional. Attempts to reduce masturbation to simple hedonism or the gratification of libidinous passions are based on misconceptions of what is taking place. Both fictional and autobiographical portrayals of the place of masturbation in the single sex schools for adolescents, in prisons, and similar total institutions reveal the place that masturbation has when social suffering becomes maximal. The Church rightly speaks out against those who would make of masturbation an absolute right or good, seeking to establish "self-pleasuring" or "self-love" in the form of masturbation as an inherent good. Masturbation is simply too complex to classify it so easily. It is often compulsive. It is sometimes pathological. It may also be said to be under certain circumstances a lesser evil, for example, where a violent or gravely immoral sexual act would occur in its absence. The task of the moral theologian or the spiritual father is to uncover what place masturbation occupies in the emotional economy and the existential situation of the person who presents it as a problem. What it means to a fourteen-year-old boy and to a married man of fifty will be worlds apart. This is as equally true for an adolescent girl as for a married woman of mature age.

To assume that a form of behavior such as masturbation has a single meaning is comparable to assuming that mere sounds can tell us the meaning of words without our knowing the various languages in which sounds are spoken. Masturbation is indeed a speaking to oneself of the sexual language. As such its significance may be no more than a waking dream since dreams are ways in which we speak to ourselves in symbolic and emotional ways. What is morally problematic is whether this form of speaking to ourselves is a refusal of the language of love or a preparation for the language of love. Indeed, it may be a way in which one would seek to speak that language because there is no love at hand. Masturbation speaks of our lack of the other. The moral question is not a matter of the waste of seed (as the reality of female masturbation shows us) or even the falling into the libidinous for those whose vocation lies in marriage. It is, rather, the question as to why one masturbates in place of loving, or, for that matter, in place of praying. To make the evil simply a matter of releasing sexual passions is far too simplistic. As Robert Solomon as revealed, the passions are not simply irrational urges and powers that defeat our rationality. They are structured and refined by our intentional orientations to others.[35]

It has become usual for modern moral theologians to recognize that freedom is often curtailed in a masturbatory act.[36] Even the Vatican Declaration *Persona Humana* bids us assess free responsibility with caution:

> Psychology helps one to see how the immaturity of adolescence (which can sometimes persist after that age), psychological imbalance or habit can influence behavior, diminishing the deliberate character of the act and bringing about a situation whereby subjectively there may not always be serious fault. But in general, the absence of serious responsibility must not presumed; this would be to misunderstand people's moral capacity.[37]

Numbers of modern Roman Catholic authors have witnessed to the frequent lack of freedom in those who masturbate. The force of the passion, the habitual character once formed, and the determining character of the motives and unconscious meanings, all would deprive the subject of sufficient freedom to commit grave sin.

Orthodox moral theologians have not investigated the character of masturbation from clinical insights as have Roman Catholics, but they are equipped with the category of "involuntary sin" which appears a number of times in liturgical formulas. This may be applied by some in a way which only increases the guilt feelings of the sinner, but I would think that this is hardly the point of the concept. The Western contrast between material and formal sin may be of help here. A sin is material to the extent that it involves an evil act but is deficient in the knowledge and freedom of the subject that commits it. This is, I think, the intention behind the distinction between voluntary and involuntary sin. Whereas the tendency among Jesuit moral theologians has been to dismiss involuntary sin as not in any sense a sin (though it may be an evil), the Orthodox recognize that we are victims of evil acts which we perpetrate without willing them. Thus, we are called to repent of them, to disengage ourselves from them. Nonetheless, we are not fully (if at all) responsible for them, and insofar as they are truly involuntary we may well expect to commit them again unless we move to make ourselves conscious of their evil and thus be able to take responsibility for them. Masturbation is clearly an act which is sinful since it misses the mark of fully developed sexual love for the other person in the context of fidelity which is marriage. Yet it is more symptomatic than causative in its disorder. Furthermore, it may well be inevitable that we masturbate prior to forming a mature sexual relationship or arriving at a vocation whereby our sexuality is taken up into a spiritual life directed toward God and heroic charity. To regret masturbation is what we are asked for in the sacrament of repentance. That regret is not found in self-hatred but in awareness that we are called to more than the flesh taking delight in itself, turned in upon itself, and reduced to a world of fantasies.

Fidelity to Orthodox faith and morals can never allow us to uphold masturbation as an inherent good or right. The reasons for this position are not merely adherence to an ancient tradition (such as remaining loyal to the canons attributed to

St. John the Faster). They are based on our fundamental perception as to what human love and existence are all about. We are made for love, not just for orgasms. On the other hand, we must not sit in judgment on the masturbator. His or her problem is rarely masturbation itself but rather a situation of conflict, immaturity, loss, or incapacity. Those guilty of masturbation are assisted by love, not by condemnation. Their guilt lies far deeper than the isolated sexual act. It is a guilt of failure in the speaking of the sexual language in the context of love. As always, the resolution of guilt lies in forgiveness and restoration to communion. It is only in the gift of love that the isolated and alienated person can once more become part of the human community of love. That is the gospel of Jesus Christ and the Orthodox Church is committed to that gospel at every point in its life.

Notes

(1) André Guindon, *The Sexual Language* (Ottawa: University of Ottawa Press, 1976), p. 252.

(2) Sacred Congregation for the Doctrine of the Faith, *Declaration on Certain Questions Concerning Sexual Ethics*, 9.

(3) Ibid., 9.

(4) John Boswell, *Christianity, Social Tolerance, and Homosexuality* (Chicago: University of Chicago Press, 1980), p. 107.

(5) John Erikson, "Penitential Discipline in the Orthodox Canonical Tradition," *St. Vladimir's Theological Quarterly*, 21, 4 (1977), p. 200.

(6) Ibid., p. 201.

(7) Ibid., p. 203.

(8) St. John Climacus, *The Ladder of Divine Ascent*, Step 15, 29, trans. Lazarus Moore, (Boston, MA: Holy Transfiguration Monastery, 1979), pp. 107-8.

(9) Ibid., Step 15, 30, p. 108.

(10) Ibid., Step 15, 33, p. 109.

(11) Michel Foucault, *The Care of the Self* (New York: Random House, 1987), p. 140.

(12) Ibid., p. 140.

(13) Michel Foucault, "Sexuality and Solitude," in M. Blonsky, ed., *In Signs* (Baltimore: Johns Hopkins University Press, 1985), pp. 365-72.

(14) *The Rudder* (*Pedalion*), p. 938.

(15) Antony Khrapovitsky, *Confession: A Series of Lectures on the Mystery of Repentance* (Jordanville, NY: Holy Trinity Monastery, 1975), p. 61.

(16) William E. Phipps, "Masturbation: Vice or Virtue?," *Journal of Religion and Health*, 16, 3 (1977).

(17) James M. Cameron, "Sex in the Head," *New York Review of Books* 23, 8 (1976).

(18) Sacred Congregation for the Doctrine of the Faith, 9.

(19) F. M. Podimattam, *A Difficult Problem in Chastity: Masturbation* (Kotagiri, Nilgris, S. India: St. Joseph's College, 1972), pp. 151-2.

(20) Bernard Häring, *Medical Ethics* (Notre Dame, IN: Fides, 1973), pp. 92-3.

(21) Ronald D. Laing, *The Self and Others: Further Studies in Sanity and Madness* (London: Tavistock Publications, 1961), pp. 38-47.

(22) Heinz Kohut, *The Restoration of the Self* (New York: International Universities Press, 1977), pp. 161, 284.

(23) Edrita Fried, *On Love and Sexuality* (New York: Grove Press, 1962), pp. 155-9.

(24) Robert Solomon, "Sex and Perversion," in *Philosophy and Sex*, R. Baker and E. Elliston, eds. (Buffalo: Prometheus Books, 1975), p. 282.

(25) Sharon Hite, *The Hite Report on Female Sexuality* (New York: Dell, 1976); *The Hite Report on Male Sexuality* (New York: Knopf, 1981).

(26) John the Faster, Penitential, Canon 5, in *The Rudder* (*Pedalion*), p. 934.

(27) Alfred Kinsey; B. Wardell; and Clyde E. Martin, *Sexual Behavior in the Human Male* (Philadelphia and London: W. B. Saunders Company, l948).

(28) Michel Foucault, "Sexuality and Solitude," in *Humanities in Review*, 1 (Cambridge: Cambridge University Press, 1982), pp. 265-72.

(29) Richard Sennett, "Sexuality and Solitude," in *Humanities in Review*, 1 (Cambridge: University Press, l982), pp. 4-5.

(30) Ibid., p. 5.

(31) Michel Foucault, *The History of Sexuality*, Vol. 1, *An Introduction* (New York: Random House, l980).

(32) Sennett, p. 7.

(33) Fried, pp. 138-48.

(34) Sheila Kitzinger, *Woman's Experience of Sex* (New York: Penguin, l985).

(35) Robert Solomon *Passions* (Garden City, NY: Doubleday, l976).

(36) One should consult R. P. O'Neil and M. A. Donovan, *Sexuality and Moral Responsibility* (Washington, DC, Corp[us, 1968) and V. Venovesi, *In Pursuit of Love: Catholic Morality and Human Sexuality* (Wilmington, DL, Michael Glazier, l986).

(37) Sacred Congregation for the Doctrine of the Faith, *Declaration on Certain Questions Concerning Sexual Ethics*, 9.

Chapter Nine:

Homosexuality and Moral Theology

The movement for the legitimation of homosexuality and its practice in North American liberal Christian circles is viewed by most Orthodox Christians as entirely alien to the practice of their faith. Not only are Orthodox Christians not in the habit of changing their moral standards in response to various secular movements, but they find the attempts to legitimize homosexuality perfidious. Many non-Orthodox Christians would say, however, that this only indicates the isolation of Orthodoxy from contemporary life. Certainly the confusion evident in some Orthodox circles between homosexuality as a condition and homosexual vice points in the direction of obscurantism. Others would say that we cannot afford to ignore psychiatric evidence and commit the grave injustice of condemning persons whose sexual orientation was determined by genetic factors or other causes beyond their control, not by a willful perversity or a surrender to the wiles of the devil. There exists among Orthodox Christians great fear as well as confusion in these matters.

There is today a widespread discussion of homosexuality. We must be very careful, however, in our use of the word "homosexuality." The term is an abstract one which needs to be deconstructed if we are to grasp a complex set of phenomena. First of all there are homosexual acts. Since there are a wide variety of acts which may be designated as "sexual" (everything from holding hands to coitus), we must define a homosexual act as a genital act between persons of the same gender. These may be carried out by those whose emotional orientation is homoerotic but also by persons who are heterosexual in their affective and erotic responses. That they act homosexually may be only by reason of a chance encounter, isolation in a same-sex institution, or by other restrictions set on heterosexual behavior. There are others who are emotionally homoerotic and, nonetheless, may never carry out a homosexual act. These persons are sexually attracted predominantly to others of the same sex. The modern awareness of the homosexual as having a decisively different sexual orientation is a move away from the assumption made among the ancient Greeks and Romans that all persons were capable of homosexual acts and that bisexuality was a permanent potentiality for human beings. This modern awareness resulted from the impact of the clinical sciences and the importance given to subjectivity by modern people. It is clear that the homoerotic person may commit homosexual acts and will have a tendency to do so unless inhibited in various ways. To perceive oneself as "a homosexual" is a form of self-identification which is in no way automatically assumed by those who carry out homosexual acts or even by those experiencing homoerotic love. To identify another or oneself as a homosexual is, in part, to accept a social construction. A person may inwardly decide that he or she is homosexual but carry out no homoerotic acts. Similarly, a person may be sexually active with a person of the same sex and yet not identify, publicly or privately as a homosexual. It is clear that the word "gay" is used today for those who have identified themselves with the social roles offered in various homophile groups. For that reason it is best to avoid the term except in the context of political movements working for the liberation from civil and moral restraints on homosexuals.

It is clear that homosexual acts are to be distinguished from the homosexual condition. By analogy we may distinguish an aggressive character from aggressive or violent acts carried out by a person with or without such a character. Whether homosexual acts are sinful or not depends on our theology of sexuality as a whole. If such acts are compulsive and predetermined by drives which are not subject to ego control their gravity is mitigated, and we must speak of involuntary sin. Many people find homosexual impulses present and strong despite their constant attempt to repress them and negate them. To condemn such people for their orientation as evil or wicked is to show oneself lacking in justice and charity. Consequently, a moral discussion of the homosexual condition must be viewed as distinct from the examination of homosexual acts. To evaluate the sinfulness of homosexual acts is quite another matter, though it remains essential to ask by what criteria such judgments may be made. It is important that Orthodox pastors and laity should be aware of why and how homosexual acts are to be rejected as immoral. Hysteria in this sphere helps no one and leads only to anxiety and injustice.

As with any ethical problem, we must first look to the Holy Scriptures. In the Old Testament the only explicit condemnation of homosexual acts is that of Lv 18:22: "You shall not lie with a male as with a woman; it is an abomination." The word *shakav* used in this passage is a term frequently used to denote sexual intercourse. The penalty in Leviticus for such an act is death. There are various other crimes in this chapter for which death is a penalty: bestiality, adultery, intercourse with a menstruating woman, incest, etc. Dt 23:17-18 may refer to cult prostitution by men, but this is unclear. The term used for such prostitution is that it is an abomination, which is a word usually cultic in meaning. It has been argued by various scholars that the word *toebah* translated from the Hebrew as "abomination" is sufficiently cultic as to place the penalties and condemnation of homosexual prostitution entirely within the context of the ceremonial Torah rather than in what later theologians would designate as the natural law. The fact remains that the designation of "abomination" and the penalty of death are part of a code of morality based on purity and cleanness as its primary characteristic. The purity laws, whether the prohibition of coitus with a woman during her menstrual period or the rejection of various foods are clearly abolished by the new covenant.

The most famous condemnation of a homosexual act is that

recorded in Gn 19:1-29. When two angels come to destroy Sodom because of its sins and are received by Lot, the wicked men of Sodom come and try to force Lot to send his guests out so that they "might know them." Lot tries to interest them in his two daughters, but they persist in wanting to know the male guests. The assumption is that "to know" means to have sexual intercourse with. This assumption has been questioned by various modern authors, notably Bailey, Boswell, and McNeill, who think that the sin for which Sodom was destroyed was the violation of the sacred bonds of hospitality. Robin Scroggs in *The New Testament and Homosexuality* and A.M.J.M. Herman van de Spijker in *Die gleichgeschlectliche Zuneigung* both reject this revised interpretation.[1] The parallel narrative in Judges 19 uses the same language of "knowing" and the context is explicitly sexual. A gang of men come demanding a male guest "in order that they may abuse him," but the man of the house offers his daughter in his place. When she is rejected his concubine is offered, and she is raped to death. The crime was what would now be called "gang rape," and it was plotted in the first place against a man. For a contrary interpretation of the Sodom story, it is clear that the Hebrew tradition did not associate Sodom with homosexual sin but, rather, with sin in general, whereby the city of the plain was destroyed as a punishment for wickedness. The reference to Sodom in the teaching of Jesus in the Synoptic gospels has to do with the refusal of hospitality by the cities of Galilee to the disciples of Jesus (Mt 10:15, Lk 10:12, and Mk 6:11). The use of the term "sodomy" to refer to a specific form of homosexual activity does not originate with the Old Testament but is a later usage. There is no reference whatsoever to female homosexuality in the Old Testament.

The New Testament references to homosexual vice are to be found in 1 Cor 6:9-10; Rom 1:26-27; and 1 Tm 1:9-10. In both 1 Cor and 1 Tm we have lists of vices. We read in 1 Cor 6:9-10: "Do you not know that the unrighteous will not inherit the kingdom of God? Do not be deceived; neither the immoral, nor idolaters, nor adulterers, not *malakoi*, or *arsenokoitai*, nor thieves, nor the greedy, nor drunkards, nor revilers, nor robbers will inherit the kingdom of God." The problematic words *malakoi* and *arsenokoitai* have been retained in the Greek since their translation is open to question. The variety of words used to translate *malakoi* includes "homosexuals," "effeminate," "sodomites," and "abusers of themselves with mankind." Quite literally *malakos* means "soft" and has even been translated "sissy." The word *arsenokoitai* has been translated as "perverts, "sodomites," and "them that defile themselves with mankind." The list of sins that appears in 1 Cor 6:9-10 has parallels in 1 Cor 5:10 ("immoral, greedy, robbers, idolaters") and 1 Cor 5:11 ("immoral, greedy, idolaters, revilers, drunkards, robbers").

None of the above translations of *malakoi* and *arsenokoitai* are supported by lexicographical evidence. Scroggs summarizes the evidence thus: "Among a long list of activities which are said to exclude one from the kingdom of God in 1 Cor 6:9-10 is the plural adjective *malakoi*, used as a noun. The word literally means "soft" and can be applied to material like cloth, as in Mt 11:8: "When then did you go out? To see a man clothed in soft raiment? Behold, those who wear soft raiment are in kings' houses." A "soft" person is presumably one who needs exercise in order to become "tough." In the Greek period, however, the word came to have the meaning of "effeminate." We must ask if St. Paul meant it in this sense. Obviously the translators of the KJV. read it in this way. That would involve a condemnation of men whose lifestyle was like that of women. The translators of the RSV connected the word *malakoi* with *arsenokoites*, a rare word which means simply "one who has intercourse with males." Many have thought that St. Paul could not have been against effeminacy as such and that there would have to be some sexual meaning in the word *malakoi*. In his extensive study of the use of the word *malakos* in Greek writers of antiquity, Scroggs concludes that *malakos* is not a technical term for pederasty. However, there are links between the word as meaning "effeminate" and pederasty in ancient literature. When *malakos* is used with words that do point to pederasty it "would almost certainly conjure up images of the effeminate call-boy, if the context otherwise suggested some form of

293

pederasty."[2] The word *arsenokoites* has a straightforward meaning for a homosexual act. The root words are *arsen* (male) and *koite* (bed), and Scroggs translates it as "lying with a male" or as a noun "one who lies with a male." Rejecting the argument of John Boswell that *arsenokoites* is a compound with the emphasis on the first word (*arsen*) rather than the second (*koite*) thus giving it the meaning of a male prostitute who serves women, Scroggs claims that the Greek word *arsenokoites* is a translation of the Hebrew term most often used to describe male homosexual acts, *mishkav zakur* "lying with a male." Scroggs produces evidence from the Septuagint to the effect that parts of the Greek compound appear in the LXX version of the laws of Leviticus. The word is unusual in Greek, but as a translation from the Hebrew it makes good sense. One must not assume the correctness of Scroggs' interpretation, however. L.W. Countryman has given reason to suggest that Boswell's interpretation may have more support than that of Scroggs, particularly since *malakos* and *arsenokoites* are not always found together in the New Testament (cf. 1 Tm 1:10). According to him, the former term may mean "masturbators" and the latter "male prostitutes." However, the lack of clear evidence makes exact translation impossible.[3]

The most extensive reference to homosexuality in the New Testament is found in Rom 1:24-32:

> Therefore God gave them up in the lusts of their hearts to impurity, to the dishonoring of their bodies among themselves, because they exchanged the truth about God for a lie and worshiped and served the creature rather than the Creator, who is blessed forever! Amen.
>
> For this reason God gave them up to dishonorable passions. Their women exchanged natural relations for unnatural, and the men likewise gave up natural relations with women and were consumed wityh passion for one another, men committing shameless acts with men and receiving in their own persons the due penalty for their error.

The context here is the universal fall of mankind. The sin which is mentioned is idolatry. God's abandonment of the human race to their passions is a consequence of their refusal to worship the true God and to their worship of idols. Hellenistic Jews had long claimed a close connection between idolatry and homosexuality.[4] The example of homosexual vice is only illustrative of the consequences of idolatry since other evils result from idolatry. St. Paul refers to "evil, covetousness, malice, full of envy, murder, strife, deceit, malignity, gossips, slanders, haters of God, insolent, haughty, boastful, inventors of evil, disobedient to parents, foolish, faithless, heartless, ruthless (Rom 1:28-31)." Paul draws a conclusion from this record of human evil, "Though they know God's decree that those who do such things deserve to die, they not only do them but approve those who practice them (Rom 1:32)." It is important to quote these passages at length since the status of homosexual vice is precisely the same as that of the other sins mentioned in Rom 1:28-31. Scroggs notes the following points of clarification: God "gave them up" to these false actions; Paul "heaps up anthropological terms - heart, body, passions, mind - apparently to indicate that this false reality permeates a person's entire existence;"[5] Finally, there appears to be no concrete illustration of what happens to the heart-body as there is for what happens when the passions (emotions) and the mind are disordered. Scroggs is persuaded that Paul (like Philo) is speaking of pederasty in verses 28-31. The judgment that males leave natural (*physiken*) intercourse for unnatural homosexual acts is an argument that was "a commonplace of the Graeco-Roman attack on pederasty and has nothing to do with any theories of natural law or with interpretation of the Genesis stories of creation."[6] The passage concerning homosexual lust (Rom 1:28-31) has been interpreted by McNeill so as not to apply to true homosexuals since those born homosexual (or made that way in childhood) have had no opportunity to change from heterosexuality to homosexuality as St. Paul appears to claim in his text.[7] Basic to the Pauline theology is the assumption that idolatry creates a false world which

295

produces a false self. The false self finds homosexual activity pleasing and manifests the fall from nature to what is unnatural. The first chapter of Romans is clearly an indictment of and illustration of the Fall as evident among the Gentiles. Homosexuality was culturally and historically more characteristic of Gentile (Greek and Roman) society than of Jewish society. Scroggs insists that St. Paul is thinking of pederasty and its more degraded forms since he knew no other form of homosexuality. St. Paul is not interested in natural law in these passages; the phrase *para physin* was a popular one and is used in a popular rather than a philosophical or theological sense.

To build a theory of natural law on the passages which speak of the natural and the unnatural here misses the point of St. Paul's dialectic between the consequences of the Fall leading to death and the justification of faith which leads to life. To read Rom 1:18-32 as an index to unnatural and immoral behavior without reference to its place within the whole of the Epistle to the Romans is to distort St. Paul's statement of justification by faith. Countryman provides a very illuminating exegesis in urging that Paul seeks to illustrate the uncleanness of the Gentiles by reference to homosexual acts and proclivities. He was not setting up a morality of natural law but uses the term *para physin* ("against nature") as he does *physis* in Rom 11:24, Rom 2:14, and 1 Cor 11:14, either to provide discontinuity with the past or to reflect social usage. Indeed, it is God who punishes the Gentiles for their idolatry with homosexual desire. The penalty which they suffer is for their error (*plane*) which is clearly idolatry rather than homosexuality.[8]

The passage of 1 Tm 1:8-10 is the latest text referring to those alleged to be homosexuals: "Now we know that the law is good, if any one uses it lawfully, understanding this, that the law is not laid down for the just but for the

    lawless, rebellious
    impious, sinner, unholy, profane
    patricide, matricide, murderer
    pornoi, arsenokoitai, andrapoidistai
    liar, perjurer."[9]

In the usual Greek usage the world *pornos* means "male prostitute." However, the usage in the Septuagint (Sirach 23:16-18) would appear to be broader. Such broader meaning might refer to a sexual criminal, but that is difficult to prove. The connection with *arsenokoites* may well give it a more precise meaning. The word *andropodistes* means "kidnaper" or "slave dealer." Scroggs suggests that the three words so fitted together could be translated as "male prostitutes, males who lie (with them), and slave dealers (who procure them)."[10] He seeks the origins of these words in Hellenistic Jewish circles rather than treating them as direct translations of words from the LXX. They would nonetheless refer to Old Testament injunctions against *arsenokoites* (Lv 18 and 20), the *pornos* (Dt 23:18) and the kidnaper (Ex 4:16; Dt 24:7). Thus he draws the conclusion that "the vice list in 1 Timothy is not condemnatory of homosexuality in general, not even pederasty as such, but that specific form of pederasty which consisted of the enslaving of boys and youths for sexual purposes, and the use of these boys by adult males."[11]

Though we must reject the thesis of John Boswell that opposition to homosexual activities in the early Church develops only in the post-biblical period, we must admit that the positions taken vis-à-vis homosexual acts in the New Testament do not condemn homosexuality as such. The very notion of homosexuality is a modern one, largely due to the emergence of clinical psychiatry. What we find in the Bible is the condemnation of behavior which was a particular form of Greco-Roman decadence: pederasty, effeminacy, and male prostitution. This does not involve a clear interdiction against all forms of homosexuality, though such a conclusion may follow if we construct from the Bible a doctrine of natural law built on a doctrine of creation. Despite the attempts of Boswell to invent a Christian tradition more friendly to homosexuality than previously imagined, the patristic tradition is clear in its condemnation of homosexual acts. It is true that the discussions and references have to do with pederasty since that was the dominant form that homosexuality took in the Greek and Roman world, which is the context for the discussion in the New Testament. The argument of John Boswell from silence regarding other forms of homosexual activity can prove nothing at all, either positively or negatively. Perhaps the earliest reference to homosexual acts outside the New Testament is that found in the *Didache (The Teaching of the Twelve Apostles)*. In chapter 2:1-2 we read: "The second commandment of the Teaching is: You shall not commit murder. You shall not commit adultery. You shall not corrupt boys (*paidophthoreseis*)." Similar is a rather esoteric passage from the Epistle of Barnabas:

> Among other things, he also says, *you are not to eat of the hare* (Lv 11: 6) by which he means you are not to debauch young boys, or become like those who do; because the hare grows a fresh orifice in its backside every year, and has as many of these holes in the years of its life. And *you are not to eat the hyena* signifies that you are to be no lecher or libertine, or copy their ways; for that creature changes its sex annually and is a male at one time and a female at another. The weasel, too, he speaks of with abhorrence, and not without good reason; his implication being that you are not to imitate those who, we are told, are filthy enough to use their mouths for the practice of vice, nor to frequent the abandoned woman who do the same - since it is through its mouth that this animal is impregnated.[12]

It is certainly correct to make the point that we have here examples of popular folklore about animals. Boswell traces the observation about hares to Aristotle's contention that hares were retromingent. Despite Aristotle's rejection of the view that the hyena was done that changed its sex every year, this was almost universally held as truth by authors of the first century of the Christian era. The Epistle of Barnabas was widely circulated in the early Christian Church and thought of as part of Holy Scripture by many Christians. There is no need to be unduly concerned with the legends regarding the various animals or the lack of scientific accuracy. Rather, in an allegorical way, Barnabas is proscribing certain behavior as contrary to the Mosaic law. The word *paidophthoros*, used in 10:6 is best translated as "boy-molester" although it could also mean "child-molester," but the reference to the anal orifice makes it likely that Barnabas was referring to anal intercourse with a boy. The other passages (7-8) refer to an adulterer and a seducer (in reference to the hyena), but they may also have homosexual overtones since the object of the unlawful intercourse was presumably alternatively male and female. So, 10:8 refers to oral intercourse of any kind whether it be with a man or a woman, with the odd suggestion that the weasel might conceive in this manner.

Apart from his use of the interpretation by Barnabas of the Mosaic prohibitions about sex, Clement of Alexandria advanced two very important reasons for rejecting homosexual activity as contrary to God's purpose. For Clement God created sexuality for procreation, and any use of the sexual powers in wasteful ways which do not lead to procreation is evil and unlawful. Clement quite consciously brought forward the Stoic teaching that the sexual organs must be ruled by wisdom. Excess is the violation of wisdom, and excess is present if sex is perverted from its wisdom, and excess is present if sex is perverted from its rational purpose. Indeed, Clement compares lawful sexual union with moderate eating habits. Enjoyment is appropriate if food is taken for nourishment. Excess clearly leads to immoral activity.[13] The idea of excess is most important since much of the criticism of homosexual (and specifically pederastic) relations in antiquity is built on this notion. Persons were not clearly designated as heterosexuals or homosexuals as in the modern world. The assumption of Clement is that each man has a wide spectrum of sexual abilities, but the norm is heterosexual because nature dictates a purpose for heterosexuality which is the good of creation. Clement advocates a mixture of the Stoic virtue of self-control (particularly in relation to sexual practices) and gender expectations. The latter include not only a horror of any passivity in a man but the expectation that men should not shave since a smooth face is like a woman's. The importance he gives to physical teleology creates a concern that copulation only be by the use of the organs that God designed for procreation.

Homosexual attraction is simply taken for granted by both St. Basil the Great and St. John Chrysostom.[14] It is not the attraction which concerns them morally but unnatural acts that might be committed by those attracted to boys and young men. St. Basil's canonical injunctions place sodomists, bestialists, murderers, sorcerers, and adulterers under the same condemnation. Fifteen years of penance were dealt out to the male who had sexual intercourse with another man. John Boswell seeks to expose to ridicule the theological traditions of the early church as they developed in relation to homosexuality by gathering up their arguments under four headings: animal behavior, unsavory associations, concepts of nature, and gender expectations. We have already observed Clement's and Barnabas' use of legends about animals in relation to the Mosaic prohibitions against eating certain animals and the allegorical interpretation of these animals in relation to unnatural sexual acts. Boswell makes much of the scientific ignorance evident here and the long legacy of bestial imagery surviving even into medieval times. Such allegory appears only fanciful and silly to the modern man. Clement's reasons for rejecting unnatural sexual behavior are clear and rational, however. When it comes to unsavory associations, homosexuality in the ancient world was closely related to child-molesting, the enslavement of children for sexual purposes, prostitution, and the possibility of incest that alarmed many people. Since homosexuality was institutionalized as pederasty in the ancient world, there is no need to be apologetic about moral concern in this regard.

Boswell's treatment of "concepts of nature" has been questioned by many of his readers. He seems to think that only the full-blown medieval doctrine of natural law as found in Thomas Aquinas' work has any claim to be called a consistent doctrine of natural law. Thus, for Boswell, all the references to nature from St. Paul to St. John Chrysostom are only "bits and pieces of 'natural' philosophies" which entered Christian thought at many points.[15] But, as Glenn W. Olson has observed, Stoic philosophies of natural law were consistent, coherent, and widely used by early Christian philosophers.

There is no reason to think that those Fathers who spoke of
nature and its laws were referring "to the characteristics of
individuals or things rather than to an ideal concept."[16] To
use the criterion of the natural as a means of resistance to the
culture of the city as Boswell does is to miss entirely the
rational and philosophical base of natural law thinking in the
ancient world. Boswell thinks that Chrysostom was
influenced by both Manichaean hatred of pleasure and Stoic
natural law thinking, which led him to condemn sexual
pleasures and at the same time to claim that homosexual acts
were not providing natural pleasures. Chrysostom held that
homosexual acts arose from a demand for excessive pleasure,
beyond the pleasures that one would have from natural
heterosexual relations.[17] He thought that there was no other
sin equal to that of homosexual intercourse, observing that
"There is nothing, absolutely nothing more demented or
noxious than this wickedness."[18] Chrysostom was not,
however, strong on consistency. He was a preacher rather
than a moral theologian.

Boswell detects in Chrysostom a horror at one man being
passively subject to another.[19] This was revealed when
Chrysostom wrote: "If those who suffer it really perceived
what was being done to them, they would rather die a thousand deaths than undergo this...For I maintain that not only
are you made (by it) into a woman, but you also cease to be a
man; yet neither are you changed into that nature, nor do you
retain the one you had." [20] Boswell draws the conclusion
that Chrysostom, like other early Christian authors, felt an
intense anxiety about violations of gender expectations. He
suggests that this is why there is so little concern about female
homosexuality in the Fathers of the Church.[21]

Chrysostom himself denounced the evil of homosexuality
as widespread in his times:

> What, then, is the evil? A new and lawless lust has
> invaded our life, a terrible and incurable disease has
> fallen upon us, a plague more terrible than all plagues
> has struck. A new and unspeakable crime has been
> devised. Not only written laws, but also the laws of

nature have been overturned. Fornication now seems like a minor offense among forms of unchastity.[22]

This contagion of homosexual activity seems to have been particularly widespread in the great city of Constantinople of which St. John Chrysostom was the bishop. In fact, Chrysostom asserts that what is most terrible is that "such a great abomination is performed with great fearlessness and lawlessness has become the law."[23] Throughout the future centuries homosexuality remained a problem in Byzantium. Laws were passed prohibiting homosexual activity in Constantinople by the emperor Justinian in 533 A.D.. These may well have been in response to earthquakes in 525 and the plague in Constantinople in 543, but Boswell does not think that the time lapse allows such a construction. The laws were justified in religious terms, but there does not appear to have been an attempt on the part of the Church to bring about such legislation. In fact, it was against certain churchmen that the laws were directed and enforced. Certainly, the people on the whole showed little enthusiasm for such laws or their enforcement, seeing them as merely excuses for obtaining money and for persecuting opposing groups such as Samaritans, pagans, unorthodox Christians, and astrologers.[24]

There appears to be no question of what the patristic norms were regarding homosexual acts. The question remains of asking whether such norms can stand in the modern world. As the research of Michel Foucault has shown, the very concept of a homosexual personality is a modern one, unknown to the ancients. It may be that modern psychology and the awareness of cultural relativity have somewhat modified the negative moral judgments made by the Fathers on homosexual acts. That is something which we must investigate. We can well admit that St. John Chrysostom erred by his excess of rhetoric (so abundant that obvious contradictions become evident). If we are to reject as immoral all homosexual activity, we must give good, solid reasons. It is not enough to appeal to authorities in the ancient world, if only because their understanding of homosexual acts apart from emotional orientation cannot be sustained in the light of modern clinical evidence.

Modern social science has given us sufficient evidence to prove that the homosexual condition exists in various shapes and degrees of intensity. The Kinsey Reports revealed that in the North American public 4 percent of the white males interviewed were exclusively homosexual throughout their lives, after the onset of adolescence.[25] On the other hand 10 percent of the American male population is more or less exclusively homosexual for at least three years between the ages of 16 and 55. We find that 18 percent of the males have at least as much homosexual as heterosexual experience in their lives for at least three years between the ages of sixteen and fifty-five. This is more than one in six of the white male population.[26] It is obvious that one cannot compare the homosexual statistics of 1948 as found in the Kinsey Reports with the poverty of our data from the sixth century A.D.. From this data, however, we can conclude that the majority of those who perform homosexual acts do not remain exclusively or predominantly homosexual. We may also set forth as a reasonable hypothesis the conclusion that cultural factors have an important influence on whether a person remains homosexually oriented. Such cultural factors may include prohibitions, punishments, disintegration of family life, moral decadence, or extreme hostility on the part of the society toward homosexual activity. People are clearly motivated by social and cultural pressures that dictate what is normal and what is abnormal. Similarly, institutions such as a predominantly male oriented society or a society in which women live in seclusion will influence the circumstances which encourage or discourage homosexual acts. None of this answers the moral question, but it reminds us that culture has a profound influence on behavior.

Christian societies have been exclusively anti-homosexual in the past. This position is questioned today by those who would argue that it leaves the homosexual with no possible sexual relationship. The traditional stance has been that continence is ethically appropriate in every case until marriage joins a man to a woman. What we have discovered in modern times, however, is that homosexuality is not in all cases a type of excess and decadence for those not willing to keep their sexual practice within the confines of marriage. Homosexuality is an erotic orientation toward one's own sex. As such it is a permanent and exclusive condition in at least 4 percent of the population. It is also clear from clinical evidence that a larger number of persons become homosexual in contexts where heterosexual activity is impossible or where powerful social influences dictate a regression or a reaction formation. We see such activity in prisons, in armies, and in single sex schools. What moral theologians should not do is to examine homosexual relations exclusively from some physical, structural, or legal context without due regard for the emotional dynamics involved. To do so is to omit the most significant movers of the act: the motives and influences that direct a person to homosexual relations. The influence of motives and emotional states upon the will is important in assessing whether a sinful act is voluntary or involuntary. For Orthodox moral theology the involuntary sin is still a sin though a lesser one in its gravity. More important is the assessment of a person's fundamental option, which for the Christian homosexual is the question of whether a life of indulgence or restraint is to be embraced in regard to sexual expression.

A traditional Christian position has been that homosexual acts are wrong because they are unnatural. This stance can be viewed from two perspectives. One would be from that of creation. The classical texts in the Bible are found in Gn 1:27, 31: "God created man in His image...male and female. He created them...God saw all that He had made and behold it was very good." We read also in Gn 2:23-4: "Therefore, a man leaves his father and his mother and cleaves to his wife, and they become one flesh." The Protestant theologian Karl Barth built into his theology the God-givenness of the duality of man and woman and the evil of every institution which would segregate the sexes and make celibate life superior to that of married life.[27] Another perspective may be found in the Roman Catholic Thomistic philosophy which makes teleological ends the norms for sexual acts. An authoritative example is found in the Vatican Declaration *Persona Humana* issued in 1976. The condemnation of homosexual acts (if not homosexual persons) is absolute in this context because any sexual act not governed by the procreative finality is wrong. That procreative finality is by its nature heterosexual. Homosexual acts violate this God-given purpose. They are sterile and reject the heterosexual context whereby God has revealed his purposes and law for mankind. The Vatican position is not only built on natural law but on Ulpian's interpretation of natural law. In other words, a physical teleology dominates it and dictates the moral norms. An Orthodox theology of nature would depend not upon narrowly conceived finalities but upon a biblical understanding of sexuality as created dual by God, something reinterated by the Lord Himself (Mt 19:4; Mk 10: 6-7). However, it would not draw the conclusions of Barth that monasticism is unnatural since the monks and nuns are as the angels, beyond sexuality, and, of course, beyond any genital expression.

The severity of Christian teaching has been felt by homosexuals for centuries, often experienced as a severe condemnation leading to persecution of the most terrible sort. In more recent times various authors, both Catholic and Protestant, have sought to mitigate the effect of such severity. A psychological argument for alleviation of sanctions was set forth in Marc Oraison's book, *Vie chrétienne et les problèmes de sexualité*, which argued that sexual behaviour was so governed by unconscious factors that no sexual sin could be formally grave since full and sufficient freedom was not present to give it that character. This book, published in 1952, was condemned by the Holy Office in 1953.[28] Oraison's thesis was condemned also in an Allocution of Pope Pius XII.[29] The Pope, in effect, assumed the reality of freedom except in those concrete cases where evidence can be provided to show the contrary. Echoes of the controversy remain in the Vatican Declaration:

> Their culpability will be judged with prudence. But no pastoral method can be employed which would give moral justification to these acts on the grounds that they would be consonant with the condition of such

> people...In Sacred Scripture they are condemned as a
> serious depravity and even presented as the sad conse-
> quence of rejecting God. This judgment of Scripture
> does not of course permit us to conclude that all those
> who suffer from this anomaly are personally responsi-
> ble for it, but it does attest to the fact that homosexual
> acts are intrinsically disordered and can in no case be
> approved of."[30]

Other Catholic authors have been more ready to accept
limitations of freedom in the area of homosexual activity.
Few have been as prepared as Oraison to make a universal
exemption from the possibility of grave sin. In the light of
the distinction between voluntary and involuntary sin which is
basic to Orthodox moral theology, it is possible to assimilate
the mitigation of responsibility and guilt to allow that much
homosexual sin is truly involuntary. The sin is to be lamented and rejected, but the gravity is not such as would exist in
full voluntary assent to such sin. Two traditions exist in
Western religious ethics regarding limitation of freedom.
There is the psychological one which we find in Oraison and
in *Persona Humana* and the other is more objective, something we find in the Jewish moral theologian Hershel Matt who
thinks that homosexual activity is involuntary since the condition of the homosexual is a given, something which he has not
chosen. Thus the Halachic principle of *me ontes* applies since
it is comparable here to the lack of freedom which a Jew has
if Sabbath duties are not possible because of the prior duty of
defense of the community and one's life in the advent of
foreign invasion.[31]

Many Christian theologians, both Catholic and Protestant
have been ready to accept homosexual relations if they were
means for expressing love. This has been the position taken
by Norman Pittenger, John McNeil, and more recently by
André Guindon. Orthodox objections to permitting homosexual acts in the name of love are that this form of love
insofar as it becomes sexual does not follow the divine pattern
which must mirror the love of Christ for His spouse the
Church. That love is built on *agape* and is reflected in the

sacrament of marriage which is based on a male-female union. It is quite true that the homosexual cannot act as a heterosexual, even if he thinks that this is the will of God for him, since his sexuality is muted by a kind of color-blindness. He is usually unaware of the specific beauty and grace of the other sex and is consequently not drawn toward it by *eros*. Marriages carried out by homosexuals with the other sex are precarious at best. Dr. John R. Cavanagh has provided us with a devastating picture of what latent homosexuality can do to a marriage.[32] Similar concerns have been voiced by Dr. Richard Isay, a psychoanalyst, who notes the dire consequences for a wife and children in those instances when homosexual men have been convinced that they can become heterosexual, marry, and have a normal life.[33]

Catholic liberal moral theologians have been ready to accept a homosexual couple in the name of a proportionalism or a theory of compromise which establish the moral character of an act by its being the lesser of evils. An example of this is found in the rather moderate Edward A Malloy:

> Homosexual couples, consciously committed to a permanent and exclusive relationship, offer the best hope for the preservation of Christian values by active homosexuals. As I have continually argued, the Christian church has not, cannot, and should not celebrate a rite of marriage for homosexual couples. But, as a number of theologians have reasoned, for those homosexuals incapable of living a celibate life, such private arrangement is surely preferable to the other alternatives of Christian homosexuals who are capable of such a commitment.[34]

Malloy is unusual among Catholic moral theologians insofar as he stakes out a claim to a specifically Christian ethic rather than one built on natural law. Central to the Christian sexual ethic for Malloy are chastity, sacrificial love and fidelity. The "gay life" is lacking on all scores. It is anarchistic, sensualist, and lacking in both love and fidelity. A very similar position has recently been taken by Richard A.

McCormick who creates a proportionalist case that homosexuals who cannot be celibate should find a partner to whom they can be committed.[35] Even if the Church cannot bless this union, it is something that the couple may morally do in good faith. It is right for them since the alternatives are decidedly very bad.

An Orthodox moral theologian must ask where Orthodoxy stands in such issues. Clearly the dominant, even exclusive, standpoint among Orthodox theologians and Church authorities has been the view that homosexuality is sinful and contrary to God's will. Nevertheless, it is important to ask theologically why this stand is taken. Furthermore, it is important to do so in the light of what modern clinical science tells us about homosexuality. The temptation is for Orthodox Christians to condemn homosexuality as diabolical and gross evil without ever understanding it. Without true knowledge we end not only in constructing spectres, ignoring the human beings who feel isolated, who suffer deeply, and who often want to live their lives both as Christians and as homosexuals. The degree of homophobia among Orthodox people is staggeringly high, if only because the Orthodox live within a pro-natalist and family-oriented milieu. While retaining these values of the Christian family and the normative character of marriage for those not committed to monastic vows, the Orthodox Church must, nonetheless, be compassionate and merciful as God is compassionate and merciful.

The theological grounds for refusing an ethical and theological justification of homosexual relationships which involves genital acts lie in the fact that such acts are appropriate only within the "one flesh" context of marriage. It is only this union of man and woman that can receive the Church's blessing. Orthodox theology does not place the degree of emphasis that Roman Catholic theology has traditionally placed on the natural law ends of sexuality. Rather, it is the ritual context of marriage which sets the norms of sexual relating. It is not necessarily because homosexual acts are not reproductive that the Orthodox Church disapproves of them but because the unitive and redeeming purposes of God are not manifest in them. One may approach these acts objectively from a theological perspective or subjectively from a psychological perspective, but they all come down to the simple fact that homosexual genital acts, even though highly symbolic in themselves, do not symbolize the unity between Christ and His Church as sacramental marriage does. Consequently, homosexual love is rarely oblative but most usually reparative. Reparative love is an attempt to compensate for what was and remains lacking. This is not to deny that true love can exist within a homosexual relationship. Whatever is authentically loving is of God. This Orthodox theology must affirm. However, the symbolic expression of that love must not be a parody of the genital union which is the coitus of marriage. Orthodox moral theology is ready to allow that many sins are involuntary, and I would strongly urge that this category applies to many, perhaps most homosexual acts.

The Orthodox Church is not ready to accept a theory of compromise or a form of proportionalism which would justify a homosexual union as a lesser of evils. It is possible, however, to recognize that a homosexual relationship may be expressive of love for some persons, if not for many. This is a fact recognized by various moralists within the Catholic tradition who reject the objective goodness of homosexual genital acts.[36]

With James Hanigan we can agree that homosexual relations should not be genital since the genital union is expressive of the "one flesh" union of marriage. To say that a form of erotic expression is inappropriate is not to deny the goodness or the appropriate nature of this form of *eros*. Love between persons of the same sex is appropriate for homoerotic persons, but the expression must not be genital. For homosexual persons love is vital if they are to exist as living, expressive persons. Without it they become depressed, angry, defeated people.

The ideal of expressive, oblative love for homosexual persons who remain predominantly homosexual stands in stark contrast to the ethos of the gay world. Here the norms are that anything goes, that anyone who is attractive is a potential sexual partner, and that multiple sexual partners are acceptable as a way of life. Writing of the gay world Susan Sontag refers to the 1970s "when many male homosexuals reconstituted themselves as something like an ethnic group, one whose distinctive folkloric custom was sexual voracity, and the institutions of urban homosexual life became a sexual delivery system of unprecedented speed, efficiency, and volume."[37] It was the anomie and chaos of the gay world that led to the rapid spread of AIDS in North America. From the Orthodox perspective the gay world constitutes an heretical community. Its beliefs, its community, and its character manifest a distinct example of the unity of falsity and moral decadence. It has exalted homosexuality as an inherent good, equal to heterosexuality, and created a lifestyle of multiple sexual partners, seduction, and hedonism. It would be wrong, I believe, to see AIDS as a judgment of God upon homosexuals except insofar as we can say that destructive activity (which may be such socially acceptable behavior as smoking tobacco or drinking alcohol to excess) brings consequences in human pathology. We must remember that AIDS is a breakdown of the human immune system resulting from infection with HIV. The virus may infect anyone who is exposed to it by the transmission of blood or body fluids such as semen and that includes hemophiliacs, infants, and a multitude of others than homosexuals. The terrible effects of the AIDS epidemic on the gay community may well result in a resolve to stop the promiscuity and form committed couples of same-sex persons. The Church, I believe, should rejoice in this but not compromise her position that homosexual genital expression is wrong since the "one flesh" union is possible only within the heterosexual context of marriage. However, the importance and the significance of the beloved friend for homosexual persons must not be negated by a false moralism.

A Christian ethic must be both good news and profoundly realistic about the deepest needs and aspirations of persons. It must not stand in judgment upon persons whom we suspect of being sinners. It must speak with comfort and sympathy for persons who have lost beloved friends. The mystery of God's love appears, as we see in the life of the Lord Jesus, in the oddest of places. It was a prostitute who washed the feet of the Lord. The Church must never seek to deprive persons, particularly persons who have been deprived from childhood, of the love of another person.

In my opinion, Dr. Elizabeth Moberly, an Orthodox theologian and psychotherapist, has taken the most informed and compassionate approach to homosexuality. She has written a clinical study of the topic in *Psychogenesis: The Early Development of Gender Identity* and a little book entitled *Homosexuality: A New Christian Ethic.* What is unique about her study of sexual inversion is her stress on the homosexual condition in contrast to the prevailing tendency to be concerned only with homosexual acts. Moberly believes that evidence does not exist to prove that homosexuality results from hormonal imbalance, genetic predisposition, or abnormal learning processes. Rather, she depends upon psychoanalytic conclusions that the condition results from "difficulties in the parent-child relationship, especially in the earlier years of life."[38] Essentially she thinks that the motivating factors depend upon a deficiency in the relationship with the parent *of the same sex.* Moberly dismisses the usual psychoanalytical opinion that male homosexuals have an unconscious fixation upon the parent of the other sex. She also holds that the male homosexual has disidentified with his father and is consequently ambivalent toward him and other members of the same sex. The female homosexual has a disidentification with other members of the same sex also. This deficit in relationship often depends on circumstances beyond anyone's control such as the father's absence during war or the parents' divorce. Moberly is too experienced a psychologist to make a direct connection between any such factor and the homosexual condition. Moberly's thesis is quite simple: "It is not that homosexuality is an independent entity or condition *caused* by difficulties in the parent-child relationship. Rather, the homosexual condition is itself a deficit in the child's ability to relate to the parent of the same sex which is carried over to members of the same sex in general."[39] From this defect comes a special need for dependency upon and love from the parent of the same sex. Insofar as this need is not fulfilled, there is a defensive detachment, which is associated with the frequent repression of the original needs. The drive for the restoration of the attachment leads to a reparative need manifested in the homosexual impulse. As Moberly puts it: "The persisting need for love from the same sex stems from and is to be correlated with the earlier unmet needs for love from the parent of the same sex, or rather, the inability to receive such love, whether or not it was offered."[40] This is what gives rise to the same sex ambivalence so evident in homosexuals. The effeminancy of the male homosexual and the quasi-masculinity of the female homosexual exist not by reason of identification with the parent of the other sex but rather, by reason of a disidentification with the parent of the same sex.

Moberly's wisdom is striking. It is found in the assertion that we cannot undertake therapy or make ethical evaluation without knowing what homosexuality is. This is in contrast to the simplistic approach that assumes the moral decadence and evil dispositions of the homosexual. The homosexual condition is fraught with difficulties because the homosexual experiences a defensive withdrawal from the same-sex parent, and this manifests itself in hostility and ambivalence. The fact that a homosexual falls in love with a member of the same sex instead of developing a paranoid psychosis depends on the strength of the reparative need for love and the positive elements in the psyche which sustain hope in place of despair and hate.

Moberly sees the homosexual orientation as a search for a love that has been lacking in childhood from the parent of the same sex. When this love is experienced, one ordinarily becomes heterosexual. For Moberly this is the norm:

> When same sex identificatory needs have been fulfilled, one has become a psychologically complete member of one's own sex and by the same fact a person who is able to relate as truly other to a member of the opposite sex. However, when the same sex identificatory process is still incomplete, there remains a need to fulfil this process. Hence, the reparative urge dictates a reparative choice of love-object, i.e., the restoration and continuation of a libidinal bond in

which same-sex identificatory love-needs may be fulfilled.[41]

The fact is, however, that such needs are only rarely fulfilled. In theory, they could and should be fulfilled, and in
practice it may be that they have been fulfilled more often
than is known. Moberly also notes that in the homosexual
relationship both partners have similar needs, and "thus each
is trying to meet his own needs through another person in
whom there is a similar lack of fulfilment."[42] Furthermore
dependency needs vary and are often very deep. Sometimes
the relationship of love between persons of the same sex is
too brief or shallow to allow dependency needs to be realized.

By centering her investigation on the condition of homosexuality, Moberly has invited us to take a new and more
optimistic look at homosexuality. It may be pathological in
its genesis but developmentally it expresses a reparative and
self-curing function in the emotional development of a person.
Does this mean that homosexual acts can be tolerated or
approved? Moberly answers: "An attachment to the same sex
is not wrong, indeed it is precisely the right thing for meeting
same-sex deficits. What is improper is the eroticisation of the
friendship. Such eroticisation is secondary and not essential
to the homosexual condition as such."[43] Dr. Moberly thinks
that the word "homosexual" is consequently misleading, and
she would prefer a word such as "homophilia."

Having discussed the psychodynamics of the homosexual
condition, Moberly turns to the traditional Christian position
on the topic. She recognizes that Holy Scripture condemns
homosexual acts. She sees no need of a reassessment on this
point. It is the homosexual condition which needs examination. In fact, she thinks that the "neglect of such understanding has been the glaring weakness of the traditional Christian
viewpoint."[44] Moberly gives examples of such misunder-
standing in various Christian authors (mostly Anglican and
Evangelical) who speak of homosexuality as violating God's
intention for men and women. Such language neglects the
fact that homosexuality is an arrested developmental process.
As she puts it: "Sexual sin is contrary to God's intention, but

homosexuality, though often an occasion for sexual sin, is essentially a state of incomplete development. It is the incompletion that is contrary to God's intention here. Homosexual acts are prohibited, "not because they repudiate the man-woman relationship but because sexual expression is not appropriate to pre-adult relationships."[45] The biblical texts that Moberly thinks are most relevent to the treatment of homosexuality are those asserting our duty to care for orphans and those denouncing the oppression of orphans (Isa 2:23; Jer 5:28 and Ez 22:7). The will of God for human growth, she writes "is checked whenever a child is orphaned. However, although being an orphan is in this sense 'against the will of God,' one does not therefore seek to punish an orphan for being an orphan."[46] The logic of Moberly at this point is inexorable and to the point:

> Rather, to seek the will of God in such a situation implies doing all that one can to make good whatever deficits are involved. By analogy, the homosexual condition, as involving deficits in the ability to relate to the parent of the same sex, is not culpable as such, but rather requires the resolution of the deficits in question. To thwart the evolution of these deficits and to hinder the fulfilment of unmet needs is comprable to oppressing the orphan, indeed is a form of such oppression.[47]

Treating homosexuality as essentially a sexual problem is misleading. Liberal theologians such as Norman Pittenger agree that love is the essential need of the homosexual, but then he moves on to assume that love will take sexual forms. Moberly rejects this opinion. She asserts that homosexuality is not at base a sexual disorder, and sexual expression ignores the authentic needs inherent in them.

Moberly devotes the last chapter of *Homosexuality: A New Christian Ethic* to healing and prayer, urging the importance of both. Healing is not magic, however, and for homosexuals it involves finding ways to fulfill the legitimate need for love shared with someone of the same sex. These healing processes must not be ignored in praying for miraculous cures. The cure will come by way of human relationships which are therapeutic and will be brought about through God the Holy Spirit who inspires them. It is perfectly permissible to pray for a cure, but we must not assume that cures are always given. It is contrary to God's will that moral imperfection exists, but God permits it because He permits free will and allows us space and time for growth. God's plan for our sexual salvation lies in marriage and in monasticism, but the sinful condition of humanity often prevents God's plan from being realized. Salvation is equally found in the struggle through illness and suffering, so one must not condemn the sick for being sick. God does not will homosexuality, but He permits it. Then homosexuality becomes a condition with which some must live and in which their salvation is to be found, by the realization of relationships full of grace, self-sacrifice, and hope. Filling the homosexual with self-hate because of desires and tendencies that straight society cannot know or approve of is surely a terrible thing. His need is to know how to love himself rightly, as God loves him for who he is rather than for what he does. Homosexuals sense very deeply that they cannot be loved unless they are loved in their need and love for the same sex. I suspect they are right in this, but this does not mean that one can accept the self-destructive ways found in the gay world, the promiscuity and lack of serious commitment create an atmosphere which is pervaded with an eroticism devoid of dialogue.

In an article published in *Salmagundi* in 1982-3, Elizabeth Moberly restated the conservative case regarding homosexuality.[48] Much of the article only repeats what was written in her books. However, certain points are made more clearly. She asserts that the wide prevalence of homosexuality in no way deprives it of its pathological character. Epidemics of influenza are equally widespread. The failure of much psychiatric treatment again does not provide evidence in favor of the normality of homosexuality as a variant orientation. Rather, treatment must be centered and relocated in the area of the pathology, something not yet done. Civil rights advocates rightly claim that homosexuals should not be discriminated against or be subject to criminal action, and Moberly is in full agreement. But one must not agree with liberals who make homosexuality normal and acceptable. It is by reassessing the significance of the homosexual *condition* that the polarized views of liberals and conservatives can be reconciled.

Dr. Moberly's work remains, in my opinion, incomplete. She does not integrate the variations in the homosexual pattern as, for example, those men whose problem is essentially a fixation on the mother. Furthermore, the tendencies to narcissism among homosexuals are largely ignored by Moberly. Such narcissism is wrongly interpreted as self-love (as by Bishop Chrysostomos in *Orthodox Tradition*).[49] The search to escape from isolation into a fusion with an idealized other is the essence of narcissism. The narcissistic homosexual seeks to become the other whom he finds so attractive rather than to relate to him in his otherness. This aspect is largely ignored in Moberly's works. The homosexual critic of Moberly's work (as well as many clinicians) would state that Moberly misses the point that eroticization has occurred in the search for love from and for persons of the same sex. Such eroticization can scarcely be reversed in most cases. This may be the most significant fact about homosexuality, despite Moberly's opinions to the contrary. Furthermore, the hope for escaping from this eroticization by the fulfillment and experience of one's needs for same-sex love from a parental substitute is remote for most homosexuals. It may be that sexual acts are inappropriate in the light of the real and deeper emotional needs of homosexuals, but the fact remains that they are a fact of life for most older (that is over the age of eighteen years) homosexuals. The fusion of frustrated emotional and sexual needs leads to an obsession that verges on compulsion. There is a closer link in the makeup of most homosexuals, particularly male homosexuals, between sexual acts and emotional needs for love than Moberly is willing to acknowledge. This is why neither homosexuals nor moralists are particularly happy with Moberly's work. The former will claim that affection and erotic experience are as closely tied together as heterosexuals find them to be. The latter will state that the homosexual condition is rarely so distinct from acts as Moberly thinks possible. In attempting to supply the affectionate needs of homosexuals one may find that eroticization of what was meant to be a non-erotic relationship often becomes inevitable.

Nevertheless, I believe that Moberly is right about homosexuality being a condition that is both indicative of a reparative need to overcome a severe lack in one's childhood from the same-sex parent and the importance of recognizing that the homosexual is seeking to make up that lack. Whether he or she will go on to become heterosexual once the lack is supplied is not at all clear. By focusing on a condition rather than on behavior, Moberly directs our attention to the affective and emotional aspects of personality rather than on acts of the will. Moberly avoids the simple dualism of the normal and the abnormal, the good and the evil. She bypasses the assessment of acts, leaving them to the confessor. Her entire understanding of homosexuality is psychological, though from a Christian perspective. She makes no moral judgments beyond the assumption that homosexuality is an immaturity.

From the confessor's viewpoint the homosexual act is symptomatic also, but what is most important is that the fundamental option of the penitent be retained as submissive to the will of God. As with masturbation, or even with sins such as lying or stealing, a fall is to be taken as something to be repudiated, and then with the assistance of God's forgiving grace the penitent stands once more firm in his Christian commitment. The homosexual must not be condemned for his or her orientation, however. That would be like condemning a person for coming down with influenza. Moreover, whenever the penitent is involved in a relationship which has genuine characteristics of love no confessor ought to demand that the relationship be terminated because either person is homosexual. The target should be the elimination of sexual acts as inappropriate to the relationship. It is easier to persuade the penitent that acts of an impersonal or promiscuous sort are sinful. Indeed, they are more obviously sinful because they are not in the context of love. It is not an open option for an Orthodox Christian to accept homosexual activity of a genital variety as morally acceptable. Yet, on the other hand, if we accept the view that expression of affection by physical means is permitted, we cannot draw exact lines as to what may or may not be permitted. Gestures exist as a language of physical expression of meaning, and though genital activity may not be morally acceptable, the exchange of affection must be acceptable between homosexual persons. The *eros* of friendship makes such gestures as holding hands or exchanging an embrace entirely good and moral as long as they do not become means to an immoral end. What is immoral within homosexual expressions of affection would be seductiveness, objectification and manipulation of another for physical satisfaction. As to genital activity, attempts at becoming "one flesh" on the part of same sex partners are often grotesque in their distortion and in their sado-masochistic undertones. Homosexual activity is more often a narcissistic self-centered search for orgasm than a speaking of the language of love. The wholeness of other-directed love in the heterosexual pattern is often lacking. Moral judgments are usually made on the basis of what is normal and good within the fullness of God's created world as it is being transformed by the Holy Spirit. This, of course, is not to say that all heterosexual acts are good, but they provide the grounding whereby love and sexual union may be joined in the sacramental mystery of marriage. Nevertheless, the only moral solution for homosexuals is that they learn to speak the language of love to one another.

Many homosexuals would say with justice that they are not heterosexual and ought not to be judged by heterosexual norms. It is important, therefore, that the Church speak to homosexuals about a norm of wholeness which is the transformation of libido into *philia* and *agape*. Homosexual activity is sinful insofar as it fails in this task. The surrender to raw sexual impulses, to impersonal and seductive cruising, to acts which parody the "one flesh" of Christian marriage - all are perverse debasements of the dignity to which God has called all human beings. But the fact remains that our fallenness has created a world where often little good can be forthcoming. The nature of life in times of war, under conditions of enslavement, in prisons, and in other such conditions makes it necessary that we recognize whatever good is expressed in affection and friendship. To impose an ideal as an absolute in a way which would permit no physical contact between two persons of the the same sex, particularly where the surrounding material evil is destructive of the realization of any ideals, is to turn moral theology into a tyranny out of touch with all reality. No person should be forced in the name of "Christian morality" to reject whatever goodness is brought into being under such circumstances. This is not to accept homosexuality as an unqualified good or homosexual acts as morally acceptable. It is to avoid passing judgment on the basis of a category with a negative significance. Judgment must always lie in examination of the concrete context of acts and depends upon a discernment at both the spiritual and the psychological levels. Whatever good may exist in disorder is a reflection of a good that lies elsewhere. The profound contrast between an intimate relationship of affection and the impersonal, self-centered, fetishistic relations of most homosexuals is clear to all who can discern it. Just lumping them all together under the category "homosexual" is of little help. Truly good sexual relations exist on the basis of the created order which reflects the threefold persons of the holy Trinity. The otherness of the other person and the otherness of the other sex reflects reality in a way that narcissistic self-indulgence can never do. Love must always be seen as something other than sentiment or desire if we continue to speak in a Christian sense. Love is for the other as a unique person. The sexual project to which every person is called involves the transformation of libido into an *eros* which seeks the other as other, affirms the other as a friend, and ultimately calls for a self-sacrificing gift of oneself as it was revealed in the life of Jesus Christ. This transformation is in no way automatic. *Eros* is not only attraction to another but just as often a desire to have or even to be the other person. This is particularly true in homosexual attraction where it is often the wish to be the other person which is paramount. The struggle against possessiveness is a struggle whose ascetic nature will be self-evident to those who comprehend the intensity of desire.

In understanding and sympathizing with the plight of the

homosexual, as with that of the orphan who cries out for help, we must not become caught in the illusions which a false toleration brings with it. That is only to harm the homosexual. The demon who is the father of lies ever comes seeking to persuade us that what is immediately attractive will fulfill our need. The libido which is so terribly disordered by our fallen condition constantly insists on its satisfaction and release. That pattern is self-destructive unless it is redeemed. If the homosexual person persists in substituting eroticism for authentic love then untold damage may result. The sad and dreary search for what is lost and never to be found becomes an obsessive preoccupation which leads only to constant repetition and never-ending disapointment

What homosexuals have in common with all humanity is the disorder in which libido becomes a dominant desire to obtain satisfaction and release. As long as the libido is predominantly physical, repressed, or restrained, the dynamisms demanding release are dominant. Then a cycle of built-up tension, release of tension, guilt, and attrition (meaning largely sorrow for what one has done) will remain intact. The disorder lies in concupiscence which has remained untouched by spiritualization. This concupiscence is split into desire versus reason, which seeks to restrain it but has little comprehension of the underlying condition. The penitential practice of the Church often just reinforces this pattern, urging the penitent into deeper self-hatred and more compulsive need to carry out acts whose inner purpose is mixed with despair, rebellion, and the attempt to avert inner disintegration. If the penitential practice is built on focusing the love of God upon the sinner, the sinner can be assisted to comprehend his obsessive patterns by experiencing the love of God. This is a love that can heal the deep wounds that the homosexual has within by way of the failure of love from the parent of the same sex. Where there is repentance for sexual activity it must be seen in the light of the true meaning of that activity rather than merely a submission to authority for breaking the laws of the Church.

Elizabeth Moberly is surely correct in affirming that homosexuals primarily need love, not sex, and once loved they are called to liberate themselves from the bondage of the narcissistic double and open themselves to a love which recognizes the otherness of the other person. The fundamental Orthodox insight remains valid: our developmental end is to become what we are, for we are made in the image of God. To realize the likeness with God is by a *theosis* whereby *agape* is born in our lives. It is impossible for us to manifest in the likeness of God while existing in a state of hedonistic and sensual indulgence. Just as marriage involves wearing the martyrs' crown, so the Christian and Orthodox homosexual will walk in the way of the cross. It is my firm belief that on the other side of that cross is the glory of the resurrection. To abandon the fundamental option of Christ in favor of the "gay" life is only to lose the hope and joy of participation in the resurrection. On the other hand, the particular and peculiar road of the Christian homosexual is a vocation similar to the monastic one. It is not a vocation to perpetual frustration but to an unfolding of love in the knowledge that God has a very special love for the outcasts, the rejected, and the eunuchs. We can remember the promise made to the eunuchs in Is 57:3-5:

Let the eunuch not say: behold, I am a withered tree; for thus says the Lord: as regards the eunuchs who keep My Sabbaths, who have chosen what I desire, and hold fast to My covenant, I will give them, in My house and within My walls, a monument and a name better than sons and daughters....an everlasting name that shall not perish.

As Christians we also reflect on the words of the Lord Christ:

For there are eunuchs, which were so born from their mother's womb: and there are eunuchs, which were made eunuchs by men: and there are eunuchs which made themselves eunuchs for the kingdom of heaven's sake. He that is able to receive it, let him receive it. (Mt 19:12)

Notes

(1) Robin Scroggs, *The New Testament and Homosexuality Contextual Background for Contemporary Debate* (Philadelphila: Fortress Press, 1983), p. 62.

(2) Ibid., p. 65.

(3) William L.Countryman, *Dirt, Greed & Sex: Sexual Ethics in the New Testament and Their Implications for Today* (Philadelphia: Fortress Press, 1988), pp. 18-20.

(4) Scroggs, pp. 92-6.

(5) Ibid., p. 113.

(6) Ibid., p. 114.

(7) John McNeill, *The Church and the Homosexual* (New York: Pocket Books, 1976), p. 67.

(8) Countryman, pp. 115-6.

(9) Translation from Scroggs, p. 118.

(10) Scroggs, p. 120.

(11) Ibid., pp. 120-1.

(12) Epistle of Barnabas 10, trans. Maxwell Staniforth, in *The Apostolic Fathers* (Harmondsworth, Middlesex, UK: Penguin Books, 1968), p. 207.

(13) Clement of Alexandria, *Paedagogus* 2:10.

(14) John Boswell, *Christianity, Social Tolerance, and Homosexuality* (Chicago: University of Chicago Press, 1980), p. 160.

(15) Ibid., p. 147.

(16) Glenn Olsen, "The Gay Middle Ages: A Response to Professor Boswell," *Communio* 8, 2 (1981), pp. 119-38.

(17) Boswell, p. 156.

(18) John Chrysostom, *Homilies on the Epistle to the Romans* 4, trans. John Boswell, p. 157.

(19) Boswell, p. 157.

(20) John Chrysostom, *On Perfect Charity* 7, trans. Boswell, p. 157.

(21) Boswell, p. 158.

(22) John Chrysostom, *Against the Opponents of the Monastic Life* 3, trans. David G. Hunter, in *Studies in the Bible and Early Christianity*, vol. 13, p. 140.

(23) Ibid., p. 140.

(24) Boswell, p. 173.

(25) Alfred C. Kinsey, et al., *Sexual Behavior in the Human Male* (Philadelphia: Saunders, 1948), pp. 650-1.

(26) Ibid., p. 650.

(27) Karl Barth, *Church Dogmatics* 3, 4, (New York: Scribners, 1956), p. 166

(28) John C. Ford and Gerald Kelly, *Contemporary Moral Theology*, Vol. I, *Questions in Fundamental Moral Theology* (Westminster, MD: Newman Press, 1960), pp. 178-9.

(29) Pope Pius XII, *A.A.S.* 45 (1953), pp. 278-86.

(30) Sacred Congregation for the Doctrine of the Faith, *Declaration on Certain Questions Regarding Sexual Ethics (Persona Humana)* 9, 10.

(31) Hershel Matt, "Sin, Crime, Sickness or Alternative Lifestyle? A Jewish Approach to Homosexuality," in Bachelor, E., ed., *Homosexuality and Ethics* (New York: Pilgrim Press, 1980), p. 118.

(32) John R. Cavanagh, "Latent Homosexuality as a Cause of Marital Discord," *Linacre Quarterly*, 43, 3 (1976), pp. 138-46.

(33) Richard A. Isay, "Analytic Therapy of Homosexual Men," *Psychoanalytic Study of the Child*, 40 (1985), pp. 235-254.

(34) Edward A. Malloy, *Homosexuality and the Christian Way of Life* (Lanham, MD: University Press of America, 1981), p. 359.

(35) Richard A. McCormick, "Homosexuality as a Moral and Pastoral Problem,"in *The Critical Calling: Reflections on Moral Dilemmas since Vatican II* (Washington, DC: Georgetown University Press, 1989), pp.289-314.

(36) Examples may be found in Marc Oraison, Edward Malloy, Andre Guindon, Richard Woods, and James P. Hanigan.

(37) Sontag, Susan, *AIDS and Its Metaphors* (New York: Farrar, Straus, Giroux, 1989), p. 76.

(38) Elizabeth Moberly, *Homosexuality: A New Christian Ethic* (Cambridge: James Clarke, 1983), p. 2.
(39) Ibid., p. 5.

(40) Ibid., p. 6.

(41) Moberly, *Psychogenesis; The Early Development of Gender Identity* (London: Kegan Paul, 1982), p. 47.

(42) Ibid., p. 37.

(43) Moberly, *Homosexuality*, p. 20.

(44) Ibid., p. 20.

(45) Ibid., p. 27.

(46) Ibid., p. 28.

(47) Ibid., p. 35-6.

(48) Moberly, "The Conservative Case," *Salmagundi*, 58-9 (1982-3), pp. 281-299.

(49) Bishop Chrysostomos, *Orthodox Tradition*, 1, 4-5 (1984), pp. 68-70.

Chapter Ten:
Eros and Transformation

Theological Foundations

When we draw the fundamental principles from the teachings of the Orthodox Church regarding the place of human sexuality in creation and in the economy of salvation, we may arrive at the following conclusions:

1. Human sexuality though created good by God after the Fall lost the coinherence between man and woman that existed in Paradise. As a consequence, the passions, having lost their coherent ends, have been unleashed in a war against the soul. In place of love, man begins to lust.

2. The transformation of the passions is a primary task of *theosis*. Ascetic ordering stands as a first step in this direction, but it is only by transformation into love that the human condition can be restored to its likeness with God.

3. By way of constraint, we can say with St. Ignatius the Godbearer that *eros* must be crucified, which is the ascetic way. But by way of transformation *eros* is ecstatically drawn into the vision of God, either directly or by way of anticipation through the revelation of the image of God in another person. Love is the opening of our eyes to see that image for what it is.

4. Sexuality is related to the baser human instincts (lusts) as well as to the higher (*eros*). Only by grace can human

sexuality undergo the transformation of *eros* into self-sacrificing love, *agape*. As lust is the perversion of what is good, so *agape* is the fulfillment of what is good.

5. Sexuality has its primary purpose not in procreation but in a union of two persons, which is the integration of desire, attraction, and personal communion in the "one flesh", a bodily union that mediates the communion of persons.

6. Within the context of the Christian revelation the union of a man and a woman becomes a sacrament when elevated into the union of Christ and His Church. The archetype of Christ who loves His Church as His body and His bride is the foundation of the sacramental bond. This sacrament is a way of entry into the kingdom of God and a participation in the *eschaton* and *telos* of all creation. The grounding of marriage in creation and its exaltation in Christ are not conflicting aspects of the reality which is Christian marriage.

7. The union of persons of male and female gender creates a loving communion in grace whereby the image of the holy Trinity is mirrored sacramentally. The offspring of the union brings into being the third person and thus creates "the little church" (St. John Chrysostom) which is the family, an image of the Trinity. This is not to exalt the family as such. By reason of the Fall the family has often become a conflicted core (as discovered by Freud and Laing) within society. By way of the restoration to grace the unity of the three persons (father, mother, and child) the family may become a reflection of the perfect equality of the Trinity rather than the model of all conflict as in the Oedipal triangle.

8. The integration of nature and the person in the sexually integrated person is analogous to the union of nature and person in Christ who is hypostatically one person in both divine and human natures. Fallen human nature apart from God loses its integration in the human person. Concupiscence occurs when the energies of nature become disoriented as passions turned against the soul. Redemption means restoration to wholeness whereby the energies are once more integrated into the person and subject to both reason and freedom. At the deepest level of our humanity freedom is not just a matter of self control or decision making but is realized in

the openness and communion with another person that comes through love. Thus the Incarnation becomes not only the symbol of human self-integration but the means of achieving *theosis* which restores humanity to its recreated integrity and wholeness by participation in God.

This vision of sexual wholeness through *theosis* stands in profound contrast to the hedonism and sexual chaos of the modern world. In responding to modernity it would be vain and useless to reply only in a negative fashion. It is true that eroticism and license have created a nightmare of disordered passion manipulated by the mass media and threatening sanity itself. There is evidence of the presence of the energies of God active in the *eros* that moves and motivates persons toward love and transformation. It is also wrong to regard *eros* as primarily nature's way of achieving reproduction of the species. This would make openness to procreation the criterion or right or wrong use of the sexual organs. A morality devised by celibates on the basis of biological teleology simply will not do. Such a simplistic approach ignores the lived experience of love. Those who know love also know that the structures imposed on them in the name of biological teleology (as natural law) are false to their experience. Similarly, the contemporary reduction of sexuality to pleasurable "outlets" (as in the works of Kinsey and Hite) ignores the mystery of *eros* in favor of physical pleasure. Such an approach may promise a liberation from restraint, but it ends in the banality of sensation, a way of despair and loneliness. The mystery of love, with all its power, has been left out. Pleasure and pain become intimately related, as St. Maximus the Confessor noted. It is only in putting on the new being of Christ that the enslavement to pleasure (and to pain) is overcome. Nevertheless, the ability of *eros* to attract and draw together is a basic force within human life and existence. Such a force remains blind and passionate unless it is tested by reality. Reality offers no negation of the erotic vision but rather the mature awareness that *eros* can only be lived in response to a person who is experienced as an other. Experiencing the otherness of the other and ultimately the other of the other sex remains the task of love when it moves beyond the narcissism of loving those who love us. *Eros* becomes *agape* insofar as it affirms the otherness of the other in his or her particularity. The affirmation of otherness becomes alienation unless it is an affirmation of the will of the other but also of the freedom of the other and the good of the other as the other perceives it. *Eros* is a way of being drawn toward, but unless otherness is affirmed the attraction is one of seeking to have or even become the other, something narcissistic. The union with another is never a fusion. The otherness must be lived out or else *eros* becomes a smothering possessiveness. Dialogue lies at the heart of authentic love, and this dialogue is established in the language of affection, achieving a union in diversity.

The argument of Olivier Clément, Robert Solomon and André Guindon, that sex is a language is worthy of serious attention. The dialogue of the body and of the soul brings forth an achievement found nowhere else in nature. This interpretation of the sexual dialogue was, as we have seen, anticipated by Vladimir Soloviev. It is very easy, under the conditions of fallen human nature, to become subject to bodily passions which may exclude any communication other than mutual sensual satisfaction. Sensuality has its own meaning in the pleasure of intoxication, excitement, and release, but it remains less than fully human when the word of dialogue is absent. Making love is quite different from mere copulation. When the physical is linked to what is said, and when what is said is mutual affection and delight in one another, a transformation of rare and vital significance takes place. The language of love may often be used only as a means of seduction, but that is deceit and deception. If the language of love is authentic there occurs glorification and celebration which have more in common with the effect of liturgical language than of any other except poetry itself. It is my basic conviction that the liturgical rite of marriage, with its giving and receiving of rings and the crowning of the man and woman, is a public participation in a grace which celebrates the energies of God already present in the integrated couple. In turn, the sacramental blessing increases the grace bestowed by bringing the couple into the mystery of Christ's love for His Church. But this blessing confirms what has already become present in the mutual affection of the couple.

The Orthodox vision, when grasped in all its richness, is not a legal permission to indulge in sexual intercourse for the sake of procreation and the prevention of fornication. It may function in either way, but it is more than either. It is, at best, a fulfillment of all that has come into being in the *eros* of the couple. The vision of sex as evil or dirty, and only to be legitimized by a sacrament is, we believe, quite foreign to a genuine Orthodox theology of transformation. We must affirm that whatever is truly loving is always of God. That, of course, does not mean that all libido, all sentiment, all passion are of God. The road to hell lies in a passion unredeemed by *agape*, unformed by due regard for the good as it exists for each partner.

It is Olivier Clément who more than any other Orthodox theologian has grasped this power of love to transform our lives. He remarks that "to fall in love" is one thing, to love truly is another. As he says, "I believe and maintain strongly against the trends of fashion that it is not a good thing to want immediate sexual realization of the fact of falling in love"[1] On the other hand, he realizes that the "old Christians" will say that sexual intercourse outside of marriage is sinful, and he hopes that they will say this out of obedience to the faith rather than from resentment. He knows that few people today understand this prohibition so that it becomes imperative to give the reasons for restraint of sexual expression on the part of those who fall in love:

> I would say that to fall in love and give immediate sexual expression to this attraction (which is largely the anonymous game of the species) is to run the risk of remaining prisoner of ourselves, of our narcissism or of an image going back to childhood, perhaps the quest for the mother, perhaps a fusional regression...It is not that sexuality is bad in itself. On the contrary: because it is fundamentally good, because it is the participation of two persons in the Breath which carries the world, because it makes them "one flesh"

331

(even, says Paul, in relation to a prostitute), it is essential for a man and a woman to become worthy of this language. Most often in these "brief encounters" we are not worthy of our sexuality, we receive a language while we have nothing to say. Sin is not the infringement of a prohibition. The gospel sets forth the meaning of life, it shows the way, it does not dictate laws. Sin is that blind encounter, that ignorance of the other in the very act which the Bible calls "knowledge," it is the face transformed into body while the body should be transformed into the face.[2]

Clément notes that the spiritual fathers, and especially the Russian spiritual fathers, held that sexual sin is no more accursed than power or wealth, for which the Lord had much harsher words. He remarks that "a woman, out of kindness, offers the gift of her presence, perhaps of her body, to a man who is about to die or to descend to the inferior circles of hell - and I say that this woman, this man, one or the other, are Christians, and even if they are not (which poses a problem), I do not call this 'fornication'."[3] For Clément the sins of sexual life lie in speaking falsely, the lie that speaks of love when it is only manipulation and self-satisfaction that are being sought. It is violence and the reduction of a person through ignorance to a thing to be used that produce fornication. Clément's central affirmation is that *to love truly means to discover the other in his or her specific identity.* He spells out the affirmation thus:

This does not necessarily mean to fall in love. Often it takes the form of a deep friendship being at peace with the other, feeling at ease, being accepted and accepting the other, having the capacity (which is a unique grace) to help the other mature and deepen, and perhaps to help him or her one day to age and to die. The otherness of the partner may even dazzle man to the point of producing the momentary suppression of desire in the genital sense: the time of being a "fiance," of offering "trust," confidence and of engaging one's "faith," according to a magnificent ancient expression.[4]

The difficulty that exists in revealing the authenticity of this vision of married love arises from the institutionalization of marriage in society. The legal and social bonds that marriage creates often prevent the vision which *eros* grants from being lived out in its fulfillment and ecstasy. Life, of course, is filled with the tedious, the boring, and the routine, but as in the liturgical worship of God, the ordinary must be the vehicle that enables us to relate to what is beyond the ordinary. Both God and the other person in the image of God are revealed to our erotic vision, and if the vision is not sustained by the leisure, the contemplation, and the enjoyment that should accompany it, the vision may eventually be lost. To exist together when the vision is lost may be possible in the hope of a renewed vision or even in memory of a vision that once was shared, but a marriage without any vision soon grows hollow and empty. To command what is no more is close to commanding the impossible.

The realism of the Orthodox Church about second marriages is important here. That realism must exist side by side with the penitential context which witnesses to the failure of vision. The birth of a new relationship of love which makes possible the second marriage must be given its due and its praise. Perhaps this is the reason that the penitential rite provided for second marriages is often neglected in Orthodox practice in favor of the celebration of matrimony as provided by the first rite, particularly if one partner has previously been unmarried.

The modern release of sexuality from the bourgeois bonds that once held it captive has scarcely been an unmitigated good. The illnesses of repression may have disappeared, but in place of the one demon exorcised, a multitude of new demons have returned to haunt our homes. The assumption that free sexual expression without ties or commitments can bring us happiness is a serious mistake with tragic dimensions. It leads to a never-ending search for whatever escapes us. The capacity to break through the flesh to the spirit is never found in the flesh itself. The terrible vision of David Plante's novel *Relatives* is that of violence done to the flesh in seeking to reach the spirit. The failure is total. The flesh may mediate the spirit but only when it is part of spiritual union. The bourgeois marriage may give one the impression that the bond of union is only a bundle of chains to provide a cage for those ensnared within.

Despite the enclosure which marriage and family have created in bourgeois society, the exclusivity of married love demands a degree of privacy in order to create an atmosphere of leisure and intimacy. Yet our fundamental conviction must be that love never opposes love. The Orthodox vision of the communion of saints is that in the end we shall all love one another fully, even if certain loves are particular. This vision is not the tragedy of romantic love, which isolates and estranges the couple from others. The bourgeois sense that the physical expression of love is only permissible in the sexual context is fatally wrong. It is true that genital expression of love belongs within the context of married love where the "one flesh" is essential and reflects the union of Christ with His body the Church. Yet insofar as all human beings are bodies, we must express affection physically. The cultural heritage of Greece and Russia expresses this most beautifully. The embraces and kisses which exist in utmost chastity express the joy of bodily love which is appropriate for those who are members of the body of Christ.

Human sexuality is certainly not just a physical matter. It has its own emotional and spiritual dynamism. Modern science has often considered it only from the physical perspective. Roger Scruton, a British philosopher, has written a devastating critique of Kinsey's interpretation of sexuality as physical "outlets."[5] Kinsey's behavioristic perspective has dominated American secular thinking about sexuality since he wrote his famous reports in the 1940s. The framework adopted for the various studies of Masters and Johnson has presented human sexuality as entirely physical since the models used were either mechanistic or bestial.[6] In an earlier age various theologians also had thought that human sexuality was something which we shared with the animals while the soul was entirely spiritual. This dualism pervaded much Christian thought. Some of the Greek Fathers (notably St. Gregory of Nyssa) held that sexuality did not exist in Paradise and that the restoration of this angelic life is the goal of *theosis*. All dualism tends to eliminate its opposite. The view of man as an angel with a bestial body demanded an exclusively spiritual life, while modern sexologists have thought man to be entirely physical and thus neglected or even negated the spiritual side of sexuality.

I have persistently held that an Orthodox doctrine of marriage must be built not on the angelic life of Paradise but on the importance of the Incarnation for Christian life. If marriage is a participation of husband and wife in the union of Christ and His Church then this vision of love as *theosis* is as valid as the monastic one. Too often in the Christian vision of sexuality there has been an absence of any potential vision of God as He appears in the image of the beloved. The whole Augustinian tradition conceived of sexuality in the light of the Fall as evil concupiscence redeemed only by God's purposes in procreation. Consequently the modern naturalistic reaction has moved almost entirely within the contours of the body as good and as needing satisfaction. The bodily status of sexuality has remained intact even if the sense of evil has been removed. It has been my belief that Orthodoxy has been deeply aware of the spiritual dimensions of sexuality, but this understanding has existed within the ambivalence set up by the Church's commitment to monasticism. The spiritual vision, presented most powerfully by those theologians writing from the tradition of sophiology, has opened doors to our understanding of sexuality comparable only to those of the great depth-psychologist C. G. Jung. Until such time as the feminine image is openly perceived as a way to God revealing the divine glory, our sexual ethic will be dominated by a masculine image that inevitably reduces sexuality to the lesser and the impure, as being remote from God.[7] The exaltation of the Holy Theotokos as the embodiment of the *sophia* of God, as the revelation of the Holy Spirit, if not hypostatically, then by a perfect manifestation of grace, is a gigantic step in this direction. A theological meditation upon the beauty of

335

married love must extend itself to a theology that takes seriously the feminine image of woman as body of Christ and as the Spirit-filled Church.

Sometimes it appears that modern Orthodox theologians take the rather "Neo-Orthodox" stance that revelation alone can give us God's answers to our questions about what is good and evil in sexuality. The difficulties inherent in all fundamentalism become acute at this point. We must know how to recognize what is revealed and what the words of revelation may mean. The puzzlement as to what *porneia* means in the New Testament is a case in point. Simply to translate the word as "fornication" does not tell us what that means. To define fornication as sex outside of marriage is inadequate since we must establish whether the word had that meaning in the New Testament. There we discover that marriage was, in a particular historical era, often something very different from the legal and ceremonial arrangements of the modern world. It is fundamental to our comprehension of Orthodox faith that what is revealed should confirm what is discovered as true by persons of wisdom and perspicacity. The Greek Fathers, from St. Justin Martyr through St. Maximus the Confessor, would, we believe, uphold this conviction. Their use of Platonic or Aristotelian philosophy points in such a direction. This is why the phenomenological studies of a philosopher such as Roger Scruton can be of much assistance to a moral theologian. It is not immediately obvious what sexual desire is, and until we know what it is, we cannot make a decision regarding its morality or immorality. To assume that it is only the search for a partner with whom to have sexual relations is false and distorting. What makes human sexual desire uniquely human must be the subject of our enquiry. What the Bible says about sexuality must be seen within a human context as what our nature seeks most profoundly. Otherwise, we fall into a biblical positivism, where what is right depends on God's permission as given in Holy Scripture, not on God's blessing of what is good in and of itself. It is in our sexual lives that we most clearly experience either blessing or curse, either ecstasy or damnation. To this extent the psychoanalytic movement has been perceptive and to the point. Consequently our sexual lives must be integrated by grace and transformed by the Holy Spirit. What is not sanctified and integrated becomes a dangerously divisive force pitted against the self and its integration in union with God.

The Search for Human Nature

The central question of moral theology must be the relation of created human nature to the perfection and fulfillment of humanity in *theosis*. To avoid theological fundamentalism, which is essentially a form of positivism admitting no place for reason in theological discourse, it is imperative that a place be given to natural law. Natural law must not be confused, however, with the versions of it which exist in Roman Catholicism built upon Aristotelian and Stoic foundations and mediated through the interpretations of the ancient philosopher Ulpian. In particular, the version of it adopted by Thomas Aquinas in his sexual ethics is to be avoided. Modern critics, notably E. Egner, C. Curran, and A. Guindon, to mention only a few, have produced devastating critiques of such teleological reductionism. Any scientific basis for the arguments set forth by Pope Paul VI in his encyclical *Humanae Vitae* has been exposed as totally unfounded by W. Wickler in his book *The Sexual Code: The Social Behavior of Animals and Men.*[8] However, an alternative understanding of natural law in a phenomenology of human nature is necessary if we are to avoid either biblical fideism or moral legalism.

Vigen Guroian has set forth the essential characteristics of Orthodox ethics: "An Eastern Orthodox ethic values virtue highly, but not rationalistically so ."[9] The Greek Fathers did, indeed, value natural law but in a very different sense from later Thomists. As Guroian observes: "Eastern fathers such as Clement of Alexandria, John Chrysostom, and Basil of Caesarea agree that the fundamental moral law is expressed in and through the creature in several forms."[10] It is true that the eternal law of God is reflected in the laws of nations which enact what is rational for human society, but one must not separate the law of nature from the eternal law of God. Guroian observes that "Nature is not an autonomous plane of existence. The *Logos* was present at Creation, and the Incarnation commences an in an infusion of grace into nature and a transfiguration of it that destroys the wall of separation between God and creature which was built up by sin."[11] A deified human existence of man already has begun in the life of the Church.

Orthodox theologians have not endeavored to define the precise ways in which the various forms of law - divine, natural, and civil - are ordered hierarchically or otherwise correspond with each other because they have not made the sharp distinctions between nature and grace which gave rise to such questions in the West.[12] In fact, natural law theory is quite underdeveloped in the moral theology of the Eastern Church. This is because nature is understood in process of being transformed by uncreated grace. St. Basil the Great sensed this when he stated: "Instruction in divine law is not from without, but simultaneously with the formation of the creature - man, I mean - a kind of rational force was implanted in us like a seed, which, by an inherent tendency, impels us toward love."[13]

Stanley Harakas has criticized Christos Yannaras for downplaying the role of the commandments following from natural law. Harakas would emphasize the place of law in Orthodox Christian ethics, and particularly the ten commandments of the Bible. To this end he quotes both St. Gregory Nazianzus and St. Maximus the Confessor on the importance of keeping the commandments. Harakas even accuses Yannaras of sharing certain characteristics of situation ethics.[14] This debate is important for our purposes since Yannaras rejects an ethics built on pure rationality as reflecting a human nature separated and distinct from the human person. His reaction to a rationalistic natural law ethic is that it is sub-personal. Because man is personal and free we cannot deduce his capacities as "generic, objective properties."[15] Yannaras admits that there are potentialities or ener-

gies of human nature viewed generally, but they reveal the
uniqueness of a person: "They have no existence other than
as manifestations of personal distinctiveness."[16] For Yannaras this makes a morality based on nature prior to the personal
reality of man impossible. As he says, "In that case, ethics is
understood as conformity by the individual to objective or
natural requirements, and violation of these has consequences
which are "destructive" to his nature." Yannaras notes that
nature is mortal as well as creative, and it does not,
therefore,"constitute a hypostasis of eternal life."

This Orthodox perspective, as set forth by Yannaras,
excludes the very possibility of a legalistic, external system of
ethics. A Christian ethic must be existential since the human
being is free and not subject to the necessities of nature. The
response of Harakas to Yannaras reveals how dangerous such
a stance can appear. Harakas thinks that Yannaras is inviting
us to embrace a situational ethic. It is clear, however, that
Yannaras is doing nothing of the sort. He is happy to acknowledge the importance of law, but its place is to be found
not in a rationalistic natural law theory but in the limits
imposed by the canons of the Orthodox Church. There individual penances for particular sins assist in the "cure of souls
and the healing of passions."[17] Law speaks to our failures
"within the context of the Church's common struggle to
delimit and avoid death, her common asceticism."[18] There
can be no justification before God by means of legal observ-
ances, and yet the canons have their place as "the measure of
the Church's ascetic consciousness."[19]

The importance of this discussion for sexual ethics is
noteworthy. An essentialist understanding of Christian ethics
is translated not only into rules and prohibitions but into laws.
The route taken by the Church of Rome is exactly a way of
abiding by what are perceived as nature's laws. Yannaras
holds that to build an ethic on static commands is only to
forget the primacy of the person and the transformation of the
person by love. Furthermore, natural law as conceived in the
West and borrowed by Orthodox theologians in their "captivity" to Western thought assumes a different view of nature
than that held by the Greek Fathers. Grace remains for

Western scholastics both supernatural and created. Nature retains its autonomy despite its elevation by grace. Such reasoning remains foreign to Orthodox theology in which creation is itself pervaded by the uncreated grace of God and is perceived dynamically rather than statically.

André Guindon, a Catholic moral theologian, gives us a personalistic interpretation of natural law and the primacy of love which is very close to the Orthodox position on natural law as it has been presented by Guroian and Yannaras. At the practical level, it is not just a matter of the commandments which forbid adultery and fornication. It is methodologically a question of knowing what these commandments mean and how they identify a failure and violation of love. Abiding by the law *of itself* does not indicate that we are doing good or being good. The law sets limits, as do the Holy Canons, which tell us that we are far from the goals of Christian life. Guindon similarly recognizes, particularly in his later work, that a pure naturalism, even if built on reason, does not account for the theological realities by which Christians live. Thus he can compare the love of human beings with the love of the divine persons of the Trinity. Theologically this means that revelation and nature are not so distinct as to forbid any overlapping and that grace and nature interpenetrate one another.

In André Guindon's moral theology it is love and the language of love which are uniquely human and reveal the deepest dimensions of human creativity. Guindon rejects any opposition between personalism and natural law theory, arguing that the primacy of the person is the central core of our comprehension of human nature. Guindon moves beyond a teleology of sexuality having its purpose in procreation to a new model of sexual relations as based on what is most uniquely human: the ability to speak to another in love. He centers his attention not on what is shared with other human beings but on how nature is individuated in each person. The potentialities which are ours are realized in communion and love. He quotes Thomas Aquinas to the effect "that which is most perfect in the whole of nature is the human person."[20] The perfection of nature thus lies in a person's freedom and

subjectivity. Indeed, for Guindon "a human being is a personal subject only through reciprocal relationship with another
subject which enables him or her to act as a self-conscious
person."[21] Indeed, he claims that "without a relation which
distinguishes them and unites them reciprocally, human sub-
stances do not exist as persons."[22] In addition to giving his
philosophy of natural law a personalist perspective he elevates
sexuality into the spiritual realm of love by his emphasis on
the person and the transformation of *eros* into *philia*. In an
extraordinary way his expansion of natural law theory almost
exactly parallels that taken by Yannaras:

> From those few elementary notions, it should be clear
> that any "natural law approach" to human fecundity
> which postulates that nature works in human persons
> as it does in beings lacking self-consciousness and
> freedom is totally inadequate. "Nature" and "natural
> law" are highly analogous notions. If human sub-
> stances find in themselves connatural inclinations, for
> instance, the inclination to establish a tender and
> sensual rapport with other human beings, not one of
> those inclinations prescribes a unique scenario of
> execution. Without out the call of some other, heard
> and heeded by each self-conscious person, nothing
> human is ever begotten.[23]

The Discovery of Human Nature in the Language of Love

Olivier Clément speaks of the language of love and of the
mutual gift of pleasure as a "language beyond words."[24]
André Guindon has similarly interpreted human sexuality as a
language. Guindon takes us beyond legalism, beyond an
interpretation of sex based on instincts, impulses, biological
determinism, or social determinism. Since Guindon's personalist version of natural law is so similar to that held by Orthodox personalists, it would be useful if Orthodox moral theolo-

gians were to pay close attention to his notion of sexuality as a language spoken in various modes, both verbally and physically. He has much in common with Michel Foucault who has taught us in his *History of Sexuality* to understand sexuality as a discourse created by various cultures over the centuries, both to interpret and to control sexual behavior.[25] Guindon, however, would take us beyond such historical relativism by a study of the grammar of the language which conforms both with ways of being human (natural law) and with the revelation given in Jesus Christ of God as the lover of mankind.[26] Since the highest activity of human beings is that of communicating with other human beings, forming bonds of love between persons in mutual understanding and sympathy, it is language which is most expressive of a natural law ethic. Indeed, virtue is established by way of language since just relations, prudence, fortitude, and other virtues cannot exist without expression and comprehension by means of a mutually comprehended language. Love-making is indeed basking in the presence of the other, communicating affection, and being lifted beyond hedonistic self-satisfaction in intimate union.

The view of sexuality as a language is shared by Robert Solomon and Roger Scruton, both philosophers. Solomon has written persuasively that we must change our Platonic understanding of the passions as invading forces threatening to destroy both reason and the self. The passions are not forces coming at us from below, as it were. They all involve the self, so that we participate in both their direction and their intentionality.[27] Solomon and Scruton owe much to phenomenology in their grasp of sexual emotion as a response to the other, indeed, as a way of speaking. In his discussion of sexual perversion, Solomon notes that the concept of the natural built on biology is inadequate as a base whereby we identify perversions with the unnatural.[28] De Sade was able to dissolve the criterion of the "unnatural" by observing that such allegedly "unnatural" acts do truly exist in nature. For Solomon perversion must be viewed within the context of sexuality as a language, not in the context of pre-genital sexuality or as an indulgence in unnatural activity. It is the nature of humankind that we as persons speak to one another, and sexuality is a mode of speaking to one another. Solomon does not view speaking to oneself as a perverse act (masturbation is the sexual mode of speaking to oneself). Masturbation is for Solomon a minimal rather than a perverse use of the sexual language. This is why it is the activity of the lonely and always frustrating if carried out in a reparative sense, i.e., as a substitute for what one really wants. Narcissistic masturbation might seem to be without conflict, but the necessity of conjuring up fantasies of an important, attractive, and powerful other person tells the lonely that sexuality is by its nature intentional, even if it is only to invoke the *other* to praise oneself. Roger Scruton is less sanguine about the autoerotic, holding that masturbation replaces sexual desire for another person with obscene images and substitutes self-satisfaction for the satisfaction of the other.[29]

Rejecting the reproductive model of sex as normative while refusing the model of tension release or sexual outlets used by Freud and Kinsey, Solomon and Guindon look instead to the ethics of speech to determine what is moral or immoral in sexual relations. We must be aware of the sins of unauthenticity, of lying, of the false presentation of the self, even of self-deception, if we are to evaluate the sexual language. Solomon notes that the concept of perversion usually is charged with moral connotations rather than naturalistic. In translating what have been considered perverse acts into those expressed in language, Solomon notes, one finds, that there is no deviation of "sexual aim or object," as Freud insisted, but rather the nonverbal equivalent of lying or insincerity, which is where perversion is really to be found. The models of sexuality as outlet and private pleasure provide us with no light with regard to setting up ethical criteria. Such models are basically amoral. Since for Solomon sexuality is primarily a way of speaking to another person, he compares it with other body languages. The language of aggression has not only words which express hostility but acts which carry them out. Fear also has a body language. Defensiveness, insecurity, domination, and self-confidence may all be expressed bodily. Such languages are learned, and the basic form of the language is the gesture. Just as one may be able to speak a foreign language only with difficulty, some persons speak the sexual language badly, but we distinguish between speaking the language falsely and speaking it badly. Solomon notes that some persons are sexual "losers" since they suffer from bodily inarticulateness. Impotence is an example of this. Others are able to speak forcefully but without elegance or creativity in their use of body language. A dancer may speak the language of dance, but might only be a solipsist. Yet for Solomon the facts are clear: "Whatever else sexuality might be and for whatever purposes it might be used or abused, it is first of all language."[30]

One must ask what is being said in a language. We can listen to operatic arias in a foreign language and know nothing of what it is about. However, the language of music may speak to the emotions so that various beautiful arias may convey the meaning of love without one knowing to whom this meaning is conveyed, or exactly what is being said. To observe the language of two lovers may be to participate in something beautiful, but their experience of the onlooker usually has the effect of disintegrating their own language of intimacy. Intimacy does not easily take place in the presence of a third person.

The language of sex is complicated like any language. The gesture, whether it be a drooping cigarette or a scratch of the body, may convey a sexual meaning or only be accidental. When picked up as a gesture a communication between two persons, it may be accepted or rejected. A gesture may be an invitation to a greater communion, or, on the other hand, to further alienation. Sexual intercourse may be the most intense form of communion between persons; on the other hand, it may be, as in cases of rape, only an violent act seeking to make another person submit. The meaning of the act is not given by the physical. Learning to be sexual is not becoming an expert in performance or in positions for intercourse. It is learning to convey and to translate meanings provided by a culture and personally assimilated.

Theosis and the Incarnation of Love

I have sought by the use of the linguistic model to provide a grounding in human nature for the making of a sexual ethic. Such a grounding seeks to determine what sexuality is so that we may speak of it normatively, that is, in terms of its authentic expression and its inauthentic expressions. This is essential before we can speak of right or wrong sexual behavior. Once realized, we will have access to the dynamics of sexuality in the created order. Procreation is only one aspect of the fecundity of men and women as sexual creators.[31] It is only on the basis of the love for one another communicated by a man and a woman that the appropriate setting is provided for the procreation of a child. If that love does not exist, the scene is set for damage to the child. From the mutual love of the man and woman comes forth the offspring of their union, a human being who is genetically 50 per cent from the man and 50 percent from the woman. Thus the child is the realization in the flesh of the union of husband and wife. By discerning in the language of love the essential way of existing which is human sexuality, we move far from the Thomistic formulation of static potentialities, which has so crippled the Vatican's understanding of natural law in relation to sexuality. Our nature is precisely to be lovers, to relate as person to person, as male to female, as I to thou. Thus the model of language provides the grounding which will admit of spiritual transformation. As "one flesh," the marital relation is analogous with the incarnation of God in Christ, united with His wife the Church. As persons related to persons, we love in a way which is not only analogous with the Holy Trinity, but is a participation in the Holy Spirit, a communion in the Spirit, sacramentally flowing from the communion with the Body and Blood of Christ. No doubt this is why receiving Holy Communion together as man and wife was the particular and special mark of the act of being married in the early Church.

Marriage is neither the beginning nor the end of the relationship but rather the attainment of a stage of integration signifying that the couple wishes to live together (even to death "us do part"). The language that is used and spoken between the couple has become an intimate language, a language speaking of love and fidelity. Indeed, the Church speaks to the couple about restraint of physical union until their commitment is made and the crowning and blessing have taken place. What has begun by erotic attraction has developed into friendship. A marriage is the consecrating of this particular friendship between this particular man and woman as a sign and symbol of the union of Christ and His Church as "one flesh." To be united in spirit and flesh is only possible through a love which is of God and blessed by God. The commitment involved is to *agape*, but in the particular mode of sacramental union in the flesh.

The language of sexuality moves to the language of love (and sometimes the language of love precedes and even anticipates the language of sex). For both Rosemary Haughton and Roger Scruton the language of incarnation provided by Christian faith is of central importance for the sexual relationship. Scruton has put it thus:

> I wish you to be your body, not in the straightforward sense in which this is always true, but in the metaphysical sense in which it can never be true, the sense of an identity between your "unity of consciousness" and the animal unity of your body. That, I believe, is the real mystery of incarnation. It is part of the genius of Christianity that it invites us to understand the relation between God and his creation in terms of a mystery that we have, so to speak, continually between our hands.[32]

Scruton points to the burning of the soul in the flesh as the symbol of all mystic unions. Indeed, at this point he directs us to the *Llama de amor viva* of John of the Cross.[33]

Rosemary Haughton similarly refers to the doctrine of the Incarnation:

> The fact that Christians know God as human, literally,

means that we have to reckon with God in every aspect of human experience. Since human beings are communal, this is a communal experience, and since human beings are inextricably enmeshed in the ecological systems of the earth (and presumably of the universe, ultimately) this is also a cosmic experience. All of material reality is affected by the Incarnation and all of material reality is caught up in the experiences of sin, and of redemption. Human beings are part of a sinful world, but a saved world, one in which the process of transformation, which took its revolutionary leap in the resurrection of Christ, is going on at all kinds of levels.[34]

I believe that Haughton is putting her finger upon the central theological affirmations of the Church. She speaks of the levels of consciousness and of the bodily. At every level sin may enter (most noticeably through the influences of the cultural milieus in which we live), but so may the transforming power of grace. The spiritual touches and sanctifies the flesh also. She mentions Charles Williams as one the few Christian writers who has been able to express the concept of the transformation of the flesh. Physical acts not only convey meaning but they help create meaning. The miraculous transformation of the act of love into the birth of a child is the foremost instance of this in human life. No matter what may become of the relationship between the man and the woman their relationship is changed, for better or for worse, by this wonderful event and can never be as it was before that event. The "one flesh" of intercourse has become the "one flesh" of the child, whose flesh is of both the father and the mother.

The transforming power of *eros*, which is to be carefully distinguished from mere sexual attraction or lust, is an effect of the energies of God changing and redeeming the world. The interior experience of love for another can be an awesome and ecstatic experience. The consecration and ratification of this desire for union bring with them the external gifts of love: social recognition, promises, rings, all one's worldly goods, even one's body. This is because the lover seeks to give to the beloved. Partially it is the commitment to share one's life in the context of constituting a family. All of this makes it inadequate and even improper to ask whether "it does any harm" for the couple to copulate. Similarly, the perennial question of the moral theologian has been "may I do it without sin?" Of human behavior Haughton tells us that we have to ask: "is it physically, emotionally, and spiritually fitted to express the human perfection to which we are called--to *be* it, at some level, to symbolize it (since symbols are the activators of the unconscious transformation) and to bear witness to the nature of our relationship to the Lord."[35]

I have explored the comments of Rosemary Haughton because her criticism of moral theology - even of the most *avant garde* variety - is based on a theology which is clearly Orthodox (despite her own Roman Catholic commitment). Human experience in its growth toward inter-relatedness, in its movement from *eros* to *agape*, in its dynamism from the narcissistic to the other-directed, inevitably reaches out for grace. As Georges Florovsky often put it, we are saved as a family, not as individuals, indeed, we are saved in God's own family. Thus the bond of union which the couple represents is consecrated at the altar of God and crowned with the promise of the Kingdom of God, which we attain not by worldly success but by way of the cross and the promised resurrection. It is true, as Rosemary Haughton states that "deeply passionate love is painful, however happy it may be. It is painful because the lovers, in the measure of their love, become aware of the limits of their unity, the way in which something prevents that complete oneness for which they long, and for which (they know) they were made."[36] Here is indeed the intimation of immortality, but bodily love also "rubs our noses in the facts of mortality, the limitation of that physical existence by which we are able to experience communion at all."[37]

The attempt to reduce reality to what moral theologians categorize as licit or illicit, right or wrong, is an attempt to map out the world and to control it. If one reads the lists of sins against purity in a Roman Catholic manual such as that of Jone-Adelman, one finds that sin permeates every pleasure or delight within the realm of sexuality and impurity.[38]   One discovers that looks, touches, kisses, conversations, songs, literature--all are gravely sinful if indulged in for the sake of the arousing influence that they may bring. The sphere of pleasure and specifically physical pleasure has become the land of damnation. The traditional teaching of the Roman Catholic Church has been that there is no parvity (lightness) of matter in any sexual pleasure willfully taken outside of the marital relationship.[39]   Little awareness is shown of pleasure as a side effect of the expression of affection or as a response of delight and joy in another.

The link between the popular sexologists and the pre-Vatican II Roman Catholic moral theologians has been graphically illustrated by André Guindon in his book, *The Sexual Language*. Both reduce sexual activity to pleasures, the former delighting in such pleasure, the latter damning it with accusations of grave sin. Both miss the point that sexuality is a language. One may speak the sexual language in fantasy and never get beyond fantasy, which is to fall away from reality into near-madness. One may speak it falsely, pretending to love when one is only lusting or sometimes only playing at love or lust.   It is the integration of physical affection with personal communion which brings that wholeness which sexual desire promises when it transcends mere bodily satisfaction. This, in turn, brings us to the brink of the mystery of sanctification where one seeks not only union but a mutual willing of good and immortality for the other. The dynamism is toward a deeper (and at the same time a higher) integration. Just as what takes place spiritually has deep resonation with the physical, so physical intimacy and union have profound implications for the spiritual. This is partly because we are symbolic creatures. The psychoanalyst will seek to understand the symbolism underlying dreams, fantasies, desires, and fears, while the poet constructs of words a network of symbols to express feelings and perceptions that remain unique in her experience.

In the end, our moral questions must refer back not only to our experience but to our theology. If we answer moral questions by a teleological physiology, we will come up with answers which to lovers are limited and seemingly far-fetched. If we portray the world as darkly evil and our sexuality as not only involved in sin but of its very nature evil, we will live in fear of our desires and attractions. Fear will - along with morbid desires and obsessions - stalk us through life. If we search our lives only to see what we can get by with, our vision of sexuality will remain childish, limited to self indulgence and subsequent resort to confession. If, on the other hand, we experience love as grace pouring into our lives, our moral theology will be affirmative of the dynamic which pulls and carries us toward fulfillment and intimations of the communion of the saints. Many people live their sexuality out in the jungle of Hobbes, where only the few succeed, where love is usually frustrated, since the strong triumph (and gain the young and the beautiful) and the weak fail by reason of their ugliness, their shyness, or their ineptitude. The Orthodox Christian vision is not one of unmitigated optimism (or pessimism), but it is one which hopes that all lovers will make their love culminate in a common and universal love, once selfishness and particularity give way to the love which the communion of the saints gives us reason to think possible. Of course, sin is present by reason of our inability to love, and our needs are often disproportionate and lead to anger when not fulfilled. But the Orthodox Christian faith bids us ever to repent and turn once more to the grace that calls us, surprises us, and fulfills us. It is in mutual repentance, mutual *metanoia*, that our sexuality can be transformed from the demand for satisfaction to the sacrificial offering which completes as well as changes us.

It is vital that Orthodox theology not isolate itself from human experience. If it does, it enters into a ghetto which allows only the very few to live within its vision of life. There is, of course, a vast abyss between the spiritual vision of sexuality and its transformation in Christ through the Holy Spirit and the secular profanation of sex which the culture of hedonism offers us today. But there is not a deep divide between the heights and depths of human experience and the ascesis and mystagogy of *theosis*. The integration of birth, marriage, and death into the sacramental life, along with the links between the nourishment of the daily table and our super-substantial food of immortality, present us with instances of consecration of the natural by the spiritual. Too often Orthodoxy has been presented as a severe puritanism, and indeed if one lived by the sanctions, prohibitions, and punishments of the *Pedalion* it would a very grim religion indeed. But the lived experience of Orthodox people, their joy and their hopes, integrated with their beliefs and their ritual, present a different picture. This was the vision that Father Alexander Schmemann gave us in his various works (though he was equally a witness to the demonic in life).

Since in Christ God gave Himself for the life of this world, the life of the world is good. Our sexuality, however devastated and twisted it may be, shares that goodness when it is personally, socially, and spiritually integrated. It is with this goodness that our moral theology must begin, and what is not good must be seen not as inherent evil but as evil which exists through lack of the good which ought to be present. The fundamental theme of Charistian ethics is that of *eros* elevated by the Holy Spirit to *agape*. Just as Freud discerned the underlying libido in all forms of love, so we must equally affirm that *eros* directs us beyond ourselves towards an other whose otherness is not foreign to us but is felt to be "our other side." The teaching of Jung that *eros* projects the *anima* (if a man) or the *animus* (if a woman) on to the other sex reveals that *eros* opens up for us an alter ego. This is, of course, why a narcissistic element remains within erotic love. It is the encounter with the otherness of the other that not only inflicts upon us a dose of reality but brings us to the crucial point of truly loving the good of the other. We will usually serve and bestow goods upon those who love us, if only for the reward of being loved, but to move toward a love of the other as other brings us to *agape* as truly self-sacrificing. By ourselves alone love is unattainable; it can be attained only by God's love for us. Vigen Guroian puts forth the transformation of the meaning of *philanthropia* as the key to the Christian revision of *eros*:

The love manifested in Jesus Christ is a love which

does not negate but sublimates and transforms all so-called natural or human loves. This explains why such Greek writers as Chrysostom and Cabasilas used *philanthropia* and *agape* (or *caritas*) interchangeably. In the hands of these theologians *philanthropia* is no longer used in the Hellenistic sense to mean a merely human love exchanged between men and redounding to them; rather, it is a divine love for man manifested in us by Christ and returning to God through man's loving acts toward his neighbors. This is also how the Greek fathers reinterpreted *eros*. *Eros* is no longer simply a human yearning for the divine. It is a divine-human love, the ascending mode of charity itself whereby the mind ravished by divine knowledge" (St. Maximus the Confessor) seeks God, but in so doing discovers from a divine point of view the infinite value and perfect equality of all persons.[40]

The admonition of Christ, taken from the teachings of the Hebrew scriptures (Lv 19:18), is "to love our neighbor as ourself" (Mt 19:19). The word translated as "love" comes from the Greek *agapao* and is distinctive insofar as the Bible uses terminology which points to something greater than *eros* or *philia*. Christ also teaches us to love our enemy (Mt 5:44). Thus we are called to love the other person even when he or she does not love us in return. The saying of the Lord found in St. John's Gospel (Jn 15:13) that "Greater love has no man than this, that a man lay down his life for his friends" confirms the centrality and importance of *agape*. It has often been thought that sexual love is higher and deeper than friendship, but this is not so. A marriage deepens, if it remains intact and healthy, into a friendship of the highest value. Friendship contains not only *philia* but *agape* if it goes beyond mere reciprocity. Each one of us develops friendships throughout our lives, but few are able to speak openly about the love of particular friends. Shakespeare had no hesitation in writing of the love of friends and making them speak in his plays of their love for one another. Modern people are deeply confused here by reason of the distance that they impose on relationships and their suspicion that all feeling is potentially sexual.

Often it is thought that *eros* cuts one off from love for others by reason of the exclusivity of the attraction to one person. This is not so if the *eros* is deep and overflowing. The love for another person becomes a channel through which love may flow not just to one person but to many. Rather than creating a situation where many relationships become sexualized, the contrary is true. *Eros* thus provides the energy, the lift, and the motivation to move toward the other. It overcomes the sense that the stranger is an alien. *Philia* develops when trust and intimacy and mutual interests are born in the lives of two persons. *Agape* brings love to maturity. The goal is not just union (and one must remember that the flow of communication between people is a form of union) but self-giving. To give gifts involves discernment and wisdom as well as a generous will. When *eros* is transformed into lust, the selfishness and possessiveness entailed may bring about a collapse of the spiritual and altruistic dimensions of the relationship. The subtle elements of *eros* and friendship which are brought to a sexual relationship demand a certain exclusivity if they are to remain intact. This is why marriage is the norm for sexual relationships, and why marriage promises *agape* in the context of the example of Christ's love for His Church. Without this context, the collapse of the couple is virtually inevitable. The Church's concern that sexual intercourse be in the context of marriage stems from an awareness that lustful drives may and often do destroy spiritual goals. Sexual union demands commitment to one another or it becomes occasional and incorporates a lie, promising love but denying it the full continuity which the commitment of marriage brings. There is a limitation in the "one flesh' which is marriage and sexual union. Friendship must be part of marriage, but the particular friendship which is marriage limits itself to the context of heterosexuality, to a sexual commitment, and to the context of the family which normally springs from the sexual union of husband and wife. Marriage remains at the level of the flesh and the body, though the love within marriage leads to a participation in the spiritual love of the Kingdom of God. Nevertheless marriage often, particularly in certain cultures, limits friendship and often inhibits a wider set of friendships. This limitation is overcome when friends become part of the community which results from the communion in the Holy Spirit.

Sublimated *eros* helps us to create friendships, which, in turn, cry out for *agape* under the conditions of fallen human life. Once a person is perceived as distinct and separate and not simply the focus of a projection of one's *animus* or *anima* (as the Jungians would put it), the task of recognition of the other as other enters the picture. *Agape* demands that reverence before the other's good, even if that good is perceived differently by the loved one, be accepted and recognized. No demands for the love and attention of the other can ever prevail without damaging the relationship. Demands of their very nature involve an element of force which violates the freedom which is the *sine qua non* of a true and mutually beneficial friendship. *Eros* must stand aside before the higher good of *agape*, since to love the other person demands that one must love the otherness of the other. Certainly only the other can make the final judgment of what his or her good may be. It is on the basis of otherness and sameness that friendship emerges. Friendship is higher than the *eros* which does not recognize any good beyond one's own need for union. Friendship is reciprocal or it is not friendship. *Agape* builds on friendship and moves beyond it, but not toward a masochism whereby a sacrifice is made of oneself in favor of the other. *Agape* moves us beyond our inherent narcissism toward the self-fulfillment which is found in reverence before the otherness of the beloved friend. The great Russian philosopher and theologian Pavel Florensky introduces the theme of friendship into his massive work of philosophy, *The Pillar and Foundation of Truth*. For Florensky friendship is the expression of the love which unifies the cosmos. Robert Slesinski, in his exposition of Fr. Pavel's thought, puts it thus:

> In the sophianic vision, God's infinite love is grasped to be the true, creative cause of the ordered beauty of

the cosmos. The creature, however, is able to understand this causal mystery; and then fully participate in
creation's own beauty, only if he has been internally
purified by the cathartic fires of love. Love is, indeed, the spark that initiates creation, and also the
energy force that sustains it. It is also, at once, the
key and the hallmark to Florensky's metaphysics of
consubstantiality in which all reality, both divine and
creatural, is bound together by dynamic interrelation-
ships of love.[41]

Florensky closely relates *eros* and *philia*. For him the
kiss, which linguistically is related in Russian to the sense of
"making whole" (the word is *tselovat*), marks the love of
friendship. There is no note of moralism in this. It is *agape*
which brings a rational love which "concentrates on the objective appraisal of the one loved."[42]   The Russian word *storge*
is also used for a love which is basically "generic," a fellow-
feeling rather than a specifically "personal" one. Long before
Martin Buber's analysis of the I-thou relation of love, Florensky said the same, that love is an overcoming, particularly in
the mode of friendship, of the boundaries of the "I". As
Florensky sees it, the "egocentric man, however, enclosed
within himself, does not partake of the plenitude of being, and
remains essentially isolated in his own world, which in turn
must be unfounded and hence meaningless."[43] Florensky
views friendship as a primary datum of reality, the achievement of which is the most important task in life. As he puts
it, "This reciprocal penetration of personalities, however, is
a task, and not an original given of friendship."[44]   What
strikes us as most odd is the place that Florensky gives to
jealousy as an authentic note of friendship. Jealousy is usually viewed as a mean and vicious phenomenon, but Florensky,
beginning with the Biblical datum of God as a jealous God,
concludes that it is legitimate for friends to be jealous for the
protection of what is unique in their experience of one another. "Authentic love, on the other hand," Florensky maintains, "can only foster dynamic identity as gained from organic ties of interdependence. Jealousy, in this perspective, is

nothing other than zeal for love and dynamic identity, and accordingly belongs to love's very nature as its safeguard and patron."[45]

It is, therefore, before the mystery of the person that love comes to its fulfillment and its transformation from desire for the other into a love for the other as such. Orthodox faith would show us how the restoration of humanity in Christ lifts up our natural aspirations for union and friendship with others and integrates them by way of the communion of persons. We see this also in Florensky's metaphysics since for him "the correlativity of the 'I' and 'Thou' is a primary datum in the homoousian universe, itself irreducibly founded upon the dynamic identity of its constitutive entities whereby no one of them is its own sufficient explanation."[46] To be of one nature (human) we must need one another. Friendship is that opening to the other in love which unifies and realizes the *homoousia* of humanity. Just as the human nature of Christ is united with His divinity by way of his divine *hypostasis*, so our humanity is integrated with that of others by way of persons in relation to one another by friendship. Christ's person is related to His Father and to the Holy Spirit as *hypostases* in a communion which is consubstantial as God, so human persons exist within a communion of friendship. Marriage is only a particular form of friendship in which the sexual energies are fully realized to become "one flesh" and to open the relationship up to the possibility (and usually the reality) of the third person, the child. Both Lossky and Zizioulas have expounded the meaning of communion as reflecting the Divine Trinity, and Dumitru Staniloae has abundantly expanded the doctrine of the Holy Trinity as it relates to our communion and union with God.[47] The ethicist Vigen Guroian, also has found in the love of the persons of the Holy Trinity the divine pattern of human love which is the foundation for all Orthodox ethics.[48] In the Trinity that love is perfect and never ending. In us it is imperfect, and *eros* reaches out for a completion which is never absent in the Trinity. In marriage the coming into being of the child is, according to Guroian, the presence of the third person, giving rise to a perfect love which is parallel to the Trinitarian love.

The "we" of the family mirrors, when it is fully present, the "we" of the Trinity. The man and the woman are integrated as the Father and the Son are integrated with the third, the Holy Spirit, in the mystery of the Trinity. Even in God the person is not lost in the other. The Father pours out from Himself the existence of the Word and Spirit, and each flows back into the other in perfect love and harmony. Unity of substance is what binds all together in the Godhead, but the three persons remain distinct. So in the flow between human persons, the male is not lost in the female, nor the female in the male. Neither sex may dominate the other but must stand in awe and reverence before the other. Each remains distinct, but the male gender and the female gender (both constituting human nature) are integrated in a person. Just as the persons of the Godhead are equally God, so human persons, ensubstantiated in a specific sex, remain in one humanity, neither being less than fully and equally human. Gender confusions in the modern world have led many to the conclusion that insofar as the persons of both men and women transcend their genders it is of little importance whether sexual relationships are homosexual or heterosexual. At the level of *philia* and *agape* this would appear to be a correct conclusion since *eros* as a mutual attraction and sympathy may legitimately and naturally exist between persons of the same sex. A friendship may involve the greatest love of all if it is marked by *agape*. But sexual relationships insofar as they are physical and become "one flesh" must be heterosexual. Even at the spiritual level the relating of the sexes involves a projection, as Jung would put it, of the man's *anima* onto the female and a woman's *animus* onto the male. A sacramental marriage necessarily reflects the created structure of male and female, since it is based on the archetype of Christ the husband united to the Church as His wife.

Marriages are often threatened with collapse by reason of the weight placed on the physical aspects and on the material concerns in the life of a couple. In the midst of these concerns the erotic is sometimes extinguished, making of marriage a way of the cross through a darkness opaque in its enveloping cloud. The erotic must not be seen as akin to the pornographic as in "erotica" but as the flow of feeling, delight, and joy in the being of the other person as he or she is revealed to the lover. The confusion between the pornographic and the erotic can be devastating in its consequences when a couple seeks to keep their love alive by acting out obscene fantasies. The confusion between sexual excitement and erotic veneration is widespread in modern culture.

My concern throughout this study has been that *theosis* as understood by Orthodox theology, both patristic and modern, is the key to an Orthodox moral theology of sexuality. It would help us to avoid legalism and a negative moralism. It helps us to appreciate and rejoice in the current of the energies of God that open our souls up to the image of God in the other person. This is the true meaning of the erotic. Furthermore, it allows us to direct our attention where many modern Orthodox theologians (such as Lossky and Zizioulas) would have us put it it, in the love of persons for one another. It helps us avoid the dark pessimism of Augustinianism (and the puritanism of either Rome or Geneva) as well as the superficial naturalism so widespread in the Christian West today. The drama of redemption is precisely that in our brokenness we find God healing and lifting us to search for life and joy. It may well be that the negativity which many have found in our contradictory drives (one thinks of Sartre, Freud, and Stoller at this point) and their self-defeating character may appear to be an expression of the nihilism of much modern thought and culture. The Christian gospel bids us look more deeply to the power of re-creation. Our vision of perfection through God's grace must acknowledge that God does good even in the most dismal and ruinous circumstances. The gospel of God's compassion evident on every page of the liturgical formulations of the Orthodox Church invites us to adopt a more positive attitude toward human possibilities in the broken circumstances of modernity. The Orthodox witness is not to brokenness but to whatever good may be realized by the Spirit of God in the midst of the world. The fact that the Church is willing to permit a second marriage and to bless it illustrates her realism and her readiness to use *economia* for the salvation of souls. It is by the power of the

Holy Spirit that *theosis* takes place, and it is in discernment of spirits that the Orthodox confessor and spiritual father must act. Such discrimination between the demonic and the spiritual is at the heart of our moral task.

Olivier Clément's most basic affirmation is that "to love truly means to discover the other in his or her specific identity."[49] Clément observes two marks which are signs of a true encounter: the proof of time and the proof of the gift of life. With regard to the former, the couple is not only moving through time rather than just living in an erotic instant, but each assumes the other's past and takes responsibility for the other's future. With regard to the latter, Clément notes that "idolatrous passion is linked to death, it is both nostalgia for an impossible fusion and war between the sexes. It exhausts the world and chases the others away."[50] There is, he urges, a need for a theology of amorous passion for our time, "corresponding to the theology of lewdness so well developed by the ascetics as they were confronted by stark temptations (for amorous passion cannot be reduced to lewdness)."[51] Clément perceives this as essential since young people are often so out of touch with the meaning of the sacrament of marriage that they cannot see its point:

> Today young people, and sometimes the most conscientious among them, tell us: "We are going to live together. Why get married, legally or in church? Why let institutions interfere with what is our own secret? And how can we commit ourselves to stay together forever when each of us will change and when life lasts much longer in our time?" The answer is that the sacrament of marriage is not a social affair but a mystery. It has meaning only within the context of the faith, of the Gospel, of the assurance that the work of Christ, shown in the Gospels, continues in the church - that is what the sacraments are about - and that even today Jesus can change water into wine. But it is not only absurd but criminal in talking with young people about sexuality to use the language of judgment, accusation and menace, to deal with it in terms

of what is permitted and forbidden, when they do not
even know whether they believe in God. It may keep
them forever away from God, Christ and the
Church.[52]

Nevertheless, there are many who love one another intensely, "passionately, with simplicity and a true purity."
Clément discerns in such love "a privileged point of evangelization, because on a primitive level it often involves a mystical experience, a sense of unity in difference, the passionate
desire for the other to exist, even beyond death, a desire for
love to be stronger than death."[53]   Here is where one can
speak to the young about Christ's victory over death. As he
puts it: "You can testify that at the bottom of things there is
love and not nothingness, and that our God, in his trinitarian
openness, constitutes the secret source of love."[54]   Indeed,
he affirms: "It is only when we make evident to the young --
and the not so young -- the sacramentality of love, that we can
make them understand the sacrament of marriage."[55]
Clément affirms that we do indeed discover God in and
through His image as revealed in the other: "The sacrament,
the entry into the light of Christ, helps me to discover the
other as God's image. It deepens and stabilizes in me the
unique grace to know someone else, soul and body as a revelation."[56]
I have quoted Clément at length because I believe that his
views, those of a professor at the Institute St. Serge in Paris
and a specialist in Orthodox theology and Russian literature,
confirm what I have been trying to say regarding the moral
and spiritual meaning of sexuality and marriage. It is the
ascesis of love that enables us to know the heights and depths
of human experience that would enable us to know the great
mystery of Trinitarian love incarnate in the love of Christ for
His beloved Church. Every lover who truly loves and who
overcomes the temptations of the flesh, the inherent narcissism which plagues our desires and attractions and the blind
projections which distort our vision, is being led into this
mystery. It is by taking account of the highest in the human
experience as well the lowest that light can be shed on the

mystery of human existence and the grace that pursues us throughout our lives. To be a lover who deeply and authentically loves is to become alive, for even in the midst of death there is the sign of the *Parousia* and the gift of life eternal present in the Holy Spirit. This is not in any way to surrender to "pan-sexualism" but rather to affirm that love, which goes beyond sexual desire, seeks for that which is eternal. It is a vision of God mediated through the image of God which has a particular and incarnate reality in the soul of each human being. The ascent to God by way of human love becomes another form of the ascetic way which overcomes self-seeking, the demands for immediate gratification, and the power of death revealed by the movement of time. The power of love to transcend all limitations is a gift of the Holy Spirit. It is the very stuff of sanctity, a holiness based on a purification of love and of all sensual delights. There the communion of the Holy Spirit prepares us for the mystical banquet where love will be fulfilled and know no end and no restraints, for God will be in all.

Notes

(1) Olivier Clément, "Life in the Body," *The Ecumenical Review*, 33 (1981), p. 141.

(2) Ibid., p. 141.

(3) Ibid., p. 142.

(4) Ibid., p. 142.

(5) Roger Scruton, *Sexual Desire* (London: Weidenfeld and Nicolson, 1986).

(6) Paul Robinson, *The Modernization of Sex* (New York: Harper & Row, 1976).

(7) One must consult Evdokimov's great book *La Femme et le Salut* to appreciate the insights that he was able to reap from sophiology by way of the thought of Jung.

(8) Wolfgang Wickler, *The Sexual Code: The Social Behavior of Animals and Men* (Garden City, NY: Doubleday Anchor, 1973).

(9) Vigen Guroian, *Incarnate Love: Essays in Orthodox Ethics* (Notre Dame, IN: University of Notre Dame Press, 1987), p. 13. It has been argued by at least one outstanding Orthodox theologian that Guroian cannot be taken seriously as an Orthodox moral theologian insofar as his ecclesiastical tradition is Armenian. It is difficult to separate the ecclesiastical and the theological issues in this matter, but this author has no hesitation in accepting Guroian's theology as Orthodox since it is deeply grounded in the patristic tradition.

(10) Ibid., p. 21.

(11) Ibid., pp. 21-2.

(12) Ibid., pp. 21-22.

(13) Basil the Great, *The Long Rules* in trans. Agnes Claire Way, in *St. Basil, Ascetical Works, The Fathers of the Church*, vol. 9 (Washington, DC: Catholic University of America, 1950), p. 233.

(14) Stanley Harakas, *Toward Transfigured Life* (Minneapolis: Light and Life, 1983), p. 137.

(15) Christos Yannaras, *The Freedom of Morality* (Crestwood, NY: St. Vladimir's Seminary Press, 1984), pp. 25-6.

(16) Ibid., p. 27.

(17) Ibid.

(18) Ibid., p. 181.

(19) Ibid.

(20) André Guindon, *the Sexual Creators: An Ethical Proposal for Concerned Christians* (Landon, MD: University Press of America, 1986), pp. 21-37.

(21) Ibid., p. 70, quoting Thomas Aquinas, *Summa Theologica* Ia, q.29, a. 3.

(22) Ibid., pp. 70-1.

(23) Ibid., pp. 70-1.

(24) Clément, op. cit., p. 142.

(25) Michel Foucault, *The History of Sexuality: An Introduction* (New York: Random House, 1978).

(26) André Guindon, *The Sexual Language* (Ottawa: University of Ottawa Press, 1976).

(27) Robert Solomon, *Passions* (Gardon City, NY: Anchor, 1973).

(28) Robert Solomon, "Sex and Perversion," in R. Baker and R. E. Ellison, eds. *Philosophy and Sex* (Buffalo: Prometheus Books, 1975), pp. 271-2.

(29) Scruton, p. 128.

(30) Solomon, p. 281.

(31) Roger Scruton, p. 128.

(32) Ibid., p. 128.

(33) Rosemary Haughton, "Toward a Christian Theology of Sexuality," *Cross Currents* 28, 3 (Fall, 1978), p. 296.

(34) Ibid., p. 296.

(35) Ibid., p. 296.

(36) Ibid., p. 297.

(37) H. Jone and U. Adelman, *Moral Theology* (Westminster, MD: Newman Press, 1953), pp. 232-42.

(38) Patrick J. Boyle, *Parvitas Materiae in Sexto in Contemporary Catholic Thought* (Lanham, MD : University Press of America, 1987).

(39) Vigen Guroian, "Notes Toward An Eastern Orthodox Ethic," *The Journal of Religious Ethics* 9, 2 (Fall, 1981), p. 232.

(40) Robert Slesinski, *Pavel Florensky: A Metaphysics of Love* (Crestwood, NY: St. Vladimir's Seminary Press, 1984), p. 212.

(41) Ibid., p. 217.

(42) Ibid., p. 225.

(43) Paul Florensky, *The Pillar and Foundation of Truth* (Russian Edition), p. 447, as quoted by Slesinski, p. 226.

(44) Slesinski, p. 230

(45) Ibid., p. 225.

(46) Vladimir Lossky, *The Mystical Theology of the Eastern Church* (London: James Clarke, 1957); J. D. Zizioulas, *Being as Communion* (Crestwood, NY: St. Vladimir's Seminary Press, 1985); Dimitri Staniloae, *Theology and the Church* (Crestwood, NY: St. Vladimir's Seminary Press, 1980).

(47) Guroian, *Incarnate Love: Essays in Orthodox Ethics*, pp. 18-9.

(48) Clément, p. 142.

(49) Ibid., p. 143.

(50) Ibid., p. 143.

(51) Ibid., p. 143.

(52) Ibid., p. 144.

(53) Ibid., p. 144.

(54) Ibid., p. 144.

(55) Ibid., p. 144.

Index

Credits

In this volume passages are quoted from the following titles with the permission of their publishers:

Rosemary Haughton, "Toward a Christian Theology of Sexuality" *Cross Currents*, Fall, 1978.

Evgueny Lampert, *The Divine Realm* (Faber & Faber, 1944).

Theodore Mackin, *Divorce and Remarriage*, copyright (c) 1984, used by permission of Paulist Press.

J. M.-F. Marique, trans., *The Shepherd of Hermas* in *The Apostolic Fathers, The Fathers of the Church*, 1 (Catholic University of America, 1947)

Stephen Miletic, *"One Flesh": Eph. 5.22-24, 5.31. Marriage and the New Creation, Analecta Biblica*, Vol. 115 (Editrice Pontificio Istituto Biblico, Piazza della Pilotta, 35 - 600187, Roma, Italy).

Richard McCormick, "Notes on Moral Theology," *Theological Studies* 36, 1 (1975).

John Meyendorff, *Marriage: An Orthodox Perspective* (St. Vladimir's Theological Seminary Press, 1970).

Elizabeth Moberly, *Homosexuality: A New Christian Ethic* (Cambridge, U.K., James Clarke & Co., Ltd., 1983).

St. Nicodemus the Hagiorite and Agapius, *The Rudder (Pedalion)*, trans., D. Cummings, published by The Orthodox Christian Educational Society, Box 287 West Brookfield, MA, 01585.

Philip Schaff, ed., *A Select Library of Nicene and Post-Nicene Fathers of the Christian Church* (William B. Eerdmans Publishing Company).

Edward Schillebeeckx, *Marriage: Sacred and Profane Reality* and *Celibacy*, used by permission of Uitgeverij H. Nelissen, 3743 Ed Baarn, The Netherlands.

Alexander Schmemann, *For the Life of the World* (St. Vladimir's Seminary Press, 1973).

Philip Sherrard, *Christianity and Eros* (Society for the Propagation of Christian Knowledge, 1976).

Philip Sherrard: "Humanae Vitae: Notes on the Encyclical Letter of Pope Paul VI," *Sobornost* 5:8 (1969).

Sally Rieger Shore, trans., *John Chrysostom: On Virginity; Against Remarriage*, Studies in Women and Religion Vol. 9, The Edwin Mellen Press, Lewiston, NY, 1983.

Kenneth Stevenson, *Nuptial Blessing* (Oxford University Press, 1983) by permission of the Society for the

Propagation of Christian Knowledge, London, U.K.

Theodore Stylianopoulos, "Toward a Theology of Marriage in the Orthodox Church," *Greek Orthodox Theological Review* 12, 3.

M. Monica Wagner, trans., *St. Basil: Ascetical Works, The Fathers of the Church*, 9 (Catholic University Press of America, 1950).

Christos Yannaras *The Freedom of Morality*, trans. Elizabeth Brière (St. Vladimir's Seminary Press, Crestwood, New York, 1984).

Chrysostomos Zaphiris, "The Morality of Contraception: An Eastern Orthodox Opinion," *The Journal of Ecumenical Studies* 11, 4 (1974).

All quotations from the Old and New Testaments are taken from the Revised Standard Version with the permission of the Division of Christian Education of the National Council of the Churches of Christ in the United States of America.